FOCUS ON GRAMMAR

An **INTERMEDIATE** Course for Reference and Practice

SECOND EDITION

Marjorie Fuchs

Margaret Bonner

Miriam Westheimer

To the memory of my parents, Edith and Joseph Fuchs—MF

To my parents, Marie and Joseph Maus, and to my son, Luke Frances—MB

To my husband, Joel Einleger, and my children, Ari and Leora—MW

FOCUS ON GRAMMAR: AN **INTERMEDIATE** COURSE FOR REFERENCE AND PRACTICE

Pearson Education, 10 Bank Street, White Plains, NY 10606

Editorial director: Allen Ascher
Executive editor: Louisa Hellegers
Director of design and production: Rhea Banker
Development editor: Françoise Leffler
Production manager: Alana Zdinak
Managing editor: Linda Moser
Senior production editor: Virginia Bernard
Senior manufacturing manager: Patrice Fraccio
Manufacturing manager: David Dickey
Photo research: Beth Boyd
Cover design: Rhea Banker
Cover image: *Elm, Middleton Woods, Yorkshire,
    6 November 1980.* Copyright © Andy Goldsworthy
    from his book *A Collaboration with Nature,*
    Harry N. Abrams, 1990.
Text design: Charles Yuen
Text composition: Preface, Inc.
Illustrators: Moffitt Cecil: pp. 17, 18, 156, 208, 359, 388; Ronald
    Chironna: pp. 24, 33 (br), 34, 191, 215, 239, 250, 251, 296, (bm), 272;
    Brian Hughes: pp. 14, 244, 247 (tl, br), 272, 292; Jock MacRae: pp. 45, 94,
    181, 183, 302, 304, 314, 316; Paul McCusker: pp. 37, 41, 44, 103; Andy
    Myer: pp. 52, 149, 184, 205; Dusan Petricic: pp. 2, 7, 8, 15, 58, 86, 171,
    176, 193, 198, 247 (tr, bl), 404; PC&F: pp. 46, 51, 398, 407, 408, 409.
Text and photo credits: see p. xiv

Library of Congress Catalog-in-Publication Data
Fuchs, Marjorie,
    Focus on grammar, An intermediate course for reference and practice /
    Marjorie Fuchs, Margaret Bonner, Miriam Westheimer.—2nd ed.
        p. cm.
    ISBN 0-201-34682-6 (alk. paper)
    1. English language textbooks for foreign speakers. 2. English language—
Grammar problems, exercises, etc. I. Bonner, Margaret, II. Westheimer, Miriam.
III. Title.

PE1128.F794 1999
428.2'4'076—dc21

                                                99-23208
                                                CIP

10—CRK—04

CONTENTS

APPENDICES

ABOUT THE AUTHORS

Marjorie Fuchs has taught ESL at New York City Technical College and LaGuardia Community College of the City University of New York and EFL at the Sprach Studio Lingua Nova in Munich, Germany. She holds a Master's Degree in Applied English Linguistics and a Certificate in TESOL from the University of Wisconsin–Madison. She has authored or co-authored many widely used ESL textbooks, notably *On Your Way: Building Basic Skills in English, Crossroads, Top Twenty ESL Word Games: Beginning Vocabulary Development, Around the World: Pictures for Practice, Families: Ten Card Games for Language Learners, Focus on Grammar: A High-Intermediate Course for Reference and Practice*, and the workbooks to the *Longman Dictionary of American English*, the *Longman Photo Dictionary*, *The Oxford Picture Dictionary*, and the *Vistas* series.

Margaret Bonner has taught ESL at Hunter College and the Borough of Manhattan Community College of the City University of New York, at Taiwan National University in Taipei, and at Virginia Commonwealth University in Richmond. She holds a Master's Degree in Library Science from Columbia University, and she has done work towards a Ph.D. in English Literature at the Graduate Center of the City University of New York. She has contributed to a number of ESL and EFL projects, including *Making Connections, On Your Way*, and the Curriculum Renewal Project in Oman, where she wrote textbooks, workbooks, and teachers manuals for the national school system. She authored *Step into Writing: A Basic Writing Text*, and co-authored *Focus on Grammar: A High-Intermediate Course for Reference and Practice* and *The Oxford Picture Dictionary Intermediate Workbook*.

Miriam Westheimer taught EFL at all levels of instruction in Haifa, Israel, for a period of six years. She has also taught ESL at Queens College, at LaGuardia Community College, and in the American Language Program of Columbia University. She holds a Master's Degree in TESOL and a doctorate in Curriculum and Teaching from Teacher's College of Columbia University. She is the co-author of a communicative grammar program developed and widely used in Israel.

INTRODUCTION

THE **FOCUS ON GRAMMAR** SERIES

Focus on Grammar: An Intermediate Course for Reference and Practice, *Second Edition,* is part of the four-level ***Focus on Grammar*** series. Written by practicing ESL professionals, the series focuses on English grammar through lively listening, speaking, reading, and writing activities. Each of the four Student Books is accompanied by an Answer Key, a Workbook, an Audio Program (cassettes or CDs), a Teacher's Manual, and a CD–ROM. Each Student Book can stand alone as a complete text in itself, or it can be used as part of the series.

BOTH CONTROLLED AND COMMUNICATIVE PRACTICE

Research in applied linguistics suggests that students expect and need to learn the formal rules of a language. However, students need to practice new structures in a variety of contexts to help them internalize and master them. To this end, ***Focus on Grammar*** provides an abundance of both controlled and communicative exercises so that students can bridge the gap between knowing grammatical structures and using them. The many communicative activities in each unit enable students to personalize what they have learned in order to talk to each other with ease about hundreds of everyday issues.

A UNIQUE FOUR-STEP APPROACH

The series follows a unique four-step approach. In the first step, **grammar in context,** new structures are shown in the natural context of passages, articles, and dialogues. This is followed by a **grammar presentation** of structures in clear and accessible grammar charts, notes, and examples. The third step is **focused practice** of both form and meaning in numerous and varied controlled exercises. In the fourth step, **communication practice,** students use the new structures freely and creatively in motivating, open-ended activities.

A COMPLETE CLASSROOM TEXT AND REFERENCE GUIDE

A major goal in the development of ***Focus on Grammar*** has been to provide Student Books that serve not only as vehicles for classroom instruction but also as resources for reference and self-study. In each Student Book, the combination of grammar charts, grammar notes, and expansive appendices provides a complete and invaluable reference guide for the student.

THOROUGH RECYCLING

Underpinning the scope and sequence of the series as a whole is the belief that students need to use target structures many times in many contexts at increasing levels of difficulty. For this reason new grammar is constantly recycled so that students will feel thoroughly comfortable with it.

COMPREHENSIVE TESTING PROGRAM

SelfTests at the end of each part of the Student Book allow for continual assessment of progress. In addition, diagnostic and final tests in the Teacher's Manual provide a ready-made, ongoing evaluation component for each student.

THE **INTERMEDIATE** STUDENT BOOK

Focus on Grammar: An Intermediate Course for Reference and Practice, Second Edition, is divided into eight parts comprising thirty-eight units. Each part contains grammatically related units with each unit focusing on a specific grammatical structure. Where appropriate, contrast units present two contrasting forms (for example, the simple present tense and the present progressive). Each unit has a major theme relating the exercises to one another. All units have the same clear, easy-to-follow format:

GRAMMAR IN CONTEXT

Grammar in Context presents the grammar focus of the unit in a natural context. The texts, all of which are recorded, present language in various formats. These include newspaper and magazine excerpts, Web sites, e-mail messages, advertisements, instructions, questionnaires, and other formats that students encounter in their day-to-day lives. In addition to presenting grammar in context, this introductory section raises student motivation and provides an opportunity for incidental learning and lively classroom discussions. Topics are varied, including employment, the weather, marriage, homelessness, the environment, and future technology. Each text is preceded by a pre-reading activity called **Before You Read.** Pre-reading questions create interest, elicit students' knowledge about the topic, help point out features of the text, and lead students to make predictions about the reading.

GRAMMAR PRESENTATION

This section is made up of grammar charts, notes, and examples. The Grammar **charts** focus on the form of the unit's target structure. The clear and easy-to-understand boxes present each grammatical form in all its combinations. Affirmative and negative statements, *yes/no* and *wh-* questions, short answers, and contractions are presented for all tenses and modals covered. These charts provide students with a clear visual reference for each new structure.

The Grammar **notes** and **examples** that follow the charts focus on the meaning and use of the structure. Each note gives a clear explanation of the grammar point, and is always accompanied by one or more examples. Where appropriate, timelines help illustrate the meaning of verb tenses and their relationship to one another. *Be careful!* notes alert students to common ESL/EFL errors. Usage Notes provide guidelines for using and understanding different levels of formality and correctness. Pronunciation Notes are provided when appropriate. Reference Notes provide cross-references to related units and the Appendices.

FOCUSED PRACTICE

The exercises in this section provide practice for all uses of the structure presented in the Grammar Presentation. Each Focused Practice section begins with a "for recognition only" exercise called **Discover the Grammar.** Here, students are expected to recognize either the form of the structure or its meaning without having to produce any language. This activity raises awareness of the structures as it builds confidence.

Following the Discover the Grammar activity are exercises that practice the grammar in a controlled, but still contextualized, environment. The exercises proceed from simpler to more complex. There is a large variety of exercise types including fill-in-the-blanks, matching, multiple choice, question and sentence formation, and editing (error analysis). Exercises are cross-referenced to the appropriate grammar notes so that students can review the notes if necessary. As with the Grammar in Context, students are exposed to many different written formats, including letters, postcards, journal entries, resumes, charts, schedules, menus, and news articles. Many exercises are art-based, providing a rich and interesting context for meaningful practice. All Focused Practice exercises are suitable for self-study or homework. A complete **Answer Key** is provided in a separate booklet.

COMMUNICATION PRACTICE

The exercises in this section are intended for in-class use. The first exercise is **Listening.** After having had exposure to and practice with the grammar in its written form, students now have the opportunity to check their aural comprehension. Students hear a variety of listening formats, including conversations, radio announcements, weather forecasts, interviews, and phone recordings. After listening to the recording (or hearing the teacher read the tapescript, which can be found in the Teacher's Manual), students complete a task that focuses on either the form or the meaning of the structure. It is suggested that students be allowed to hear the text as many times as they wish to complete the task successfully.

The listening exercise is followed by a variety of activities that provide students with the opportunity to use the grammar in open-ended, interactive ways. Students work in pairs or small groups in interviews, surveys, opinion polls, information gaps, discussions, role plays, games, and problem-solving activities. The activities are fun and engaging and offer ample opportunity for self-expression and cross-cultural comparison. The final exercise in this section is always **Writing,** in which students practice using the structure in a variety of written formats.

REVIEW OR SELFTEST

After the last unit of each part, there is a review feature that can be used as a self-test. The exercises in this section test the form and use of the grammar content of the part. These tests include questions in the format of the Structure and Written Expression sections of the TOEFL®. An **Answer Key** is provided after each test, with cross-references to units for easy review.

FROM GRAMMAR TO WRITING

At the end of each part, there is a writing section called From Grammar to Writing in which students are guided to use the grammar structures in a piece of extended writing. Formats include a personal letter, a business letter, instructions, an informal note, and an essay. Students practice pre-writing strategies such as brainstorming, word-mapping, tree-diagramming, and outlining. Each writing section concludes with peer review and editing.

APPENDICES

The Appendices provide useful information, such as lists of common irregular verbs, common adjective-plus-preposition combinations, and spelling and pronunciation rules. The Appendices can help students do the unit exercises, act as a springboard for further classroom work, and serve as a reference source.

NEW IN THIS EDITION

In response to users' requests, this edition has:

- new and updated texts for Grammar in Context
- pre-reading questions
- a new easy-to-read format for grammar notes and examples
- cross-references that link exercises to corresponding grammar notes
- more photos and art
- more recorded exercises
- more information gap exercises
- more editing (error analysis) exercises
- a writing exercise in each unit
- a From Grammar to Writing section at the end of each part

SUPPLEMENTARY **COMPONENTS**

All supplementary components of *Focus on Grammar, Second Edition,* —the Audio Program (cassettes or CDs), the Workbook, and the Teacher's Manual—are tightly keyed to the Student Book. Along with the CD-ROM, these components provide a wealth of practice and an opportunity to tailor the series to the needs of each individual classroom.

AUDIO PROGRAM

All of the Listening exercises as well as the Grammar in Context passages and other appropriate exercises are recorded on cassettes and CDs. The symbol ▭ appears next to these activities. The scripts appear in the Teacher's Manual and may be used as an alternative way of presenting these activities.

WORKBOOK

The Workbook accompanying *Focus on Grammar: An Intermediate Course for Reference and Practice, Second Edition,* provides a wealth of additional exercises appropriate for self-study of the target grammar of each unit in the Student Book. Most of the exercises are fully contextualized. Themes of the Workbook exercises are typically a continuation or a spin-off of the corresponding Student Book unit themes. There are also eight tests, one for each of the eight Student Book parts. These tests have questions in the format of the Structure and Written Expression section of the TOEFL®. Besides reviewing the material in the Student Book, these questions provide invaluable practice to those who are interested in taking this widely administered test.

TEACHER'S MANUAL

The Teacher's Manual, divided into five parts, contains a variety of suggestions and information to enrich the material in the Student Book. The first part gives general suggestions for each section of a typical unit. The next part offers practical teaching suggestions and cultural information to accompany specific material in each unit. The Teacher's Manual also provides ready-to-use diagnostic and final tests for each of the eight parts of the Student Book. In addition, a complete script of the Listening exercises is provided, as is an answer key for the diagnostic and final tests.

CD-ROM

The *Focus on Grammar* CD-ROM provides individualized practice with immediate feedback. Fully contextualized and interactive, the activities broaden and extend practice of the grammatical structures in the reading, listening, and writing skill areas. The CD-ROM includes grammar review, review tests, and all relevant reference material from the Student Book. It can also be used alongside the *Longman Interactive American Dictionary* CD-ROM.

CREDITS

TEXT

Grateful acknowledgment is given to the following publishing companies and individuals for permission to print, reprint, or adapt materials for which they own copyrights:

The Warrior Workout. Adapted from "Body Jolt" by Laurie Tarkin. Published in *Fitness Magazine,* July/August 1998. Copyright © 1998 by Laurie Tarkin. Used by permission of Laurie Tarkin. **"This Used to Be My Playground,"** by Madonna Ciccone and Shep Pettibone © 1992 WB Music Corp., Webo Girl Publishing, Inc., MCA Music Publishing, a Division of MCA Inc. and Shepsongs Inc. All Rights o/b/o Webo Girl Publishing, Inc. administered by WB Music Corp. All Rights o/b/o Shepsongs, Inc. administered by MCA Music Publishing, a Division of MCA Inc. All Rights Reserved. Used by Permission.

PHOTOGRAPHS

Grateful acknowledgment is given to the following for providing photographs:

p. 11 *(left)* Eyewire, Inc.; **p. 11** *(center, right)* MEDIAFOCUS International, LLC; **p. 12** Stephen Danelian/ Exposure New York; **p. 19** Corbis/Asian Art & Archeology, Inc.; **p. 24** Corbis; **p. 26** Copyright © 1994 by Barbara Seyda. Reprinted by permission of Susan Bergholz Literary Services, New York; **pp. 27, 29** RubberBall Productions; **p. 30** Corbis/Bettmann; **p. 35** *(left)* Seth Poppel Yearbook Archives; **p. 35** *(right)* Corbis/Jim Lake; **p. 36** PhotoDisc Inc.; **p. 58** Corbis/Jennie Woodcock; **p. 65** Reflections Photolibrary; **p. 95** Cornell University Photography, photo by Frank DiMeo; **p. 99** Courtesy of Dr. Eloy Rodriguez; **p. 100** Courtesy of Corel and IWEC (International Wildlife Education & Conservation; **p. 114** Courtesy of Professional Flair and Mary Verdi Fletcher; **p. 118** Courtesy of Professional Flair and Mary Verdi Fletcher; **p. 142** Comstock; **p. 150** *(left)* HI-AYH Photo by Joe Hochner; **p. 150** *(right)* Swedish YHA; **p. 156** Courtesy of Hong Kong Youth Hostel Association; **p. 166** Corbis/S. Carmona; **p. 201** Courtesy of Robert Stolarick; **p. 208** PhotoDisc Inc.; **p. 213** PhotoDisc Inc.; **p. 216** *(left)* Corbis/Yogi, Inc.; **p. 216** *(right)* PhotoDisc Inc.; **pp. 226, 231, 234** Courtesy of Beth Boyd; **p. 235** Corbis/Bob Krist; **p. 254** AP/Wide World Photos; **p. 259** Corbis/Kevin R. Morris; **p. 260** AP/Wide World Photos; **p. 277** Centers for Disease Control and Prevention; **p. 281** *(1–7)* PhotoDisc Inc.; **p. 281** *(8)* RubberBall Productions; **p. 285** RubberBall Productions; **p. 291** Courtesy of PNI; **p. 298** RubberBall Productions; **p. 306** Copyright The New Yorker Collection, 1995, Robert Mankoff from cartoonbank.com; **pp. 312, 332** Courtesy of PNI; **p. 340** Courtesy of the New York State Governor's Traffic Safety Committee; **p. 344** Courtesy of Ben Leonard; **p. 350** Courtesy of Beth Boyd and Marjorie Fuchs; **p. 352** Spencer Grant/Photo Researchers, Inc.; **p. 358** Corbis/Ric Ergenbright; **p. 365** PhotoDisc Inc.; **p. 378** Copyright R. Calentine/Visuals Unlimited, Inc.; **p. 388** Corbis/Bettmann; **p. 394** PhotoDisc Inc.

ACKNOWLEDGMENTS

Before acknowledging the many people who have contributed to the second edition of *Focus on Grammar: An Intermediate Course for Reference and Practice*, we wish to express our gratitude to those who worked on the **FIRST EDITION**, and whose influence is still present in the new work.

Our continuing thanks to:

- **Joanne Dresner,** who initiated the project and helped conceptualize the general approach of *Focus on Grammar*.

- **Nancy Perry, Penny Laporte, Louisa Hellegers,** and **Joan Saslow,** our editors, for helping to bring the first edition to fruition.

- **Sharon Hilles,** our grammar consultant, for her insight and advice.

Writing a **SECOND EDITION** has given us the wonderful opportunity to update the book and implement valuable feedback from teachers who have been using *Focus on Grammar*.

We wish, first of all, to acknowledge the following consultants and reviewers for reading the manuscript and offering many useful suggestions:

- CONSULTANTS: **Marcia Edwards Hijaab**, Henrico County Schools, Richmond, Virginia; **Kevin McClure**, ELS Language Center, San Francisco; **Tim Rees**, Transworld Schools, Boston; **Alison Rice**, Director of the International English Language Institute, Hunter College, New York; **Ellen Shaw**, University of Nevada, Las Vegas.

- REVIEWERS: **Lynn Alfred**, William Rainey Harper College, Palatine, Illinois; **Sandra Banke**, Clark College, ESL, Vancouver, Washington; **Judy Cleek**, University of Tennessee-Martin; **Julie Cloninger**, English Language Program, Virginia Commonwealth University; **Mary Coiner**, J. Sargeant Reynolds Community College, Richmond, Virginia; **Diane De Echeandia**, Delhi Technical College, Delhi, New York; **Meg Flynn**, Avila College, Intensive Language and Culture Program, Kansas City, Missouri; **Irene Frankel**, Assistant Director of New School University, English Language Studies, New York; **Andrea Whitmore**, Applied Language Institute at Penn Valley Community College, Kansas City, Missouri.

(continued on next page)

We are also grateful to the following editors and colleagues:

- **Françoise Leffler**, editor *extraordinaire*, for her dedication, her keen ear, and her sense of style. We also appreciate her unstinting attention to detail and her humor, which had us looking forward to her calls. The book is undoubtedly better for her efforts.

- **Louisa Hellegers**, for being accessible and responsive to individual authors while coordinating the many complex aspects of this project.

- **Virginia Bernard**, for piloting the book through its many stages of production.

- **Irene Schoenberg**, author of the Basic level of *Focus on Grammar*, for generously sharing her experience in teaching our first edition and for her enthusiastic support.

- **Dr. Eloy Rodriguez**, for contributing his time and expertise as we developed the content for Unit 10. Much of the art in that unit is based on photographs from his fieldwork.

- **Andréa Cook, Gretchen Flint, Sharon Goldstein, Ian Harvey, Molly Heron, Vicky Julian, Lee Kurchinski, Phyllis Neumann, Thomas Saunders Pyle, Miriam Shakter**, and **Mark Smith**, for sharing with us their native-speaker intuition.

Finally, we are grateful, as always, to **Rick Smith** and **Luke Frances**, for their helpful input and for standing by and supporting us as we navigated our way through another *FOG*.

M.F. and M.B.

THE STORY BEHIND THE COVER

The photograph on the cover is the work of **Andy Goldsworthy**, an innovative artist who works exclusively with natural materials to create unique outdoor sculpture, which he then photographs. Each Goldsworthy sculpture communicates the artist's own "sympathetic contact with nature" by intertwining forms and shapes structured by natural events with his own creative perspective. Goldsworthy's intention is not to "make his mark on the landscape, but to create a new perception and an evergrowing understanding of the land."

So, too, *Focus on Grammar* takes grammar found in its most natural context and expertly reveals its hidden structure and meaning. It is our hope that students using the series will also develop a new perception and an "evergrowing" understanding of the world of grammar.

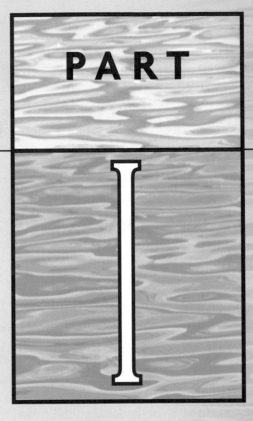

PART I

PRESENT, PAST, AND FUTURE:
REVIEW AND EXPANSION

PRESENT PROGRESSIVE AND SIMPLE PRESENT TENSE

GRAMMAR **IN CONTEXT**

BEFORE YOU READ Look at the cartoons. What are the people doing? How do they feel?

Read this article about cross-cultural communication.

WHAT'S YOUR CROSS-CULTURAL IQ?

Are you **living** in your native country or in another country? **Do** you ever **travel** abroad? **Do** you **understand** the misunderstandings below? *(Explanations appear at the bottom of the page.)*

SITUATION 1

WHY IS SHE WEARING HER ROBE!? IT'S 7:00 P.M.!

EVA!

KARL!

WHAT IS HE DOING HERE ALREADY!? IT'S ONLY 7:00 P.M.!

SITUATION 2

WHY IS HE LEANING BACK LIKE THAT?

HI. HOW ARE YOU DOING?

FINE, THANKS, HOW ARE YOU?

WHY IS HE STANDING SO CLOSE?

EXPLANATIONS

SITUATION 1:

Eva invited Karl to a seven o'clock party.

Karl **is arriving** at exactly 7:00 P.M. That**'s** polite in his culture.

In Eva's culture, people usually **arrive** at least a half an hour later than the scheduled time. That**'s** polite in her culture.

SITUATION 2:

Sami and Taro **are having** a conversation. They **are** both **feeling** uncomfortable.

In Sami's culture, people usually **stand** quite close to each other.

In Taro's culture, people **like** to stand farther apart, and they almost never **touch**.

GRAMMAR **PRESENTATION**

PRESENT PROGRESSIVE   **SIMPLE PRESENT TENSE**

AFFIRMATIVE STATEMENTS

SUBJECT	BE	BASE FORM OF VERB + -ING	
I	am*		
You	are		
He She It	is	traveling	now.
We You They	are		

AFFIRMATIVE STATEMENTS

SUBJECT		VERB
I You		travel.
He She It	often	travels.
We You They		travel.

*For contractions of *I am, you are,* etc., see Appendix 20, page A-8.

NEGATIVE STATEMENTS

SUBJECT	BE	NOT + BASE FORM OF VERB + -ING	
He	is	not traveling	now.

NEGATIVE STATEMENTS

SUBJECT	DO NOT / DOES NOT + BASE FORM OF VERB	
He	does not travel	often.

YES / NO QUESTIONS

BE	SUBJECT	BASE FORM OF VERB + -ING	
Is	he	traveling	now?

YES / NO QUESTIONS

DO / DOES	SUBJECT	BASE FORM OF VERB	
Does	he	travel	often?

SHORT ANSWERS

Yes,	he	is.
No,		isn't.

SHORT ANSWERS

Yes,	he	does.
No,		doesn't.

WH- QUESTIONS

WH-WORD	BE	SUBJECT	BASE FORM OF VERB + -ING	
Where	are	you	traveling	now?

WH- QUESTIONS

WH-WORD	DO / DOES	SUBJECT		BASE FORM OF VERB
Where	do	you	usually	travel?

NOTES	EXAMPLES

1. Use the **present progressive** (also called the present continuous) to describe something that is happening <u>right now</u>.

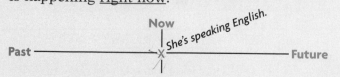

Use the **simple present tense** to describe what <u>regularly</u> happens, what <u>usually</u> happens, or what <u>always</u> happens.

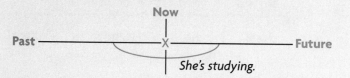

- Eva **is talking** to Karl.
- At the moment, she**'s wearing** a robe.
- She**'s speaking** English right now.

- Eva **talks** to Karl every day.
- She usually **wears** jeans.
- She **speaks** Spanish at home.

REFERENCE NOTE

For **spelling rules** on forming the **present progressive,** see Appendix 15 on page A-6.

For **spelling rules** on forming the third person singular of the **simple present** tense, see Appendix 16 on page A-6.

For **pronunciation rules** for the **simple present** tense, see Appendix 22 on page A-10.

---

2. Use the **present progressive** to describe something that is happening in the <u>extended present time</u> (for example, *nowadays, this month, these days, this year*), even if it's not happening at the moment of speaking.

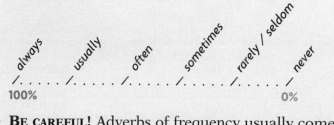

Use the **simple present tense** with <u>adverbs of frequency</u> to express how often something happens.

always | usually | often | sometimes | rarely / seldom | never

/. . . . . /. . . . . /. . . . . /. . . . . /. . . . . /
100%   0%

▶ **BE CAREFUL!** Adverbs of frequency usually come before the main verb, but they go after the verb *be*.

- We**'re studying** U.S. customs *this month*.
- Laura**'s studying** in France *this year*.
- **Are** you **studying** hard *these days*?

- In Spain, women *always* **kiss** on both cheeks.
- In France, women *often* **kiss** on both cheeks.
- We *rarely* **stand** very close to each other.
- In China, children *never* **call** adults by their first name.

- They *never* **come** late.
- They **are** *never* late.

3. The **present progressive** is often used to show that the action is <u>temporary</u>.

- **I'm staying** with friends, but I plan to leave soon.

---

4. REMEMBER! **Non-action verbs** (also called stative verbs) usually <u>describe states or situations</u> but not actions. Most non-action verbs are <u>not</u> usually <u>used in the present progressive</u> even when they describe a situation that exists at the moment of speaking.

- Jane **wants** to go home right now.
  NOT ~~Jane is wanting to go home now.~~

Non-action verbs:

a. express **emotions**
(*hate, like, love, want, feel*)

- I'm hungry. I **want** a hamburger.
  NOT ~~I'm wanting a hamburger.~~

USAGE NOTE: Unlike other verbs that express emotion, *feel* is often used in the progressive form.

- Ricki **feels** homesick.
  OR
- Ricki **is feeling** homesick.

b. describe **mental states**
(*know, remember, believe, think [= believe], suppose, understand*)

- I **know** a lot of U.S. customs now.
- Ari **remembers** your number.

c. show **possession**
(*have, own, possess, belong*)

- Cesar **has** two brothers.
- Some students **own** cars.

d. describe **perceptions** and **senses**
(*hear, see, smell, taste, feel, notice, seem, look [= seem], be, appear, sound*)

- I **hear** the telephone.
- Dina **seems** tired.

▶ **BE CAREFUL!** Some verbs that describe perceptions and senses such as *taste, smell, feel,* and *look* can have both a non-action and an action meaning.

- The soup **tastes** good. Try some.
- She**'s tasting** the soup to see if it needs more salt.

(See Appendix 2, page A-2, for a list of non-action verbs.)

---

5. Use the **simple present tense** to talk about situations that are <u>not connected to time</u>—for example, scientific facts and physical laws.

- Stress **causes** high blood pressure.
- Water **boils** at 212° F=100° C.

REFERENCE NOTE
You can also use the present progressive and the simple present to talk about the **future**.
(See Unit 6.)

FOCUSED PRACTICE

1 DISCOVER THE GRAMMAR

*Read these journal entries by Brian, a Canadian summer exchange student studying in Argentina. Circle all the verbs that describe what is happening **now**. Underline the verbs that describe what **generally** happens.*

June 28: I'm sitting in a seat 30,000 feet above the earth en route to Argentina! I usually have dinner at this time, but right now I have a headache from the excitement. My seatmate is eating my food. She looks happy.

June 30: It's 7:30. My host parents are still working. Carlos, my father, works at home. My little brother Ricardo is cute. He looks (and acts) a lot like Bobby. Right now, he's looking over my shoulder and trying to read my journal.

July 4: The weather is cold here. I usually spend the first weekend of July at the beach. Today I'm walking around in a heavy sweater.

August 6: I feel so tired tonight. Everyone else feels great in the evening because they take long naps in the afternoon.

2 SCHEDULE CHANGES

Grammar Note 1

Look at Brian's schedule. Complete the sentences below. Use the present progressive or the simple present tense. Choose between affirmative and negative forms.

○	8:30–12:30	~~Attend class~~	Go on field trip to the Museum of the City	○
○	2:00–3:00	Eat lunch		○
○	3:00–5:00	~~Take a nap~~	Work on my Web page	○
○	5:00–6:30	~~Do homework~~	(Call home at 5:00 sharp today!)	○
○	6:30–8:30	~~Play tennis~~	Watch a video with Eva	○
○	9:00	Have dinner		○

1. Brian usually _____attends class_____ between 8:30 and 12:30, but today he
   ___is going on a field trip to the Museum of the City.___

2. He always _____ between 2:00 and 3:00.

3. He normally _____ after lunch, but today he _____

   _____

4. It's 5:00, but he _____ homework now. He _____

_____ instead.

5. It's 6:20. He _____

6. It's 6:45, but he _____ tennis. He _____

_____ with Eva.

7. It's 9:00. Brian _____

---

3 DIFFERENT MEANINGS   **Grammar Notes 1–4**

Complete these conversations that take place outside of a classroom. Choose between the present progressive and the simple present tense of the verbs in parentheses.

1. **LI-WU:** Hi, Paulo. What _____are_____ you _____doing_____ ?
                                                          a. (do)

PAULO: Oh, I _____ for class to begin.
                          b. (wait)

LI-WU: How are you? You _____ tired.
                                    c. (look)

PAULO: I am a little. I _____ evenings this semester. Hey, is that your
                                    d. (work)

teacher over there?

LI-WU: Yes. She _____ to one of my
                              e. (talk)

classmates.

PAULO: I wonder what's wrong. He _____ at
                                          f. (not look)

her. He _____ uncomfortable.
                  g. (look)

LI-WU: Oh. That _____ anything. In Taiwan
                              h. (not mean)

it's not respectful to look directly at your teacher.

2. MORIKO: Look, there's Miguel. He _____ to Luisa.
                                                  a. (talk)

NINA: Yes. They _____ a class together
                              b. (take)

this semester.

MORIKO: They _____ very close to each other.
                            c. (stand)

_____ you _____ they
                          d. (think)

_____ ?
      e. (date)

(continued on next page)

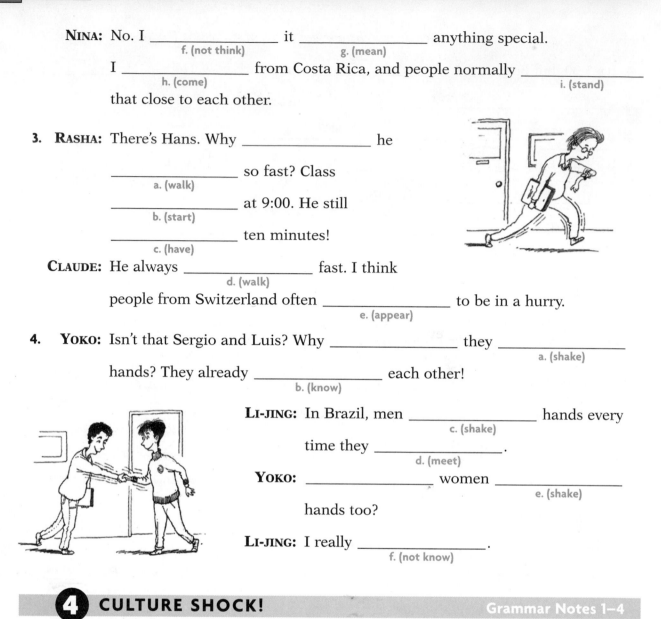

NINA: No. I _____ it _____ anything special.
f. (not think)   g. (mean)

I _____ from Costa Rica, and people normally _____
h. (come)   i. (stand)

that close to each other.

3. RASHA: There's Hans. Why _____ he

_____ so fast? Class
a. (walk)

_____ at 9:00. He still
b. (start)

_____ ten minutes!
c. (have)

CLAUDE: He always _____ fast. I think
d. (walk)

people from Switzerland often _____ to be in a hurry.
e. (appear)

4. YOKO: Isn't that Sergio and Luis? Why _____ they _____
a. (shake)

hands? They already _____ each other!
b. (know)

LI-JING: In Brazil, men _____ hands every
c. (shake)

time they _____.
d. (meet)

YOKO: _____ women _____
e. (shake)

hands too?

LI-JING: I really _____.
f. (not know)

④ CULTURE SHOCK!   Grammar Notes 1–4

Complete this paragraph. Use the correct form of the verbs in the box.

cause	feel	live	~~make~~	travel

New food, new customs, new routines—they all _____make_____ international travel
                                                    1.

interesting. But they also _____ culture shock in many travelers.
                                 2.

_____ you now _____ or _____ in a culture
                         3.   4.

different from your own? If so, why _____ you _____ so good
                                                              5.

(or so bad)? Take the quiz on the next page and learn more about the four stages of

culture shock.

Complete the following statements, using the correct form of the verbs in the box. Then, check the statements that are true for you now.

annoy	feel	improve	love	make	treat	understand	want

a. I _____ it here! ☐
6.

b. People always _____ me very kindly. ☐
7.

c. The customs here often _____ me. ☐
8.

d. I _____ to go home! ☐
9.

e. My language skills _____ a lot this month. ☐
10.

f. I _____ a lot of new friends these days. ☐
11.

g. I still _____ everything, but I _____ at home. ☐
12. (negative)   13.

QUIZ RESULTS:

If you checked . . .	You may be in the . . .	
a and **b**	**Honeymoon Stage:**	In the first weeks everything seems great.
c and **d**	**Rejection Stage:**	You have negative feelings about the new culture.
e and **f**	**Adjustment Stage:**	Things are getting better these days.
g	**Adaptation Stage:**	You are finally comfortable in the new culture.

⑤ EDITING

Read this student's journal. Find and correct eleven mistakes in the use of the present progressive or simple present tense. The first mistake is already corrected.

> ○ 　　　　　　　　　　　　　　　'm sitting
> It's 12:30 and I ~~sit~~ in the library right now. My classmates are eating lunch together,
>
> but I'm not hungry yet. At home, we eat never this early. Today our journal topic is
>
> culture shock. It's a good topic for me right now because I'm being pretty homesick.
>
> I miss my old routine. At home we always are eating a big meal at 2:00 in the
>
> afternoon. Then we rest. But here in Toronto I'm having a 3:00 conversation class.
>
> Every day, I almost fall asleep in class, and my teacher ask me, "Are you bored?"
>
> Of course I'm not bored. I just need my afternoon nap! This class always is fun.
>
> This semester, we work on a project with video cameras. My team is filming groups
>
> of people from different cultures. We are analyze "social distance." That means how
>
> close to each other these people stand. According to my new watch, it's 12:55,
>
> so I leave now for my 1:00 class. Teachers here really aren't liking tardiness!

COMMUNICATION PRACTICE

6 LISTENING

A school newspaper is interviewing a new foreign student. Listen. Then listen again and check the things the student usually does and the things she is doing now or these days.

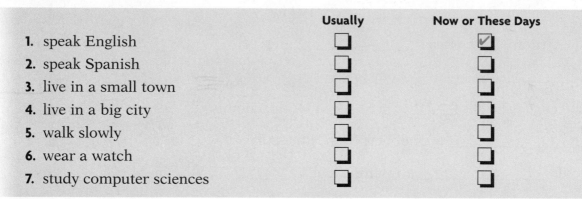

	Usually	Now or These Days
1. speak English	☐	☑
2. speak Spanish	☐	☐
3. live in a small town	☐	☐
4. live in a big city	☐	☐
5. walk slowly	☐	☐
6. wear a watch	☐	☐
7. study computer sciences	☐	☐

7 GETTING TO KNOW YOU

Walk around your classroom. Ask your classmates questions. Find someone who . . .

Name(s)

likes visiting foreign countries _____

isn't wearing a watch _____

speaks more than two languages _____

is studying something besides English _____

doesn't watch sports on TV _____

is planning to travel this year _____

_____   _____
        (add your own)

EXAMPLE:
A: Do you like visiting foreign countries?
B: Yes, I do. What about you?

Report back to the class.

EXAMPLE:
Tania and José like visiting foreign countries.

8 WHAT'S HAPPENING?

Work in pairs. Look at the photographs. Describe them. What's happening?
Discuss possible explanations for each situation. Compare your answers to those
of your classmates.

EXAMPLE:

A: He's pointing. He looks angry.

B: Maybe he's just explaining something.

9 QUESTIONABLE QUESTIONS?

Work in small groups. Look at these questions. In your culture, which questions
are appropriate to ask someone you just met? Which are not appropriate?
Compare your choices with those of your classmates. Discuss appropriate and
inappropriate questions in an English-speaking culture you know.

Where do you come from?   Do you have any children?

How old are you?   Where do you live?

What do you do?   Are you living alone?

How much rent do you pay?   How much do you weigh?

What are you studying?   Why do you have only one child?

Are you married?   Are you wearing perfume?

10 WRITING

Write a paragraph about a new experience you are having. Maybe you are living
in a new country, taking a new class, or working at a new job. Describe the
situation. How is it different from what you usually do? How do you feel in
the situation?

EXAMPLE:

I usually live at home with my parents, but this month I'm living
with my aunt and uncle. Everything seems different. My aunt . . .

UNIT

2 IMPERATIVE

GRAMMAR IN CONTEXT

BEFORE YOU READ Look at the pictures. What is the woman doing? What do *you* do to stay fit?

Read part of an exercise routine presented in a fitness magazine.

THE WARRIOR WORKOUT

Having a bad day? **Don't let** it get you down. **Try** our kickboxing workout instead. You'll feel better *and* build your strength. **Do** it three times a week for fast results.

THE JAB

Get into the basic position: **Bend** your knees and **place** your right foot in front. **Raise** your fists with your right hand in front. Now **punch** with your right fist. **Don't stand** straight as you punch. Instead, **lean** forward for more power. **Bring** your fist back immediately. Then **change** sides.

THE POWER KICK

Get into the basic position and **move** your weight onto your right foot. **Bring** your left knee as high as your hip. Then **kick** to the side. **Point** your toes as you kick.

GRAMMAR **PRESENTATION**
IMPERATIVE

AFFIRMATIVE	
BASE FORM OF VERB	
Bend	your knees.
Raise	your fists.

NEGATIVE		
DON'T	**BASE FORM OF VERB**	
Don't	**stand**	straight.
	kick	to the front.

NOTES

EXAMPLES

1. Use the imperative to:

  a. give **directions** and **instructions**.

- **Get** into the basic position.
- **Turn** left at the light.

  b. give **orders** or **commands**.

- **Get up!**
- **Don't move!**

  c. make **requests** (use *please* in addition to the imperative).

- *Please* **read** this article.
- **Read** this article, *please*.

  d. give **advice** or make **suggestions**.

- Always **warm up** first.
- **Don't exercise** when you're sick.

  e. give **warnings**.

- **Be** careful!
- **Don't trip**!

  f. extend an **informal invitation**.

- **Work out** with us tomorrow.
- **Bring** a friend.

▶ **BE CAREFUL!** Do not use the imperative in formal situations (for example, when inviting a boss or a teacher).

- Would you like to join us, Mrs. Rivera?
  NOT ~~Join us, Mrs. Rivera.~~

2. Note that the <u>subject</u> of an imperative statement is *you*. However, *you* is <u>not said or written</u>.

- **Stand up** straight.
- **Don't hold** your breath.

▶ **BE CAREFUL!** The imperative form is the same in both the singular and the plural.

- John, **point** your toes.
- John and Susan, **point** your toes.

FOCUSED PRACTICE

① DISCOVER THE GRAMMAR

Match the imperative in column A with a situation in column B.

Column A	Column B
_g_ **1.** Don't touch that!	**a.** Someone is visiting a friend.
_____ **2.** Look both ways.	**b.** Someone is going out into the cold.
_____ **3.** Dress warmly!	**c.** Someone is crossing a street.
_____ **4.** Don't bend your knees.	**d.** Someone is taking an exam.
_____ **5.** Mark each answer true or false.	**e.** Someone is exercising.
_____ **6.** Come in. Make yourself at home.	**f.** Someone is tasting some food.
_____ **7.** Try a little more pepper.	**g.** Something is hot.

② HEALTH SHAKE   Grammar Notes 1a and 2

Match a verb from column A with a phrase from column B to give instructions for making a banana-strawberry smoothie. Then put the sentences in order under the correct pictures.

Column A	Column B
Add	the ingredients until smooth.
Slice	six strawberries.
Wash	a banana.
Cut	orange juice into the blender.
Blend	the strawberries in half.
Pour	the fruit to the orange juice.

1. _____Slice a banana._____

2. _____

3. _____

4. _____

5. _____

6. _____

③ MARTIAL ARTS

Complete the advertisement for a martial arts school. Use the affirmative or negative imperative form of the verbs in the box.

become	choose	decrease	~~increase~~	learn
miss	register	take	~~think~~	wait

MARTIAL ARTS ACADEMY

_____ Don't think _____ that martial arts is only about physical training. A good
a.

martial arts program offers many other benefits as well. _____
b.

self-defense and more at the Martial Arts Academy:

◆ _____ stress. Martial arts training helps you relax.
c.

◆ _____ concentration. Martial arts students focus better.
d.

◆ _____ fit. Strength and flexibility improve as you learn.
e.

We are offering an introductory trial membership. _____ this special
f.

opportunity. _____ classes with Master Lorenzo Gibbons,
g.

a ninth-level Black Belt Master. _____ classes
h.

from our convenient schedule. _____!
i.

_____ now for a two-week trial.
j.

ONLY $20. ◆ UNIFORM INCLUDED.

④ EDITING

Read this martial arts student's essay. Find and correct five mistakes in the use of the imperative. The first mistake is already corrected.

For the Black Belt essay, Master Gibbons gave us this assignment: ~~You write~~ ^{Write}
about something important to you. My topic is *The Right Way*, the rules of
life for the martial arts. First, respects other people—treat them the way
you want them to treat you. Second, helped people in need. In other words,
use your strength for others, not to use it just for your own good. Third,
no lie or steal. You can't defend others when you feel guilty. There are
many rules, but these are the most important ones to me.

COMMUNICATION PRACTICE

5 LISTENING

A TV chef is describing how to make pancakes. Listen. Then listen again and number the instructions in the correct order.

_____ Heat a frying pan and melt a small piece of butter in it.

__1__ Beat two egg whites in a large bowl.

_____ Add one and a quarter cups of whole wheat flour to the egg whites.

_____ Flip the pancakes over.

_____ Blend in some fruit.

_____ Mix thoroughly.

_____ Top them with fruit or yogurt.

_____ Pour some of the pancake mixture into the frying pan.

_____ Add a cup of low-fat milk.

6 RECIPE EXCHANGE

Work in groups. Write down one of your favorite recipes. List the ingredients and write the directions. Read it to your group. Answer any questions they have.

EXAMPLE:

> **QUICK AND EASY BEAN TACOS**
>
> **Ingredients:** 1 can of beans (black, kidney, or pinto), 4 hard corn taco shells, 1 tomato, 1 onion, lettuce, salsa, spices (cumin, chili powder)
>
> **Directions:** Rinse and drain the beans. Add the spices. Simmer for 10 minutes. Chop the tomato and onion. Shred the lettuce. Fill the taco shells with the beans, tomatoes, and onion. Top with the lettuce and salsa.

A: How long do you rinse the beans?

B: Until the water looks clear. Use cold water. Don't use hot water.

7 CALM DOWN!

Work in small groups. Imagine you have been in a traffic jam for an hour. Someone is waiting to meet you on a street corner. What can you say to yourself to calm yourself down? Share your list with the other groups.

EXAMPLE:

A: Take a deep breath.

B: Don't think about the traffic.

C: . . .

8 INFORMATION GAP: FIND THE WAY

Work in pairs (A and B). You are both going to give driving directions to places on the map. Student B, turn to page 18 and follow the instructions there. Student A, trace the route from Carter and Adams to the Sunrise Gym. Be careful! One-way streets are marked → or ←. Don't go the wrong way on one-way streets! Give your partner directions. Ask your partner for directions to the Martial Arts Academy. Trace the route. Use sentences like these:

Start at Carter and Adams.	Go straight.	Continue on 9th Street.
(Don't) turn right.	Make a left turn.	Stay on Founders.

EXAMPLE:

A: I want to go to the Martial Arts Academy. Can you give me directions?

B: Sure. Start at Carter and Adams.

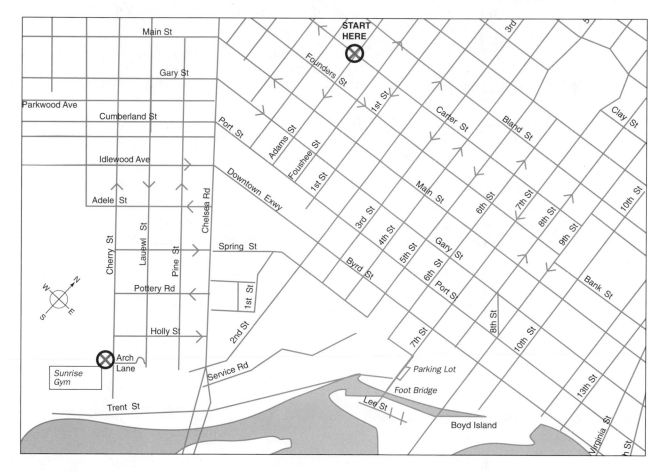

When you are finished, compare routes. Are they the same?

9 WRITING

Write directions from your school to another location. It can be your home, a store, the train station, or any place you choose.

INFORMATION GAP FOR STUDENT B

Student B, trace the route from Carter and Adams to the Martial Arts Academy. Give your partner directions. Ask your partner for directions to the Sunrise Gym. Trace the route. Be careful! One-way streets are marked → or ←. Don't go the wrong way on one-way streets! Use sentences like these:

Start at Carter and Adams.	**Go straight.**	**Continue on 9th Street.**
(Don't) turn right.	**Make a left turn.**	**Stay on Founders.**

EXAMPLE:

A: I want to go to the Martial Arts Academy. Can you give me directions?

B: Sure. Start at Carter and Adams.

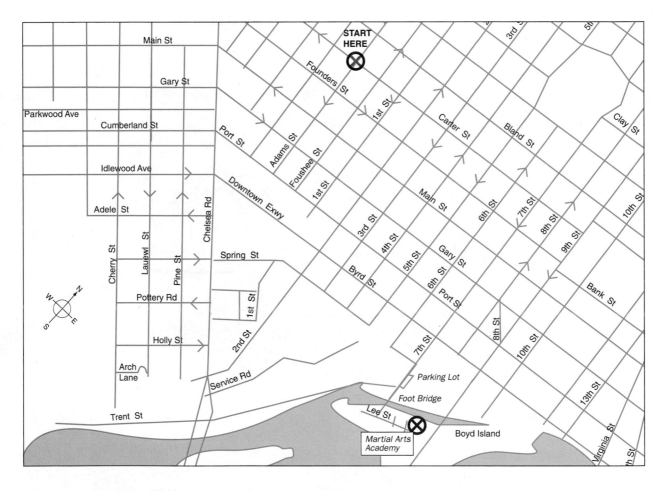

When you are finished, compare routes. Are they the same?

SIMPLE PAST TENSE

GRAMMAR **IN CONTEXT**

BEFORE YOU READ Look at the picture and the text next to it. What did Matsuo Basho do? How long did he live?

Read this excerpt from a biography of Japanese poet Matsuo Basho.

The old pond;
the frog.
Plop!

As for that flower
By the road—
My horse ate it!

First day of spring—
I keep thinking about
the end of autumn.

Matsuo Basho, 1644–1694

Matsuo Basho **wrote** more than 1,000 three-line poems called "haiku." He **chose** topics from nature, daily life, and human emotions. He **became** one of Japan's most famous poets, and his work **established** haiku as an important art form.

Matsuo Basho **was born** near Kyoto in 1644. He **did not want** to become a samurai (warrior) like his father. Instead, he **moved** to Edo (present-day Tokyo) and **studied** poetry. By 1681, he **had** many students and admirers.

Basho, however, **was** restless. Starting in 1684, he **traveled** on foot and on horseback all over Japan. Sometimes his friends **joined** him and they **wrote** poetry together. Travel **was** difficult in the seventeenth century, and Basho often **got** sick. He **died** in 1694, during a journey to Osaka. At that time he **had** 2,000 students.

GRAMMAR **PRESENTATION**
SIMPLE PAST TENSE: *BE*

AFFIRMATIVE STATEMENTS

SUBJECT	*BE*	
I	**was**	
You	**were**	
He She It	**was**	famous.
We You They	**were**	

NEGATIVE STATEMENTS

SUBJECT	*BE NOT*	
I	**wasn't**	
You	**weren't**	
He She It	**wasn't**	famous.
We You They	**weren't**	

YES / NO QUESTIONS

BE	SUBJECT	
Was	I	
Were	you	
Was	he she it	famous?
Were	we you they	

SHORT ANSWERS
AFFIRMATIVE

Yes,	you	**were.**
	I	**was.**
	he she it	**was.**
	you we they	**were.**

SHORT ANSWERS
NEGATIVE

No,	you	**weren't.**
	I	**wasn't.**
	he she it	**wasn't.**
	you we they	**weren't.**

WH- QUESTIONS

WH- WORD	*BE*	SUBJECT	
	was	I	
	were	you	
Where When Why	**was**	he she it	famous?
	were	we you they	

SIMPLE PAST TENSE: REGULAR AND IRREGULAR VERBS

AFFIRMATIVE STATEMENTS

SUBJECT	VERB	
I You He She It We You They	**moved** **traveled**	to Japan.
	came* **left***	in 1684.

NEGATIVE STATEMENTS

SUBJECT	DID NOT	BASE FORM OF VERB	
I You He She It We You They	**didn't**	**move** **travel**	to Japan.
		come **leave**	in 1684.

Come (came) and *leave (left)* are irregular verbs.
  See Appendix 1 on page A-1 for a list of irregular verbs.

YES / NO QUESTIONS

DID	SUBJECT	BASE FORM OF VERB	
Did	I you he she it we you they	**move** **travel**	to Japan?
		come **leave**	in 1684?

SHORT ANSWERS

	AFFIRMATIVE	
Yes,	you I he she it you we they	**did.**

SHORT ANSWERS

	NEGATIVE	
No,	you I he she it you we they	**didn't.**

WH- QUESTIONS

WH- WORD	DID	SUBJECT	BASE FORM OF VERB	
When Why	**did**	I you he she it we you they	**move** **travel**	to Japan?
			come? **leave?**	

NOTES	EXAMPLES

1. Use the **simple past tense** to talk about actions, states, or situations that are now **finished**.

Now
Past ——X—————————— Future
He was a poet.

- Basho **lived** in the seventeenth century.
- He **was** a poet.
- He **wrote** *haiku*.
- He **didn't stay** in one place.
- Where **did** he **travel**?

2. You can use the simple past tense with **time expressions** that refer to the past. Some examples of past time expressions are *last week, by 1681, in the seventeenth century, 300 years ago*.

- ***By 1681,*** he had many students.
- He lived ***in the seventeenth century***.
- He died more than ***300 years ago***.

3. REMEMBER: the simple past tense of **regular verbs** is formed by adding *–d* or *–ed*.

BASE FORM		SIMPLE PAST
live	→	live**d**
join	→	join**ed**
travel	→	travel**ed**
want	→	want**ed**
study	→	stud**ied**
hop	→	hop**ped**
prefer	→	prefer**red**

▶ **BE CAREFUL!** There are often <u>spelling changes</u> when you add *-d* or *-ed* to the verb.

REFERENCE NOTE
For **spelling rules** for the simple past tense of regular verbs, see Appendix 17 on page A-7.
For **pronunciation rules** for the simple past tense of regular verbs, see Appendix 23 on page A-10.

4. Many common English verbs are **irregular.** Their past tense is not formed by adding *-d* or *-ed*.

(See Appendix 1, page A-1, for a list of irregular verbs.)

BASE FORM		SIMPLE PAST
be	→	**was / were**
build	→	**built**
choose	→	**chose**
have	→	**had**
get	→	**got**
go	→	**went**

FOCUSED PRACTICE

1 DISCOVER THE GRAMMAR

Read more about Basho. Underline all the verbs in the past tense.
Then complete the time line on the left.

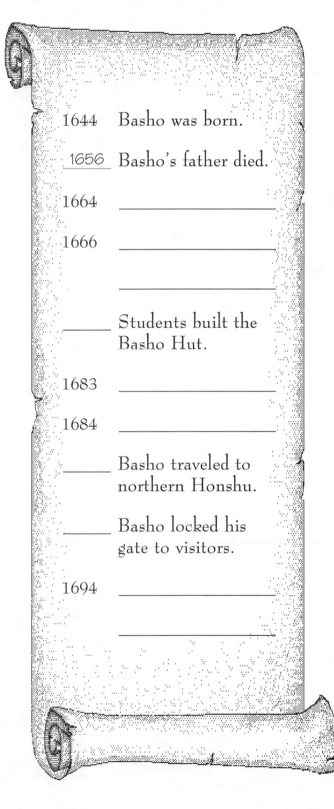

1644	Basho was born.
1656	Basho's father died.
1664	_____
1666	_____
_____	_____
_____	Students built the Basho Hut.
1683	_____
1684	_____
_____	Basho traveled to northern Honshu.
_____	Basho locked his gate to visitors.
1694	_____
	_____

As a son of a samurai, Basho grew up in the household of Todo Yoshitada, a young lord. After his father's death in 1656, Basho stayed on in the Yoshitada household. He and Todo wrote poetry together, and in 1664 they published some poems. Two years later, Todo died suddenly. Basho left the area.

Basho moved around for several years. In the 1670s, he went to Edo and stayed there. He found friendship and success once again. Basho judged poetry contests, published his own poetry, and taught students. His students built him a home outside the city in 1681. They planted a banana tree (a *basho*) in front and called his home Basho Hut. That is how the poet got his nickname: *Basho*.

In spite of this success, Basho became unhappy. He often wrote about loneliness. His mother died in 1683, and he began his travels a year later. His trip to the northern part of Honshu in 1689 was difficult, but his travel diary about this journey, *Narrow Road to the Deep North*, became one of Japan's greatest works of literature.

As a famous poet, Basho had many visitors—too many, in fact. In 1693 he locked his gate for a month, stayed alone, and wrote. The following year he took his final journey, to Osaka. He died there among his friends.

➋ ANOTHER POET

Complete this biography of another poet. Use the simple past tense form of the verbs in the boxes.

address appear be become happen lead leave ~~live~~ receive wear write write

Emily Dickinson, one of the most popular American poets,

_____lived_____ from 1830 to 1886. She _____ about
1.   2.

love, nature, and time. These _____ her favorite themes.
3.

Dickinson _____ an unusual life. After just one year
4.

of college, she _____ a recluse—she almost never
5.

_____ her house in Amherst, Massachusetts. At home,
6.

she _____ visitors, and she only _____ white.
7. (negative)   8.

In addition to her poetry, Dickinson _____ many letters. Other people
9.

always _____ the envelopes for her. During her lifetime only seven of
10.

her 1,700 poems _____ in print—and this _____ without
11.   12.

her knowledge or permission.

Now complete these lines from a poem by Emily Dickinson. Use the simple past tense form of the verbs in the box.

bite   ~~come~~   drink   eat   hop   see

A bird _____came_____ down the walk:
13.

He did not know I _____;
14.

He _____ an angle-worm in halves
15.

And _____ the fellow raw.
16.

And then he _____ a dew
17.

From a convenient grass,

And then _____ sidewise to the wall
18.

To let a beetle pass.

3 TWO POETS

Read about Basho. Ask questions about Dickinson. Write **yes / no** *questions about the underlined verbs. Write* **wh-** *questions about other underlined words. Then answer the questions with information from Exercise 2.*

1. Basho <u>was</u> a poet.

   A: ___Was Dickinson a poet?___

   B: ___Yes, she was.___

2. He was born <u>in 1644</u>.

   A: ___When was Dickinson born?___

   B: ___She was born in 1830.___

3. He <u>became</u> famous during his lifetime.

   A: _____

   B: _____

4. Basho <u>received</u> many visitors.

   A: _____

   B: _____

5. He <u>traveled</u> a lot.

   A: _____

   B: _____

6. Basho wrote <u>more than 1,000 poems</u>.

   A: _____

   B: _____

7. He wrote <u>about nature</u>.

   A: _____

   B: _____

8. He died <u>in 1694</u>.

   A: _____

   B: _____

4 ANA CASTILLO   Grammar Notes 1–4

Read the article about a modern writer.

⌒Ana Castillo is a modern poet, novelist, short story writer, and teacher. She was born in Chicago in 1953, and she lived there for thirty-two years. *Otro Canto,* her first book of poetry, appeared in 1977. In her work, she uses humor and a lively mixture of Spanish and English (Spanglish). She got her special writer's "voice" in a neighborhood with many different ethnic groups. She also thanks her father. "He had an outgoing and easy personality, and this . . . sense of humor. I got a lot from him. . . ."

Castillo attended high school, college, and graduate school in Chicago. In the 1970s, she taught English as a Second Language and Mexican history. She received a Ph.D. in American studies from Bremen University in Germany in 1992.⌒

Read the statements. Write **That's right** *or* **That's wrong**. *Correct the wrong statements.*

1. Ana Castillo was born in Mexico City.

   That's wrong. She wasn't born in Mexico City. She was born in Chicago.

2. She lived in Chicago until 1977.

   _____

3. Her father was very shy.

   _____

4. She grew up among people of different cultures.

   _____

5. Castillo got most of her education in Chicago.

   _____

6. She taught Spanish in the 1970s.

   _____

7. She went to France for her Ph.D.

   _____

COMMUNICATION PRACTICE

5 LISTENING

Listen to part of an interview with a poet. Listen again, and write the years on the time line.

| was born | parents left Turkey | moved to U.S. | began to write poetry | graduated from college | won poetry award | became a teacher |

1970

6 INFORMATION GAP: COMPLETE THE BIOGRAPHY

Work in pairs (A and B). Student B, turn to page 29 and follow the instructions there. Student A, read the short biography below. Ask your partner questions to complete the missing information. Answer your partner's questions.

> **EXAMPLE:**
> **A:** Where was Vladimir born?
> **B:** He was born in Kiev.
>   When was he born?
> **A:** He was born on May 6, 1975.

Vladimir Liapunov was born on May 6, 1975, in

_____Kiev_____. His mother was a

_____, and his father made shoes. At home

they spoke _____. In 1993 Vlad and his

family moved to _____. At first Vlad felt

_____. Then he got a part-time job as a

_____. He worked in a Russian restaurant.

He met _____ at work, and they got married

in 1995. They had a baby in 1997. _____ ago Vlad enrolled at the

community college. His goal is to own his own restaurant someday.

When you are finished, compare biographies. Are they the same?

 7 DIFFERENT LIVES

Work in pairs. Reread the information about Matsuo Basho (see pages 19 and 23)
and Emily Dickinson (see page 24). In what ways were the two poets similar?
How were they different? With your partner, write as many ideas as you can.
Compare your ideas with your classmates.

> **EXAMPLES:**
>
> **A:** Both Basho and Dickinson were poets.
>
> **B:** Basho lived in the seventeenth century. Dickinson lived in the nineteenth century.

8 HAIKU FOR YOU

Work in pairs. Write a three-line haiku poem. Make an observation about nature.
Try to use the simple past tense. Share your poem with your classmates.

> **EXAMPLE:**
>
> Early spring petals
>
> Fell on rain-wet ground—
>
> A hint of autumn?

9 RHYMING PAIRS

In poetry the last word of a line sometimes rhymes with the last word of another
line. For example, look at these first two lines of a famous poem by Joyce Kilmer.
In these lines, **see** *rhymes with* **tree***.*

> I think that I shall never see
>
> A poem lovely as a tree.

Work with a partner. Write down as many past-tense verbs as you can that rhyme
with the verbs in the box.

sent	bought	drew	kept	spoke

> **EXAMPLE:**
>
> Sent rhymes with <u>bent</u>, <u>lent</u>, <u>meant</u>, <u>spent</u>, and <u>went</u>.

Compare your lists with those of another pair of students. Who has the most
rhyming pairs? Now try to write two lines that rhyme. Use one of the rhyming
pairs from the lists you made with your partner. Share your rhymes with
your class.

 WRITING

Write a short autobiography. Do not put your name on it. Your teacher will collect all the papers, mix them up, and redistribute them to the class. Read the autobiography your teacher gives you. Then ask your classmates questions to try to find its writer.

EXAMPLES:

Did you come here in 1990?

OR

When did you come here?

INFORMATION GAP FOR STUDENT B

Student B, read the short biography below. Answer your partner's questions. Ask your partner questions to complete the missing information.

EXAMPLE:

A: Where was Vladimir born?

B: He was born in Kiev.

When was he born?

A: He was born on May 6, 1975.

Vladimir Liapunov was born on _____May 6, 1975_____,

in Kiev. His mother was a dressmaker, and his father made

_____. At home they spoke Russian.

In _____ Vlad and his family moved to

Boston. At first Vlad felt lonely. Then he got a part-time job as a

cook. He worked in a _____. He met Elena

at work, and they got married in _____.

They had a baby in _____. A month ago Vlad

enrolled at the _____. His goal is to own his own restaurant someday.

When you are finished, compare biographies. Are they the same?

USED TO

GRAMMAR **IN CONTEXT**

BEFORE YOU READ Why are jeans so popular throughout the world? What questions can you ask about jeans?

Read this FAQ (Frequently Asked Questions) about blue jeans.

FAQ ABOUT JEANS

◉ *Where are blue jeans from, anyway?*
Gold miners in the California Gold Rush **used to get** a lot of holes in their pants. In the 1850s, Levi Strauss, a recent immigrant from Germany, solved their problem. He used tent material to make extra-strong pants. In this way, the 24-year-old businessman also made his fortune.

◉ *Why do we call them "jeans" and not "strausses"?*
"Jeans" was the name of the strong cotton fabric Strauss used. The material **used to come** mainly from Genoa, Italy. The French called it "gênes" after that city. Today the fabric is called denim, and the pants are called jeans.

◉ *Jeans **didn't use to be** so popular. What happened?*
Jeans **used to be** just work clothes. Then they began to appear on movie stars. James Dean, a 1950s movie actor, **used to wear** jeans. So did Marlon Brando. You know the rest.

◉ ***Did** they **use to come** in so many colors and fabrics?*
No. Blue **used to be** the only color, and denim the only fabric. But not anymore. Today you can buy jeans in many colors and materials. (But they still have to have five pockets or they're not really jeans!)

James Dean

GRAMMAR **PRESENTATION**
USED TO

STATEMENTS

SUBJECT	*USED TO*	BASE FORM OF VERB	
I You He She It We You They	**used to didn't use to**	**be**	popular.

YES / NO QUESTIONS

DID	SUBJECT	*USE TO*	BASE FORM OF VERB	
Did	I you he she it we you they	**use to**	**be**	popular?

SHORT ANSWERS

AFFIRMATIVE		
Yes,	you I he she it you we they	**did**.

SHORT ANSWERS

NEGATIVE		
No,	you I he she it you we they	**didn't**.

WH- QUESTIONS

WH- WORD	*DID*	SUBJECT	*USE TO*	BASE FORM OF VERB
What	**did**	I you he she it we you they	**use to**	**do**?

NOTES

EXAMPLES

1. Use *used to* + base form of the verb to talk about **past habits** or **past situations** that <u>no longer exist in the present</u>.

- Lea **used to buy** tight jeans. (*It was her habit to buy tight jeans, but now she doesn't buy tight jeans.*)

(continued on next page)

Now

Past ———————————————— Future

used to hate

▶ **BE CAREFUL!** *Used to* always refers to the past. There is <u>no present tense form</u>.

- She **used to hate** loose jeans.
  (She hated loose jeans, but now she doesn't hate loose jeans.)

- In the past, Todd **used to wear** jeans.
  NOT ~~Today Todd uses to wear jeans.~~

2. We usually use *used to* in sentences that **contrast the past and the present**. We often emphasize this contrast by using time expressions such as *now, no longer,* and *not anymore* with the present tense.

- Jeans only **used to come** in blue. *Now* you can buy them in any color.

- They **used to live** in Genoa, but they *no longer* live there.

- She **used to wear** a size 6, but she does*n't anymore*.

3. BE CAREFUL! Form the **questions** for all persons with *did + use to*.

Form the **negative** with *didn't + use to*.

USAGE NOTE: *Used to* is more common in affirmative statements than in negative statements or questions.

- **Did** you **use to wear** jeans?
  NOT ~~Did you used to wear jeans?~~

- They **didn't use to come** in different colors.
  NOT ~~They didn't used to come . . .~~

4. BE CAREFUL! Do not confuse *used to* + base form of the verb with the following expressions:

-*be used to* (be accustomed to)

OR

-*get used to* (get accustomed to)

- I **used to wear** tight jeans.
  (It was my past habit to wear tight jeans.)

- I'm **used to wearing** tight jeans.
  (It is normal for me to wear tight jeans.)

- I can't **get used to wearing** them loose.
  (It still seems strange to me to wear them loose.)

PRONUNCIATION NOTE
Used to and *use to* are pronounced the same: / ˈyustə /

FOCUSED PRACTICE

1 DISCOVER THE GRAMMAR

Read this fashion article. Underline **used to** + *the base form of the verb only when it refers to a habit in the past.*

In many ways, fashion used to be much simpler. Women didn't use to wear pants to the office, and men's clothes never used to come in bright colors. People also used to dress in special ways for different situations. They didn't use blue jeans as business clothes or wear jogging suits when they traveled. Today you can go to the opera and find some women in evening gowns while others are in blue jeans. Even buying jeans used to be easier—they only came in blue denim. I'm still not used to buying green jeans and wearing them to work!

2 TIMES CHANGE
Grammar Note 1

Look at these pictures from an old magazine. Use the verbs in the box with **used to**. *Write one sentence about each picture.*

~~be~~ carry dance dress have wear

1. Women's skirts ____used to be____ long and formal.

2. All men _____ long hair.

3. Children _____ like adults.

4. Men and women _____ at formal balls.

5. Women _____ many petticoats under their skirts.

6. Men _____ walking sticks.

3 SNEAKER FAQ

Look at the information about sneakers from 1922. Complete the FAQ. Use the correct form of **used to**.

STYLE	HIGH-TOP	LOW-TOP
MEN'S	98¢	89¢
WOMEN'S	38¢ WHITE	79¢
	95¢ BLACK	
BOYS' AND GIRLS'	85¢ SMALL	73¢ SMALL
	89¢ LARGE	79¢ LARGE
CHILDREN'S	—	65¢

1. Q: ___Did sneakers use to come in many colors?___

　　　　(sneakers / come in many colors?)

　A: ___No. Only in white and black.___

2. Q: How many styles did they use to come in?

　A: _____

3. Q: _____

　　　　(How much / pair of men's high-tops / cost?)

　A: _____

4. Q: What about women's sneakers? Did they use to cost the same as men's?

　A: _____

5. Q: What kind of sneakers did children use to wear?

　A: _____

6. Q: How many sizes did there use to be for boys and girls?

　A: _____

4 EDITING

Read this student's journal. Find and correct five mistakes in the use of **used to**.
The first mistake is already corrected.

> 　　　　　　　　　　　　　　　　　　use
> 　　　　When I was younger, clothing didn't ~~used~~ to be a problem. All the girls at my
>
> school used to wore the same uniform. I used to think that it took away from my
>
> freedom of choice. Now I can wear what I want, but clothes cost so much! Even blue
>
> jeans, today's "uniform," used to be cheaper. My mom uses to pay less than $20
>
> for hers. I guess they didn't used to sell designer jeans back then. You know, I ~~was~~
>
> used to be against school uniforms, but now I'm not so sure!

COMMUNICATION PRACTICE

5 LISTENING

Two friends are talking about their teenage years. Listen to their conversation. Listen again. Check the things they used to do in the past and the things they do now.

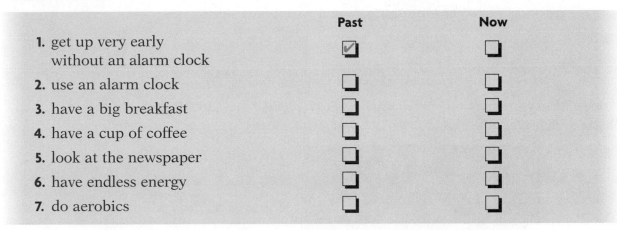

	Past	Now
1. get up very early without an alarm clock	☑	☐
2. use an alarm clock	☐	☐
3. have a big breakfast	☐	☐
4. have a cup of coffee	☐	☐
5. look at the newspaper	☐	☐
6. have endless energy	☐	☐
7. do aerobics	☐	☐

6 THEN AND NOW

Work with a partner. Look at the photos of pop star Madonna, and read the information about her. Write sentences about Madonna's life in the past, and her life now. Compare your sentences with your classmates' sentences.

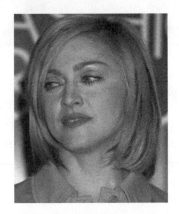

Then

- was called Madonna Louise Ciccone
- student, University of Michigan
- sang in bands
- lived in Michigan
- worked in a donut shop

Now

- is called Madonna
- singer, dancer, actress
- sings solo
- owns homes in New York City, Los Angeles, Miami
- has her own music company

EXAMPLE:
She didn't use to wear a lot of makeup.
Now she wears lipstick and eye makeup.

THE WAY I USED TO BE

Work in small groups. Bring in a picture of yourself when you were much younger. Talk about the differences in how you used to be and how you are now. What did you use to do? How did you use to dress?

> **EXAMPLE:**
> I used to wear long skirts. Now I wear short skirts.

8 THIS USED TO BE MY PLAYGROUND

Work with a partner. Read part of the lyrics to a popular song by Madonna. Discuss their meaning.

This used to be my playground
This used to be my childhood dream
This used to be the place I ran to
Whenever I was in need
Of a friend
Why did it have to end?

9 THINGS CHANGE

Work in small groups. Think about how things used to be ten, fifteen, and twenty years ago. Think about the changes in science, business, and your daily life. Share your ideas with each other.

> **EXAMPLE:**
> A local phone call used to cost ten cents everywhere. Now it costs at least twenty-five cents in most places.

10 WRITING

Write a two-paragraph composition. Contrast your life in the past and your life today. In the first paragraph, describe how your life used to be at some time in the past. In the second paragraph, describe your present life.

> **EXAMPLE:**
> I used to live in Russia. I attended a university in St. Petersburg. . . .

PAST PROGRESSIVE AND SIMPLE PAST TENSE

GRAMMAR **IN CONTEXT**

BEFORE YOU READ Look at the picture. What do you think happened at "Ligo Diamonds" last Friday night? What was the weather like that night?

Read part of The Alibi, *a radio play.*

> *[Ding-dong!]*

SANDERS: Coming!

OFFICER: Officer Barker. City Police. I'd like to ask you a few questions.

SANDERS: Sure. Sorry I took so long. I **was taking** a shower when the bell **rang**.

OFFICER: Is your wife home?

SANDERS: No, she's at work. Eve's a manager at Ligo Diamonds. She **was** very upset when she **heard** about the burglary.

OFFICER: **Was** your wife **working** that night?

SANDERS: No, she **wasn't**. We **were staying** at Cypress Ski Lodge when it **happened**. Don't tell me we're suspects!

OFFICER: Just for the record, what **were** you and Mrs. Sanders **doing** between 6:00 P.M. and 9:00 P.M. last Friday?

SANDERS: We **were having** dinner in our room.

OFFICER: **Were** you still **eating** at 7:00?

SANDERS: No. My wife **was making** a call from her cell phone.

OFFICER: What **were** you **doing** while your wife **was talking**?

SANDERS: I **was watching** *Wall Street Watch*.

OFFICER: Hmm . . . But the electricity was out because of the blizzard.

GRAMMAR **PRESENTATION**
PAST PROGRESSIVE

STATEMENTS				
SUBJECT	WAS / WERE	(NOT)	BASE FORM OF VERB + -ING	
I	was			
You	were			
He She It	was	(not)	working eating sleeping	yesterday at 7:00 P.M. when Eve **called**. while Sal **was watching** TV.
We You They	were			

YES / NO QUESTIONS			
WAS / WERE	SUBJECT	BASE FORM OF VERB + -ING	
Was	I		
Were	you		
Was	he she it	working eating sleeping	yesterday at 7:00 P.M.? when Eve **called**? while Sal **was watching** TV?
Were	we you they		

SHORT ANSWERS		
AFFIRMATIVE		
	you	**were.**
	I	**was.**
Yes,	he she it	**was.**
	you we they	**were.**

SHORT ANSWERS		
NEGATIVE		
	you	**weren't.**
	I	**wasn't.**
No,	he she it	**wasn't.**
	you we they	**weren't.**

WH- QUESTIONS				
WH- WORD	WAS / WERE	SUBJECT	BASE FORM OF VERB + -ING	
	was	I		
	were	you		
Why	was	he she it	working eating sleeping	yesterday at 7:00 P.M.? when Eve **called**? while Sal **was watching** TV?
	were	we you they		

NOTES

EXAMPLES

1. Use the **past progressive** (also called the past continuous) to describe an action that was <u>in progress at a specific time in the past</u>. The action began before the specific time and may or may not continue after the specific time.

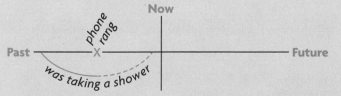

▶ **BE CAREFUL!** Non-action verbs are not usually used in the progressive.
(See Appendix 2, page A-2, for a list of non-action verbs.)

- My wife and I **were eating** at 6:00.
- What **were** you **doing** at 7:00?
- They **weren't skiing**.

- I **had** a headache last night. NOT ~~I was having a headache last night.~~

2. Use the **past progressive with the simple past tense** to talk about an action that was <u>interrupted by another action</u>. Use the simple past tense for the interrupting action.

Use **when** to introduce the simple-past-tense action OR use **while** to introduce the past-progressive action.

- I **was taking** a shower *when* the phone **rang**.
  (The phone call came in the middle of what I was doing.)

- They **were skiing** *when* the storm **started**. OR
- *While* they **were skiing**, the storm **started**.

(continued on next page)

3. Use the **past progressive with** *while* (or *when*) to talk about <u>two actions in progress at the same time in the past</u>.
Use the past progressive in both clauses.

Now

Past —————⌣———————— Future
      was watching
      was talking

• *While* I **was watching** TV, my wife **was talking** on the phone.
    OR
• My wife **was talking** on the phone *while* I **was watching** TV.

---

4. Notice that the **time clause** (the part of the sentence with *when* or *while*) can come at the <u>beginning or the end</u> of the sentence. The meaning is the same.
Use a comma after the time clause when it comes at the beginning.

• *When* you **called,** I was eating.
    OR
• I was eating *when* you **called**.

---

5. **BE CAREFUL!** Sentences with both clauses in the simple past tense have a very <u>different meaning</u> from sentences with one clause in the simple past tense and one clause in the past progressive.

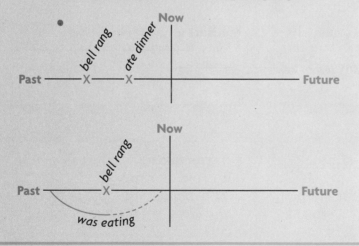

• When the bell **rang, I ate** dinner.
(First the bell rang; then I ate dinner.)

• When the bell **rang, I was eating** dinner.
(First I was eating dinner, then the bell rang.)

---

6. Use the **past progressive** to focus on the <u>duration</u> of an action, not its completion.

Use the **simple past tense** to focus on the <u>completion</u> of an action.

• Paul **was reading** a book last night.
(We don't know if he finished the book.)

• Paul **read** a book last night.
(He probably finished it.)

FOCUSED PRACTICE

1 DISCOVER THE GRAMMAR

Circle the letter of the correct answer.

1. In which sentence do we know that the diamond necklace is gone?
   a. He was stealing a diamond necklace.
   b. He stole a diamond necklace.

2. Which sentence tells us that the people arrived at the mountains?
   a. They were driving to the mountains.
   b. They drove to the mountains.

3. Which sentence talks about an interruption?
   a. When the phone rang, he answered it.
   b. When the phone rang, he was looking for the safe.

4. Which sentence talks about two actions that were in progress at the same time?
   a. While the officer was questioning Sal, Eve was leaving town.
   b. When the officer questioned Sal, Eve left town.

5. In which sentence did the friends arrive before lunch began?
   a. When our friends arrived, we were eating lunch.
   b. When our friends arrived, we ate lunch.

2 DESCRIBE THE SUSPECTS

Grammar Note 1

Look at the picture of the suspects in last Friday afternoon's burglary. Write about them. Use the past progressive.

1. He __was wearing a hat.__
   (wear / a hat)

2. She __wasn't wearing a hat.__
   (wear / a hat)

3. They _____
   (wear / sunglasses)

4. They _____
   (wear / gloves)

5. She _____
   (smile)

6. She _____
   (hold / a cell phone)

7. They _____
   (sit / outside)

8. They _____
   (eat)

3 A TRAFFIC ACCIDENT

Complete the conversation with the simple past tense or the past progressive form of the verbs in parentheses.

REPORTER: What was the cause of the accident, Officer?

OFFICER: Well, it looks like there were many causes. First of all, when the accident

_____occurred_____, the driver ____was driving____ much too fast. The driver
　　1. (occur)　　　　　　　　　2. (drive)

is a suspect in a burglary, and she _____ town. While she
　　　　　　　　　　　　　　　　　3. (leave)

_____, she _____ to someone on her car phone.
　　4. (drive)　　　　　5. (speak)

When she _____ the pedestrian, she immediately _____
　　　　　6. (see)　　　　　　　　　　　　　　　7. (step)

on the brakes, but it was too late. The victim wasn't paying attention, either.

First of all, he didn't wait for the traffic light to change. He _____
　　　　　　　　　　　　　　　　　　　　　　　　　　8. (cross)

against a red light when the car _____ him. He _____
　　　　　　　　　　　　　9. (hit)　　　　　　　10. (not see)

the approaching car because he _____ to his friend. The friend
　　　　　　　　　　　　　11. (talk)

wasn't paying attention, either. He _____ an ice cream cone while
　　　　　　　　　　　　　　12. (eat)

he _____ the street. When he _____ the car, he
　　13. (cross)　　　　　　　　　　14. (notice)

_____ to push his friend out of the way, but it was too late.
　15. (try)

REPORTER: How is the victim doing?

OFFICER: Well, when the ambulance _____, he _____ from a
　　　　　　　　　　　　　16. (arrive)　　　　　17. (bleed)

head wound, but the doctors stopped the bleeding and they think he'll be OK.

4 ANSWER CAREFULLY

The police are questioning another suspect in last Friday's burglary. Read this suspect's answers. Use the words in parentheses and the past progressive or simple past tense to write the police officer's questions.

1. **POLICE:** __What were you doing Friday night?_____
　　　　　　　　　(What / do / Friday night?)

    SUSPECT: I was visiting a friend.

2. **POLICE:** _____
　　　　　　　　　(Who / exactly / you visit?)

    SUSPECT: My girlfriend. I got to her house at 5:30 and drove her to work.

3. **POLICE:** _____
　　　　　　　　　(she / work / at 7:00?)

    SUSPECT: Yes, she was working the late shift.

4. POLICE: _____

(anyone else / work / with her?)

SUSPECT: No. She was working alone.

5. POLICE: _____

(What / you / do / while / she / work?)

SUSPECT: I was reading the paper in her office.

6. POLICE: But there was a terrible blizzard Friday night. The lights went out.

_____

(What / do / when / lights go out?)

SUSPECT: I was still reading the paper.

7. POLICE: _____

(What / do / when / lights go out?)

SUSPECT: When the lights went out, we left the building.

8. POLICE: _____

(Why / run / when / the police / see you?)

SUSPECT: We were running because we wanted to get out of the storm.

---

5 BLIZZARD

*Combine these pairs of sentences. Use the simple past tense or the past
progressive form of the verb. Remember to use commas when necessary.*

1. The blizzard started.   Mr. Ligo attended a party.

When _the blizzard started, Mr. Ligo was attending a party._

2. It began to snow.   The electricity went out.

When _____

3. He drove home.   He listened to his car radio.

While _____

4. He pulled over to the side of the road.   The visibility got very bad.

_____ when _____

5. He listened to the news.   He heard about the burglary.

While _____

6. The police began the investigation.   It snowed.

_____ while _____

7. It stopped snowing.   Mr. Ligo went to the police station.

When _____

COMMUNICATION PRACTICE

6 LISTENING

The police are trying to draw a detailed picture of an accident. Listen to a witness describe the accident. Then listen again. According to the witness, which set of pictures is the most accurate? Circle the number.

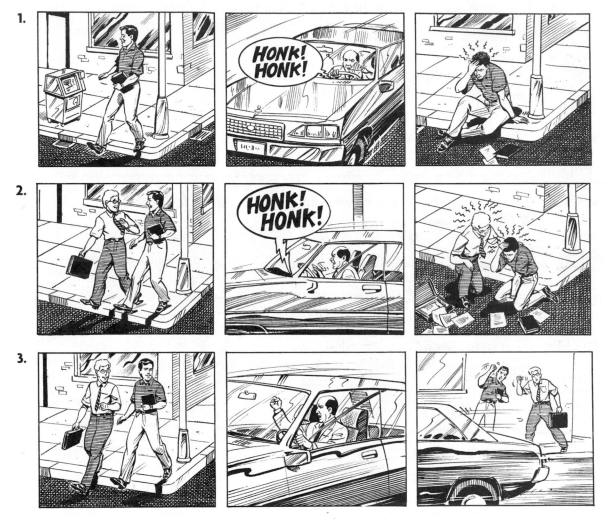

7 ROLE PLAY: THE REAL STORY

Work in groups of four. Follow these steps:

1. Three students are witnesses; the fourth is a police officer. Look at the pictures above.

2. The police officer asks the witnesses questions to describe the accident.

3. Each of the witnesses chooses one set of pictures to describe.

EXAMPLE:

A: Can you describe the accident?

B: Yes. Two men were crossing the street.

A: Were they paying attention?

B: No, they weren't; they were talking.

8 WHAT'S YOUR ALIBI?

Work in small groups. Reread the alibi in the story on page 37. Do you think it is a good alibi? Pretend that you are a suspect in the burglary. What were you doing last Friday night between 6:00 and 9:00 P.M.? Give your alibi to the class. The class will decide which alibis are good and which are bad.

EXAMPLE:

I work from midnight until 7:00 A.M., so between 6:00 and 9:00 P.M. I was sleeping.

9 ARE YOU A GOOD WITNESS?

Look at this picture for ten seconds. Close your book and write down what was happening. See how many details you can remember. What were the people doing? What were they wearing?

EXAMPLE:

A man and woman were standing by the fireplace. The woman was wearing . . .

Compare your list with a classmate's.

10 WRITING

Write a description of an event that you witnessed: an accident, a crime, a reunion, a wedding, or any other event. Use the past progressive and the simple past tense to describe what was happening and what happened during the event.

EXAMPLE:

While I was going to lunch today, I saw a wedding party. People were waiting for the bride and groom outside a temple. They were holding bags of rice. When they saw the couple, they . . .

6 FUTURE

GRAMMAR **IN CONTEXT**

BEFORE YOU READ Look at the picture. Describe the car. What's new about it? What's the same?

Read an article about future transportation.

Highway to the Future

On the road to exciting new changes in car design

By Harry Vroom
SPECIAL TO THE AUTO GAZETTE

Get ready! We're on the road to exciting new changes in car design. How **will** the vehicle of the future **look**? Well, it **will** probably still **have** four wheels, but it**'s going to come** in many more colors and patterns. You**'ll be able to choose** a green and yellow polka-dotted model or **design** your very own personal look! It**'s going to be** environmentally friendly, too. The material **will be** 100 percent recyclable, and the car **will run** on solar energy.

What about speed? The car of the future **will go** a lot faster than current cars. One day, it **will** even **fly**! But it **will** also **be** safe. An electronic shield around the car **will warn** of danger and automatically **avoid** accidents. And you **won't get** lost anymore! You**'ll** just **say** the destination and the car **will give** you directions.

One manufacturer, Smart Transport, Inc., **is holding** a press conference next week. At the conference you**'ll see** actual models of these fantastic new cars. And before very long, you**'ll be able to zip** around town in the real thing! So, full speed ahead to the future! It**'s going to be** a great trip!

GRAMMAR **PRESENTATION**
BE GOING TO FOR THE FUTURE

STATEMENTS

SUBJECT	BE	(NOT) GOING TO	BASE FORM OF VERB	
I	am*			
You	are			
He She It	is	(not) going to	leave	soon.
We You They	are			

*For contractions of *I am, you are,* etc., see Appendix 20, p. A-8.

YES / NO QUESTIONS

BE	SUBJECT	GOING TO	BASE FORM OF VERB	
Am	I			
Are	you			
Is	he she it	going to	leave	soon?
Are	we you they			

SHORT ANSWERS

	AFFIRMATIVE		
		you	are.
		I	am.
Yes,		he she it	is.
		you we they	are.

SHORT ANSWERS

	NEGATIVE		
		you're	
		I'm	
No,		he's she's it's	not.
		you're we're they're	

WH- QUESTIONS

WH- WORD	BE	SUBJECT	GOING TO	BASE FORM OF VERB
When Why	are	you	going to	leave?

PRESENT PROGRESSIVE FOR THE FUTURE

STATEMENTS

SUBJECT + BE	(NOT) + BASE FORM OF VERB + -ING	
I'm	(not) leaving	soon.

See page 3 in Unit 1 for a complete presentation of present progressive forms.

(continued on next page)

WILL FOR THE FUTURE

STATEMENTS			
SUBJECT	*WILL (NOT)*	BASE FORM OF VERB	
I You He She It We You They	**will (not)***	**leave**	soon.

*For contractions of *I will, you will*, etc., see Appendix 20, page A-8.

YES / NO QUESTIONS			
WILL	SUBJECT	BASE FORM OF VERB	
Will	I you he she it we you they	**leave**	soon?

SHORT ANSWERS		
AFFIRMATIVE		
Yes,	you I he she it you we they	**will**.

SHORT ANSWERS		
NEGATIVE		
No,	you I he she it you we they	**won't**.

WH- QUESTIONS			
WH- WORD	*WILL*	SUBJECT	BASE FORM OF VERB
When	**will**	you	**leave**?

THE SIMPLE PRESENT TENSE FOR THE FUTURE

STATEMENTS		
SUBJECT	VERB	
We	**leave**	Monday at 6:45 A.M.
It	**leaves**	

See page 3 in Unit 1 for a complete presentation of simple present tense forms.

NOTES

EXAMPLES

1. There are several ways to talk about actions and states **in the future.** You can use:

–*be going to*

–**present progressive**

–*will*

–**simple present tense**

```
                    Now
                     |
                     |         conference
Past ────────────────┼──────────X──────── Future
                     |
                     |
```

USAGE NOTE: Sometimes only one form of the future is appropriate, but in many cases more than one form is possible.

- They**'re going to hold** a press conference.

- It**'s taking** place next week. *[handwritten: it takes]*

- I think **I'll go.**

- It **starts** at 9:00 A.M. on Monday. *[handwritten: it's starting]*

2. To make **predictions or guesses** about the future, use:

–*be going to*

  OR

–*will*

Use *be going to* instead of *will* when there is something in the present that leads to the prediction.

- People **are going to travel** differently.
                    OR
- People **will travel** differently.

- Look at those cars! They**'re going to crash**!
NOT ~~They'll crash.~~

(continued on next page)

3. To talk about future **intentions or plans**, use:

–*be going to*

OR

–*will*

OR

–**present progressive**

- He**'s going to hold** a conference next week.

OR

- He **will hold** a conference next week.

OR

- He **is holding** a conference next week.

a. We often use *will* when we decide something at the <u>moment of speaking</u>.

A: The car show is opening next week.
B: I love new cars. I think **I'll go**.

Will can also be used for making a request. *(See Unit 13.)*

b. We often use the **present progressive** when we talk about future plans that have already been <u>arranged</u>.

- Jana and I **are buying** a new car next week. We've already chosen the model.

4. Use the **simple present** to talk about <u>scheduled future events</u> (such as timetables, programs, and schedules). Verbs such as *start, leave, end,* and *begin* are often used this way.

- The press conference **begins** at 9:00 A.M.
- It **ends** promptly at 9:45.

PRONUNCIATION NOTE
In informal speech, ***going to*** is often pronounced *gonna* /ɡɔnə/.

FOCUSED PRACTICE

1 DISCOVER THE GRAMMAR

Read this transcript and listen to a radio interview with Professor Harry Vroom, a well-known researcher of the Future Watch Institute. There are fifteen verb forms that refer to the future. Find and underline them.

INTERVIEWER: For those of you who are just tuning in, this is "Looking Into the Future." I am Will Bee, and we are talking with Professor Harry Vroom. Good afternoon, Professor. I understand you <u>are going to tell</u> our listeners about the cars of the future.

VROOM: That's right. I believe there will be some surprising changes in the next century. Let me give you some examples. Cars of the future are going to have "brains." They'll start themselves, and they'll adjust the seats, mirrors, and steering wheels automatically. Luxury cars will even ask you where you want to go and will tell you the best route to take.

INTERVIEWER: That certainly is amazing! I'm sure lots of our listeners have questions for you, but, unfortunately, we only have time today for a few call-ins.

VROOM: Well, you know, I am speaking at the annual Car Show next week. The show begins at 10:00 A.M. on August 11. I'm going to talk more about the plans for cars of the future. I'm also going to show some models. I hope many of your listeners will be there.

INTERVIEWER: I'm sure they will. We have to pause for a commercial break. But don't go away, listeners. We'll be right back—and Professor Vroom will be ready to answer some of your questions.

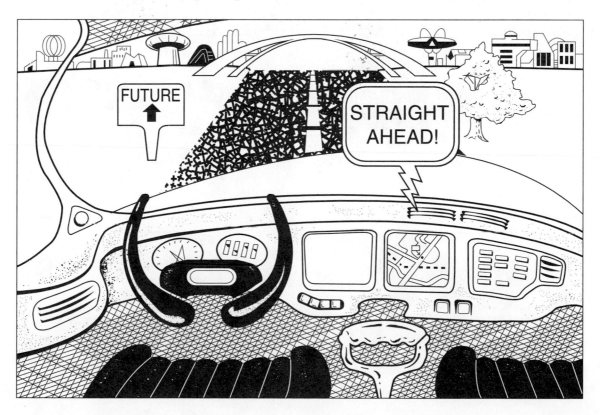

2 IT'S GOING TO HAPPEN

Look at the pictures. They show events from a day in Professor Vroom's life.
Write predictions or guesses. Use the words in the box and a form of **be going to**
or **not be going to**.

answer the phone	drive	get very wet	give a speech
have dinner	rain	take a trip	watch TV

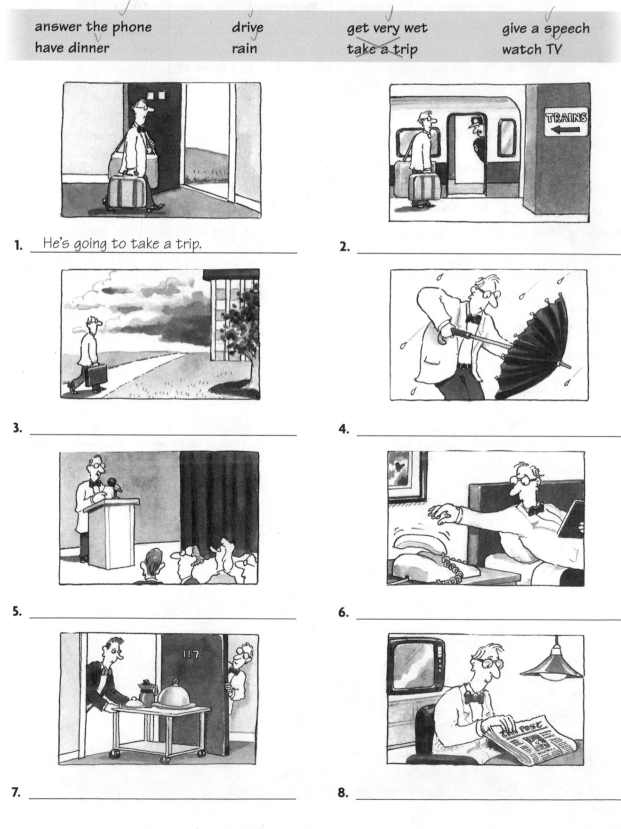

1. He's going to take a trip.

2. _____

3. _____

4. _____

5. _____

6. _____

7. _____

8. _____

③ PROFESSOR VROOM'S SCHEDULE

Write about Professor Vroom's plans for next week. Use the information from his calendar and the present progressive. Add **the** *and* **a** *when necessary.*

	Monday	**Tuesday**	**Wednesday**	**Thursday**	**Friday**
A.M.	take train to New Haven	go to Washington (8:00 A.M.)	work in research lab all day	attend annual Car Show	talk on radio show
P.M.	give lecture at Yale		↓		

1. On Monday morning ___he's taking the train to New Haven.___

2. On Monday evening _____

3. On Tuesday morning _____

4. All day Wednesday _____

5. On Thursday morning _____

6. On Friday morning _____

④ RADIO CALL-IN QUESTIONS

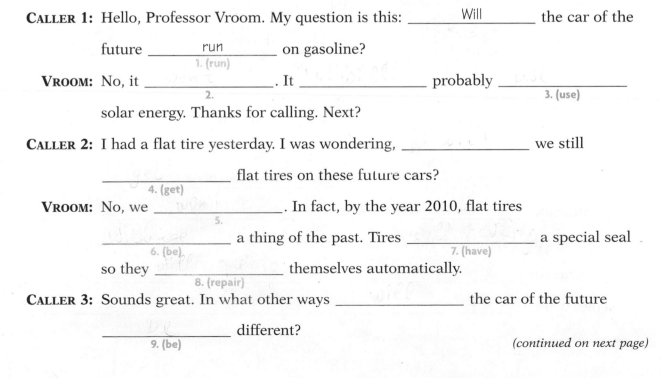

Radio listeners are calling in with questions for Professor Vroom. Complete the questions and answers. Use the words in parentheses and **will** *or* **won't**.

CALLER 1: Hello, Professor Vroom. My question is this: _____Will_____ the car of the

future _____run_____ on gasoline?
  1. (run)

VROOM: No, it _____. It _____ probably _____
  2.   3. (use)

solar energy. Thanks for calling. Next?

CALLER 2: I had a flat tire yesterday. I was wondering, _____ we still

_____ flat tires on these future cars?
  4. (get)

VROOM: No, we _____. In fact, by the year 2010, flat tires
  5.

_____ a thing of the past. Tires _____ a special seal
  6. (be)   7. (have)

so they _____ themselves automatically.
  8. (repair)

CALLER 3: Sounds great. In what other ways _____ the car of the future

_____ different?
  9. (be)

(continued on next page)

VROOM: Well, instead of keys, cars _____ smart cards. These
                                    10. (have)

_____ a lot like credit cards. They _____ doors,
   11. (look)   12. (open)

and they _____ the seats, mirrors, and steering wheels. They
              13. (adjust)

_____ even _____ the inside temperature.
                        14. (control)

CALLER 3: _____ they _____ prevent car thefts?
                                15. (help)

VROOM: Yes, they _____ ! OK, next caller?
                    16.

CALLER 4: Hello. I'm curious. How much _____ these cars

_____ ?
  17. (cost)

VROOM: I don't know exactly, but they certainly _____ cheap.
                                      18. (not be)

---

5 **ALL ABOARD**   **Grammar Note 4**

Professor Vroom is going to take the train from New York to New Haven on Monday. He is asking questions at the information booth. Write his questions. Then look at the train schedule and write the answers. Use the simple present tense.

NEW YORK TO NEW HAVEN					
MONDAY TO FRIDAY, EXCEPT HOLIDAYS					
Leave	Arrive	Leave	Arrive	Leave	Arrive
New York	New Haven	New York	New Haven	New York	New Haven
AM	AM	PM	PM	PM	PM
12:35	2:23	3:22	4:55	6:04	7:46
1:30	3:37	3:37	5:17	6:30	8:16
6:02	7:48	4:02	5:44	7:06	8:51
7:05	8:55	4:07	5:58	7:37	9:28
8:07	9:57	4:22	6:06	8:07	9:55
9:07	10:53	4:35	6:17	9:07	10:55
10:07	11:53	4:45	6:49	10:07	11:55
11:07	12:53	5:02	6:40	11:20	1:08
12:07	1:53	5:13	7:26	12:35	2:23
1:07	2:54	5:18	7:03	1:30	3:37
2:07	3:55	5:35	7:11	——	——
3:02	4:38	5:39	7:55	——	——
PM	PM	PM	PM	PM	AM

1. When / the first train to New Haven / leave New York?

    VROOM: When does the first train to New Haven leave New York?

  INFORMATION: It leaves New York at 12:35 A.M.

2. How long / the trip to New Haven / take?

    VROOM: _____

  INFORMATION: _____

3. So, what time / the 9:07 train / arrive in New Haven?

VROOM: _____

INFORMATION: _____

4. About how often / trains / depart for New Haven after that?

VROOM: _____

INFORMATION: _____

5. And what time / the last morning train / leave New York?

VROOM: _____

INFORMATION: _____

6 **CHOOSE THE FUTURE**   Grammar Notes 1–4

Two people are traveling to the Car Show. Read their conversation and circle the most appropriate future forms.

JASON: I just heard the weather report.

ARIEL: Oh? What's the forecast?

JASON: It's raining / (It's going to rain) tomorrow.
                            1.

ARIEL: Oh, no. I hate driving in the rain. And it's a long drive to the Car Show.

JASON: Wait! I have an idea. We'll take / We're going to take the train instead!
                                           2.

ARIEL: Good idea! Do you have a train schedule?

JASON: Yes. Here's one. There's a train that will leave / leaves at 7:00 A.M.
                                                       3.

ARIEL: What about lunch? Oh, I know, I'll make / I'm making some sandwiches for us to
                                               4.

take along. I don't like train food.

JASON: Sounds good. You know, it's a long trip. What are we doing / are we going to do all
                                                                              5.

those hours?

ARIEL: Don't worry. We'll think / We're thinking of something.
                           6.

JASON: You know, we have to get up really early.

ARIEL: That's true. I think I'm going / I'll go home now.
                              7.

JASON: OK. I'm seeing you / I'll see you tomorrow. Good night.
              8.

COMMUNICATION PRACTICE

⑦ LISTENING

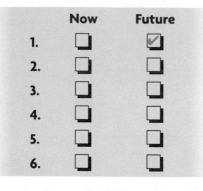 *Listen to the short conversations. Decide if the people are talking about something happening now or in the future. Listen again and check the correct column.*

	Now	Future
1.	☐	☑
2.	☐	☐
3.	☐	☐
4.	☐	☐
5.	☐	☐
6.	☐	☐

⑧ FORTUNE COOKIES

Most Chinese restaurants in the United States give you fortune cookies at the end of your meal. Inside each cookie is a small piece of paper with a prediction about the future.

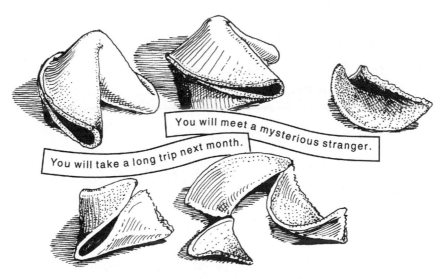

You will meet a mysterious stranger.

You will take a long trip next month.

On a piece of paper, write down a fortune. Now work in small groups. Put all the fortunes in a pile and have each person take one. Discuss your fortunes with the group.

EXAMPLE:

A: "You will take a long trip next month."
That's not possible. I'm starting my new job next week.

B: "You will meet a mysterious stranger."
It's possible. I'm going to a party tomorrow night.

9 WHEN ARE YOU FREE?

Complete your weekend schedule. If you have no plans, write **free**.

	Friday	Saturday	Sunday
12:00 P.M.			
1:00 P.M.			
2:00 P.M.			
3:00 P.M.			
4:00 P.M.			
5:00 P.M.			
6:00 P.M.			
7:00 P.M.			
8:00 P.M.			
9:00 P.M.			

Now work with a partner. Ask questions to decide on a time when you are both free to do something together.

EXAMPLE:

A: What are you doing Friday afternoon? Do you want to go to the movies?

B: I'm studying at the library. How about Friday night? Are you doing anything then?

10 CHOOSE A TIME

Work with the same partner as in Exercise 9. Look at this movie schedule. Then look at your schedules from Exercise 9. Decide which movie to see and when.

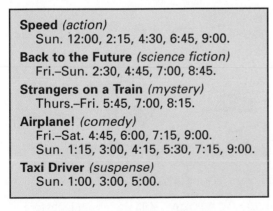

Speed *(action)*
Sun. 12:00, 2:15, 4:30, 6:45, 9:00.
Back to the Future *(science fiction)*
Fri.–Sun. 2:30, 4:45, 7:00, 8:45.
Strangers on a Train *(mystery)*
Thurs.–Fri. 5:45, 7:00, 8:15.
Airplane! *(comedy)*
Fri.–Sat. 4:45, 6:00, 7:15, 9:00.
Sun. 1:15, 3:00, 4:15, 5:30, 7:15, 9:00.
Taxi Driver *(suspense)*
Sun. 1:00, 3:00, 5:00.

EXAMPLE:

A: There are three good movies Friday night. *Back to the Future* is playing at 7:00. Is that OK?

B: That's a little early. When does the next show begin?

11 WRITING

Write a paragraph describing the ideal car of the future. Use your imagination. What material will it be made of? What form of energy is it going to use? How fast will it go? What features is it going to have?

7 FUTURE TIME CLAUSES

GRAMMAR **IN CONTEXT**

BEFORE YOU READ Look at the picture. What is the child thinking?

 *Read this article about setting goals.*

GO FOR IT!
What are your dreams for your future?

Are you **going to get** your degree *by the time you're twenty-two*? **Will** you **start** your own business *before you turn forty*? We all have dreams, but they **won't become** reality *until we change them to goals*. Here's how.

■ **PUT YOUR DREAMS ON PAPER.** *When you write a dream down,* it **will start** to become a goal. Your path will be a lot clearer.

■ **NOW LIST BENEFITS.** For example, Latoya Jones **is going to go back** to school *as soon as she saves enough* money. One benefit: She**'ll get** the job she wants *when she has her degree.* *When things get tough,* Latoya **will read** her list and **remember** the benefits.

■ **WRITE DOWN SMALLER GOALS.** It's easier to reach a goal when you break it down into steps. *Before Latoya applies,* she's **going to look** at school catalogs. She **won't decide** on a school *until she visits several of them.*

■ **ACT TODAY.** Will you watch TV before dinner tonight or read school catalogs? *After you know your smaller goals,* it **will be** easier to make these small decisions every day.

GRAMMAR **PRESENTATION**
FUTURE TIME CLAUSES

STATEMENTS

MAIN CLAUSE			TIME CLAUSE	
I **will** I **am going to**			I **graduate**	
She **will** She **is going to**	**get** a job	**when**	she **graduates**	next June.
They **will** They **are going to**			they **graduate**	

YES / NO QUESTIONS

MAIN CLAUSE			TIME CLAUSE	
Will I **Am** I **going to**			I **graduate**	
Will she **Is** she **going to**	**get** a job	**when**	she **graduates**	next June?
Will they **Are** they **going to**			they **graduate**	

SHORT ANSWERS

AFFIRMATIVE		
Yes,	you	**will.** **are.**
	she	**will.** **is.**
	they	**will.** **are.**

SHORT ANSWERS

NEGATIVE		
No,	you	**won't.** **aren't.**
	she	**won't.** **isn't.**
	they	**won't.** **aren't.**

WH- QUESTIONS

MAIN CLAUSE			TIME CLAUSE	
Where	**will** I **am** I **going to**		I **graduate**	
	will she **is** she **going to**	**get** a job	**when** she **graduates**	next June?
	will they **are** they **going to**		they **graduate**	

NOTES	EXAMPLES

1. When a sentence about future time has two clauses, the verb in the <u>main clause</u> is often in the **future** (*will* or *be going to*). The verb in the <u>time clause</u> is often in the **present tense**.

▶ **BE CAREFUL!** Do not use *will* or *be going to* in a future time clause.

The **time clause** can come at the beginning or the end of the sentence. The meaning is the same. Use a <u>comma</u> after the time clause when it comes at the beginning. Do not use a comma when it comes at the end.

• main clause time clause
  He**'ll look** for a job *when he graduates*.

• main clause time clause
  I**'m going to work** *after I graduate*.

NOT ~~when he will graduate.~~
NOT ~~after I will graduate.~~

• time clause
  Before she applies, she'll visit schools.

                    OR

• She'll visit schools ***before she applies***.
  NOT ~~She'll visit schools, before she applies.~~

2. Here are some **common time expressions** you can use to begin future time clauses.

a. ***When***, ***after***, and ***as soon as*** often introduce <u>the event that happens first</u>.

b. ***Before***, ***until***, and ***by the time*** often introduce <u>the event that happens second</u>.

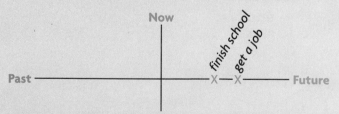

c. ***While*** introduces an event that will happen <u>at the same time</u> as another event.

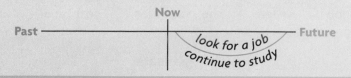

• ***When*** I graduate, I'll look for a job.

• I'll look for a job ***after*** I graduate.

• ***As soon as*** I graduate, I'll look for a job.
  (*First I'm going to graduate. Then I'll look for a job.*)

• ***Before*** I get a job, I'll finish school.

• I won't get a job ***until*** I finish school.

• ***By the time*** I get a job, I'll be out of school.
  (*First I'll finish school. Then I'll get a job.*)

• ***While*** I look for a job, I'll continue to study.
  (*I will look for a job and study during the same time period.*)

FOCUSED PRACTICE

1 DISCOVER THE GRAMMAR

Read the first sentence in each set. Then circle the letter of the sentences whose meaning is similar.

1. Amber will open her own business when she finishes school.
   a. Amber will open her own business. Then she'll finish school.
   (b.) Amber will finish school. Then she'll open her own business.

2. Denzell won't quit until he finds another job.
   a. Denzell will find another job. Then he'll quit.
   b. Denzell will quit. Then he'll find another job.

3. Jake will retire as soon as he turns sixty.
   a. Jake will retire. Then he'll turn sixty.
   b. Jake will turn sixty. Then he'll retire.

4. After the Morrisons sell their house, they'll move to Florida.
   a. The Morrisons will sell their house. Then they'll move to Florida.
   b. The Morrisons will move to Florida. Then they'll sell their house.

5. Marisa will call you when she gets home.
   a. Marisa will call you. Then she'll get home.
   b. Marisa will get home. Then she'll call you.

6. Demetri and Iona are going to look for an apartment before they get married.
   a. Demetri and Iona are going to get married. Then they'll look for an apartment.
   b. Demetri and Iona are going to look for an apartment. Then they'll get married.

7. While Li-jing is in school, she'll work part-time.
   a. Li-jing will finish school. Then she'll get a part-time job.
   b. Li-jing will go to school. At the same time she'll have a part-time job.

8. By the time Marta gets her diploma, she'll be twenty-one.
   a. Marta will get her diploma. Then she'll turn twenty-one.
   b. Marta will turn twenty-one. Then she'll get her diploma.

2 WHAT'S NEXT? Grammar Notes 1–2

Combine these sentences.

1. Sandy and Jeff will get married. Then Sandy will graduate.

   _____Sandy and Jeff will get married_____ before _____Sandy graduates._____

2. Jeff is going to get a raise. Then they are going to move to a larger apartment.

   _____ as soon as _____

3. They're going to move to a larger apartment. Then they're going to have a baby.

   After _____

(continued on next page)

4. They'll have their first child. Then Sandy will get a part-time job.

_____ after _____

5. Their child will be two. Then Sandy will go back to work full-time.

By the time _____

6. Sandy will work full-time, and Jeff will go to school.

_____ while _____

7. Jeff will graduate. Then he'll find another job.

_____ when _____

3 **LOOKING AHEAD**   **Grammar Notes 1–2**

Complete this student's worksheet. Use the correct form of the verbs in parentheses.

GOAL PLANNING WORKSHEET

I. Write your major goal.

I __'ll get__ a job after I _____.
  (get)   (graduate)

II. List three benefits of achieving your goal.

1. When I _____ a job, I _____ more money.
           (get)   (have)

2. When I _____ enough money, I _____ a used car.
           (save)   (buy)

3. I _____ happier when I _____ employed.
       (feel)   (be)

III. How will you reach your goal? Write down smaller goals.

1. As soon as I _____ in the morning, I _____ the
                   (get up)   (buy)
newspaper to look at the employment ads.

2. When I _____ to my friends, I _____ them if they
            (speak)   (ask)
know of any jobs.

3. I _____ at the job notices board when I _____ to the
       (look)   (go)
supermarket.

4. Before I _____ on an interview, I _____ my
             (go)   (improve)
computer skills.

COMMUNICATION PRACTICE

4 LISTENING

 *A woman is calling Jobs Are Us Employment Agency. Listen. Read the sentences that follow. Then listen again and number the events in order.*

_____ **a.** speak to a job counselor   _____ **d.** receive more job training

_____ **b.** have interview at the agency   _____ **e.** go to companies

__1__ **c.** send a resume   _____ **f.** take a word-processing test

5 THE NEXT STEP

Fill out this questionnaire. Check (✓) the appropriate boxes.

When I finish this course, I'm going to . . .

☐ take another English course.   ☐ take some time off.

☐ apply to another school.   ☐ go on vacation.

☐ look for a new job.   ☐ Other: _____

Now work in a small group. Take a survey. What are your classmates going to do when they finish this course? Compare your group's answers with the other groups' answers.

> **EXAMPLE:**
> **A:** Ten students are going to take another English course when they finish this course.
> **B:** Two students are going to look for a new job.

6 UNTIL THEN

Complete these three sentences. Then compare your answers with your classmates' answers. How many different answers are there? Remember that all sentences refer to future time.

a. I'm going to continue studying English until _____

b. While I'm in this class, _____

c. I'll stay in this country until _____

> **EXAMPLE:**
> I'm going to continue studying English until I pass the TOEFL® exam.

7 **INTERVIEW**

Work with a partner. Interview him or her about some future plans. Ask questions such as:

What will you do when . . . ?

Where will you go after . . . ?

Will you . . . while you . . . ?

Take notes and then write a short paragraph about your classmates' plans.

EXAMPLE:

Soo Mi is going to get married next year. Before she gets married, she's going to return home to visit her family. While she's away she'll miss her boyfriend, but she'll write to him every day.

8 **WRITING**

Complete this worksheet for yourself. Use future time clauses.

GOAL PLANNING WORKSHEET _____

I. Write your major goal.

I _____

II. List three benefits of achieving your goal.

1. _____

2. _____

3. _____

III. How will you reach your goal? Write down smaller goals.

1. _____

2. _____

3. _____

4. _____

WH- QUESTIONS: SUBJECT AND PREDICATE

GRAMMAR **IN CONTEXT**

BEFORE YOU READ Look at the photograph. Where is the man? What is he doing?

A lawyer is questioning a crime witness. Read part of the court transcript.

STATE OF ILLINOIS V. HAROLD M. ADAMS   March 31, 2000
_____

LAWYER: **What happened on the night of May 12?** Please tell the court.

WITNESS: I went to Al's Grill.

LAWYER: **Who did you see there?**

WITNESS: I saw one of the defendants.

LAWYER: **Which one did you see?**

WITNESS: It was that man.

LAWYER: Let the record show that the
witness is pointing to the
defendant, Harry Adams.
OK, you saw Mr. Adams.
Did he see you?

WITNESS: No, he didn't see me.

LAWYER: But somebody saw you.
Who saw you?

WITNESS: A woman. He was talking to
a woman. She saw me.

LAWYER: OK. **What happened next?**

WITNESS: The woman gave him a package.

LAWYER: A package! **What did it look like?**

WITNESS: It was about this long . . .

LAWYER: So, about a foot and a half. **What did Mr. Adams do then?**

WITNESS: He took the package. He looked frightened.

LAWYER: **Why did he look frightened? What was in the package?**

WITNESS: I don't know. He didn't open it. He just took it and left in a hurry.

LAWYER: **Where did he go?**

WITNESS: Toward the parking lot.

LAWYER: **When did the woman leave?**

WITNESS: She was still there when we heard the explosion in the parking lot.

GRAMMAR **PRESENTATION**
WH- QUESTIONS: SUBJECT AND PREDICATE

QUESTIONS ABOUT THE SUBJECT

WH- WORD SUBJECT	VERB	PREDICATE
Who	**saw**	you?

ANSWERS

SUBJECT	VERB	PREDICATE
He	saw	me.

QUESTIONS ABOUT THE PREDICATE

WH- WORD PREDICATE	AUXILIARY VERB OR *BE*	SUBJECT	VERB
Who(m)	**did**	you	**see**?

ANSWERS

SUBJECT	VERB	PREDICATE
I	saw	**him**.

NOTES

EXAMPLES

1. Use *wh-* **questions** (also called information questions) to <u>ask for specific information</u>.

Wh- questions begin with question words such as *who, what, where, when, why, which, whose, how, how many, how much,* and *how long*.

- **Who** did you see at Al's Grill?
- **Why** did you go there?
- **How many** people saw you there?
- **How long** did you stay there?

2. When you are **asking about the subject** (usually the first part of the sentence), use a *wh-* question word in place of the subject.

<u>Someone</u> saw you.
↓
- **Who** saw you?

<u>Something</u> happened.
↓
- **What** happened?

3. When you are **asking about the predicate** (usually the last part of the sentence), the word order is similar to the word order of a *yes / no* question, but the question begins with a *wh-* word.

You saw <u>someone</u>.
Did you see <u>someone</u>?
- **Who** did you see?

She said <u>something</u>.
Did she say <u>something</u>?
- **What** did she say?

▶ **BE CAREFUL!** When you ask a *wh-* question about something in the predicate, you need either:

a. a form of the verb *be* (*am, is, are, was, were*).

OR

b. an **auxiliary** ("helping") verb such as *do, does, did, have, has, had, can, will*.

- Who **is** Harry Adams?
- Why **was** he at Al's Grill?

- Why **does** she want to testify?
  NOT ~~Why she wants to testify?~~
- When **did** she arrive?
  NOT ~~When she arrived?~~

4. USAGE NOTE: In <u>formal</u> English when asking about people in the predicate, **whom** is sometimes used instead of *who*.

FORMAL
- **Whom** did you see?
INFORMAL
- **Who** did you see?

▶ **BE CAREFUL!** If the main verb is a form of *be*, you cannot use *whom*.

- **Who is** the next witness?
  NOT ~~Whom is the next witness?~~

FOCUSED PRACTICE

1 DISCOVER THE GRAMMAR

Match the questions and answers.

__f__ **1.** Who did you see?

_____ **2.** Who saw you?

_____ **3.** What hit her?

_____ **4.** What did she hit?

_____ **5.** Which man did you give the money to?

_____ **6.** Which man gave you the money?

a. His wife saw me.

b. She hit a car.

c. Harry gave me the money.

d. A car hit her.

e. I gave the money to Harry.

f. I saw the defendant.

2 CROSS-EXAMINATION   Grammar Notes 1–4

Complete the cross-examination. Write the lawyer's questions.

1. LAWYER: ___What time did you return home?___
                           (What time / you / return home?)
  WITNESS: I returned home just before midnight.

2. LAWYER: _____
                           (How / you / get home?)
  WITNESS: Someone gave me a ride.

3. LAWYER: _____
                           (Who / give / you / a ride?)
  WITNESS: A friend from work.

4. LAWYER: _____
                           (What / happen / next?)
  WITNESS: I opened my door and saw someone on my living room floor.

5. LAWYER: _____
                           (Who / you / see?)
  WITNESS: Deborah Collins.

6. LAWYER: _____
                         (Who / be / Deborah Collins?)
  WITNESS: She's my wife's boss. I mean, she *was* my wife's boss. She's dead now.

7. LAWYER: _____
                          (What / you / do?)
  WITNESS: I called the police.

8. **LAWYER:** _____

   (When / the police / arrive?)

   WITNESS: In about ten minutes.

9. **LAWYER:** _____

   (How many police officers / come?)

   WITNESS: I don't remember. Why?

   LAWYER: I'm asking the questions here. Please just answer.

---

3 Q AND A   **Grammar Notes 1–4**

Read the answers. Then ask questions about the underlined words.

1. The witness recognized Harry Adams.

   Who recognized Harry Adams?

2. The witness recognized <u>Harry Adams</u>.

   _____

3. Court begins <u>at 9:00 A.M.</u>

   _____

4. <u>Five</u> witnesses testified.

   _____

5. The jury found Adams guilty <u>because he didn't have an alibi</u>.

   _____

6. <u>Something horrible</u> happened.

   _____

7. The trial lasted <u>two weeks</u>.

   _____

8. <u>The judge</u> spoke to the jury.

   _____

9. Adams paid his lawyer <u>$2,000</u>.

   _____

10. The district attorney questioned <u>the restaurant manager</u>.

   _____

COMMUNICATION PRACTICE

4 LISTENING

You are on the phone with a friend. There is a bad connection. Listen to the following sentences. Then listen again. Circle the letter of the question you need to ask in order to get the correct information.

1. **a.** Who did you see at the restaurant?
   b. Who saw you at the restaurant?

2. **a.** Which car did the truck hit?
   b. Which car hit the truck?

3. **a.** When did it happen?
   b. Why did it happen?

4. **a.** Whose mother did you call?
   b. Whose mother called you?

5. **a.** Who did you report it to?
   b. Who reported it?

6. **a.** How many people heard the shouts?
   b. How many shouts did you hear?

7. **a.** Who saw the man?
   b. Who did the man see?

8. **a.** Why do you have to hang up?
   b. When do you have to hang up?

5 WHAT HAPPENED NEXT?

Work with a partner. Look at the court transcript on page 65 again. Read it aloud. Then continue the lawyer's questioning of the witness.

> **EXAMPLE:**
> **LAWYER:** When did the woman leave?
> **WITNESS:** She was still there when we heard the explosion in the parking lot.
> **LAWYER:** What happened next?

6 STAR REPORTERS

Work in small groups. You are going to interview a ten-year-old child genius who is attending law school. You have five minutes to think of as many wh- questions as you can. One student should write down all the questions.

> **EXAMPLES:**
> When did you decide to become a lawyer?
> Who influenced you to become a lawyer?

You will be allowed to ask only six questions. Choose the six best questions. Compare questions with the rest of the class. Now work in pairs. Role-play the interview. Use the six questions your group chose. Then write up the interview for a magazine article.

7 INFORMATION GAP: POLICE CRIME BOARD

Two detectives are investigating a case. All the suspects work at the same office. The detectives interviewed Mary Rogers, the office manager, and wrote her answers on a board. Work in pairs (A and B). Student B, look at the Information Gap on p. 72. Student A, look at the chart below. Ask your partner for the information you need to complete the chart. Answer your partner's questions.

> **EXAMPLE:**
> **A:** Who did she see at 8:00 P.M.?
> **B:** Rick Simon. Where did she see him?
> **A:** At Al's Grill. Who else saw him?

Suspect	Time	Location	Other Witnesses
Rick Simon	8:00 P.M.	Al's Grill	
Alice May		Fifth Avenue	Bob May
Jake Bordon	6:30 P.M.		the janitor
	7:15 P.M.		some children
John Daniels	7:00 P.M.		

When you are finished, compare your charts. Are they the same?

8 WRITING

Work with a partner. Think of something exciting or interesting that you once saw. Tell your partner. Then write a list of questions and interview your partner to get more information. Write up the interview.

> **EXAMPLE:**
> **A:** What did you see?
> **B:** It was a famous person in a restaurant.
> **A:** Who was it?
> **B:** . . .

INFORMATION GAP FOR STUDENT B

Student B, ask your partner for the information you need to complete the chart.
Answer your partner's questions.

EXAMPLE:
A: Who did she see at 8:00 P.M.?
B: Rick Simon. Where did she see him?
A: At Al's Grill. Who else saw him?

Suspect	Time	Location	Other Witnesses
Rick Simon	8:00 P.M.	Al's Grill	the waiter
Alice May	7:30 P.M.		
Jake Bordon	6:30 P.M.	the office	
Lilly Green	7:15 P.M.	in the park	
		Tony's Pizza	two customers

When you are finished, compare your charts. Are they the same?

REVIEW OR SELFTEST

I. *Complete each sentence with the simple present tense or present progressive form of the verb in parentheses.*

1. You _____'re breathing_____ hard. Sit down and rest for a while.
   (breathe / are breathing)

2. Dolphins and whales are mammals. They have lungs and they

   _____ air.
   (breathe / are breathing)

3. Fred just left. He _____ to his biology class right now.
   (goes / is going)

4. He _____ to biology class twice a week.
   (goes / is going)

5. In our area, it _____ a lot in March.
   (rains / is raining)

6. It _____ right now, and I don't have my umbrella.
   (rains / is raining)

7. We _____. Is the music too loud for you?
   (dance / are dancing)

8. We _____ every day. It's good exercise.
   (dance / are dancing)

II. *Complete the conversations with short answers and the present progressive or simple present tense of the verbs in parentheses.*

1. A: _____Are_____ you _____getting_____ ready for school? It's 7:45.
                              1. (get)

   B: Yes, I _____am_____. I _____ my teeth right now.
                       2.   3. (brush)

   A: How about Sue? _____ she _____ dressed?
                                              4. (get)

   B: I _____ so. She _____ for her shoes.
           5. (think)   6. (look)

2. A: Something _____ good. What _____ you
                        7. (smell)
   _____?
       8. (cook)

   B: Pancakes. Hey, _____ you _____ your book bag?
                                              9. (have)

   A: No, I _____. _____ you _____ where it is?
               10.   11. (know)

   B: You _____ it in your room these days, right?
             12. (keep)

   A: I _____ in my room right now, but I _____ it.
           13. (stand)   14. (not see)

(continued on next page)

3. A: Yuck. This milk _____ awful. I'm going to have juice instead.
  15. (taste)

   B: Look, I _____ one sandwich for lunch. _____ that enough?
  16. (pack)   17. (be)

   A: I _____ any lunch. I _____ hungry today.
  18. (not want)   19. (not be)

   B: You _____ pale. _____ you _____ OK?
  20. (look)   21. (feel)

   A: Yes, I _____. I'm just a little nervous about my spelling test.
  22.

   B: Oh, no! Look at the time. I think I _____ the school bus.
  23. (hear)

   A: Don't worry. We _____ right now.
  24. (leave)

   B: Bye. Have a great day!

III. *Complete each sentence with a negative or affirmative imperative. Use the verbs in the box. Use some verbs more than once.*

forget	enjoy	lock	call	walk	have	put

1. Please _____walk_____ the dog in the morning and afternoon.

2. But _____ her near the Wongs' house. She chases their cat.

3. Please _____ the back door before you go out. The key is in the door.

4. Also, _____ to turn out the lights. We have high electric bills.

5. _____ newspapers in the garbage. They go in the green bin. We recycle them.

6. _____ the garbage cans on the sidewalk on Tuesday morning.

7. _____ me if you have any problems.

8. But _____ after 11:00. We go to bed early when we're on vacation.

9. _____ fun, and _____ the house.

IV. *Complete the conversation with short answers or the simple past tense form of the verbs in parentheses.*

   A: Are you from Baltimore?

   B: No, I'm not. I _____was born_____ in China, but I _____ here ten years ago.
  1. (be born)   2. (move)

   A: Where _____ you _____ in China?
  3. (live)

   B: In Shanghai.

A: Oh, really? I _____ in Shanghai last year. I _____ English
there for three years.

4. (be)   5. (teach)

B: That's interesting. _____ you _____ it?

6. (like)

A: Yes, I _____. Very much.

7.

B: _____ the United States _____ strange to you after China?

8. (appear)

A: Yes, it _____. I _____ comfortable in Baltimore for months.

9.   10. (not be)

For one thing, my students here _____ very polite.

11. (not seem)

B: I think it's called reverse culture shock. I _____ uncomfortable when I

12. (be)

_____ back to China a few years ago.

13. (go)

A: _____ you uncomfortable for a long time?

14. (be)

B: No, I _____. Things _____ to feel normal again after a
few weeks.

15.   16. (begin)

A: _____ you _____ to feel culture shock in your own culture?

17. (expect)

B: No, I _____! But I'll be prepared the next time I visit!

18.

V. *Circle the correct verbs to complete the conversation.*

A: When you were young, did you use to ate / eat in restaurants a lot?

1.

B: No, not that often. We used to cooking / cook dinner at home.

2.

A: How about prices? Were / Did they lower when you were a kid?

3.

B: They sure were. Here's an example. A movie got used to / used to cost a dollar.

4.

A: Wow! Did you go / went to the movies a lot?

5.

B: Yes. We were going / went every Saturday afternoon. Hey, how about eating that

6.

hamburger?

A: OK—but one last question. Did / Are you like everything better in those days?

7.

B: Nope. In those days, I wasn't having / didn't have you to talk to. I like things much

8.

better now.

VI. *Complete the telephone conversation with the simple past tense or past progressive form of the verbs in parentheses.*

A: Hi, I'm glad you're home! No one _____answered_____ a few minutes ago.
1. (answer)

B: I _____ the lawn when the phone _____. What's up?
2. (mow)   3. (ring)

A: I _____ a little accident with the car. Nothing serious—no injuries.
4. (have)

B: Oh, that's good. How about the car?

A: It's OK. There _____ much damage. I _____ fast when
5. (not be)   6. (not drive)

I _____ the bus.
7. (hit)

B: The bus! How _____ you _____ that?
8. (do)

A: I _____ to find a special radio station, so I _____ attention.
9. (try)   10. (not pay)

B: _____ you _____ the police?
11. (call)

A: No. It _____ right in front of the police station. An officer
12. (happen)

_____ before I even _____ out of the car. After they
13. (appear)   14. (get)

_____, I _____ the insurance company.
15. (leave)   16. (call)

B: Well, I'm just glad you're OK.

VII. *Circle the correct verb to complete each conversation.*

1. A: Do you and Nora have plans for the weekend?
B: Yes, we('re going to)/ 'll go to a concert on Saturday. I just bought the tickets.

2. A: I can't believe I got into medical school.
B: You are / 'll be a doctor in just a few years!

3. A: Oh, no! I forgot to deposit my paycheck yesterday.
B: I'll / 'm going to deposit it for you. It's on my way.

4. A: I'm taking the train to Boston tomorrow.
B: Oh. What time does / did it leave?

5. A: Take your umbrella. It's going to / 'll rain.
B: Thanks. I didn't listen to the weather report this morning.

6. A: My son is really interested in science fiction.
B: Maybe he has / 'll have a career in space exploration when he grows up.

7. A: Look at Rachel's face. I think she's going to / 'll cry.
B: Poor kid. She really wants to come with us today.

8. A: It's almost June. What are we going to / do we do for the summer?
B: How about summer school?

9. **A:** <u>Will / Does</u> Mahmoud call back this afternoon?
   B: He promised to call, but he's usually in class all afternoon.

10. **A:** Should I make a reservation at Dino's for tonight?
    B: It's already arranged. We <u>are / were</u> meeting there at 6:00.

VIII. _Complete the sentences with the correct forms of the verbs in parentheses. Use_ will _in one clause of each sentence._

1. Laila _____will need_____ some new furniture when she _____moves_____.
   a. (need)   b. (move)

2. As soon as you _____ to Oak Street, you _____ the library.
   a. (get)   b. (see)

3. We _____ here tonight until we _____ the report.
   a. (stay)   b. (finish)

4. After Sid _____ next June, he _____ in the city.
   a. (graduate)   b. (live)

5. I _____ the newspaper while I _____ breakfast.
   a. (read)   b. (eat)

6. They _____ a car when they _____ enough money.
   a. (buy)   b. (save)

7. Carmen _____ me before she _____.
   a. (call)   b. (leave)

8. By the time you _____ thirty, there _____ a shuttle
   a. (turn)   b. (be)
   to the moon.

IX. _Complete the conversations with_ **Wh-** _questions._

1. **A:** ___Where did you go_____ last night?
        a.

   B: I went to the movies.

   A: Really? _____ with you?
                       b.

   B: Mona did. She goes every weekend.

   A: _____?
           c.

   B: We saw _Earthquake._

2. **A:** You look upset. _____?
                              a.

   B: Nothing happened. I'm just tired.

   A: _____ on the math test?
                       b.

   B: I got an A.

   A: Wow! Big improvement. _____ with?
                                      c.

   B: I studied with Ana. It really helped.

X. *Circle the letter of the correct answer to complete each sentence.*

1. What _____? You look fascinated.   (A) B C D
   (A) are you reading   (C) will you read
   (B) do you read   (D) did you read

2. I am reading a history of the Internet. Did you know it _____   A B C D
   in the 1960s?
   (A) begins   (C) began
   (B) 's going to begin   (D) is beginning

3. Jill, please _____ me your e-mail address again. I lost it.   A B C D
   (A) gives   (C) give
   (B) is giving   (D) gave

4. My e-mail address is jillski4@data.com. _____ it again!   A B C D
   (A) Not lose   (C) Aren't losing
   (B) Won't lose   (D) Don't lose

5. How are you, Naruyo? You _____ a little tired these days.   A B C D
   (A) 'll seem   (C) were seeming
   (B) seem   (D) seemed

6. I _____ some evening classes this semester, and I have a lot   A B C D
   of homework.
   (A) 'm taking   (C) 'm going to take
   (B) take   (D) was taking

7. I remember you. You _____ to go to school here.   A B C D
   (A) used   (C) using
   (B) were used   (D) use

8. You have a good memory. I _____ here for only a month.   A B C D
   (A) go   (C) was going to go
   (B) went   (D) 'm going

9. Will you buy an electric car when they _____ available?   A B C D
   (A) will become   (C) became
   (B) are becoming   (D) become

10. I think I _____ until electric cars are really cheap.   A B C D
    (A) waited   (C) wait
    (B) 'll wait   (D) was waiting

11. _____ when it started to rain?   A B C D
    (A) Were you driving   (C) Do you drive
    (B) Are you driving   (D) Will you drive

12. We were having dinner while it _____.   A B C D
    (A) rains   (C) raining
    (B) 's going to rain   (D) was raining

XI. *Each sentence has four underlined words or phases. The four underlined parts of the sentence are marked A, B, C, or D. Circle the letter of the <u>one</u> underlined word or phrase that is NOT CORRECT.*

1. <u>Before</u> I <u>moved</u> to Chicago, I <u>use to</u> <u>live</u> in the country.   A B Ⓒ D
    A   B   C   D

2. We <u>are going to</u> <u>study</u> tonight <u>until</u> we <u>finished</u> the chapter.   A B C D
         A   B   C   D

3. It<u>'s</u> a one-way street, <u>so</u> <u>no</u> <u>turn</u> left here.   A B C D
   A   B C   D

4. <u>When</u> Sid <u>will graduate</u> next June<u>,</u> he <u>will live</u> in the city.   A B C D
    A   B   C   D

5. <u>Where</u> <u>you went</u> <u>after</u> you <u>left</u> last night?   A B C D
    A   B   C   D

6. Who <u>did</u> <u>saw</u> you <u>while</u> you <u>were leaving</u> the bank?   A B C D
     A B   C   D

7. <u>Usually,</u> <u>it's raining</u> a lot here every winter, <u>but</u> last year it <u>didn't</u>.   A B C D
    A   B   C   D

8. <u>Were</u> you <u>watching</u> TV <u>when</u> I <u>call</u> you last night?   A B C D
    A   B   C   D

9. You<u>'ll see</u> the bank<u>,</u> <u>when</u> you <u>get</u> to Main Street.   A B C D
    A   B C   D

10. We <u>didn't hear</u> the doorbell <u>when</u> he <u>arrived</u> because we <u>ate</u>.   A B C D
      A   B   C   D

11. Years <u>ago</u>, I didn't <u>used to</u> like rock music, <u>but</u> now I <u>love</u> it.   A B C D
      A   B   C   D

12. The movie <u>starts</u> <u>at</u> 7:30, so I <u>think</u> I <u>go</u>.   A B C D
         A B   C D

13. <u>Are you wanting</u> to <u>go</u> with me, or <u>are you</u> <u>studying</u> tonight?   A B C D
    A   B   C   D

▶ *To check your answers, go to the Answer Key on page 83.*

PART

FROM GRAMMAR TO WRITING
COMBINING SENTENCES with time words

Y ou can often improve your writing by combining two short sentences into one longer sentence that connects the two ideas. The two sentences can be combined by using a time word such as *while, when, as soon as, before, after,* or *until.* The resulting longer sentence is made up of a main clause and a time clause.

> **EXAMPLE:**
> I was shopping. I saw the perfect dress for her. ⟶
>
> time clause   main clause
> **While** I was shopping, I saw the perfect dress for her.

The time clause can come first or second. When it comes first, a comma separates the two clauses.

---

1 *Read this paragraph. Underline all the sentences that are combined with a time word. Circle the time words.*

> I always exchange holiday presents with my girlfriend, Shao Fen. Last year, while I was shopping for her, I saw an umbrella in her favorite color. As soon as I saw it, I thought of her. I bought the umbrella and a scarf in the same color. When Shao Fen opened the present, she looked really upset. Later she explained that in Chinese the word for "umbrella" sounds like the word for "separation". When she saw the umbrella, she misunderstood. She thought I wanted to end the relationship. Next year, before I buy something, I'm going to check with her sister!

2 *Look at this student's paragraph. Combine the pairs of underlined sentences with time words such as **when, while, as soon as, before**, and **after**. Use your own paper.*

I usually keep my wallet in my back pocket when I go out. <u>Two weeks ago, I was walking on a crowded street. I felt something.</u> I didn't pay any attention to it at the time. <u>I got home. I noticed that my wallet was missing.</u> I was very upset. It didn't have much money in it, but my credit card and my driver's license were there. <u>I was thinking about the situation. My brother came home.</u> He told me to report it to the police. <u>I called the police. They weren't very encouraging.</u> They said that wallets often get "picked" from back pockets. They didn't think I would get it back. <u>Tomorrow, I'm going to the movies. I'll keep my new wallet in my front pocket.</u>

EXAMPLE:
Two weeks ago, **while** I was walking on a crowded street, I felt something.

3 *Before you write . . .*

- We often say, "Learn from your mistakes." Think about a misunderstanding or a mistake that you experienced or observed. How did your behavior or thinking change because of it?

- Describe the experience to a partner. Listen to your partner's experience.

- Ask and answer questions about your experiences, for example: *When did it happen? Why did you . . . ? Where were you when . . . ? What will you do . . . ?*

4 *Write a draft of your story. Follow the model below. Remember to use some of these time words and include information that your partner asked about.*

when	while	as soon as	before	until

I (OR My friend) always / often / usually / never_____

_____

_____

Last week / Yesterday / In 1998,_____

_____

_____

_____

_____

In the future / Next time, _____

_____

5 *Exchange paragraphs with a different partner. Complete the chart.*

a. The writer used time words to connect ideas.   Yes _____   No _____

b. What I liked in the story:

_____

_____

_____

c. Questions I'd like the writer to answer about the story:
(Note: Write only the questions you want to ask.)

Who _____?

What _____?

When _____?

Where _____?

How _____?

(*Other*) _____?

Discuss the chart with your partner. Revise your paragraph according to the chart.

REVIEW OR SELFTEST
ANSWER KEY

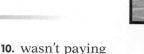

I. (Unit 1)
2. breathe
3. 's going*
4. goes
5. rains
6. 's raining
7. 're dancing
8. dance

II. (Unit 1)
3. 'm brushing
4. Is . . . getting
5. think
6. 's looking
7. smells
8. are . . . cooking
9. do . . . have
10. don't
11. Do . . . know
12. 're keeping *or* keep
13. 'm standing
14. don't see
15. tastes
16. 'm packing
17. Is
18. don't want
19. 'm not
20. look
21. Do . . . feel *or* Are . . . feeling
22. do *or* am
23. hear
24. 're leaving

III. (Unit 2)
2. don't walk
3. lock
4. don't forget
5. Don't put
6. Put
7. Call
8. don't call
9. Have . . . enjoy

IV. (Unit 3)
2. moved
3. did . . . live
4. was
5. taught
6. Did . . . like
7. did
8. Did . . . appear
9. did
10. wasn't
11. didn't seem
12. was
13. went
14. Were
15. wasn't
16. began
17. Did . . . expect
18. didn't

V. (Units 3 and 4)
2. cook
3. Were
4. used to
5. go
6. went
7. Did
8. didn't have

VI. (Unit 5)
2. was mowing
3. rang
4. had
5. wasn't
6. wasn't driving
7. hit
8. did . . . do
9. was trying
10. wasn't paying
11. Did . . . call
12. happened
13. appeared
14. got
15. left
16. called

VII. (Unit 6)
2. 'll be
3. 'll
4. does
5. 's going to
6. 'll have
7. 's going to
8. are we going to
9. Will
10. are

VIII. (Unit 7)
2. a. get
   b. 'll see
3. a. 'll stay
   b. finish
4. a. graduates
   b. 'll live
5. a. 'll read
   b. eat
6. a. 'll buy
   b. save
7. a. will call
   b. leaves
8. a. turn
   b. 'll be

IX. (Unit 8)
1. b. Who went
   c. What did you see?
2. a. What happened?
   b. What did you get
   c. Who(m) did you study

X. (Units 1–8)
2. C
3. C
4. D
5. B
6. A
7. A
8. B
9. D
10. B
11. A
12. D

XI. (Units 1–8)
2. D
3. C
4. B
5. B
6. A
7. B
8. D
9. B
10. D
11. B
12. D
13. A

*Where a contracted form is given, the long form is also correct.

83

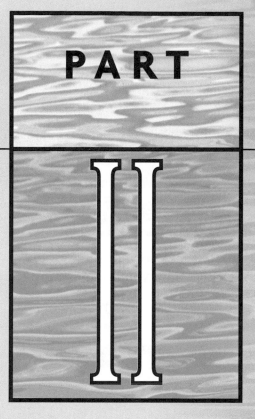

PART

II

PRONOUNS AND PHRASAL VERBS

REFLEXIVE AND RECIPROCAL PRONOUNS

GRAMMAR **IN CONTEXT**

BEFORE YOU READ What do you think *self-talk* is? Look at the examples of self-talk in the cartoons. Which are positive? Which are negative?

Read this excerpt from a psychology magazine.

SELF-TALK

IT WAS ALL MY FAULT.

I'LL NEVER FIND ANOTHER JOB.

I'M THE BEST WORKER THEY HAD.

I'LL FIND A BETTER JOB SOON.

Self-talk is the way we explain a problem to **ourselves**. It can affect how we feel and how we act. Take the case of Tom and Sara. They both got laid off from their jobs, but their reactions were very different. Sara frequently called her friends, continued her free-time activities, and kept **herself** fit. Tom, on the other hand, spent all his time **by himself**, didn't allow **himself** to have a good time, and gained ten pounds.

Why were their reactions so different from **one another**? They both lost their jobs, so the situation **itself** can't explain

Tom's problems. The main difference was the way Tom and Sara explained the problem to **themselves**. Sara told **herself** that the problem was temporary and that she **herself** could change it. Tom saw **himself** as helpless and likely to be unemployed forever.

Tom and Sara both got their jobs back. Their reactions when they talked to **each other** were, again, very different. For his part, Tom grumbled, "Oh, I guess they were really desperate." Sara, on the other hand, smiled and said, "Well! They finally realized that they need me!"

GRAMMAR **PRESENTATION**
REFLEXIVE AND RECIPROCAL PRONOUNS

REFLEXIVE PRONOUNS			
SUBJECT PRONOUN		**REFLEXIVE PRONOUN**	
I		**myself**	
You		**yourself**	
He		**himself**	
She	looked at	**herself**	in the mirror.
It		**itself**	
We		**ourselves**	
You		**yourselves**	
They		**themselves**	

RECIPROCAL PRONOUNS		
SUBJECT PRONOUN		**RECIPROCAL PRONOUN**
We You They	looked at	**each other**. **one another**.

NOTES

1. Use a **reflexive pronoun** when the <u>subject and object</u> of a sentence refer to the <u>same people or things</u>.

(See Appendix 3, page A-2, for a list of verbs and expressions that often take reflexive pronouns.)

2. In **imperative sentences** with reflexive pronouns, use:

–*yourself* when <u>the subject is singular</u>.

–*yourselves* when <u>the subject is plural</u>.

REMEMBER: In imperative sentences, the <u>subject is *you*</u>, and *you* can be either singular or plural.

EXAMPLES

subject   =   object
- **Sara** looked at *herself* in the mirror. *(Sara looked at her own face.)*

subject   =   object
- **They** felt proud of *themselves*. *(They were proud of their own actions.)*

- "Don't push *yourself* so hard, **Tom**," Sara said.

- "Don't push *yourselves* so hard, **guys**," Sara said.

(continued on next page)

3. Use a **reflexive pronoun** to <u>emphasize</u> a noun. In this case, the reflexive pronoun usually follows the noun directly.

- Tom was upset when he lost his job. The **job** *itself* wasn't important to him, but he needed the money.
  (*Tom didn't care about the job; he just needed the money.*)

---

4. *By* + **a reflexive pronoun** means *alone* or *without any help.*

- Sara lives **by** *herself*.
  (*Sara lives alone.*)
- We painted the house **by** *ourselves*.
  (*No one helped us.*)

Be + **a reflexive pronoun** means *act in the usual way.*

- Just **be** *yourself* at your interview.
- He **wasn't** *himself* after he lost his job.

---

5. Use a **reciprocal pronoun** when the subject and object of a sentence refer to the <u>same people</u>, and these people have a <u>two-way relationship</u>.

subject   =   object
- **Tom and Sara** met *each other* at work.
  (*Tom met Sara, and Sara met Tom.*)

subject   =   object
- **We all** told *one another* about our jobs.
  (*Each person exchanged news with every other person.*)

USAGE NOTE: The traditional grammar rule says to use *each other* when the subject refers to two people, and *one another* when the subject refers to more than two people. Most people, however, use *each other* and *one another* <u>in the same way</u>.

- **Sara and Tom** talked to *each other*.
- **Sara and Tom** talked to *one another*.
- **Sara, Tom, Fred, and Jane** talked to *one another*.
- **Sara, Tom, Fred, and Jane** talked to *each other*.

▶ **BE CAREFUL!** Reciprocal pronouns and plural reflexive pronouns have <u>different meanings</u>.

- Fred and Jane blamed *each other*.
  (*Fred blamed Jane, and Jane blamed Fred.*)
- Fred and Jane blamed *themselves*.
  (*Fred blamed himself, and Jane blamed herself.*)

---

6. Reciprocal pronouns have <u>possessive forms</u>: *each other's, one another's.*

- Tom and Sara took *each other's* telephone number.
  (*Tom took Sara's phone number, and Sara took Tom's.*)

FOCUSED PRACTICE

1 DISCOVER THE GRAMMAR

Read the rest of the article about self-talk. Underline the reflexive pronouns once and the reciprocal pronouns twice. Draw an arrow to the words that these pronouns refer to.

continued

Positive self-talk can make the difference between winning and losing. Many athletes use self-talk to help <u>themselves</u> succeed. For example, golf pro Jack Nicklaus used to imagine himself making a winning shot just before he played. Olympic swimmer Summer Sanders prepares herself for a race by smiling.

One sports psychologist believes that Olympic athletes are not very different from <u>one another</u>— they are all the best in their sports. When two top athletes compete against each other, the winner is the one with the most powerful positive "mental movies."

Psychologists say that ordinary people themselves can use these techniques as well. We can create "mental movies" to help ourselves succeed in difficult situations.

2 THE OFFICE PARTY   Grammar Notes 1–2, 4–5

 *Tom and Sara's company had an office party. Choose the correct reflexive or reciprocal pronouns to complete the conversations.*

1. A: Listen guys! The food and drinks are over here. Please come and help

  _____yourselves_____.
  (yourselves / themselves)

  B: Thanks. We will.

2. A: Isn't that the new head of the accounting department over there?

  B: I think so. Let's go over and introduce _____.
  (himself / ourselves)

3. A: I'm really nervous about my date with Nicole after the party. I cut

  _____ twice while shaving, and then I lost my car keys.
  (herself / myself)

  B: Come on. This is a party. Just relax and be _____. You'll do fine.
  (yourself / yourselves)

4. A: What are you giving your boss for the holidays this year?

  B: We always give _____ the same holiday gifts. Every year I give him
  (ourselves / each other)
  a book and he gives me a scarf.

(continued on next page)

5. A: What do you think of the new computer program?

   B: I'm not sure. In our department, we're still teaching _____ how
   (ourselves / themselves)

   to use it.

6. A: Jessica looks upset. Didn't she get a promotion?

   B: No, and she keeps blaming _____. I'll lend her that article
   (herself / himself)

   about self-talk.

7. A: The Aguayos are going to Japan on vacation this year.

   B: Are they going by _____ or with a tour group?
   (each other / themselves)

8. A: This was a great party.

   B: Yeah. We really enjoyed _____.
   (ourselves / myself)

---

③ WE LEARN FROM ONE ANOTHER   Grammar Notes 1–6

*Read this interview with George Prudeau, a high-school French teacher. Complete
the interview with the correct reflexive or reciprocal pronouns.*

INTERVIEWER: What do you like best about your profession?

   GEORGE: One of the great things about teaching is the freedom I have. I run the class

   by _____*myself*_____—just the way I want to. I also like the way my
              1.

   students and I learn from _____. My students teach me a lot.
                                      2.

INTERVIEWER: What about discipline? Is that a problem?

   GEORGE: We have just a few rules. I tell my students, "Keep _____ busy.
                                                                           3.

   Discuss the lessons, but don't interfere with _____'s work."
                                                           4.

INTERVIEWER: What do you like to teach best?

   GEORGE: I love French, but the subject _____ really isn't that important.
                                                      5.

   A good teacher helps students learn by _____ and encourages
                                                   6.

   them not to give up when they have problems. For instance, John, one of

   my students, just taught _____ how to bake French bread. The
                                    7.

   first few loaves were failures. I encouraged him to use positive self-talk, and

   in the end he succeeded.

INTERVIEWER: What teaching materials do you use?

GEORGE: Very simple ones. I pride _____ on the fact that I can teach
8.

anywhere, even on a street corner.

INTERVIEWER: What do you like least about your job?

GEORGE: The salary. I teach French culture, but I can't afford to travel to France.

I have to satisfy _____ with trips to French restaurants!
9.

---

4 **EDITING**

Read this woman's diary. Find and correct six mistakes in the use of reflexive and reciprocal pronouns. The first mistake is already corrected.

> ✦ Thursday
>
>   Jan's birthday was Wednesday, and I forgot to call him.
>   myself
>   I reminded ~~me~~ all day, and then I forgot anyway! I felt
>   terrible. My sister Anna said, "Don't be so hard on
>   yourselves," but I didn't believe her. She prides herself
>   on remembering everything. Then I remembered the
>   article on self-talk. It said that people can change the
>   way they explain problems to theirselves. Well, I listened
>   to the way I talked to me, and it sounded really
>   insulting—like the way our high school math teacher
>   used to talk to us. I thought, Jan and I are good friends,
>   and we treat each other well. In fact, he forgave
>   myself for my mistake right away. And I forgave him for
>   forgetting our dinner date two weeks ago. Friends can
>   forgive themselves, so I guess I can forgive myself.

COMMUNICATION PRACTICE

5 LISTENING

Listen to the conversations at an office party. Then listen again and circle the pronouns that you hear.

1. **A:** Mark's department did a great job this year.

   B: I know. They're really proud of <u>themselves</u> / <u>each other</u>.

2. **A:** What's wrong? You look upset.

   B: I just heard Ed and Jeff talking. You know Ed blames <u>him / himself</u> for everything.

3. **A:** I hear you're going to Japan on vacation this year. Are you going by <u>yourself /</u> <u>yourselves</u> or with a tour?

   B: Oh, with a tour.

4. **A:** Hillary looks happy tonight. Did Meredith give her the promotion?

   B: No, not yet. Meredith keeps asking <u>herself / her</u> if she can do the job.

5. **A:** How do you like the new computer system?

   B: I'm not sure. In our department, we're still teaching <u>each other / ourselves</u> how to use it.

6. **A:** So long, now. Thanks for coming. It was good to see you.

   B: Oh, it was a great party.

   A: I'm glad you enjoyed <u>yourself / yourselves</u>.

6 CHEER YOURSELF UP!

What do you tell yourself in a difficult situation? Work with a partner and discuss each other's self-talk in the situations below. Then report to the class.

- you're going to take a big test
- you're stuck in traffic
- you have a roommate you don't like
- you're going to compete in a sport or other event
- you're having an argument with a friend or relative
- you forgot something important

> **EXAMPLE:**
> **A:** What do you tell yourself when you're going to take a big test?
> **B:** I tell myself that I prepared myself well and that I'll do fine.

7 THE OPTIMIST TEST

Test yourself by completing the questionnaire.

Are you an optimist or a pessimist?

What do you tell yourself when things go wrong? Check your most likely self-talk for each situation below. Then find out if you're an optimist or pessimist.

1. Your boss doesn't say good morning to you.
   - ☐ **a.** She isn't herself today.
   - ☐ **b.** She doesn't like me.

2. Your family forgets your birthday.
   - ☐ **a.** Next year we should keep in touch with one another more.
   - ☐ **b.** They only think about themselves.

3. You gain ten pounds.
   - ☐ **a.** I promise myself to eat properly from now on.
   - ☐ **b.** Diets never work for me.

4. Your romantic partner decides to go out with other people.
   - ☐ **a.** We didn't spend enough time with each other.
   - ☐ **b.** We're wrong for each other.

5. You're feeling tired lately.
   - ☐ **a.** I pushed myself too hard this week.
   - ☐ **b.** I never take care of myself.

6. Your friend forgets an appointment with you.
   - ☐ **a.** He sometimes forgets to read his appointment book.
   - ☐ **b.** He never reminds himself about important things.

> **Score you questionnaire . . .**
> Optimists see bad situations as temporary or limited. Pessimists see them as permanent. All the **a** answers are optimistic, and all the **b** answers are pessimistic. Give yourself 0 for every **a** answer and 1 for every **b** answer.
>
> | If You Scored | You Are |
> | --- | --- |
> | 0–2 | very optimistic |
> | 3–4 | somewhat optimistic |
> | 5–6 | pessimistic |

Now interview five classmates and find out how they answered the questions. Report the results to another group. Use reflexive and reciprocal pronouns in your descriptions.

EXAMPLE:
For Question 5, three people said they pushed themselves too hard. Two people said they never take care of themselves . . .

8 THE MEMORY GAME

Work with a partner. First look at the picture carefully for thirty seconds. Then shut your books. Tell each other as many things as you can remember about what people in the picture are doing. Use reciprocal and reflexive pronouns in your description. Take notes. When you are finished, open your books and check your answers. Who remembered the most?

EXAMPLE:

A: Two men are waving at each other.

B: No, I think the people waving at each other are women.

9 WRITING

Imagine you receive a letter from a friend who attends school in another city. Your friend is not doing well at school and is having problems with a boyfriend or girlfriend. Write your friend a letter. Explain the kind of self-talk you use when things are not going well.

EXAMPLE:

Dear Annette,

I'm sorry you are having problems in school. Here's what I tell myself when I have problems . . .

PHRASAL VERBS

GRAMMAR **IN CONTEXT**

BEFORE YOU READ Look at the photograph. What kind of work do you think the man does?

▭ *Read this article about Dr. Eloy Rodriguez.*

PLANTING IDEAS ❧

*A*s a child, Eloy Rodriguez picked cotton to help support his family. He also **picked up** an interest in plants. Now a famous scientist, Dr. Rodriguez is still interested in plants. Every summer he **takes off** his lab coat, **puts on** his mosquito repellent, and travels to the Amazon region of Venezuela with his students. There, they search for medicinal plants.

Rodriguez **grew up** in Texas. The adults in his large family (sixty-seven cousins lived nearby) **brought** their children **up** to be honest, fair, and *vivo,* or quick-thinking. These values **helped** him **out** in high school. His counselor tried to **talk** him **into** a career in auto mechanics. Rodriguez, however, loved chemistry and went to college instead. He took a job there **cleaning up** a laboratory. He became a science major and then **went on** to graduate school. Soon he was managing the lab.

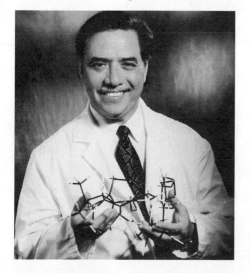

Eloy Rodriguez and anthropologist Richard Wrangham once noticed that sick animals often **pick out** plants to use as medicine. They **turned** their observations **into** a new area of science —zoopharmacognosy. Today Rodriguez is one of the most brilliant scientists in the United States. Rodriguez thanks his family. He **points out** that sixty-four of his cousins graduated from college, eleven with advanced degrees. "Although poverty was there, family was what helped us **get by** in life."

GRAMMAR **PRESENTATION**
PHRASAL VERBS

SEPARABLE TRANSITIVE PHRASAL VERBS			
SUBJECT	VERB	PARTICLE	DIRECT OBJECT (NOUN)
He	put	on	his lab coat.
	helped	out	his students.

		DIRECT OBJECT (NOUN / PRONOUN)	
SUBJECT	VERB	DIRECT OBJECT (NOUN / PRONOUN)	PARTICLE
He	put	his lab coat it	on.
	helped	his students them	out.

INTRANSITIVE PHRASAL VERBS			
SUBJECT	VERB	PARTICLE	
She	started	over.	
He	grew	up	in Texas.
They	got	back	early.

NOTES

EXAMPLES

1. Phrasal verbs (also called two-part or two-word verbs) consist of <u>a verb and a particle</u>. *On, off, up,* and *down* are common particles.

Verb + Particle = Phrasal Verb

Particles and prepositions look the same. However, particles are <u>part of the verb phrase</u>, and they often <u>change the meaning</u> of the verb.

verb + particle
• He **put on** his lab coat.

verb + particle
• She **looked up** the word "zoopharmacognosy."

verb + preposition
• She's **looking up** at the sky.
(*She's looking in the direction of the sky.*)

verb + particle
• She's **looking up** the word.
(*She's searching for the word in the dictionary.*)

2. USAGE NOTE: Many **phrasal verbs** and one-word verbs have similar meanings. The phrasal verbs are <u>more informal</u> and much <u>more common</u> in everyday speech.

PHRASAL VERB (informal)	ONE-WORD VERB (more formal)
bring up	raise
figure out	solve
go on	continue
pick out	select
take off	remove
wake up	awaken

3. Phrasal verbs can be transitive or intransitive. **Transitive phrasal verbs** <u>have direct objects</u> (d.o).

Most transitive phrasal verbs are **separable**. This means that when the <u>direct object is a noun</u>, it can come:

–<u>after</u> the verb + particle

OR

–<u>between</u> the verb and its particle.

▶ **BE CAREFUL!** When the <u>direct object is a pronoun</u>, it must come <u>between</u> the verb and the particle.

(See Appendix 4, page A-3, for a list of transitive phrasal verbs and their meanings.)

- He **set up** <u>an experiment</u>.
  (phrasal verb / d.o.)
- They **figured out** <u>the problems</u>.
  (phrasal verb / d.o.)

- We **dropped off** <u>Mary</u> at the lab.
  (verb + particle / d.o.)

OR

- We **dropped** <u>Mary</u> **off** at the lab.
  (verb / d.o. / particle)
- We **dropped** <u>her</u> **off**.
  NOT ~~We dropped off her.~~
  (d.o.)
- He **cleaned** <u>them</u> **up**.
  NOT ~~He cleaned up them.~~
  (d.o.)

REFERENCE NOTE
Some transitive phrasal verbs are inseparable. See *Focus on Grammar: High-Intermediate Student Book,* Unit 12.

4. Some phrasal verbs are intransitive. **Intransitive phrasal verbs** <u>do not take objects</u>.

(See Appendix 5, page A-3, for a list of intransitive phrasal verbs and their meanings.)

- Dr. Rodriguez **grew up** in Texas.
- He **stood up** to receive the award.

FOCUSED PRACTICE

1 DISCOVER THE GRAMMAR

Read the article. Underline the phrasal verbs. Circle the direct objects of the transitive phrasal verbs.

In Eloy Rodriguez's elementary school in Edinburg, Texas, teachers passed (Chicano* students) over for special honors classes and punished them for speaking Spanish. When Rodriguez became the first U.S.-born Chicano biology instructor at his university, he worked eighteen hours a day and slept in his lab. "I was very aware that I was the first this, and the first that, and I knew that some people were waiting for me to slip up." Rodriguez didn't slip up. However, he knows that poor treatment turns students off education. Many of them just give up.

Today, Dr. Rodriguez is passing his own success on. When he became a professor at Cornell University, he set out to find Latino** graduate students. He takes these students with him on many of his trips and works hard to turn them into top scientists. In 1990 he set up KIDS (Kids Investigating and Discovering Science)—a science program for minority elementary school children. They put on white lab coats and investigate science with university teachers who treat them like research scientists. They observe nature and figure out problems. In interviews, Rodriguez always brings up role models. "I saw my first snowflake before I saw my first Chicano scientist," he says. Because of Rodriguez's efforts, many students will not face the same problem.

* Chicano—Mexican-American
** Latino—from a Spanish-speaking country in Central or South America

Read these sentences and decide if they are **True (T)** *or* **False (F)**.

  F   **1.** In Rodriguez's elementary school, teachers chose many Chicano students for honors classes.

_____ **2.** When Rodriguez became a biology instructor, some people expected him to fail.

_____ **3.** Poor treatment makes minority students less interested in education.

_____ **4.** Today, Rodriguez wants to forget his own success.

_____ **5.** He searches for Latino graduate students for his program at Cornell.

_____ **6.** In 1990, Rodriguez visited a program called KIDS.

_____ **7.** Children in KIDS wear the same lab clothes as the scientists.

_____ **8.** Rodriguez rarely mentions role models.

2 COME ALONG!

Complete the flyer. Choose the phrasal verb from the box that is closest in meaning to the verb in parentheses. Use the correct form of the phrasal verb. Use Appendices 4 and 5 on page A-3 for help.

fill out	find out	get up	hand in	pass up
pick up	set up	~~sign up~~	talk over	work out

Two Weeks in the Amazon! ____Sign up____ Now!
1. (register)

The Biology Department is now _____ its summer field trip
2. (preparing)

to the Amazonian rain forest in Venezuela. _____ your
3. (get)

application from the Department Office (Room 215), and _____

it _____ right away. _____ it _____
4. (complete)   5. (submit)

by May 1.

Last summer we collected plants and identified them. This summer we

plan to talk to local people and _____ how they use plants in
6. (discover)

traditional medicine. This trip is very challenging. We travel to our camp by

canoe. When there are problems, we _____ them

_____ by ourselves. We _____ very early and we
7. (solve)   8. (arise)

work hard. There is also some danger, so _____ the trip

_____ with
9. (discuss)

your families before you

decide. We hope you won't

_____ this
10. (reject)

chance to do important

"hands-on science."

3 FOOD FOR THOUGHT   Grammar Notes 1–2

Circle the correct particle to complete each phrasal verb.

Eat some leaves and call me in the morning

In 1972, Richard Wrangham of Harvard University set (out)/ up to study some strange behavior of chimpanzees in
1.
Tanzania. According to Wrangham, the chimps get by / up at
2.
dawn and look for *Aspilia,* plants with furry leaves. They pick
them and swallow them whole. Wrangham's observations
brought back / up a question. Chimps clearly hated the taste
3.
of *Aspilia.* Why do they pick out / over this plant but pass out / up delicious fruit nearby?
4.   5.
Wrangham thought this question over / up for several years. He then asked Eloy Rodriguez
6.
to help him in / out with the analysis. Together, they worked on / out the puzzle: *Aspilia*
7.   8.
contains an antibiotic. Zoopharmacognosy—the study of how animals "doctor" themselves
with plants—was born.

4 IN THE FIELD   Grammar Note 3

Complete these conversations. Use phrasal verbs and pronouns.

1. A: Don't forget to put on your mosquito repellent!

   B: Don't worry! I _____put it on_____ as soon as we got here.

2. A: Can we take off our hats? It's really hot.

   B: Don't _____. They protect you from the sun.

3. A: How do you turn on the generator?

   B: It's easy. You _____ with this switch.

4. A: Did you cover up the leftover food? We don't want the ants to get at it.

   B: Don't worry. We'll _____.

5. A: Is Dr. Rodriguez going to call off the field trip tomorrow?

   B: He'll only _____ if someone gets sick.

6. A: Good night. Oh, can someone wake Mike up tomorrow morning?

   B: No problem. I'll _____.

5 IN THE LAB   Grammar Notes 3–4

Unscramble the words to make sentences. In some cases, more than one answer is possible.

1. on / Put / your lab coats   <u>Put your lab coats on. **OR** Put on your lab coats.</u>

2. the experiment / Set / up   _____

3. out / it / Carry   _____

4. down / Sit / when you're done   _____

5. to page 26 / on / Go   _____

6. up / your reports / Write   _____

7. in / them / Hand   _____

8. off / Take / your lab coats   _____

9. them / Put / away   _____

10. the lab / Clean / up   _____

6 EDITING

Read this student's journal notes. Find and correct nine mistakes in the use of phrasal verbs. The first mistake is already corrected.

○	Sept. 2

I just got <del>from Venezuela</del> ^{back} back! I spent two weeks in the Amazon rain forest with
Dr. Rodriguez's research group. We carried out research there on plants that the Piaroa
people use as medicine. We made down a list of these plants, and we're going to analyze
them when we get back to school next week.

    We set down camp near the Orinoco River, hundreds of miles from any major city.
Life there is hard. You get very early up every morning. You must always watch up and
never touch a new insect or plant. If you pick up it, you can get a bad skin rash. But
plants can also cure. One day, I felt sick. One of the Piaroa gave me the stem of a
certain plant to chew. It worked! Later I found at that the same plant helps cure insect
bites. And believe me, insects are a big problem in the rain forest. I used up many
bottles of repellent. But even when I put on it, it didn't totally keep the insects away.

    This trip changed my life! I'm now thinking about switching my major to
pharmacology. I want to find over more about how people can use the same plants that
animals use as medicine.

COMMUNICATION PRACTICE

7 LISTENING

Listen to these short conversations that take place in a college science lab. Circle the phrasal verbs that you hear. Then listen again and check your answers.

1. **A:** What's Terry doing?
   B: She's <u>handing in</u> / <u>(handing out)</u> some lab reports.

2. **A:** Are you done with your report, Rea?
   B: Almost. I just have to <u>look up</u> / <u>look over</u> some information.

3. **A:** Hey, guys. That music is disturbing us.
   B: Sorry. We'll <u>turn it down</u> / <u>turn it off</u>.

4. **A:** Jason is discouraged.
   B: I know. He says he can't <u>keep on</u> / <u>keep up</u> in class.

5. **A:** Did you hear about Lila?
   B: Yes, we were all surprised when she <u>dropped in</u> / <u>dropped out</u> yesterday.

6. **A:** OK, class. It's time to <u>take back</u> / <u>take off</u> your lab coats.
   B: Oh, could we have a few more minutes? We're almost done.

Now look at your completed sentences. Decide if the statements below are **True (T)** *or* **False (F).**

___F___ **7.** Terry is giving some reports to the teacher.

_____ **8.** Rea is going to look for some information in a reference book.

_____ **9.** They're going to make the music lower.

_____ **10.** Jason feels that the class is going too fast for him.

_____ **11.** Lila visited the class yesterday.

_____ **12.** It's time to return the lab coats.

8 LET'S TALK IT OVER

Work in groups. Imagine that you are going to take a class field trip. Decide where to go—for example, the zoo, a museum, a park. Then assign tasks and make a To Do list. Try to include some of these phrasal verbs.

call up	clean up	drop off	empty out	figure out	hand out
look over	look up	make up	pass out	pick out	pick up
put away	set up	take back	talk over	turn on	write down

EXAMPLE:
A: I'll write down the To Do list.
B: Good idea. I'll call up to find out the hours.
C: I can pick up a bus schedule.

❾ A NEW LEAF

Discuss the pictures below with a partner. Who are the people, and what are they doing in each picture? Then make up a story about the pictures, and write a number under each picture to show the sequence. Then write your story. Compare your story to your classmates' stories. Talk over any differences. There is more than one way to tell a story!

EXAMPLE:
In this picture, three people are talking to a plant doctor . . .

a. _____   b. _____   c. _____

d. _____   e. _____   f. _____

❿ WRITING

Dr. Eloy Rodriguez is a role model to his students. Who was your most important role model when you were growing up? Why did you pick this person? What problems did your role model help you out with? What ideas and actions did you pick up from this person? Write a paragraph. Use phrasal verbs.

EXAMPLE:
When I was growing up, my role model was my high school chemistry teacher. I picked Ms. Suarez because she was a good teacher. She helped me out when I didn't understand the lesson, and she . . .

PART II · REVIEW OR SELFTEST

I. *Circle the correct pronouns to complete the article.*

When Marta's company laid (her) / herself off, she told her / herself it was time

1.   2.

to start her own business. Like Marta, a lot of people dream about starting

(their) / one another's own businesses and working for them / themselves.

3.   4.

Unfortunately, very few succeed. Are you a self-starter? Read about the

qualities of successful business owners and decide for you / yourself.

                                                     5.

- Do you have a lot of energy? Self-starters have lots of energy. They push

  itself / (themselves) very hard, and their families often have to force

         6.

  them / itself to take a break.

  7.

- How well do you work in groups? Good team members work well with

  each other / themselves, but a self-starter must lead them / themselves.

        8.   9.

- Do you like to challenge you / yourself? Self-starters get bored when things

                                   10.

  are too easy.

- Are you self-confident? Self-starters have lots of self-confidence. You need to

  believe in herself / yourself even when nobody else believes in

                   11.

  you / yourself.

  12.

- Do you have social support? Self-starters need good friends and family, so

  don't forget themselves / them when you get busy. Even independent people

             13.

  listen to each other's / his problems.

        14.

II. *Complete the article. Choose the phrasal verb from the box that is closest in meaning to the words in parentheses. Use the correct form of the phrasal verb.*

find out	get back	get by	go on	grow up	hand over
help out	look up	pass over	pick out	set up	turn into

When you were _____growing up_____ , did you think that tomatoes grew in supermarkets?
  1. (becoming an adult)

Did you realize that cotton was a plant before it _____ your new gym
                                          2. (changed into)

socks? New Yorker Wendy Dubit _____ that a lot of city kids don't
                                    3. (learned)

know anything about farms. She used her own money to _____
                                                      4. (establish)

Farm Hands/City Hands. This organization buses city people to small farms.

Children and adults from all social classes _____ on family farms and
                                              5. (assist)

receive room and food in exchange. They also learn things you can't _____.
                                                                    6. (try to find in a book)

One lawyer noted, "I worked with the tomatoes for weeks. Now I can

_____ the perfectly ripe ones and _____ the ones that
    7. (select)   8. (decide not to use)

need a few more days on the vine." Many people start small gardens of their own

when they _____ to the city.
          9. (return)

    After the success of Farm Hands/City Hands, Dubit _____ to invent
                                                      10. (continued)

Project Ongoing to train homeless people in farm work and food services. The project has

been so successful that participants _____ on the food that they grow. They
                                      11. (survive)

sell any extra. They _____ the profits _____ to the program.
                                                12. (give)

III. *Complete each conversation with a phrasal verb and a pronoun.*

1. A: This field trip will be difficult. Please think over your decision carefully.

   B: OK. I'll _____think it over_____ this weekend and let you know on Monday.

2. A: Did you write down the flight number for our trip?

   B: Yes, I _____ on an envelope. Now where did I put the envelope?

3. A: Are we going to pick up Pam on the way to the airport?

   B: No. We don't have to _____ . She has a ride.

(continued on next page)

4. A: Don't forget to put on your hat. That sun is hot.

   B: I'll _____ before I leave.

5. A: Someone please help out Ramón. That pack's too heavy for one person.

   B: OK. I'll _____. We can carry it together.

6. A: Let's set up our camp near the lake.

   B: Too many mosquitoes there. Let's _____ on the hill.

7. A: Why did you pick out cat's claw to study? It's such a common plant.

   B: I _____ because people use it for a lot of different things.

8. A: When are you going to write up your notes?

   B: I'll _____ as soon as we get back.

IV. *Circle the letter of the correct answer to complete each sentence.*

1. Maria often goes to the movies by _____.   A B C Ⓓ
   (A) themselves   (C) alone
   (B) her   (D) herself

2. Paul set _____ his own business in 1999.   A B C D
   (A) out   (C) down
   (B) up   (D) at

3. That frog is poisonous. Don't _____!   A B C D
   (A) pick it up   (C) pick up
   (B) pick up it   (D) pick it

4. Sharon didn't want to study, but she talked _____ into it.   A B C D
   (A) each other   (C) them
   (B) himself   (D) herself

5. We're going your way. Do you want us to _____ at home?   A B C D
   (A) drop you off   (C) drop you down
   (B) dropping you off   (D) drop off you

6. When Brad and I study together, we help _____ a lot.   A B C D
   (A) us   (C) each other
   (B) them   (D) her

7. After Toni graduated from high school, she went _____ to college.   **A B C D**

   (A) over   (C) on

   (B) herself   (D) himself

8. Pat borrowed three books from me, and he hasn't given _____ yet.   **A B C D**

   (A) them back   (C) back them

   (B) it back   (D) back it

9. Please put _____ your lab coats before you leave the laboratory.   **A B C D**

   (A) off   (C) up

   (B) away   (D) in

10. Could you turn _____ the music so we can sleep?   **A B C D**

   (A) down   (C) over

   (B) away   (D) up

11. We'll turn _____ and go to sleep, too.   **A B C D**

   (A) it off   (C) it away

   (B) off it   (D) away it

V. *Read this student's essay. Find and correct eight mistakes in the use of pronouns and phrasal verbs. The first mistake is already corrected.*

> I have three older brothers, but my role model is my next oldest brother,
>
>   me
> Orlando. Orlando was always there for ~~myself~~ when we were growing up. I was
>
> very small, and he always kept the bullies away. When I couldn't figure up *out*
>
>   *me*
> homework problems by myself, he helped out me. Orlando never gave up when he
>
>   *me*
> had problems. Once in high school, my baseball team passed myself up for
>
>   *into*
> pitcher. I wanted to quit the team, but he talked me over playing. In fact, he
>
>   *up*
> woke early every morning up to practice with me. When they chose me for pitcher
>
>   *each other*
> the following year, we were really proud of ourselves—he was proud of me for
>
> succeeding, and I was proud of himself for being such a great coach.

▶ **To check your answers, go to the Answer Key on page 111.**

FROM GRAMMAR TO WRITING
USING PRONOUNS FOR COHERENCE

When you write a paragraph, it is usually better to use pronouns than to repeat the same noun. Pronouns can make your writing smoother and more connected.

EXAMPLE:

<u>My apartment</u> is pretty comfortable. I hope you enjoy staying in <u>my apartment</u>. ⟶

<u>My apartment</u> is pretty comfortable. I hope you enjoy staying in **it**.

1 *Read this note from Ted, thanking Felicia in advance for housesitting. Circle all the pronouns. Above each pronoun, write the noun that it refers to.*

Dear Felicia,

Thanks for staying in my apartment next weekend and taking care of the dog. Help (yourself) to the food in the fridge—you can use it all up if you like. I rented some videos for you. They're on top of the TV. I picked out some action movies. I hope you like them. The VCR is easy to use, but remember to turn it down at 11:00 P.M. My upstairs neighbor is very touchy about noise. There are just a few other things to remember. Red's friendly, but please keep her away from my neighbor's poodle. They don't like each other. Her bowl is on the kitchen counter. Fill it up once a day with dry food. Please walk her twice a day. When you go out, remember to turn on the answering machine. It's in the living room. The Sunday newspaper arrives at about 8:00 A.M. Pick it up early—sometimes it disappears! When you leave for work Monday, just leave the keys with Mrs. Delgado next door. I'll get them from her when I get back.

Thanks again!

Ted

2 *Read this note. Change the nouns to pronouns when you can. With phrasal verbs, remember to put the pronoun between the main verb and the particle.*

Dear Dara,

Welcome! I hope you enjoy staying here this week. Here are a few things to keep in mind: The mail is delivered every day around noon. You'll find
~~the mail~~ ^{it} in the mailbox in front of the building. Please pick up the mail and put the mail on the dining room table. Feel free to use the air conditioner, but please turn off the air conditioner when you leave the house. There's plenty of food in the refrigerator! Please feel free to use up the food. I'm expecting a few phone calls. If you're home, could you please take a message? Just write down the message on the yellow pad in the top left desk drawer. I think the apartment is pretty comfortable. I hope you enjoy staying in the apartment. Make yourself at home!

See you in a week.

Rachel

3 *Before you write . . .*

- Imagine that a friend is going to take care of your home while you are away. What will your friend's responsibilities be? What special things do you need to tell him or her about your home or neighborhood? Make a list.

- Exchange lists with a partner. Ask questions about your partner's list. Answer your partner's questions.

    EXAMPLE:
    A: How often should I take out the garbage?
    B: Oh, you can take it out every other day. Where do you keep the dog food?

4 *Write a note to your friend on another piece of paper. Give instructions about taking care of your home. Include answers to your partner's questions in Exercise 3. Use pronouns and phrasal verbs.*

5 *Exchange notes with a different partner. Complete the chart.*

a. Did the writer use pronouns where necessary?   Yes _____ No _____

b. Put a question mark (?) over each pronoun you think is in the wrong place.

c. Complete this chart of daily tasks. If you have a question, ask your partner, and write the answer on the chart.

EXAMPLES:
Sunday: water the plants, feed the pets, pick up the newspaper
Monday: feed the pets, pick up the mail and put it on the hall table

Day	**Tasks**

Rewrite your note. Make any necessary changes in your use of pronouns.
Add information that your partner requested.

REVIEW OR SELFTEST
ANSWER KEY

I. (Unit 9)

2. herself
3. their
4. themselves
5. yourself
6. themselves
7. them
8. each other

9. them
10. yourself
11. yourself
12. you
13. them
14. each other's

II. (Unit 10)

2. turned into
3. found out
4. set up
5. help out
6. look up
7. pick out

8. pass over
9. get back
10 went on
11. get by
12. hand . . . over

III. (Unit 10)

2. wrote it down
3. pick her up
4. put it on
5. help him out

6. set it up
7. picked it out
8. write them up

IV. (Units 9 and 10)

2. B
3. A
4. D
5. A
6. C

7. C
8. A
9. B
10. A
11. A

V. (Units 9 and 10)

I have three older brothers, but my role model is my next oldest brother, Orlando. Orlando was always there for ~~myself~~ *me* when we were growing up. I was very small, and he always kept the bullies away. When I couldn't figure ~~up~~ *out* homework problems by myself, he helped ~~out me~~ *me out*. Orlando never gave up when he had problems. Once, in high school, my baseball team passed ~~myself~~ *me* up for pitcher. I wanted to quit the team, but he talked me ~~over~~ *into* playing. In fact, he woke me early every morning ~~up~~ *up* to practice with me. When they chose me for pitcher the following year, we were really proud of ~~ourselves~~ *each other*—he was proud of me for succeeding, and I was proud of ~~himself~~ *him* for being such a great coach.

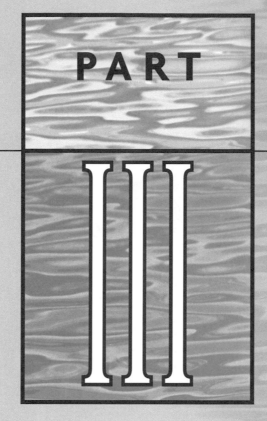

PART III

MODALS
AND
RELATED VERBS
AND EXPRESSIONS

ABILITY:
CAN, COULD, BE ABLE TO

GRAMMAR **IN CONTEXT**

BEFORE YOU READ What are the people in the photograph doing? Look at the title of the article. Guess the main point.

Read this newspaper article.

Born to Dance

by V. Gupta

"**W**ho made up the rule that you **can** only **dance** on your two feet . . . ?" asks Mary Verdi-Fletcher, president and founding director of Cleveland Ballet Dancing Wheels. She is also one of its main dancers. Verdi-Fletcher was born with a medical condition that affects the nervous system. By the age of twelve, she **was not able to stand** or **walk**. That didn't stop her from dancing. People said, "You **can't walk**; how **can** you **be** a dancer?" Verdi-Fletcher, however, *knew* it was possible to dance in her wheelchair because, as she says, "Dance is an emotion that comes from within."

When she entered her first dance competition, the audience was confused. "She's in a wheelchair. How **can** she **dance**?" But at the end of the performance, they stood and applauded. Not only **could** she **dance**, but she **could hypnotize** an audience with her talent. When the artistic director of the Cleveland Ballet first saw her, he thought, "*That* is a dancer. . . . You **can't take** your eyes off her."

Dancing Wheels has both "sitdown dancers" and "standup dancers." The group offers a new definition of dance. It also changes the perception of what people **can** or **cannot do**. "Through our dance," says Verdi-Fletcher, "we want to show that anything is possible and achievable. . . . People need to see they **can achieve** their dreams and aspirations—but not without a lot of hard work and dedication."

GRAMMAR **PRESENTATION**
ABILITY: *CAN AND COULD*

STATEMENTS			
SUBJECT	**CAN / COULD* (NOT)**	**BASE FORM OF VERB**	
I You He She We You They	**can (not)**	**dance**	now.
	could (not)		last year.

CONTRACTIONS		
cannot OR can not	=	**can't**
could not	=	**couldn't**

*Can and *could* are modals. Modals have only one form. They do not have *-s* in the third-person singular.

YES / NO QUESTIONS		
CAN / COULD	**SUBJECT**	**BASE FORM OF VERB**
Can	I you he she we you they	**dance?**
Could		

SHORT ANSWERS		
AFFIRMATIVE		
Yes,	you I he she you we they	**can.**
		could.

SHORT ANSWERS		
NEGATIVE		
No,	you I he she you we they	**can't.**
		couldn't.

WH- QUESTIONS			
WH- WORD	**CAN / COULD**	**SUBJECT**	**BASE FORM OF VERB**
How well	**can** **could**	she you	**dance?**

(continued on next page)

ABILITY: *BE ABLE TO*

STATEMENTS			
SUBJECT	BE	(NOT) ABLE TO	BASE FORM OF VERB
I	am		
You	are		
He She	is	(not) able to	practice.
We You They	are		

YES / NO QUESTIONS			
BE	SUBJECT	ABLE TO	BASE FORM OF VERB
Is	she	able to	practice?
Are	you		

SHORT ANSWERS		
AFFIRMATIVE		
Yes,	she	**is.**
	I	**am.**

SHORT ANSWERS		
NEGATIVE		
No,	she	**isn't.**
	I'm	**not.**

WH- QUESTIONS				
WH- WORD	BE	SUBJECT	ABLE TO	BASE FORM OF VERB
When	**is**	she	able to	practice?
How often	**are**	you		

NOTES

1. Use *can* to describe an <u>ability in the present</u>.

2. You can also use *be able to* to describe an <u>ability in the present or future</u>.

USAGE NOTE: In everyday speech, *can* is much <u>more common</u> than *be able to* in the <u>present</u> tense.

EXAMPLES

• She **can dance**, but she **can't skate**.
• **Can** she **swim**?

• The new student **is able to park** a car, but she**'s not able to drive** in traffic yet.
• They**'ll be able to get** tickets for Friday's dance performance, but they **won't be able to get** front-row seats.
• I **can park** a car, but I **can't drive** in traffic yet.

3. Use either *could* or *was / were able to* to describe a <u>general ability in the past</u>.

- Mary **could drive** a car with special hand controls.

  OR

- Mary **was able to drive** a car with special hand controls.

4. You must use *was / were able to* to describe a <u>special achievement</u> or a <u>single event in the past</u>.

- In 1979, they **were able to win** second prize in a dance competition. NOT ~~In 1979, they could win second prize in a dance competition.~~

5. You can use either *couldn't* or *wasn't / weren't able to* for any negative sentence <u>describing past ability</u>—either general or specific.

GENERAL ABILITY

- She **couldn't walk**.

  OR

- She **wasn't able to walk**.

SPECIAL ACHIEVEMENT

- They **couldn't win** their first competition.

  OR

- They **weren't able to win** their first competition.

6. For forms and tenses <u>other than the present or past</u>, you must use *be able to*.

- Al wants **to be able to take** dance lessons next year. *(infinitive form)*
- By June he**'ll be able to dance** at his wedding. *(future)*

REFERENCE NOTE
Can and *could* are also used to ask and give permission *(see Unit 12)*, make requests *(see Unit 13)*, and make assumptions *(see Unit 36)*.
Could is also used to make suggestions *(see Unit 15)* and express future possibility *(see Unit 35)*.

FOCUSED PRACTICE

1 DISCOVER THE GRAMMAR

Look at this information about Mary Verdi-Fletcher. Then decide whether the statements below are **True (T)** *or* **False (F)**. *Put a question mark* **(?)** *if there isn't enough information.*

Mary Verdi-Fletcher	
1955	born in Ohio
1975	graduated from high school
	got job as keypunch operator
1978	learned to drive
1979	entered Dance Fever Competition
1980	began Dancing Wheels
	enrolled in Lakeland Community College, Ohio
	took course in public speaking
1980–1988	worked for Independent Living Center
1984	married Robert Fletcher
1989–90	tour director for Cleveland Ballet
1990–present	founding director and dancer, Cleveland Ballet Dancing Wheels
	teaches dance to people with and without disabilities
Awards:	Outstanding Young Clevelander Award (1990)
	Oracle Merit Award (1991)
	Invacare Award of Excellence in the Arts (1994)
	Governor's Award for Outreach (1998)
Other Interests:	watching football and soccer games

___T___ **1.** Mary was able to get a job after high school.

_____ **2.** She can't drive a car.

_____ **3.** She couldn't participate in dance competitions.

_____ **4.** She can speak foreign languages.

_____ **5.** She was able to start a dance company.

_____ **6.** She couldn't finish college.

_____ **7.** She can probably speak well in front of large groups of people.

_____ **8.** She'll be able to help people with disabilities learn to dance.

_____ **9.** She can play the piano.

2 NOW I CAN

Grammar Notes 1, 3, and 5

Complete the paragraphs with **can, can't, could,** *or* **couldn't.**

1. For a long time, Jim and Marie _____couldn't_____ agree on a family sport. Jim
   a.

loves tennis, and Marie takes lessons, but she still _____ play. Marie
   b.

_____ swim, but Jim hates the water. They recently took up dancing.
   c.

Soon, they _____ tango beautifully together.
   d.

2. Stefan has made a lot of progress in English. Last semester he _____

   a.

   order a meal in a restaurant or talk on the telephone. His friends helped him do

   everything. Now he _____ speak English in a lot of situations.

   b.

3. Bill almost _____ make his class presentation last semester because he

   a.

   was so nervous. He _____ communicate well in small groups, but not in

   b.

   big ones. He plans to take a course in public speaking soon. I'm sure he

   _____ improve quickly.

   c.

4. Last year I _____ dance at all, but when I met Stan, I signed up for a

   a.

   class right away. He _____ really dance, and I wanted to dance with him.

   b.

   Now I _____ do the basic steps. I _____ do the waltz yet, but

   c.   d.

   we're planning to waltz at our wedding next month.

❸ AT THE DANCE STUDIO
Grammar Notes 2–6

Complete each conversation with the correct form of **be able to** *and the verb in parentheses.*

1. **A:** I heard your sister wanted to take lessons. _____Was_____ she ___able to start___ ?

   a. (start)

   B: Yes, she was. She started last month. She can do the fox-trot now, but she still

   _____ the waltz.

   b. (do)

2. **A:** Why are you taking dance lessons?

   B: I want to _____ at my wedding!

   a. (dance)

3. **A:** _____ you _____ Russian as a child, Mrs. Suraikin?

   a. (speak)

   B: Yes, I was. We spoke it at home, so I _____ it fluently.

   b. (speak)

   A: _____ your children _____ Russian, too?

   c. (speak)

   B: No, unfortunately my children never learned Russian. They only speak English.

4. **A:** I _____ last weekend. I hurt my ankle.

   a. (not practice)

   B: That's too bad. _____ you _____ next week?

   b. (practice)

   A: I hope so. I'll call you on Monday. Maybe we _____ on Tuesday.

   c. (get together)

4 **ACHIEVEMENT** Grammar Notes 1–6

Complete the advertisement. Use the appropriate form of **can**, **could**, *or* **be able to** *with each verb. Use* **can** *or* **could** *when possible.*

WILL B. HAPPY®
Professional Development Courses

Time Management   Presentations   Career Development   Teamwork

Think about your last presentation: ___Were___ you ___able to prepare___ on time?
1. (prepare)

_____ you _____ your ideas?
2. (communicate)

    Will B. Happy® has helped others, and he _____ YOU!
3. (help)

    "Before I took Will B. Happy's course, my work was always late because

I _____ a schedule. I also had big piles on my desk because I
4. (follow)

_____ what was important. Now I _____ my time
5. (decide) **6. (manage)**

effectively. Next month, when my workload gets heavy, I _____ it and
7. (organize)

do the important things first."

—Scott Mathis, student

    "I didn't use to _____ in front of groups. Now I can!"
8. (speak)

—Mary Zhang, sales manager

5 **EDITING**

Read this student's journal. Find and correct seven mistakes in the use of modals. The first mistake is already corrected.

◯	Today in my Will. B. Happy Teamwork course, I learned about work styles—"Drivers" and "Enthusiasts." I'm a Driver, so I can make decisions, but I'm not able ^{to} listen to other people's ideas. The Enthusiast in our group can communicates well, but you can't depend on her. Now I understand what was happening in my business class last year, when I couldn't felt comfortable with my team. I thought that they all talked too much and didn't able to work efficiently. I could get an A for the course, but it was hard. I can do a lot more alone, but some jobs are too big for that. Our instructor says that soon Drivers will able to listen, and the Enthusiasts could be more dependable.

COMMUNICATION PRACTICE

6 LISTENING

Karl is interviewing for the job of office manager at Carmen's Dance Studio. Listen to the conversation. Then listen again and check all the things that Karl can do now.

- ☑ answer the phones
- ☐ speak another language
- ☐ use a computer
- ☐ type 50 words per minute
- ☐ design a monthly newsletter
- ☐ schedule appointments
- ☐ drive
- ☐ dance

7 INFORMATION GAP: CAN THEY DO THE TANGO?

Students at Carmen's Dance Studio are preparing for a dance recital in June. It is now the end of April. Can students do all the dances featured in the recital by now?

Work in pairs (A and B). Student B, look at the Information Gap on page 123 and follow the instructions there. Student A, ask your partner for the information you need to complete the schedule. Answer your partner's questions.

EXAMPLE:

A: Can your students do the Argentine tango?

B: No, they can't. But they'll be able to do it by the end of May. Can they do the cha-cha?

A: Yes, they can. They could do it in March.

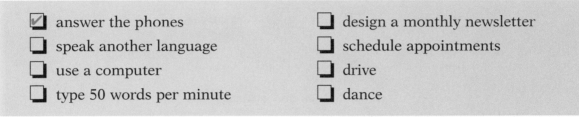

CARMEN'S DANCE STUDIO
Schedule of Dance Classes

Dances	March	April	May
Argentine Tango			✓
Cha-Cha	✓		
Fox-Trot			
Hustle			✓
Mambo			
Merengue	✓		
Salsa			✓
Swing			
Tango		✓	
Waltz			

When you are finished, compare schedules. Are they the same?

8 CLASS PRESENTATION

Work in a small group. Imagine you are planning a class presentation. Look at the list of skills and tell each other what you **can** *and* **can't** *do. Add to the list. Then assign tasks to the group members.*

do library research

do research online

type on a computer

make charts and graphs

photocopy handouts

take photographs

interview people

make the presentation

_____

_____

EXAMPLE:
A: Can you do library research?
B: Yes, but I can't do research online yet.

9 WRITING

Write one or two paragraphs about a person who has succeeded in spite of some kind of difficulty or problem. You can choose a famous person whom you have never met or anyone you know. Use **can**, **could**, *and* **be able to**.

INFORMATION GAP FOR STUDENT B

Student B, answer your partner's questions. Ask your partner for the information you need to complete the schedule.

EXAMPLE:

A: Can your students do the Argentine tango?

B: No, they can't. But they'll be able to do it by the end of May. Can they do the cha-cha?

A: Yes, they can. They could do it in March.

CARMEN'S DANCE STUDIO
Schedule of Dance Classes

Dances	March	April	May
Argentine Tango			✓
Cha-Cha	✓		
Fox-Trot		✓	
Hustle			
Mambo		✓	
Merengue			
Salsa			
Swing	✓		
Tango			
Waltz	✓		

When you are finished, compare schedules. Are they the same?

12 PERMISSION:
MAY, COULD, CAN,
DO YOU MIND IF . . . ?

GRAMMAR IN CONTEXT

BEFORE YOU READ What do you know about the TOEFL® test? What's your opinion about this test?

Read this excerpt from a booklet about the Test of English as a Foreign Language (TOEFL®).

SOME FREQUENTLY ASKED QUESTIONS ABOUT THE TOEFL® TEST

Q: **Can I take** the TOEFL test more than once?

A: Yes. **You can take** the TOEFL test as many times as you want, but **you may** only **take** it one time per calendar month.

Q: **May I register** for the test on the same day as the test?

A: No, **you may not.** You must register before the test.

Q: I'm a doctor. **Could I wear** my beeper during the test?

A: Sorry, but no cell phones, beepers, pagers, or watch alarms are permitted.

Q: My students are going to take the test for the first time. They don't want schools to see bad test scores. **Can they cancel** their scores after the test?

A: Immediately following the test, **they may choose** to see their scores on the screen OR **they may cancel** them. Once they see their scores, **they cannot cancel** them. However, **they may** always **choose** not to send them to any schools.

Structure

Directions: Click on the one word or phrase that best completes the sentence.

How many times may a student _____ the TOEFL?

- ● take
- ○ takes
- ○ to take
- ○ taking

| TIME | HELP | Confirm Answer | NEXT |

GRAMMAR **PRESENTATION**
PERMISSION: *MAY, COULD, CAN, DO YOU MIND IF . . . ?*

QUESTIONS: *MAY / COULD / CAN*

MAY / COULD / CAN*	SUBJECT	BASE FORM OF VERB	
May **Could** **Can**	I he she we they	**start**	now?

May, could, and *can* are modals. Modals have only one form. They do not have *-s* in the third-person singular.

SHORT ANSWERS

	AFFIRMATIVE	
Yes,	you he she they	**may**. **can**.
Sure. Certainly. Of course. Why not?		

SHORT ANSWERS

	NEGATIVE	
No,	you he she they	**may not**. **can't**.

NOTE: *May not* is not contracted.

QUESTIONS: *DO YOU MIND IF . . . ?*

DO YOU MIND IF	SUBJECT	VERB
Do you mind if	I we they	**start**?
	he she it	**starts**?

SHORT ANSWERS

AFFIRMATIVE
Not at all.   **No, I don't**.   Go right ahead.

SHORT ANSWERS

NEGATIVE
Yes, I do.

STATEMENTS: *MAY / CAN*

SUBJECT	MAY / CAN (NOT)	BASE FORM OF VERB	
You He They	**may (not)** **can (not)**	**start**	now.

NOTES	EXAMPLES
1. Use *may, could* and *can* to <u>ask permission</u>.	• **May** I **call** you next Friday? • **Could** we **use** our dictionaries? • **Can** he **come** to class with me next week?
USAGE NOTE: Some people feel that *may* is more formal than *can* and *could*. You can use *may* when you ask <u>formal permission</u> to do something.	• **May** I **leave** the room, Professor Lee?
▶ **BE CAREFUL!** Requests for permission always <u>refer to the present or the future</u>. When you use *could* to ask for permission, it is not past tense.	**A:** **Could** I register for the test *tomorrow*? **B:** Certainly. The office will be open at 9:00 A.M.

2. We often say *please* when we ask permission. Note the word order.	• **Could** I ask a question, *please*? • **May** I *please* ask a question?

3. Use *Do you mind if . . . ?* to ask for permission when it is possible your action will inconvenience someone or make someone uncomfortable.	**A:** **Do you mind if** I clean up tomorrow? **B:** Yes, actually, I do mind. I hate to see a mess in the kitchen in the morning.
▶ **BE CAREFUL!** A <u>negative answer</u> to the question *Do you mind if . . . ?* gives permission to do something. It means "It's OK. I don't mind."	**A:** **Do you mind if** my brother comes to class with me? **B:** *Not at all.* *(Your brother may come with you.)*

4. Use *may* or *can* to <u>answer requests for permission</u>. Don't use *could* in answers.

A: **Could** I borrow this pencil?
B: Yes, of course you **can**.
   NOT ~~Yes, you could.~~
   ~~No, you couldn't.~~

▶ **BE CAREFUL!** Do not contract *may not*.

• No, you **may not**.
   NOT ~~No, you mayn't.~~

We also frequently use certain **expressions** instead of modals to <u>answer requests for permission</u>.

A: **Could** I close the window?
B: *Sure.*
   Certainly.
   Go ahead.
   No, please don't. It's hot in here.

5. When people **refuse permission**, they usually do so indirectly. They soften the refusal <u>with an apology and an explanation</u>.

Sometimes, when the <u>rules are very clear</u>, someone will refuse permission without an apology or an explanation.

STUDENT: Can I please have five more minutes to answer this question?
TEACHER: *I'm sorry, but the time is up.*

DRIVER: Can I park here?
OFFICER: *No, you can't.*

REFERENCE NOTE
May, can, and *could* are also used to express possibility. *(See Unit 35.)*
Can and *could* are also used to talk about ability and to make requests. *(See Units 11 and 13.)*

FOCUSED PRACTICE

1 DISCOVER THE GRAMMAR

Write the letter of the correct response to each request for permission.

a. No, he can't. He has to complete an accident report first.

b. Not at all. There's plenty of time.

c. Sure they can. There's plenty of room.

d. Yes, you may. The test starts in ten minutes.

e. I'm sorry, he's not in. Can I take a message?

f. Certainly. Here they are.

1. ___d___

2. _____

3. _____

4. _____

5. _____

6. _____

② GIVING THE GO-AHEAD   Grammar Notes 1–2, 4–5

Mr. Hamad is supervising a test. Complete each conversation with the word in parentheses and the correct pronouns.

1. (can)

> **MR. HAMAD:** It's 9:00. _____<u>You can</u>_____ come into the room now. Please show me
> a.
>
> your registration forms as you come in.

> **SOFIA:** My brother isn't taking the test. _____ come in with me?
> b.

> **MR. HAMAD:** No, I'm sorry, _____. Only people with tickets are permitted
> c. (negative)
>
> in the exam room.

2. (may)

> **MR. HAMAD:** I'm going to hand out the tests now. Write your name on the front in
>
> pencil, but don't start the test yet. Remember, _____ start
> a. (negative)
>
> the test until I tell you to.

> **AHMED:** I'm sorry I'm late. _____ come in?
> b.

> **MR. HAMAD:** Yes, _____. We haven't started the test yet.
> c.

3. (could)

> **ROSA:** _____ use a pen to write my name?
> a.

> **MR. HAMAD:** No, you have to use a pencil.

> **ROSA:** Jamie, _____ borrow this pencil, please? I only
> b.
>
> brought a pen.

> **JAMIE:** Sure, take it. I brought a few.

4. (can)

> **MR. HAMAD:** OK. We're ready to start. Open your test booklets and read the
>
> instructions.

> **JEAN:** Excuse me. We're late because our train broke down. _____
> a.
>
> still come in?

> **MR. HAMAD:** I'm sorry, _____. We've already started the test.
> b. (negative)

3 **TAKING THE TEST**

Read the directions to this section of a test similar to part of the TOEFL®.
Then complete the test questions.

Directions: These conversations take place on a train. Each conversation has four underlined words or phrases. They are marked (A), (B), (C), and (D). Find the underlined word or phrase that is incorrect. Fill in the space that corresponds to the letter of the incorrect word or phrase.

Example   **Sample Answer**

<u>May</u> we <u>board</u> the train yet?   Ⓐ Ⓑ Ⓒ ⬤
  A   B
No, you <u>mayn't</u> board until 12:30.
  C   D

1.   Can he <u>comes</u> on the train with me?   Ⓐ Ⓑ Ⓒ Ⓓ
     <u>A</u>   B
     I'm <u>sorry</u>, but only passengers <u>can</u> board the train.
            C   D

2.   Do you <u>mind</u> if I sit <u>here</u>?   Ⓐ Ⓑ Ⓒ Ⓓ
     A   B   C
     <u>No, I don't</u>. This seat is taken.
         D

3.   <u>Could</u> I <u>looked</u> at your newspaper?   Ⓐ Ⓑ Ⓒ Ⓓ
       A   B
     <u>Yes</u>, of course you <u>can</u>.
       C   D

4.   <u>Can</u> I <u>to get</u> through, <u>please</u>?   Ⓐ Ⓑ Ⓒ Ⓓ
       A   B   C
     Yes, <u>of course</u>. I'll move my bag.
             D

5.   <u>Could</u> we <u>change</u> seats? I'd like to sit next   Ⓐ Ⓑ Ⓒ Ⓓ
       A   B
     to my daughter.

     <u>Yes</u>, <u>we could</u>. No problem.
       C   D

6.   <u>Do you mind</u> if <u>she</u> <u>play</u> her computer game?   Ⓐ Ⓑ Ⓒ Ⓓ
         A   B   C
     It's a little noisy.

     <u>No</u>, not at all.
       D

7.   Can <u>we'll</u> get a sandwich soon, <u>please</u>?   Ⓐ Ⓑ Ⓒ Ⓓ
           A   B
     I'm hungry.

     <u>Sure</u> we <u>can</u>. Let's go find the club car.
       C   D

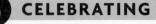 **CELEBRATING**

Lucy got high TOEFL® scores. She's going to celebrate by attending a concert with some friends. Write questions to ask for permission. Use the words in parentheses.

1. Lucy's friend Carl came to pick her up for the concert. He wants his friend Bob to come along.

   CARL: I have an extra ticket. ___Do you mind if Bob comes along?___

   (Do you mind if)

   LUCY: Not at all.

2. Carl decides to call Bob and invite him. He wants to use Lucy's phone.

   CARL: Great. I'll call him right now. _____

   (Could)

   LUCY: Sure. It's in the kitchen.

3. Carl, Bob, and Lucy want to park in front of the stadium. Lucy asks a police officer.

   LUCY: Excuse me, officer. We're going to the concert.

   _____

   (Can)

   OFFICER: No, you can't. It's a tow-away zone.

4. The usher at the concert wants to see their tickets.

   USHER: _____

   (May / please)

   CARL: Certainly. Here they are.

5. Lucy, Bob, and Carl want to move up a few rows. Bob asks an usher.

   BOB: All those seats are empty. _____

   (Could / please)

   USHER: Sure. Go right ahead.

6. Bob and Carl want to tape the concert. Lucy asks the usher first.

   LUCY: My friends brought their tape recorder.

   _____

   (Can)

   USHER: No, they can't. No one is allowed to record the concert or take pictures.

7. Lucy hates the music, and she wants to leave. Bob and Carl don't seem to like it either.

   LUCY: This music is giving me a headache.

   _____

   (Do you mind if)

   BOB: I don't mind.

   CARL: Me neither. Let's *all* leave.

COMMUNICATION PRACTICE

5 LISTENING

Listen and write the number of each conversation. Then listen again and decide if permission was given or refused. Check the appropriate column.

		permission given	permission refused
_____	**a.** child / parent	❑	❑
_____	**b.** travel agent / customer	❑	❑
1	**c.** police officer / driver	✓	❑
_____	**d.** boyfriend / girlfriend's mother	❑	❑
_____	**e.** employee / employer	❑	❑

6 ASKING PERMISSION

Work in small groups. Read the following situations and decide what to say. Think of as many things to say as possible.

1. You're visiting some good friends. The weather is very cold, but they don't seem to mind. Their windows are open, and the heat is off. You're freezing.

   EXAMPLES:
   Do you mind if I close the windows?
   May I borrow that sweater?
   Can I turn on the heat?
   Could I make some hot tea?

2. Your teacher is explaining something to the class, and you're getting completely confused. The teacher is very friendly, and he has office hours several times a week. He also spends a lot of time talking to students after class.

3. You have a small apartment. Two friends are coming to visit your town for a week, and they want to stay with you. What can you say to your roommate?

4. You're at a concert with some friends. You like the performer very much. You have your tape recorder and your camera with you. Sometimes this performer talks to fans and signs programs after the concert.

5. You have formed a TOEFL® study group with some classmates. You want to use a classroom on Thursday evenings to study. You would like to use your school's large cassette player for listening practice. Some of your classmates come directly from work. They would like permission to eat a sandwich in the classroom. Write a note to your teacher and ask for permission.

7 ROLE PLAY

Work in pairs. Read the following situations. Take turns being Student A and Student B.

Student A

1. You were absent from class yesterday. B, your classmate, always takes good notes.

Student B

1. A is in your class. You are always willing to help your classmates.

EXAMPLE:

A: May I copy your notes from class yesterday?

B: Sure. Here they are.

A: And could you tell me the assignment?

B: It's pages 20 through 25 in the textbook.

2. You're at work. You have a terrible headache. B is your boss.

2. A is your employee. You have a lot of work for A to do today.

3. You're a teenager. You and your friend want to travel to another city to see a concert. You want to borrow your family's car. Your friend has a license and wants to drive.

3. A is your son / daughter. You like this friend, and you have no objection to lending him or her the car. However, you want the friend to be careful.

4. B has invited you to a small party. At the last minute, your two cousins show up. They have nothing to do the night of the party.

4. Your party is at a restaurant, and you have already arranged for a certain number of people to attend. Besides, this is supposed to be a small party for a few of your close friends.

8 WRITING

Write two short notes asking permission. Choose situations from Exercise 7, or use situations of your own.

13 REQUESTS: *WILL, WOULD, COULD, CAN, WOULD YOU MIND . . . ?*

GRAMMAR **IN CONTEXT**

BEFORE YOU READ What is Marcia's e-mail address? Who did Marcia send e-mail to?

Read Marcia Jones's e-mail messages.

From: John Sanchez@dataline.com
To: Marciajones@dataline.com
Marcia:
I'll be out of town until Thursday. **Would** you please **photocopy** the monthly sales report for me? Thanks a lot!
John

From: MarciaJones@dataline.com
To: AnnChen@dataline.com
Hi, Ann—
I'm sending you a copy of our sales report. **Could** you **make** 25 copies? And **would you mind delivering** them to me when you're finished? It's a rush!
Thanks.
Marcia

From: RheaJones@island.net
To: MarciaJones@dataline.com
Marcia, dear—
Can you **drive** me to the Burtons after work today? They've invited me for dinner. Oh, and **will** you **pick up** something special at the bakery before you come? I told them I'd bring dessert.
Thanks, honey. —Mom

From: MarciaJones@dataline.com
To: RheaJones@island.net
Mom,
I'm sorry, but tonight I **can't**. I have to work late. Should I ask your favorite son-in-law if he can drive you? Let me know.
M.

GRAMMAR **PRESENTATION**

REQUESTS: *WILL, WOULD, COULD, CAN, WOULD YOU MIND . . . ?*

QUESTIONS: *WILL / WOULD / COULD / CAN*

WILL / WOULD COULD / CAN*	SUBJECT	BASE FORM OF VERB	
Will **Would** **Could** **Can**	you	**mail**	this letter for me?
		drive	me to the doctor?
		pick up	some groceries?

Will, would, could, and *can* are modals. Modals do not have *-s* in the third-person singular.

SHORT ANSWERS

AFFIRMATIVE

Sure Certainly Of course	(I **will**). (I **can**).

SHORT ANSWERS

NEGATIVE

I'm sorry, but I **can't**.

QUESTIONS: *WOULD YOU MIND . . . ?*

WOULD YOU MIND	GERUND	
Would you mind	**mailing**	this letter for me?
	driving	me to the doctor?
	picking up	some groceries?

SHORT ANSWERS

AFFIRMATIVE

No, not at all.
I'd be glad to.

SHORT ANSWERS

NEGATIVE

I'm sorry, but I can't.

NOTES	EXAMPLES

1. Use *will*, *would*, *could*, and *can* to <u>ask someone to do something</u>.

We often use *will* and *can* for <u>informal requests</u>.

We use *would* and *could* to <u>soften requests</u> and make them sound less demanding.

SISTER: **Will** you **bring** dessert?
Can you **turn on** the TV?

BOSS: **Would** you **answer** my phone for me, Marcia?
Could you **give** me a copy of the sales report?

---

2. Use *please* to make the request <u>more polite</u>. Note the word order.

- **Could** you *please* close the door?

OR

- **Could** you close the door, *please*?

---

3. We also use *Would you mind +* **gerund** to make polite requests. Note that a <u>negative answer</u> means that you <u>will do what the person requests</u>.

A: **Would you mind waiting** for a few minutes? Mr. Caras is still in a meeting.

B: *Not at all.*
(OK. I'll do it.)

---

4. People usually expect us to say *yes* to polite requests. When we **cannot say yes**, we usually <u>apologize and give a reason</u>.

▶ **BE CAREFUL!** Do not use *would* or *could* in response to polite requests.

A: **Could** you **take** this to Susan Lane's office for me?

B: **I'm sorry, I can't.** I'm expecting an important phone call.

A: I'm cold. **Would** you **shut** the window, please?

B: *Certainly.*
NOT ~~Yes, I would.~~

FOCUSED PRACTICE

1 DISCOVER THE GRAMMAR

Marcia has a new co-worker. Read their conversations. Underline all the polite requests.

1. **MARCIA:** Hi. You must be the new secretary. I'm Marcia Jones. Let me know if you need anything.

   LORNA: Thanks, Marcia. <u>Could you show</u> me the coat closet?

   MARCIA: Certainly. It's right over here.

2. **LORNA:** Marcia, would you explain these instructions for the fax machine? I don't understand them.

   MARCIA: Sure. Just put your letter in here and dial the number.

3. **MARCIA:** I'm leaving for lunch. Would you like to come?

   LORNA: Thanks, but I can't right now. I'm really busy.

   MARCIA: Do you want a sandwich from the coffee shop?

   LORNA: That would be great. Can you get me a tuna sandwich and a soda?

   MARCIA: Sure. Will you answer my phone until I get back?

   LORNA: Certainly.

4. **MARCIA:** Lorna, would you mind making a pot of coffee? Some clients are coming in a few minutes, and I make terrible coffee.

   LORNA: I'm sorry, but I can't do it now. I've got to finish this letter before 2:00.

   MARCIA: That's OK. Thanks anyway.

5. **MARCIA:** I'm going home now. Don't forget to turn off the printer before you leave.

   LORNA: I won't.

   MARCIA: By the way, I'm not coming to work tomorrow. Could you give this report to Joan Sanchez for me?

   LORNA: Sure.

2 ASKING FOR FAVORS
Grammar Notes 3 and 4

Mike's roommate, Jeff, is having problems today. Check the appropriate response to each request.

1. Mike, would you please drive me to class today? My car won't start.

   a. _____ Yes, I would.   **b.** __✔__ I'd be glad to.

2. Would you mind lending me five dollars? I'm getting paid tomorrow.

   a. _____ Not at all.   **b.** _____ Yes.

(continued on next page)

3. Mike, can you take these books back to the library for me? I'm running late this morning.

    a. _____ I'm late for class, too. Sorry.   **b.** _____ No, I can't.

4. Could you lock the door on your way out? My hands are full.

    a. _____ Yes, I could.   **b.** _____ Sure.

5. Can you turn the radio down? I need to study for my math quiz this morning.

    a. _____ Certainly.   **b.** _____ Not at all.

6. Will you pick up some milk on the way home this afternoon?

    a. _____ No, I won't.   **b.** _____ I'm sorry, I can't. I'll be at work until 8:00.

 **EDITING**

Read Marcia Jones' response to an e-mail from her boss. (Her answers are in **bold** *print.) Find and correct six mistakes in making and responding to requests. The first mistake is already corrected.*

Subj: sales meeting—Reply
Date: 04-11-01 12:14:39 EST
From: MarciaJones@dataline.com
To: JohnSanchez@dataline.com
CC: AnnChen@dateline.com

>>> <JohnSanchez@dataline.com> 04/11/01 10:37am>>>

The meetings are going well but they have been extended a day. Could you ~~call please~~ *please call*
Doug Rogers to try to reschedule our sales meeting?

Not at all. I'll do it right away.

We'll need three extra copies of the monthly sales report. Would you ask Ann to take
care of that?

Yes, I would. (Ann—could you do this?)

I hate to ask, but would you mind to work on Saturday? We'll need the extra time to go
over the new information I've gotten.

**Sorry, but I couldn't. My in-laws are coming for a visit. But Rob Lin says he can come in to
the office to help out.**

One last thing. I was going to pick up those new business cards, but I won't be back in time.
Would you mind doing that for me?

Yes, I would. I'll stop at the printers during my lunch break.

4 WOULD YOU MIND?

Look at the pictures. What is each person thinking? Write the letter of the correct sentence from the box.

a.	Buy some cereal.
b.	Call back later.
c.	Close the window.
d.	~~File these reports.~~
e.	Shut the door.
f.	Wait for a few minutes.

1. _d_

2. ___

3. ___

4. ___

5. ___

6. ___

What do the people say? Complete their polite requests. Use the words in parentheses and the information from the pictures.

1. ___Can you please close the window?___ It's freezing in here.
   (Can)

2. _____ I've finished reading them.
   (Could)

3. _____ Mr. Rivera is still in a meeting.
   (Would you mind)

4. _____ on the way home? We don't have any left.
   (Will)

5. _____ Miss Sanchez is on another call right now.
   (Could)

6. _____ I can't think with all that noise in the hall.
   (Would)

COMMUNICATION PRACTICE

5 LISTENING

Marcia Jones has planned a busy weekend. Listen to the conversations. Then listen again and check the things that belong on her schedule.

__✔__ **a.** take Mark to the dentist

_____ **b.** take kids to the library

_____ **c.** babysit for Sally's daughter

_____ **d.** go to Sally's party

_____ **e.** go to the movies

_____ **f.** walk Mom's dog

_____ **g.** pick up the car at the garage

_____ **h.** go to the gym with Pat

6 I'D BE GLAD TO

Work in a group. Make out your own schedule for the weekend. Then ask group members to help you out. Use polite requests.

SATURDAY OCTOBER 18	SUNDAY OCTOBER 19
Morning	Morning
Afternoon	Afternoon
Evening	Evening

EXAMPLE:

A: Can you drive me to the mall Saturday morning?

B: Sorry, I can't. I'm working Saturday morning.

OR

Sure, I'd be glad to.

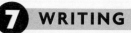 **WRITING**

Read the following situations. For each one, write a note making one or more requests.

1. Your roommate is going away for the weekend. Your sister from out of town will be visiting you. Write a note to your roommate.

 EXAMPLE:

 > Hi Viktor,
 >
 > My sister is visiting this weekend. Would you mind lending her your bike? I'd like to take her for a ride in the park.
 >
 > Thanks,
 >
 > Kunio

2. You work at a restaurant on Mondays, Wednesdays, and Fridays. You have to go to the dentist, but he or she can only see you on Wednesday. Write a note to a co-worker.

3. You're in school. You have to leave class early in order to help your parents. Write a note to a classmate.

4. You're going to have a party at your home. You've invited twenty people. Write a note to your neighbor.

14

ADVICE: *SHOULD*, *OUGHT TO*, *HAD BETTER*

GRAMMAR **IN CONTEXT**

BEFORE YOU READ Look at the photograph. What type of job is the woman training for? What skills does she need?

🔊 *Read this page from an advertisement for Capital Training Institute.*

Capital

Training Institute

Here are the answers to questions our students often ask:

Q: I can't go to college. Will I still find a job?

A: Many jobs don't require a college education. For example, administrative assistants and travel agents often move up to better positions. But be careful—you **shouldn't take** a job unless it offers you a good future. At Capital, you can get the skills you need for a job with a future.

Q: What are the best jobs these days?

A: For the next ten years, the best opportunities will be in service jobs. High school graduates **ought to think** about fields like health care and restaurant services.

Q: How **should** I **prepare** for a service job?

A: You will need a high school education for any good job. That means you**'d better not quit** high school if you want to get ahead. In fact, you **should plan** to get more education after you graduate. And, of course, computer skills are important for almost any job.

Q: I want to start my own business. **Should** I **get** a job first?

A: Yes. You **should** definitely **get** some experience before you start your own business. Appliance repairers and truck drivers often start their own companies after a few years on the job.

GRAMMAR **PRESENTATION**
ADVICE: *SHOULD, OUGHT TO, HAD BETTER*

STATEMENTS

SUBJECT	SHOULD / OUGHT TO / *HAD BETTER**	BASE FORM OF VERB	
I You He She We You They	**should (not)** **ought to** **had better (not)**	**look for**	a job.
		quit	school.

CONTRACTIONS

should not = **shouldn't**

had better = **'d better**

*Should and *ought to* are modals. *Had better* is similar to a modal. These forms do not have -s in the third-person singular.

YES / NO QUESTIONS

SHOULD	SUBJECT	BASE FORM OF VERB	
Should	I he she we they	**look for**	a job?
		quit	school?

SHORT ANSWERS

AFFIRMATIVE		
Yes,	you he she you they	**should.**

SHORT ANSWERS

NEGATIVE		
No,	you he she you they	**shouldn't.**

WH- QUESTIONS

WH- WORD	SHOULD	SUBJECT	BASE FORM OF VERB	
How When Where	**should**	I he she we they	**prepare**	for a job?

NOTES

1. Use *should* and *ought to* to say that <u>something is advisable</u>.

USAGE NOTE: We do not usually use the negative of *ought to* in American English. We use *shouldn't* instead.

EXAMPLES

- Fred and Tara **should answer** that want ad soon.
- They **ought to go** on some job interviews.
- They **shouldn't wait**.
  NOT COMMON ~~They ought not to wait.~~

(continued on next page)

2. Use *had better* for <u>urgent advice</u>—when you believe that something bad will happen if the person does not follow the advice.

- Kids, you**'d better leave** now, or you'll miss the school bus.

USAGE NOTE: The full form *had better* is very formal. We usually <u>use the contraction</u>.

- You**'d better apply** for more than one job.
  NOT ~~You had better apply . . .~~

The negative of *had better* is **had better not**.

- You**'d better not be** late.
  NOT ~~You'd not better be late.~~

▶ **BE CAREFUL!** *Had better* always refers to the <u>present</u> or the <u>future</u>, never to the past (even though it uses the word *had*).

- We**'d better take** the bus *now*.
- You**'d better call** them back *tomorrow*.

3. Use *should* for <u>questions</u>. We do not usually use *ought to* or *had better* for questions.

- ***Should* I go** to secretarial school?
- When ***should* I apply**?

4. It is usually considered impolite to <u>give advice to people</u> of equal or higher status (such as friends or bosses) unless they ask for it. However, it is polite to give advice to these people <u>when they ask for it</u>.

FRIEND: **Should I shake** hands with the interviewer?

   YOU: Yes, you **should**.

  BOSS: Where **should I take** our client to lunch?

   YOU: I think you **should go** to the Tuscan Grill.

When we give <u>unasked-for advice</u>, we often soften it with *maybe*, *perhaps*, or *I think*.

- Myra, *maybe* you **ought to call** Capital Training Institute.

REFERENCE NOTE
Sometimes we use *must* or *have to* to give very <u>strong advice</u>. This kind of advice is similar to talking about necessity or obligation *(see Unit 33)*.

FOCUSED PRACTICE

1 DISCOVER THE GRAMMAR

Two students are looking at the bulletin board at Capital Training Institute. Read their conversations and underline the words and phrases that give advice. Then complete each conversation with the number of the correct job notice.

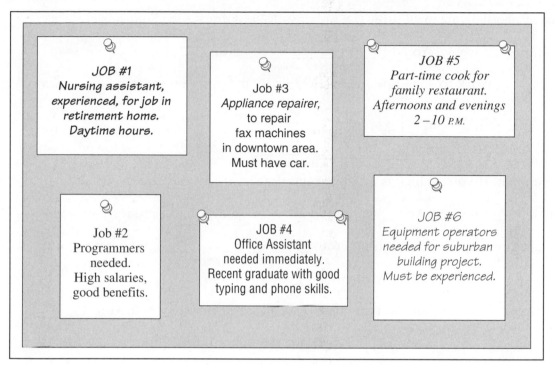

JOB #1
Nursing assistant, experienced, for job in retirement home. Daytime hours.

Job #3
Appliance repairer, to repair fax machines in downtown area. Must have car.

JOB #5
Part-time cook for family restaurant. Afternoons and evenings 2 – 10 P.M.

Job #2
Programmers needed. High salaries, good benefits.

JOB #4
Office Assistant needed immediately. Recent graduate with good typing and phone skills.

JOB #6
Equipment operators needed for suburban building project. Must be experienced.

1. **A:** Jake just finished a job for CTX builders. He's looking for work.

   B: He <u>should call</u> about number ___6___. He's got a lot of experience now.

2. **A:** I want a part-time job this semester. I think I'll apply for number _____.

   B: Maybe you shouldn't apply for that one. You have night classes, remember?

3. **A:** Pam quit her job at City Hospital because she couldn't work at night.

   B: She ought to apply for number _____. Older people really like her.

4. **A:** The company offered Cindy number _____.

   B: Well, she'd better not take it. She hates to drive in the city.

5. **A:** Kate and Denny are always complaining about their salaries.

   B: Programmers can make good money. They should call and find out about

   number _____.

6. **A:** Tom's just finished his course in office administration.

   B: Really? We'd better tell him about number _____. They need someone right away.

2 SHOULD'S AND SHOULD NOT'S   Grammar Notes 1–2

Choose the correct words to complete this advice for job-seekers.

Want or need a new job? When's the best time to start looking? Right now! You

_____'d better not_____ delay, or you'll start to feel "stuck." These tips will help:
1. (ought to / 'd better not)

- A lot of people wait until after the holidays to look for a job. That means less

  competition for you. You _____ wait!
  2. (shouldn't / should)

- Too busy at work to schedule interviews? Early morning interviews have fewer

  interruptions. You _____ ask for interviews before nine o'clock.
  3. (should / 'd better not)

- If you are laid off, you _____ immediately take a lower-paying job just
  4. ('d better / shouldn't)

  to get work. If your salary is low, your employer won't appreciate your skills. If possible,

  you _____ wait and look for a salary that matches your skills.
  5. ('d better not / should)

- However, money isn't everything! You _____ take a position with a
  6. (ought to / 'd better not)

  company you dislike, or you won't do a good job there.

- The best way to ruin an interview is to talk about salary too soon. You

  _____ wait—learn about the job and talk about your skills first.
  7. ('d better / shouldn't)

3 FRIENDLY ADVICE   Grammar Note 4

Read the conversations. Write advice with **maybe**, **perhaps**, *or* **I think**. *Use the words in parentheses. Choose between affirmative and negative statements.*

1. **A:** I'm tired. I studied all weekend for my exam.

   B: _____Maybe you'd better not study all night._____ You need to rest.
   ('d better study all night)

2. **A:** I'm hungry. I haven't eaten since breakfast.

   B: _____ The snack bar is open now.
   (ought to have a sandwich)

3. **A:** I have a headache, but I just took two aspirins an hour ago.

   B: _____ Lie down instead.
   ('d better take another one)

4. **A:** My brother hasn't made any progress in English this semester.

   B: _____ Watching TV really helps my English.
   (should watch more TV)

5. **A:** I'm not earning enough money as a waitress.

   B: _____ Then you could find a better job.
   (should learn some new skills)

4 WHAT SHOULD I DO?   Grammar Notes 1–4

Kim Yee has just started working in the United States. His boss has invited him to dinner at his home, and Kim is asking his English teacher, Scott, some questions. Complete their conversation with **should, ought to,** *or* **had better** *and the words and phrases in parentheses. Choose between affirmative and negative forms.*

KIM: _____How should I dress?_____ In a suit?
           1. (How / dress?)

SCOTT: You don't have to wear a suit. I think _____, but you
                                                  2. (look / neat)

        can wear casual clothes.

KIM: _____
           3. (What time / arrive?)

SCOTT: It's really important to be on time. They're expecting you at 7:00, so

        _____. It's OK to be a little late, but don't make your
           4. (arrive after 7:15)

        new boss wait too long for you!

KIM: _____
           5. (bring a gift?)

SCOTT: That's a good idea. But get something small. _____ It
                                                            6. (buy an expensive gift)

        would embarrass him.

KIM: _____
           7. (What / buy?)

SCOTT: I think _____.
                      8. (get some flowers)

5 EDITING

Read this letter. Find and correct six mistakes in the use of modals that express advice. The first mistake is already corrected.

Dear Son,

We are so happy to hear about your new job. Congratulations! Just remember—you shouldn't ~~to~~ work
too hard. The most important thing right now is your schoolwork. Maybe you only oughta work two
days a week instead of three. Also, we think you'd better ask your boss for time off during exams. That
way you'll have plenty of time to study. You would better give this a lot of careful thought, OK? Please
take good care of yourself. You'd not better start skipping meals, and you definitely shouldn't worked
at night. At your age, you will better get a good night's sleep. Do you need anything from home?
Should we send any of your books? Let us know.

With love,

Mom and Dad

COMMUNICATION PRACTICE

6 LISTENING

A teacher at Capital Institute is giving his students advice about taking their final exam. Listen. Then listen again and check the sentences that agree with his advice.

___✔___ **1.** Sleep well the night before the test.

_____ **2.** Stay up late and study the night before the test.

_____ **3.** Sleep late and skip breakfast.

_____ **4.** Leave plenty of time to get to school.

_____ **5.** Start answering questions right away.

_____ **6.** Read the exam completely before you start.

_____ **7.** Do the difficult sections first.

_____ **8.** Be sure to finish the test.

7 NEW COUNTRY, NEW CUSTOMS

Work with a partner. Imagine that your partner has been offered a job in a country that you know very well. Give some advice about customs there. Then switch roles. Use the topics below and some of your own.

- Calling your boss by his or her first name

- Shaking hands when you first meet someone

- Calling a co-worker by a nickname

- Bringing a gift to your host or hostess

- Asking for a second helping of food when you are a guest

- Crossing the street before the light turns green

Add your own topics.

- _____

- _____

        EXAMPLES:
        You'd better not call your boss by her first name.
        You should shake hands when you first meet someone.

8　PROBLEM SOLVING

Work in small groups. Take turns telling each other about problems you are having. They can be real problems or invented problems, or you can choose from the examples below. Let the others in the group give advice.

EXAMPLES:

Problem: I'm having trouble making friends.

Advice: Maybe you should come to the students' lounge. I think you ought to spend more time with the rest of us . . .

Other problems: I don't think I'm earning enough money.
I don't have enough free time.

9　THIS PLACE NEEDS WORK!

Look at a classroom at Mo's Training Institute. Working in pairs, give advice for ways that Mo can improve his institute. Then compare your ideas with the ideas of another pair.

EXAMPLE:

A: He should empty the trash.

B: Yes, and he ought to . . .

10　WRITING

Look at Exercise 9. Imagine you are a student at Mo's Training Institute. Write a letter of complaint. Give advice on improvements Mo should make.

15 SUGGESTIONS: LET'S, COULD, WHY DON'T ... ?, WHY NOT ... ?, HOW ABOUT ... ?

GRAMMAR **IN CONTEXT**

BEFORE YOU READ What do you know about hosteling? Would you like to stay in one of the hostels pictured below?

 Read this youth hostel brochure.

Let's Travel!

HOSTELLING INTERNATIONAL

A LOT OF INTERNATIONAL STUDENTS WANT TO TRAVEL—but it's too expensive, or they don't want to travel alone.

Are you spending your vacation in the dorm? If so, **why don't** you **travel** and stay at youth hostels? Hosteling is cheap, and you'll meet friendly people from all over the world.

Altena Castle, Germany

There are more than 6,000 hostels in over 70 different countries. They vary from simple buildings to magnificent old castles such as the Altena castle in Germany.

Do you like cities? **Why not stay** at the Ma Wai Hall overlooking the harbor in exciting Hong Kong? Or **maybe** you **could spend** the night at the historic Clay Hotel in Miami Beach. (Gangsters used to meet there.)

Tired of being on land? **How about a room** on the *af Chapman* in Stockholm, Sweden? Built in 1888, this sailing ship has been rocking tired hostelers to sleep for more than fifty years.

af Chapman, Sweden

Wherever you go, you'll meet talkative travelers, share stories with them, and gain a greater understanding of the world and its people. So what are you waiting for?

LET'S GO!

GRAMMAR **PRESENTATION**
SUGGESTIONS: *LET'S, COULD, WHY DON'T . . . ?,*
WHY NOT . . . ?, HOW ABOUT . . . ?

LET'S		
LET'S (NOT)	**BASE FORM OF VERB**	
Let's (not)	take	the ferry.
	stay	in a castle.

COULD				
(MAYBE)	**SUBJECT**	**COULD***	**BASE FORM OF VERB**	
(Maybe)	I you he she we they	could	take	the ferry.
			stay	in a castle.

*Could is a modal. Modals have only one form. They do not have *-s* in the third-person singular.

WHY DON'T . . . ?				
WHY	**DON'T / DOESN'T**	**SUBJECT**	**BASE FORM OF VERB**	
Why	don't	I we you they	take	the ferry?
	doesn't	he she	stay	in the castle?

WHY NOT . . . ?		
WHY NOT	**BASE FORM OF VERB**	
Why not	take	the ferry?
	stay	in a castle?

HOW ABOUT . . . ?		
HOW ABOUT	**GERUND / NOUN**	
How about	staying	in the castle?
	the castle?	

NOTES	EXAMPLES
1. Use *Let's*, *(Maybe) . . . could*, *Why don't / doesn't*, *Why not*, and *How about* to make <u>suggestions</u>.	**A:** *Let's* **take** a trip this summer. **B:** *Maybe* we *could* **go** to Costa Rica. **A:** *Why don't* we **ask** Luke to go with us? **B:** Good idea. *Why doesn't* Tom **call** him tonight? **A:** *Why not* **call** him right now? **B:** *How about* **staying** at youth hostels? **A:** Yes. *How about* **the hostel** in the rain forest?
USAGE NOTE: We usually use these expressions when we are speaking in <u>informal situations</u> or in an informal note or letter. We don't usually use them in formal situations.	**INFORMAL** • *Why don't* you visit Paris? **FORMAL** • May I suggest that you visit Paris?
► **BE CAREFUL!** When someone uses *Why not* and *Why don't / doesn't* to <u>make a suggestion</u>, these expressions are not information questions. The speaker does <u>not expect to receive information</u> from the listener.	**SUGGESTION** **A:** *Why don't* you **visit** Jill in New York? **B:** That's a good idea. **INFORMATION QUESTION** **A:** *Why don't* you **eat** meat? **B:** Because I'm a vegetarian.
2. *Let's* always <u>includes the speaker</u>. It means *Here's a suggestion for you and me.*	• *Let's* **go** to Miami. We need a vacation. *(I suggest that we go to Miami.)* • *Let's not* **stay** at a hostel. *(I suggest that we don't stay at a hostel.)*

3. Note the **different forms** to use with these expressions.

BASE FORM OF THE VERB

- *Let's* **take** the ferry.
- *Maybe* we *could* **take** the ferry.
- *Why don't* we **take** the ferry to Hong Kong island?
- *Why doesn't* she **take** the ferry to Hong Kong island?
- *Why not* **take** the ferry?

GERUND OR A NOUN

- *How about* **taking** the ferry?
- *How about* **the ferry**?

4. Notice the **punctuation** at the end of each kind of suggestion.

STATEMENTS

- *Let's* go to a concert.
- *Maybe* we *could* go to a concert.

QUESTIONS

- *Why don't* we go to a concert?
- *Why not* go to a concert?
- *How about* going to a concert?
- *How about* a concert?

REFERENCE NOTE
Making suggestions is sometimes similar to giving advice. *(See Unit 14.)*

FOCUSED PRACTICE

1 DISCOVER THE GRAMMAR

Emily and Megan are visiting Hong Kong. Read their conversation. Underline all the suggestions.

EMILY: <u>Why don't we go to the races?</u> I hear they're really exciting.

MEGAN: I'd like to, but I need to go shopping.

EMILY: Then let's go to the Temple Street Market tonight. We might even see some Chinese opera in the street while we're there.

MEGAN: That sounds like fun. If we do that, why not go to the races this afternoon?

EMILY: OK, but let's get something to eat first in one of those floating restaurants.

MEGAN: I don't think we'll have time. Maybe we could do that tomorrow. Right now, how about getting *dim sum* at the Kau Kee Restaurant next door? Then we could take the Star Ferry to Hong Kong Island and the racecourse.

EMILY: Sounds good. Here's an idea for tomorrow. Why not take one of those small boats—*kaido*—to Lantau Island? When we come back, we could have dinner at the Jumbo Palace.

MEGAN: Let's do that. It's a little expensive, but it floats.

Now look at this page from a Hong Kong guidebook and check the places Emily and Megan will visit and the transportation they will take.

Hong Kong Highlights

- **Hong Kong Space Museum.** One of the world's most advanced. See the Sky Show and a movie on the Omnimax movie screen.
- ✔ **Temple Street Night Market.** Find great bargains, visit a fortuneteller, and, with luck, hear Chinese opera performed in the street.

- **Harbour City.** Shop for clothing, electronics, and antiques in this huge, modern mall. Beautiful harbor views from the open rooftop.
- **Happy Valley Racecourse.** Watch Hong Kong's favorite sport. Feel the excitement as millions of Hong Kong dollars ride on every race.

Transportation

- **Railway lines** make local stops in both Kowloon and on Hong Kong Island. Use the Kwung Tong Line in Kowloon and the Island Line on Hong Kong Island.
- **The Star Ferry** is the queen of Hong Kong water transportation, and it's a bargain, too. There are several routes connecting Kowloon and Hong Kong Island.
- *Kaido* are small wooden ferries that carry 20–40 passengers.

Places to Eat

- **Jumbo Palace** ($$$) A traditional-style floating restaurant specializing in seafood.
- **Broadway Seafood Restaurant** ($) A friendly restaurant. Try the fresh scallops in black bean sauce.
- **Kau Kee Restaurant** ($) A favorite place for *dim sum*—a great way to try a variety of dishes.

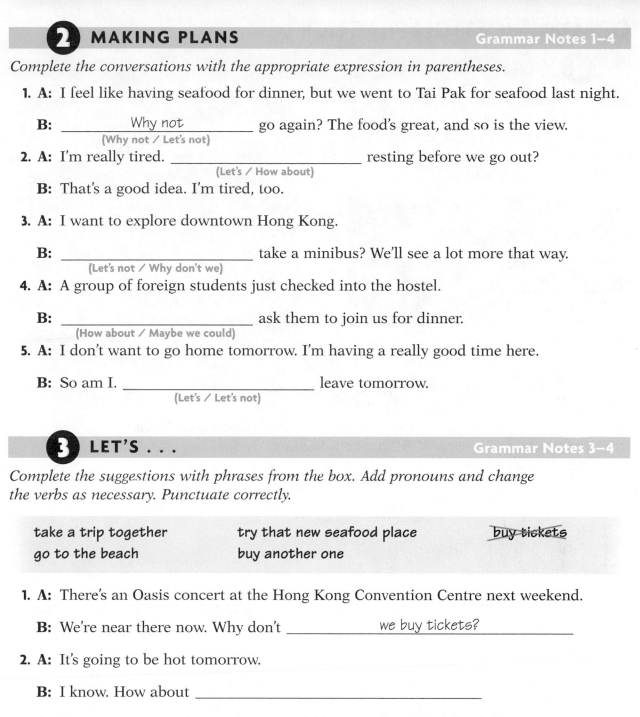

2 MAKING PLANS
Grammar Notes 1–4

Complete the conversations with the appropriate expression in parentheses.

1. A: I feel like having seafood for dinner, but we went to Tai Pak for seafood last night.

   B: _____ Why not _____ go again? The food's great, and so is the view.
   <u>(Why not / Let's not)</u>

2. A: I'm really tired. _____ resting before we go out?
   <u>(Let's / How about)</u>

   B: That's a good idea. I'm tired, too.

3. A: I want to explore downtown Hong Kong.

   B: _____ take a minibus? We'll see a lot more that way.
   <u>(Let's not / Why don't we)</u>

4. A: A group of foreign students just checked into the hostel.

   B: _____ ask them to join us for dinner.
   <u>(How about / Maybe we could)</u>

5. A: I don't want to go home tomorrow. I'm having a really good time here.

   B: So am I. _____ leave tomorrow.
   <u>(Let's / Let's not)</u>

3 LET'S . . .
Grammar Notes 3–4

Complete the suggestions with phrases from the box. Add pronouns and change the verbs as necessary. Punctuate correctly.

take a trip together	**try that new seafood place**	~~buy tickets~~
go to the beach	**buy another one**	

1. A: There's an Oasis concert at the Hong Kong Convention Centre next weekend.

   B: We're near there now. Why don't _____ we buy tickets? _____

2. A: It's going to be hot tomorrow.

   B: I know. How about _____

3. A: Sweaters are on sale. Maybe we could buy one for Brian's birthday.

   B: We got him a sweater last year. Let's not _____

4. A: I don't know what to do on spring vacation. I'm sick of staying in the dorm.

   B: Me too. Maybe _____

5. A: I'm hungry.

   B: Let's _____

COMMUNICATION PRACTICE

4 LISTENING

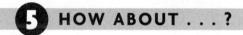 *Emily and Megan have just arrived on Lantau Island in Hong Kong. Look at the map. Then, listen to the conversation. Listen again. On the map, check the things they decide to do and places they decide to see.*

The S. G. Davis Hostel

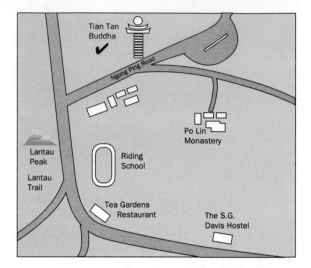

5 HOW ABOUT . . . ?

Work with a partner. Imagine you are both visiting Hong Kong. Look at the guidebook on page 154 and talk about what you like to do or want to do. Make suggestions about activities.

EXAMPLE:

A: I want to buy some souvenirs.

B: Let's go to the Temple Street Night Market.

6 THINGS TO DO

Work with a group to plan a trip to an interesting place in your area. Discuss the following:

- where to go
- when to go
- how to get there
- what to do there
- who will call or write for more information

EXAMPLES:

How about visiting San Diego?
Maybe we could go next weekend.
How about going to the zoo?

Why not take the bus?
Why don't the two of you call for information?

7 WRITING

Write a letter to someone who is going to visit you. Make suggestions about the things you can do together.

REVIEW OR SELFTEST

I. *Circle the letter of the appropriate response to each question.*

1. Could you speak English when you were a child?
   a. I'd be glad to.
   b. Yes, I could.

2. Can you swim?
   a. Yes, I can. I'd be glad to.
   b. Yes, I can. I really enjoy it.

3. Would you turn off the lights before you leave?
   a. Of course.
   b. Yes, I would.

4. May I ask a question?
   a. Yes, you may. What is it?
   b. You may. I'm not sure.

5. Would you mind lending me some money? I left my wallet at home.
   a. Yes, I would. Here's $10.
   b. Not at all. Here's $10.

6. Why don't we go to the beach today?
   a. Good idea.
   b. Because the car broke down.

7. Could you explain this word to me?
   a. Sorry, but I don't understand it, either.
   b. No, I couldn't. I never heard it before!

8. Maybe I'll wear a suit. What do you think?
   a. Maybe you shouldn't.
   b. Maybe you won't.

II. *Read each sentence. Write its function. Use the words in the box.*

ability	advice	permission	request	suggestion

1. Could I call you tonight? _____permission_____

2. Could you please turn the light out before you leave? _____

3. Why not take the train? _____

(continued on next page)

4. Of course you can use my pen. _____

5. When Eva was little, she couldn't reach the elevator button. _____

6. Do you mind if my sister comes with us? _____

7. Let's take a taxi. _____

8. You'd better work harder or you won't pass your test. _____

9. Would you mind calling back in about half an hour? _____

10. Will you please explain that to me again? _____

11. I can't lift that box by myself. _____

12. Maybe we could go to a later movie. _____

III. *Circle the correct words to complete the conversations.*

1. A: This apartment is depressing me.

   B: May we / (Why not) redecorate? We have some free time.
                1.

   A: OK. Where should we / were we able to start?
                       2.

   B: Maybe we could / couldn't start with the hall. It's easy to put up wallpaper.
                  3.

   A: How much wallpaper do we need?

   B: We can't / 'd better measure the walls and find out.
             4.

   A: This wallpaper is pretty. Let's / How about start putting it up.
                       5.

   B: We may / should clean the walls first.
             6.

   A: OK. The walls are clean. How about / Can putting up the wallpaper now?
                          7.

2. A: Dancing Wheels is performing at City Center next weekend. Let's / Would you mind
                                                           1.

   get tickets.

   B: Good idea. Could / Should you pick them up? I'm really busy this week.
                 2.

   A: No problem. I'll can / be able to get them after class today.
                   3.

   Do you mind if / How about I get a ticket for Carlos, too?
             4.

   B: Yes, I do. / Not at all. I haven't seen him in ages. Maybe we could / will all go out
             5.   6.

   to dinner before the theater. I hear that new Indian restaurant is very good.

   A: OK, but we could / 'd better make a reservation. It's very popular.
               7.

3. A: I'm taking the TOEFL exam this year. Any suggestions?

    B: <u>How about / Why don't</u> you ask Anatol? He took it last year.
                        1.

    A: Good idea. <u>Could / Should</u> you give me his phone number?
                      2.

    B: I don't have it, but you <u>'d better / could</u> ask Karin. She'll have it.
                              3.

    A: <u>Do you mind if / Would you mind</u> asking her for me? You know her better than I do.
                      4.

    B: Sure.

IV. *Each sentence has four underlined words or phrases. The four underlined parts of the sentences are marked A, B, C, or D. Circle the letter of the <u>one</u> underlined word or phrase that is NOT CORRECT.*

  1. <u>When</u> I was young, I <u>could</u> hit a baseball very far, but I <u>wasn't</u> able   A   B   C   Ⓓ
     A   B   C
    <u>run</u> fast.
     D

  2. Why <u>don't</u> we <u>have</u> dinner and then <u>go</u> see *Possible Dreams.*   A   B   C   D
         A   B   C   D

  3. You <u>drove</u> for seven hours today, so <u>maybe</u> you'd <u>not better</u>   A   B   C   D
        A   B   C
    <u>drive</u> tonight.
     D

  4. <u>Will</u> you mind <u>bringing</u> your camera to the graduation party   A   B   C   D
     A   B
    <u>tomorrow</u> <u>?</u>
      C   D

  5. Dad, <u>may</u> I <u>borrow</u> the car tomorrow or <u>does</u> Mom <u>has</u> to use it?   A   B   C   D
         A   B   C   D

  6. I <u>can't</u> <u>help</u> you with this math problem, so <u>maybe</u> you should <u>to talk</u>   A   B   C   D
        A   B   C   D
    to your teacher tomorrow.

  7. <u>Should</u> I <u>bring</u> flowers for my host tonight, or <u>should</u> I <u>giving</u> her   A   B   C   D
      A   B   C   D
    something more expensive?

  8. <u>May be</u> you <u>ought</u> <u>to</u> just <u>bring</u> flowers.   A   B   C   D
     A   B   C   D

  9. Silva <u>wasn't</u> a strong child, but she <u>could</u> win first prize in gymnastics   A   B   C   D
           A   B
    <u>when</u> she <u>was</u> ten.
      C   D

10. <u>I maybe</u> <u>will</u> be able <u>to</u> <u>finish</u> my homework early tonight.   A   B   C   D
     A   B   C   D

11. <u>It's</u> really late, so <u>let's</u> <u>us</u> <u>go</u> out to dinner tonight, OK?   A   B   C   D
     A   B   C   D

V. *Find and correct the mistake in each conversation.*

1. **A:** Can Elena ~~dances~~? *dance*

   B: Yes, she's great. She's able to do all kinds of difficult steps.

2. **A:** When you were a child, were you able to skate?

   B: Yes. In fact, I once could win a competition in my school.

3. **A:** Could please you help me?

   B: Sure. What seems to be the problem?

4. **A:** Would you mind giving me a ride home?

   B: Yes, I would. When would you like to leave?

5. **A:** We really ought see the movie that's playing at the Quad.

   B: OK. Let's go Friday night.

6. **A:** We would better hurry, or we'll be late.

   B: Don't worry. We can still get there on time.

7. **A:** Could I borrow the car tonight?

   B: Sorry, but you couldn't. I need it myself.

8. **A:** Do you mind if my friend coming to the party with me?

   B: Not at all. There's always room for one more!

▶ *To check your answers, go to the Answer Key on page 163.*

FROM GRAMMAR TO WRITING USING APPROPRIATE MODALS

When you write a note, you do more than give information. You perform social functions such as asking for permission and making requests. Modals help you perform these functions politely.

> **EXAMPLE:**
> I want you to call me in the morning. ⟶
> **Could** you **please** call me in the morning?

1 *Read this note from Ed to his co-worker, Chen. Work with a partner and decide which sentences should have modals. Underline the sentences.*

From The Desk of Ed Hansen . . .

Chen,

Here is our project summary. <u>Read it.</u> I think it's too long. What do you think? Tell me whether to shorten it. We will meet tomorrow to discuss it. My advice is that we finish the draft by Friday. By the way, Nadia is in town. I want to invite her to our meeting.

Ed

---

2 *Complete a second draft of the note. Use modals to express the functions in parentheses.*

From The Desk of Ed Hansen . . .

Chen,

Here is our project summary. <u>Would you mind</u> reading it? I think
                   (make a request)

it's too long. What do you think? _____ I shorten it?
                             (ask advice)

_____ meet tomorrow to discuss it. We _____
(make a suggestion)   (give advice)

finish the final draft by Friday. By the way, Nadia is in town.

_____ I invite her to our meeting?
(ask permission)

Ed

161

Complete Chen's note to Ed. Use modals to express the following ideas:

- Shorten the summary. (advice)
- I want to meet tomorrow morning instead. (suggestion)
- Reserve the conference room for the meeting. (request)
- Of course Nadia will come to the meeting. (permission)
- We're going to have lunch together after the meeting. (suggestion)

From the Desk of Chen Wu . . .

Ed—

Sorry, I was very busy this morning, so I wasn't able to finish reading the summary until now.

I think you should shorten it.

_____

_____

_____

_____

See you tomorrow morning.

Chen

---

4 *Before you write . . .*

- Work with a partner. Choose one of the situations below. Role-play the situation. Use modals to express the ideas.

a. You work in a sales office. Recently a customer complained to your boss because he had to wait for service. You want to meet with your boss to explain what happened. You'd like to bring a co-worker who saw the incident. You think the company needs another receptionist for busy times.

b. You would like your English teacher to write a letter of recommendation for you. You want her to mention that you have good computer skills and are an A student in her class. You're not sure how many hours to work a week, so you ask her. You want to miss class so that you can go to your job interview.

- Work with another pair of partners. Watch their role play. Make a list of functions they expressed and the modals they used to express those functions. Discuss your list with them—did they express what they wanted to?

- Perform your role play and discuss it with the other pair.

 Write a note as one of the characters in the role play. Use social modals and information from the feedback you received from your role play.

REVIEW OR SELFTEST
ANSWER KEY

PART III

I. (Units 11–15)
2. b   6. a
3. a   7. a
4. a   8. a
5. b

II. (Units 11–15)
2. request   8. advice
3. suggestion   9. request
4. permission   10. request
5. ability   11. ability
6. permission   12. suggestion
7. suggestion

III. (Units 11–15)
CONVERSATION 1
2. should we   5. Let's
3. could   6. should
4. 'd better*   7. How about

CONVERSATION 2
1. Let's   5. Not at all.
2. Could   6. could
3. be able to   7. 'd better
4. Do you mind if

CONVERSATION 3
1. Why don't
2. Could
3. could
4. Would you mind

IV. (Units 11–15)
2. D   7. D
3. C   8. A
4. A   9. B
5. D   10. A
6. D   11. C

V. (Units 11–15)

2. **A:** When you were a child, were you able to skate?
   B: Yes. In fact, I once ~~could~~ *was able to* win a competition in my school.

3. **A:** Could ~~please you~~ *you please* help me?
   OR
   Could you help me, please?
   B: Sure. What seems to be the problem?

4. **A:** Would you mind giving me a ride home?
   B: ~~Yes, I would.~~ *Not at all.* OR *No, I wouldn't.* When would you like to leave?

5. **A:** We really ought ^*to* see the movie that's playing at the Quad.
   B: OK. Let's go Friday night.

6. **A:** We ~~would~~ *'d* better hurry, or we'll be late.
   B: Don't worry. We can still get there on time.

7. **A:** Could I borrow the car tonight?
   B: Sorry, but you ~~couldn't.~~ *can't.* I need it myself.

8. **A:** Do you mind if my friend ~~coming~~ *comes* to the party with me?
   B: Not at all. There's always room for one more!

*Where a contracted form is given, the long form is also correct.

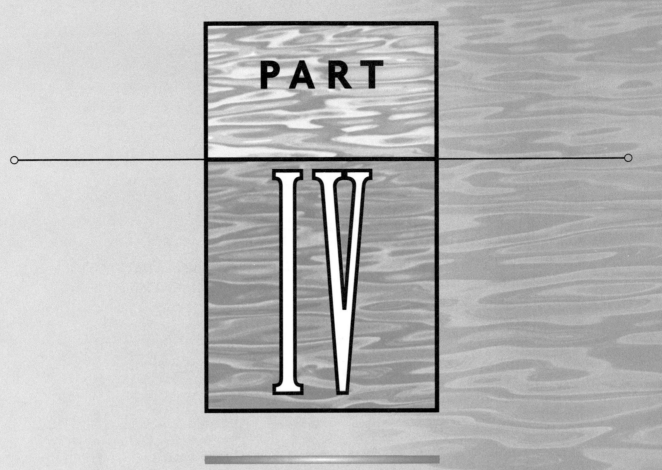

PART IV

PRESENT PERFECT

16

PRESENT PERFECT: SINCE AND FOR

GRAMMAR IN CONTEXT

BEFORE YOU READ Where can you find an article like this? Look at the information next to the photo. How long has Martina Hingis been a professional?

Read this article about tennis player Martina Hingis.

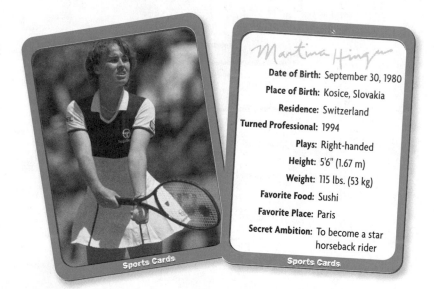

Date of Birth: September 30, 1980
Place of Birth: Kosice, Slovakia
Residence: Switzerland
Turned Professional: 1994
Plays: Right-handed
Height: 5'6" (1.67 m)
Weight: 115 lbs. (53 kg)
Favorite Food: Sushi
Favorite Place: Paris
Secret Ambition: To become a star horseback rider

Sports Cards   Sports Cards

Martina Hingis first picked up a tennis racket at the age of two. **Since then,** she **has become** one of the greatest tennis players in the world. Martina was born in Slovakia, but she and her mother **have lived** in Switzerland **for many years.** Martina became the outdoor Swiss champion at age nine. Then, in 1993, she became the youngest person ever to win the French Open Junior title. In 1996, she was the youngest player ever to win a Wimbledon event (Women's Doubles). A year later, she won almost all the major international tournaments—Wimbledon, the U.S. Open, and both singles and doubles matches at the Australian Open.

Many people criticize the lifestyle of very young tennis stars like Martina. Martina, for example, **hasn't attended** school **since 1994,** the year she turned professional. **Since then,** she **has played** tennis all over the world and **has earned** millions of dollars. As a result, she speaks several languages (English is her language on the court), and she is famous for her self-confidence. But what about a *normal* childhood? Like any young person, Martina enjoys shopping, going to parties, and listening to music. Tennis, however, **has been** the most important part of her life **since she was a little girl**. As she once told a reporter, "the life I'm living right now playing tennis is normal."

GRAMMAR **PRESENTATION**
PRESENT PERFECT: *SINCE* AND *FOR*

STATEMENTS

SUBJECT	HAVE / HAS (NOT)	PAST PARTICIPLE OF VERB		SINCE / FOR
I You* We They	**have (not)**	**been**[†] **lived**	here	**since** May. **for** a long time.
He She It	**has (not)**			

YES / NO QUESTIONS

HAVE / HAS	SUBJECT	PAST PARTICIPLE OF VERB		SINCE / FOR
Have	I you* we they	**been**[†] **lived**	here	**since** May? **for** a long time?
Has	he she it			

SHORT ANSWERS

AFFIRMATIVE		
Yes,	you I / we you they	**have.**
	he she it	**has.**

SHORT ANSWERS

NEGATIVE		
No,	you I / we you they	**haven't.**
	he she it	**hasn't.**

WH- QUESTIONS

WH- WORD	HAVE / HAS	SUBJECT	PAST PARTICIPLE	
How long	**have**	I you* we they	**been**[†] **lived**	here?
	has	he she it		

SHORT ANSWERS

Since January.
For a few months.

You is both singular and plural.
[†]*Been* is an irregular past participle. See Grammar Notes on page 169 and Appendix 1 on page A-1 for a list of irregular verbs.

CONTRACTIONS

AFFIRMATIVE				
I have	= **I've**	he has	= **he's**	
you have	= **you've**	she has	= **she's**	
we have	= **we've**	it has	= **it's**	
they have	= **they've**			

CONTRACTIONS

NEGATIVE		
have not	= **haven't**	
has not	= **hasn't**	

NOTES	EXAMPLES
1. Use the **present perfect** with *since or for* to talk about something that began in the past <u>and continues into the present</u> (and may continue into the future). Past ——— has been ——→ Future 1994 Now	• Martina **has been** a professional tennis player *since* 1994. • She **has been** a professional tennis player *for* several years. *(She began her professional career several years ago, and she is still a professional player.)*
2. Use the present perfect with *since + point in time* *(since 5:00, since Monday, since 1994, since yesterday)* to show <u>when something started</u>.	• She **has earned** millions of dollars *since 1994*.
3. *Since* can also introduce a **time clause**. When the action in the time clause ended in the past, use the <u>simple past tense</u>. When the action in the time clause began in the past but continues to the present, use the <u>present perfect</u>.	• Martina **has loved** sports *since she was a child*. • She **has won** many tournaments *since she moved* from Slovakia. *(She doesn't live there anymore.)* • She **has become** very successful *since she has been* in Switzerland. *(She still lives in Switzerland.)*
4. Use the present perfect with *for + length of time* *(for ten minutes, for two weeks, for years, for a long time)* to show <u>how long a present condition has lasted</u>.	• Martina's mother **has been** her coach *for many years*.

5. The present perfect is formed with *have* or *has* + **past participle**.

- She *has* **lived** there for years.

The **regular form of the past participle** is the base form of the verb + *-d* or *-ed.* This form is the same as the regular simple past form of the verb.

- They *have* **played** together many times since 1998.

There are many **irregular past participles**. Some common ones are listed below.

- She *has* **bought** two new rackets since March.
- They *haven't* **won** a tournament for several years.

(See Appendix 1, page A-1, for a more complete list.)

BASE FORM OF THE VERB	PAST PARTICIPLE	BASE FORM OF THE VERB	PAST PARTICIPLE
be	**been**	come	**came**
see	**seen**	do	**done**
bring	**brought**	go	**gone**
buy	**bought**	win	**won**
meet	**met**	drive	**driven**
sleep	**slept**	eat	**eaten**
hang	**hung**	get	**gotten**
sing	**sung**	give	**given**
sell	**sold**	take	**taken**
tell	**told**	write	**written**
put	**put**	find	**found**
read	**read**	have	**had**
run	**ran**	make	**made**

FOCUSED PRACTICE

1 DISCOVER THE GRAMMAR

Read the information about Gigi and Emilio. Then circle the letter of the sentence (**a** *or* **b**) *that best describes the situation.*

1. Gigi has been a tennis player since 1995.
   a. She still is a tennis player.
   b. She is not a tennis player anymore.

2. Gigi has had long hair since she was a little girl.
   a. She has short hair now.
   b. She has long hair now.

3. Gigi has lived in the same apartment for ten years.
   a. She lived in a different apartment eleven years ago.
   b. She moved a few years ago.

4. Gigi and Emilio have been married for twenty-five years.
   a. They got married twenty-five years ago.
   b. They are not married now.

5. Gigi and Emilio haven't been on a vacation since 1996.
   a. They were on a vacation in 1996.
   b. They are on a vacation now.

6. Gigi hasn't won a tennis championship for two years.
   a. She won a championship two years ago.
   b. She didn't win a championship two years ago.

2 WINNERS

Grammar Charts

Look at these tennis sports statistics. Use short answers to answer the questions.

AUSTRALIAN OPEN DOUBLES CHAMPIONS		
YEAR	**MEN**	**WOMEN**
1998	Jonas Bjorkman and Jacco Eltingh	Martina Hingis and Mirjana Lucic
1997	Todd Woodbridge and Mark Woodforde	Martina Hingis and Natasha Zvereva
1996	Stefan Edberg and Petr Korda	Chanda Rubin and Arantxa Sanchez Vicario
1995	Jared Palmer and Richey Reneberg	Jana Novotna and Arantxa Sanchez Vicario
1994	Jacco Eltingh and Paul Haarhuis	Gigi Fernandez and Natasha Zvereva
1993	Danie Visser and Laurie Warder	Gigi Fernandez and Natasha Zvereva
1992	Todd Woodbridge and Mark Woodforde	Arantxa Sanchez Vicario and Helevna Sukova

1. Martina Hingis won the Australian Open Doubles Championship in 1997. Has she won again since then?

   Yes, she has.

2. Danie Visser won the Australian Open Doubles Championship in 1993. Has he won again since then?

_____

3. Arantxa Sanchez Vicario won in 1992. Has she won again since then?

_____

4. Jared Palmer and Richey Reneberg won the Australian Open Doubles Championship in 1995. Have they won again since then?

_____

5. Helevna Sukova won in 1992. Has she won again since then?

_____

6. Gigi Fernandez and Natasha Zvereva won in 1993. Have they won as partners since then?

_____

7. Todd Woodbridge won in 1992. Has he won again since then?

_____

③ CHILD GENIUS   Grammar Notes 1–4

Read this magazine excerpt and complete it with **since** *or* **for***.*

Thirteen-year-old Ronnie Segal has loved math _____*since*_____ he was a little boy.
                                                        1.
"I have been interested in numbers _____ nine years, five months, three weeks, and
                                                 2.
two days," says Ronnie. _____ the past year, Ronnie has attended graduate-level
                              3.
classes at the university. _____ January he has taken five exams and has gotten
                                 4.
grades of 100 on all of them. _____
                                    5.
Ronnie began classes, he has met an average

of 1.324 people a month. And his future?

Thirteen-year-old Ronnie has known

_____ years that he is
      6.

going to become a famous

sports announcer, get married,

and have exactly 2.2 children.

MARTINA HAS SERVED 52.3% OF THE TIME. SHE HAS WON 81% OF HER 1st SERVES AND 7.8% OF HER 2nd SERVES.

Ingrid Schwab is applying for a job as a college sports instructor. Look at her resume and the interviewer's notes. Complete the interview. Use the words in parentheses to write questions. Then answer the questions. The year is 2004.

Ingrid Schwab
2136 East Travis Street
San Antonio, Texas 78284

INTERVIEWED
09/11/04

Education:

1996 Certificate (American College of Sports Medicine)
1995 MA Physical Education (University of Texas)

moved to San Antonio in 1989

Employment:

1995—present   part-time physical education teacher
                     (high school)

1993—present   sports trainer (private)   *teaches tennis, swimming*

Skills:

speak Spanish, German, and Korean

martial arts   *—got black belt in Tae Kwon Do 2 mos. ago*

Awards:

1996 Teacher of the Year Award

1993 Silver Medal in Texas Tennis Competition

Memberships:

1996–present   member of National Education Association (NEA)

---

1. (How long / live in San Antonio?)

   INTERVIEWER: How long have you lived in San Antonio?

        INGRID: I've lived in San Antonio for 15 years.

                         OR

   I've lived in San Antonio since 1989.

2. (How long / have your MA degree?)

   INTERVIEWER: _____

        INGRID: _____

3. (have any more training since you got your MA?)

> INTERVIEWER: _____

> INGRID: _____

4. (How long / be a physical education teacher?)

> INTERVIEWER: _____

> INGRID: _____

5. (How long / work as a sports trainer?)

> INTERVIEWER: _____

> INGRID: _____

6. (How long / have a black belt in Tae Kwon Do?)

> INTERVIEWER: _____

> INGRID: _____

7. (win any awards since then?)

> INTERVIEWER: I see you won a tennis award. _____

> INGRID: _____. I won the Teacher of the Year Award in 1996.

8. (How long / be a member of the NEA?)

> INTERVIEWER: _____

> INGRID: _____

5 EDITING

Read this student's journal entry. Find and correct nine mistakes in the use of the present perfect. The first mistake is already corrected.

> learned
> I've ~~learn~~ a lot since Ms. Schwab became my teacher. I've been in her physical education
> class since two months. I've only miss two classes since the beginning of the semester.
> I've became a much better player since Ms. Schwab started teaching us. We don't play
> much since November because the weather have been too cold. Instead, we switched to
> volleyball. My team has winned two games since we started to compete. Next month
> we start swimming. I've been afraid of the water since many years, but now I think I can
> learn to swim. I got so confident since I've been in this class.

COMPLICATION PRACTICE

6 LISTENING

*Antonio Serrano is looking for a job as a radio sports announcer. Listen to this interview. Then, listen again and complete the interviewer's notes. Use **since** and **for**.*

WSPR Radio

Antonio Serrano   interviewed 9/11

He's been a sports announcer ___for 20 years___ .
                                    a.

He's had 2 jobs _____ .
                        b.

He's lived in Los Angeles _____ .
                                    c.

He hasn't worked _____ .
                        d.

He's been a student at UCLA _____ .
                                    e.

7 THE BEST PERSON FOR THE JOB

*A business college needs a new math teacher. Look at these two resumes. In small groups, decide who to hire and why. Use **since** and **for**.*

EXAMPLE:

A: Wu Hao has had the same job since he got his PhD.

B: Erika Jones has a lot of experience. She's been a teacher since 1976.

Wu Hao

Education:
1990 PhD in Mathematics (UCLA)

Teaching Experience:
1990–present Bryant College

Courses Taught:
Algebra
Trigonometry
Calculus
Business Mathematics

Publications:
"Introducing Computers into the College Math Class" (*The Journal of Mathematics*, 1992)

Awards:
Teacher of the Year, 1992
Distinguished Professor, 1999

Erika Jones

Education:
1976 PhD in Mathematics (UCLA)

Teaching Experience:
1996–present   NYC Technical College
1991–1995   UCLA
1982–1990   University of Wisconsin, Madison
1979–1981   Brown University
1976–1978   UCLA

Courses Taught:
Mathematical Analysis 1
Mathematical Analysis 2

Publications:
"Imaginary Numbers" (*MJS*, 1981)
"Number Theory" (*Mathematics*, 1981)
"How Real Are Real Numbers?" (*Math Education*, 1984)

8 ROLE PLAY: A JOB INTERVIEW

Write a resume. Use Ingrid's resume on page 172 as a model. You can use real or imaginary information. Then, role-play a job interview with a partner. Take turns being the interviewer and the candidate. Use the script below to help you complete the interview.

EXAMPLE:

A: How long have you been a lab technician?

B: I've been a lab technician for five years.

INTERVIEWER: How long have you been a(n) _____?

CANDIDATE: I've _____

INTERVIEWER: And how many jobs have you had since _____?

CANDIDATE: I've _____

INTERVIEWER: I see from your resume that you live in _____
How long have you lived there?

CANDIDATE: _____

INTERVIEWER: Your English is quite good. How long have you studied it?

CANDIDATE: _____

INTERVIEWER: How long _____?

CANDIDATE: _____

INTERVIEWER: Well, thank you very much. We'll be in touch with you.

9 WRITING

Write a paragraph about someone's accomplishments. It can be someone famous or someone you know. Use the present perfect with **since** *or* **for**.

EXAMPLE:

Ingrid has been a high school physical education teacher and a private sports trainer for many years. She has received two awards since 1993, one for teaching and the other for tennis. She has been a member of the National Education Association since 1996. Ingrid speaks four languages. She has been a student of martial arts for a long time, and she has had her black belt in Tae Kwon Do since the summer.

17 PRESENT PERFECT: ALREADY AND YET

GRAMMAR IN CONTEXT

BEFORE YOU READ Look at the chart and the cartoon. What do you think this interview is about? What is happening in the cartoon?

Read this transcript of a television interview.

TOM: Good morning! I'm Tom Mendez, and this is "A.M. America." Dr. Helmut Meier has joined us to talk about the flu season. Dr. Meier, the real flu season **hasn't arrived yet,** but we**'ve already heard** about a number of serious cases.

DR. MEIER: Yes. As this chart shows, it *is* early for so many cases.

TOM: I got my shot two weeks ago. **Has** it **started** to work **yet?**

DR. MEIER: **Yes,** it **has.** It starts working in about a week.

TOM: See that guy over at the sports desk? That's our sportscaster, Randy Marlow. Hey Randy, **have** you **gotten** your flu shot **yet?**

RANDY: **Not yet!**

TOM: Randy's afraid of needles. I think he'd rather catch the flu.

DR. MEIER: Well, our lab is testing bananas that can produce vaccines.

TOM: No more needles! **Have** they **started** to sell them **yet?**

DR. MEIER: **No,** they **haven't.** But . . .

TOM: Oops! We**'ve already run out** of time. Thanks, Dr. Meier.

Get the flu shot
... not the flu.
FLU SEASON
CASES
Best time for vaccination
Oct. Nov. Dec. Jan. Feb.
MONTH

GRAMMAR **PRESENTATION**
PRESENT PERFECT: *ALREADY* AND *YET*

AFFIRMATIVE STATEMENTS: *ALREADY*

SUBJECT	*HAVE / HAS*	*ALREADY*	PAST PARTICIPLE OF VERB	
They	**have**	**already**	**developed**	a new flu vaccine.
It	**has**		**saved**	many lives.

NEGATIVE STATEMENTS: *YET*

SUBJECT	HAVE NOT / HAS NOT	PAST PARTICIPLE OF VERB		*YET*
They	**haven't**	**finished**	the interview	**yet**.
It	**hasn't**	**ended**		

YES / *NO* QUESTIONS: *YET*

HAVE / HAS	SUBJECT	PAST PARTICIPLE OF VERB		*YET*
Have	they	**tested**	the new vaccine	**yet**?
Has	it	**gotten**	approval	

SHORT ANSWERS

AFFIRMATIVE	
Yes,	they **have.**
	it **has.**

SHORT ANSWERS

NEGATIVE	
No,	they **haven't.**
	it **hasn't.**
No, not yet.	

NOTES	**EXAMPLES**

1. We often use the **present perfect** with *already* in affirmative sentences to talk about events that happened some time <u>before now</u>. It is possible that the event happened earlier than expected.

▶ **BE CAREFUL!** Do not use the present perfect with *already* when you mention a specific past point in time or a past time expression.

Already usually comes between *have / has* and the past participle.

Already can also come at the end of the clause.

A: Is your daughter going to get her flu shot?

B: She**'s** *already* **gotten** it.

DON'T SAY: ~~She's already gotten it last month.~~

- Researchers **have** *already* **discovered** cures for many diseases.

- They**'ve made** a lot of progress *already*.

---

2. Use the **present perfect** with ***not yet*** to talk about events that have not happened <u>before now</u>. It is possible that we expected the event to have happened earlier, and it is still possible that the event will happen in the future.

Notice that ***yet*** usually comes at the end of the clause.

Yet can also come between *have not / has not* and the past participle.

- They **haven't discovered** a cure for the common cold *yet*, but they hope to discover one in the future.

- The flu season **hasn't arrived** *yet*.

- They **haven't** *yet* **discovered** a cure for the common cold.

---

3. We usually use ***yet*** **in questions** to find out if something has happened <u>before now</u>.

USAGE NOTE: Sometimes we use ***already*** **in a question** to express surprise that something happened sooner than expected.

- **Has** your son **gotten** his flu shot *yet*?

- **Has** he *already* **gotten** his flu shot? The flu season hasn't begun yet.

FOCUSED PRACTICE

1 DISCOVER THE GRAMMAR

Match the cause with the result.

Cause

___e___ **1.** Tom has already gotten his flu shot, so he probably

_____ **2.** Dr. Meier has already finished his interview, so he

_____ **3.** Dr. Meier hasn't had lunch yet, so he

_____ **4.** Randy hasn't gotten his shot yet, so he

_____ **5.** Randy has already had lunch, so he

Result

a. is really hungry.

b. may get the flu.

c. has left the TV studio.

d. isn't very hungry.

e. won't get the flu this year.

2 ASK DR. MEIER   Grammar Notes 1–3

*Complete these questions and answers from a magazine article. Use the present perfect form of the verbs in parentheses with **already** or **yet** and short answers.*

smallpox vaccine	tetanus vaccine	flu vaccine	polio vaccine	measles vaccine	world smallpox vaccination program	last case of smallpox	AIDS vaccine	cancer vaccine	malaria vaccine	common cold vaccine
1796	1880	1945	1954	1963	1966	1980	NOW			

Q: We plan to travel to the rain forest next year. _____Have_____ they _____found_____ a

1. (find)

malaria vaccine _____yet_____ ?

A: _____ , they _____ . Talk to your doctor about ways to prevent this

2.

disease.

Q: My doctor told me I won't need another smallpox vaccination. I was surprised.

_____ smallpox completely _____ ?

3. (disappear)

A: _____ , it _____ .

4.

Q: They _____ vaccines against the flu. What about the common cold?

5. (develop)

A: No. Because there are so many different cold viruses, they _____ to develop

6. (be able)

a vaccine _____ .

Q: There has been so much cancer research. _____ anyone _____ a

7. (make)

successful vaccine _____ ?

A: _____ , they _____ . Researchers *have* made a lot of progress in

8.

recent years, however.

3 **MEDICAL RECORD**

Look at Rita's immunization chart. Use the words in parentheses to write statements with the present perfect and **already** *or* **yet***.*

LIFETIME IMMUNIZATIONS					
NAME: Rita Meier					

		(2 mos.)	(4 mos.)	(6 mos.)	(15–18 mos.)	(4–6 yrs.)
		Date Given	Date Given	Date Given	Date Given	Date Given
D **P** **T**	Diphtheria Pertussis Tetanus	12/14/98	2/2/99	4/16/99		
P **O** **L** **I** **O**		12/14/98	2/2/99	4/16/99		

(12–15 mos.)	Date Given	Date Given	(18–24 mos.)	Date Given
M **M** **R** Measles Mumps Rubella	10/19/99		**H** **I** **B** Hemophilus Influenzae Type B	

(Booster every 10 yrs.)	Date	Date	Date
Tetanus Diphtheria			

1. (The Meiers / take Rita to the doctor)

    The Meiers have already taken Rita to the doctor.

2. (The doctor / give Rita her 15–18 month DPT injection)

    The doctor hasn't given Rita her 15–18 month DPT injection yet.

3. (Rita / get her 6-month DPT injection)

    _____

4. (Rita / receive / her 15–18 month polio immunization)

    _____

5. (Rita / be to the doctor for her MMR immunization)

    _____

6. (She / get a tetanus booster)

    _____

7. (The doctor / vaccinate Rita against the mumps)

    _____

8. (Rita / receive / an HIB vaccine)

    _____

COMMUNICATION PRACTICE

4 LISTENING

Dr. Meier is speaking to his wife, Gisela. Listen to their conversation. Listen again and check the things that Dr. Meier has already done.

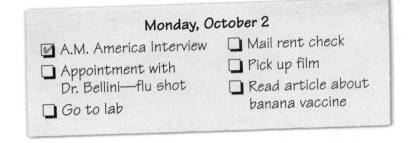

Monday, October 2

- ☑ A.M. America Interview
- ☐ Appointment with Dr. Bellini—flu shot
- ☐ Go to lab
- ☐ Mail rent check
- ☐ Pick up film
- ☐ Read article about banana vaccine

5 INFORMATION GAP: CHORES

Work in pairs (A and B). Student B, look at the Information Gap on p. 183 and follow the instructions there. Student A, look at the picture of the Meiers' dining room on this page. Cross out the chores Gisela has already done. Ask your partner about Helmut's chores and cross out the chores he's already done. Answer your partner's questions about Gisela's chores.

EXAMPLE:

A: Has Helmut bought film yet?

B: Yes, he has. OR Yes, he's already bought film. Has Gisela vacuumed the carpet yet?

A: No, she hasn't. OR No, not yet.

To Do—Helmut

- ~~buy film~~
- bake the cake
- put the turkey in the oven
- mop the floor
- wash the dishes
- cut up the vegetables

To Do—Gisela

- vacuum the carpet
- ~~buy flowers~~
- wash the windows
- set the table
- hang the balloons
- wrap the gift

Now compare lists with your partner. Are they the same?

6 WHAT ABOUT YOU?

Write a list of things that you planned or wanted to do by this time (for example: find a new job, paint the apartment). Include things that you have already done and things that you haven't done yet. Exchange lists with a classmate, and ask and answer questions about the items on the lists.

EXAMPLE:
A: Have you found a new job yet?
B: No, not yet. I'm still looking. OR Yes, I have.

7 INVENTIONS AND DISCOVERIES

Work in pairs. Decide together if the following things have already happened or have not happened yet. Check the appropriate column. Discuss your answers with your classmates.

EXAMPLE:
A: Researchers haven't discovered a cure for the common cold yet.
B: They've already found a test for the virus that causes AIDS, but they haven't found a cure yet.

	Already	Not Yet
1. a cure for the common cold	☐	☑
2. a test for the AIDS virus	☑	☐
3. a successful heart transplant (animal to human)	☐	☐
4. a successful heart transplant (human to human)	☐	☐
5. a cure for tooth decay (cavities)	☐	☐
6. a pillow that helps prevent snoring	☐	☐
7. liquid sunglasses (in the form of eye drops)	☐	☐
8. electric cars	☐	☐
9. flying cars	☐	☐
10. light bulbs that can last ten years	☐	☐

Add your own list of inventions and discoveries.

	Already	Not Yet
11. _____	☐	☐
12. _____	☐	☐
13. _____	☐	☐

8 WRITING

Imagine you and a friend are giving a party tonight. Leave a note for your friend to explain what you've already done and what you haven't done yet.

EXAMPLE:

I've already bought the soda, but I haven't gotten the potato chips yet . . .

INFORMATION GAP FOR STUDENT B

Student B, look at the Meiers' kitchen. Cross out the chores Helmut has already done. Answer your partner's questions about Helmut's chores. Ask your partner about Gisela's chores and cross out the chores she's already done.

EXAMPLE:

A: Has Helmut bought film yet?

B: Yes, he has. OR Yes, he's already bought film.
    Has Gisela vacuumed the carpet yet?

A: No, she hasn't. OR No, not yet.

To Do—Helmut

~~buy film~~
bake the cake
put the turkey in
    the oven
mop the floor
wash the dishes
cut up the vegetables

To Do—Gisela

vacuum the carpet
buy flowers
wash the windows
set the table
hang the balloons
wrap the gift

Now compare lists with your partner. Are they the same?

18 PRESENT PERFECT: INDEFINITE PAST

GRAMMAR **IN CONTEXT**

BEFORE YOU READ What kind of a TV show is "Feldstein"? Where can you find a message like this?

Read this online journal message from TV star Jimmy Feldstein to fans of his show, "Feldstein."

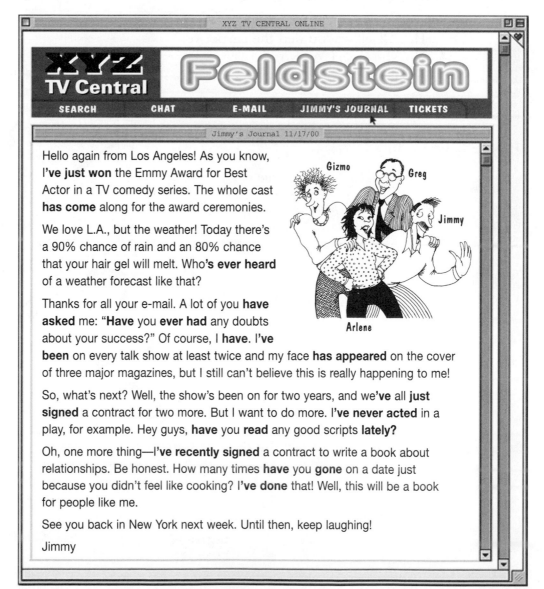

XYZ TV CENTRAL ONLINE

XYZ TV Central — **Feldstein**

SEARCH   CHAT   E-MAIL   JIMMY'S JOURNAL   TICKETS

Jimmy's Journal 11/17/00

Hello again from Los Angeles! As you know, I**'ve just won** the Emmy Award for Best Actor in a TV comedy series. The whole cast **has come** along for the award ceremonies.

We love L.A., but the weather! Today there's a 90% chance of rain and an 80% chance that your hair gel will melt. Who**'s ever heard** of a weather forecast like that?

Thanks for all your e-mail. A lot of you **have asked** me: "**Have** you **ever had** any doubts about your success?" Of course, I **have**. I've **been** on every talk show at least twice and my face **has appeared** on the cover of three major magazines, but I still can't believe this is really happening to me!

So, what's next? Well, the show's been on for two years, and we**'ve** all **just signed** a contract for two more. But I want to do more. I**'ve never acted** in a play, for example. Hey guys, **have** you **read** any good scripts **lately?**

Oh, one more thing—I**'ve recently signed** a contract to write a book about relationships. Be honest. How many times **have** you **gone** on a date just because you didn't feel like cooking? I**'ve done** that! Well, this will be a book for people like me.

See you back in New York next week. Until then, keep laughing!

Jimmy

GRAMMAR **PRESENTATION**
PRESENT PERFECT: INDEFINITE PAST

STATEMENTS			
SUBJECT	HAVE / HAS (NOT)	PAST PARTICIPLE OF VERB	
They	**have (not)**	**appeared**	on TV.
It	**has (not)**	**been**	

See page 167 in Unit 16 for a complete presentation of present perfect forms.

STATEMENTS WITH ADVERBS					
SUBJECT	HAVE / HAS	ADVERB	PAST PARTICIPLE OF VERB		ADVERB
They	**have**	*never* *just* *recently*	**appeared** **been**	on TV.	
It	**has**				
They	**have (not)**		**appeared** **been**	on TV	*lately*. *recently*.
It	**has (not)**				

YES / NO QUESTIONS				
HAVE / HAS	SUBJECT	(EVER)	PAST PARTICIPLE OF VERB	
Have	they	*(ever)*	**appeared** **been**	on TV?
Has	it			

SHORT ANSWERS	
AFFIRMATIVE	
Yes,	they **have.**
	it **has.**

SHORT ANSWERS	
NEGATIVE	
No,	they **haven't.**
	it **hasn't.**
No, *never*.	

WH- QUESTIONS				
WH- WORD	HAVE / HAS	SUBJECT	PAST PARTICIPLE OF VERB	
How often	**have**	they	**appeared** **been**	on TV?
	has	it		

NOTES	**EXAMPLES**
1. Use the **present perfect** to talk about things that happened at an <u>indefinite time in the past</u>. You can use the present perfect when you don't know when something happened, when you do not want to be specific, or when the specific time is not important. Now *have won* Past —X——————————— Future	• They**'ve won** several awards. • I**'ve interviewed** the whole cast. • She**'s been** in a Hollywood movie.
2. Use the **present perfect** to talk about <u>repeated actions</u> at some indefinite time in the past. *saw show saw show saw show* Now Past —X–X–X——————————— Future	• He**'s been** on a lot of talk shows over the past two weeks. • I**'ve seen** his show many times.
3. You can use *ever* with the **present perfect** to <u>ask questions</u>. It means *at any time up until the present.* Use *never* to answer <u>negatively</u>.	**A:** **Have** you **won** an award? OR **Have** you *ever* **won** an award? **B:** No, I**'ve** *never* **won** one. OR No, *never*.
4. Use the **present perfect** with certain **adverbs of time** to emphasize that something happened in the <u>very recent</u> (but still indefinite) <u>past</u>. USAGE NOTE: In spoken American English people often use *just* and *recently* with the <u>simple past tense</u> to refer to indefinite time.	• We**'ve** *just* **gotten** back from LA. • I**'ve** *recently* **signed** a contract to write a book. • He **hasn't had** time *lately*. • We *just* **got** back from LA.

FOCUSED PRACTICE

1 DISCOVER THE GRAMMAR

*Read the first sentence. Then decide if the second sentence is **True (T)** or **False (F)**.*

1. I've recently joined the show.
___T___ I am a new cast member.

2. I have never been to Los Angeles.
_____ I went to Los Angeles a long time ago.

3. I've just finished Jimmy's book.
_____ I finished it a little while ago.

4. Greg asks, "Have you ever seen this movie?"
_____ Greg wants to know when you saw the movie.

5. Arlene asks you, "Have you read any good books lately?"
_____ Arlene wants to know about a book you read last year.

6. She's visited New York several times.
_____ This is her first visit to New York.

7. She has become very popular.
_____ She is popular now.

2 BLIND DATE
Grammar Notes 1–3

 *In this scene from "Feldstein," Jimmy and Ursula are on a blind date—they have never met before. Complete the sentences using the present perfect form of the verbs in the box. Some verbs are used more than once.*

have	make	stop	talk	travel	want

URSULA: This is a nice restaurant. _____Have_____ you _____had_____ their steak?
                                                                     1.

JIMMY: No, but I _____ the eggplant parmigiana. In fact, I always have that.
                        2.

URSULA: Then try some of my steak tonight.

JIMMY: Actually, I _____ eating meat.
                          3.

URSULA: Oh, really? Are you a Save the Animals person?

JIMMY: Oh, no. It's not that I love animals. I just hate plants. _____ you ever

really _____ to a plant? They have absolutely nothing to say.
               4.

URSULA: Right. So, _____ you ever _____ to live outside of
                                                         5.
New York?

(continued on next page)

JIMMY: Outside of New York? Where's that? But seriously, I _____ never

_____ to try any other place. I love it here.
   6.

URSULA: But _____ you ever _____ to a different city?
                                                    7.

JIMMY: Why should I do that? No, traveling is definitely not for me. You like it here

too, right?

URSULA: It's OK, but I _____ to other places too. It's a big world out there.
                        8.

JIMMY: I like it right here. Say, _____ you _____ plans
                                                          9.

for tomorrow night? How about dinner? Same time, same place, same

eggplant parmigiana . . .

---

③ BRAINSTORMING   Grammar Note 3

*Two writers are brainstorming story ideas for Jimmy's show. They want to do
something different, so they are trying to remember what they have done in past
shows. Use the words in parentheses to write questions and answers. Use **ever**
with the questions and, when appropriate, use **never** with the answers.*

1. A: (we / do / a story about a blind date?)

   Have we ever done a story about a blind date?

   B: Yes, _____ we have _____. Jimmy went out with Ursula, remember?

2. A: Oh, yeah. Well, here's another idea.

   (Greg's parents / stay / in his apartment?)

   _____

   B: No, _____. But they've been on the show recently.

3. A: OK. Then we need something with Gizmo.

   (Gizmo / look for / a job?)

   _____

   B: No, _____. That might be funny. Gizmo finds a job, and his new

boss sends him on a trip. Maybe to Europe.

4. A: That sounds familiar.

(the characters / travel / to Europe?)

_____

B: Yes, _____, but not recently. Arlene went to Spain last year.

5. A: So let's develop this one.

(Gizmo / take / a plane?)

_____

B: No, _____. This can be his first flight.

6. A: Good. That will get lots of laughs.

(he / study / a foreign language?)

_____

B: Yes, _____. When he fell in love with the Italian tour guide.

7. A: So he goes to Rome, and he *thinks* he understands everything.

(you / write / anything like this?)

_____

B: No, _____. I'd better buy an Italian dictionary.

---

4 **EDITING**

Read this message from Jimmy Feldstein's online message board. Find and correct
five mistakes in the use of the present perfect. The first mistake is already corrected.

| **Feldstein Fan Chat** |

Subj.: Re: Jimmy's Blind Date
Date: 00-11-22
From: Yikes123

I've just ~~watch~~ *watched* the Blind Date episode on Feldstein! Have you never seen anything so

funny? I LOVE this show! It's the best show I have ever saw in my life. I really enjoyed it

lately. By the way, have you notice that Jimmy and Arlene are beginning to get along? I

can't wait to see what happens next episode. Does anyone know when Jimmy's book is

coming out?

⑤ ONLINE WITH GIZMO

Complete the XYZ Network online interview with Jake Stewart, the actor who plays the part of Gizmo on Jimmy's show.

XYZ TV'S LIVE STUDIO

XYZ online LIVE STUDIO Feldstein

ONLINE INTERVIEW WITH JAKE STEWART OF XYZ'S FELDSTEIN

XYZ:

Welcome to Live Studio, Jake. Your character, Gizmo, has become famous.

How many online interviews have you done?
1. (How many / online interviews / do?)

JAKE:

None! _____ Very exciting!
2. (Never even / be / in a chat room)

XYZ:

You used to do stand-up comedy. _____ on TV?
3. (How / change / as an actor)

JAKE:

I work with a group, so _____
4. (become / a better team player / lately)

XYZ:

As a comic actor, _____
5. (who / be / your role model?)

JAKE:

Hard to say. _____
6. (Charlie Chaplin / have / a great influence on me)

XYZ:

Yes, I can see that. _____
7. (What / be / your best moment on Jimmy's show?)

JAKE:

_____ That was a great moment for all of us.
8. (Jimmy / just / win / the Emmy)

XYZ:

All in all, _____
9. (what / enjoy / the most about this experience?)

JAKE:

Free coffee! No, really, _____
10. (meet / some fantastic people on this show)

6 ALL IN A DAY'S WORK

Look at some of Jimmy's things. Write statements using the present perfect form of the verbs in the box.

| be | meet | perform | see | win | write |

1. _____ He's been on three _____ magazine covers. _____

2. _____

3. _____

4. _____

5. _____

6. _____

COMMUNICATION PRACTICE

7 LISTENING

 *Lynette Long is a TV star. She is talking to her travel agent about different vacation possibilities. The travel agent is asking questions about where she has traveled before. Read the choices that follow. Listen to their conversation. Then listen again and check the travel package her agent is going to offer her.*

_____ **a.** Switzerland—$1,220 includes: round-trip ticket, five nights in a beautiful hotel, day trips in the mountains, fresh air, and lots of exercise

_____ **b.** Jamaica—$600 includes: round-trip ticket, six days and five nights in a beautiful hotel, all meals, lots of beaches

_____ **c.** Egypt—$2,500 group tour includes: eight days and seven nights, beautiful hotel, all meals, bus tours to the pyramids

8 HAVE YOU EVER?

*Ask your classmates questions. Find out how many people have ever done any of the following things. If the answer is **yes**, ask more questions. Get the stories behind the answers. Share your answers and stories with the class.*

- Meet a famous TV or movie star
- Take a long trip by car
- Climb a mountain
- Dream in a foreign language
- Walk in the rain
- Drive cross-country

Add your own:

- _____

- _____

> **EXAMPLE:**
> **A:** Have you ever met a famous movie star?
> **B:** Yes, I have. I was visiting Hollywood, and I saw . . .

9 WRITING

*Write a paragraph about a character on a TV show that you watch regularly. What has the show been like lately? Has the character changed recently? Use the present perfect with **lately**, **recently**, and **never**.*

> **EXAMPLE:**
> I watch "Frasier" every Thursday night. Recently, the show has been funnier than usual . . .

PRESENT PERFECT AND SIMPLE PAST TENSE

GRAMMAR **IN CONTEXT**

BEFORE YOU READ   What do you think a "commuter marriage" is? What is happening in the cartoon? How do you think the people feel?

Read this excerpt from an article in Modern Day *magazine.*

◆ LIFESTYLES ◆

Commuter Marriages

Many modern marriages are finding interesting solutions to difficult problems. Take Joe and Maria Tresante, for example. Joe and Maria **married** in June 1995. They **lived** in Detroit for three years. Then in 1998 Joe, a college professor, **got** a great job offer in Los Angeles. At the same time Maria's company **moved** to Boston. They are still married, but they **have lived** apart ever since. They **have decided** to travel back and forth between Boston and Los Angeles until one of them finds a different job. Sociologists call this kind of marriage a "commuter marriage." "It **hasn't been** easy," says Maria. "Last month I **saw** Joe three times, but this month I**'ve** only **seen** him once."

It also **hasn't been** inexpensive. In addition to the cost of frequent air flights, their phone bills **have been** sky high. December's bill **was** almost $400. This month, they**'ve started** to communicate by e-mail with the hope of lowering their expenses. Is all this trouble and expense worth it? "Yes," says the couple. "It **was** a difficult decision, but so far it **has worked out** for us. It's better for both of us to have jobs that we like." The Tresantes **have had to** work hard to make their marriage succeed, but the effort **has paid off.** Joe notes, "We**'ve been** geographically separated, but we**'ve grown** a lot closer emotionally."

GRAMMAR **PRESENTATION**
PRESENT PERFECT AND SIMPLE PAST TENSE

PRESENT PERFECT
She **has been** here since 1980.
They**'ve lived** here for twenty years.
We**'ve spoken** once today.
He **hasn't flown** this month.
Has she **called** him today?

SIMPLE PAST TENSE
She **was** in Caracas in 1975.
They **lived** there for ten years.
We **spoke** twice yesterday.
She **didn't fly** last month.
Did she **call** him yesterday?

NOTES

EXAMPLES

1. The **present perfect** is used to talk about things that started in the past, <u>continue up to the present</u>, and may continue into the future.

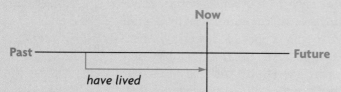

The **simple past tense** is used to talk about things that happened in the past and have <u>no connection to the present</u>.

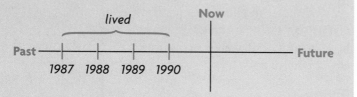

- They **have lived** apart for the past three years.
  (They started living apart three years ago and are still living apart.)

- They **lived** in Detroit for three years.
  (They lived in Detroit until 1990. They no longer live in Detroit.)

2. The **present perfect** is also used to talk about things that happened at an <u>unspecified</u> time in the past.

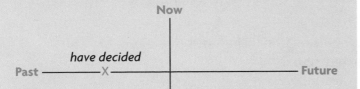

The **simple past tense** is used to talk about things that happened at a <u>specific</u> time in the past. The exact time is known and sometimes stated.

Now

Past ———X——— | ———— Future
lived
1990

▶ **BE CAREFUL!** Do not use specific past time expressions with the present perfect except after *since*.

- They **have decided** to travel back and forth.
  (*We don't know exactly when the decision was made, or the timing of the decision is not important.*)

- They **lived** in Detroit *in 1990*.

- I **lived** in Detroit in 1997.
  NOT ~~I've lived in Detroit in 1997.~~

3. Use the **present perfect** to talk about things that have happened in a time period that is <u>not finished</u>, such as *today, this morning, this month, this year.*

Use the **simple past tense** to talk about things that happened in a time period that is <u>finished</u>, such as *yesterday, last month, last year.*

▶ **BE CAREFUL!** Some time expressions like *this morning, this month,* or *this year* can refer to a finished or unfinished time period. Use the present perfect if the time period is unfinished. Use the simple past tense if the time period is finished.

- She**'s had** three cups of coffee *this morning*.
  (*It's still this morning, and it's possible that she will have some more.*)

- She **had** three cups of coffee *yesterday*.
  (*Yesterday is finished.*)

- It's 10:00 A.M. She**'s had** three cups of coffee *this morning*.
  (*The morning is not over.*)
- It's 1:00 P.M. She **had** three cups of coffee *this morning*.
  (*The morning is over.*)

FOCUSED PRACTICE

① DISCOVER THE GRAMMAR

Read the information about Joe and Maria. Then circle the letter of the sentence
*(**a** or **b**) that best describes the situation.*

1. It's 1999. Joe's family moved to Houston in 1989. They still live there.
   a. Joe's family lived in Houston for ten years.
   b. Joe's family has lived in Houston for ten years.

2. Last year Joe and Maria enjoyed their vacation in Canada.
   a. They had a good time.
   b. They've had a good time.

3. Joe is telling his friend about his wife, Maria.
   a. His friend asks, "How long were you married?"
   b. His friend asks, "How long have you been married?"

4. Joe is telling Maria that the weather in Los Angeles has been cloudy and hot for the past five days.
   a. Five days ago the weather started to be cloudy and hot, and it is still that way.
   b. Sometime in the past year the weather was cloudy and hot for five days.

5. Joe studied the piano for ten years, but he doesn't play anymore.
   a. Joe has played the piano for ten years.
   b. Joe played the piano for ten years.

6. Maria wants to move to Los Angeles from Boston but must find a job first. She is interviewing for a job in Los Angeles.
   a. She says, "I lived in Boston for two years."
   b. She says, "I've lived in Boston for two years."

7. This month Maria and Joe have met once in Boston and once in Los Angeles and will meet once more in New York.
   a. They've seen each other twice.
   b. They saw each other twice.

② IT HASN'T BEEN EASY   Grammar Notes 1–3

Circle the correct verb forms to complete this entry in Maria's journal.

Thursday, September 28

It's 8:00 P.M. It <u>has been</u> / was a hard day, and it's not over yet! I still have to work on that report.
                   1.
I <u>ve begun</u> / began it last night, but so far I <u>ve written</u> / wrote only two pages. And it's due tomorrow!
        2.   3.
Work <u>has been</u> / was so difficult lately. I <u>ve worked</u> / worked late every night this week. I feel exhausted
         4.   5.
and I <u>haven't gotten</u> / didn't get much sleep last night. And, of course, I miss Joe. Even though
              6.
I <u>ve seen</u> / saw him last week, it seems like a long time ago. Oh, there's the phone—
       7.

3 PHONE CONVERSATION

 *Use the words in parentheses to complete the phone conversation between Maria and Joe. Use the present perfect or the simple past tense.*

JOE: Hi, honey! How are you?

MARIA: I'm OK—a little tired, I guess. I only _____ slept _____ a few hours last night.
1. (sleep)

I'm writing this big report for tomorrow's meeting, and I _____
2. (not stop)

worrying about it all week.

JOE: You need to rest. Listen—maybe I'll come see you this weekend. We

_____ each other twice this month.
3. (only see)

MARIA: OK. But I really have to work. Remember the last time you _____
4. (come)

here? I _____ any work at all.
5. (not do)

JOE: OK. Now, why don't you go make yourself a cup of coffee and just relax?

MARIA: Coffee! You must be kidding! I _____ five cups today. And
6. (already have)

yesterday I _____ at least six. No more coffee for me.
7. (drink)

JOE: Well then, get some rest, and I'll see you tomorrow.

MARIA: OK. Good night!

4 AN INTERVIEW

Read the magazine article on page 193 again. Imagine that you wrote the article. You asked Joe and Maria questions to get your information. What were they? Use the words below and write the questions.

1. How long / be married?

　How long have you been married?

2. How long / have your job?

_____

3. How long / live in Detroit?

_____

4. When / get a job offer?

_____

(continued on next page)

5. When / your company move?

_____

6. How long / live apart?

_____

7. How often / see each other last month?

_____

8. How often / see each other this month?

_____

5 CHANGES

Joe and Maria met in the 1980s. Since then Joe has changed. Use the words below and write down how Joe has changed.

In the 1980s	Since then
1. have / long hair	become / bald
2. be / clean shaven	grow / a beard
3. be / thin	get / heavy
4. be / a student	become / a professor
5. live / in a dormitory	buy / a house
6. be / single	get / married

1. _In the 1980s Joe had long hair._

   Since then, he has become bald.

2. In the 1980s _____

   Since then, _____

3. _____

   _____

4. _____

   _____

5. _____

   _____

6. _____

   _____

COMMUNICATION PRACTICE

6 LISTENING

A school newspaper is interviewing two college professors. Listen to the interview. Then listen again and check the items that are now true.

The professors . . .

☑ **1.** are married ☐ **2.** live in different cities ☐ **3.** are at the same university

☐ **4.** live in Boston ☐ **5.** are in Austin ☐ **6.** have a house

7 MARRIAGE AND DIVORCE

Look at the chart. Work in pairs and discuss the marriage and divorce statistics in the United States. Use the words in the box.

↑ increase | decrease
get higher | get lower
go up | ↓ go down

	1980	1990	1995
Marriage	2,406,708	2,948,000	2,336,000
Divorce	1,189,000	1,175,000	1,169,000
Percentage of men (age 20–24) never married	68.8%	79.7%	80.7%
Percentage of women (age 20–24) never married	50.2%	64.1%	66.7%
Average age of first marriage: men	24.7	26.1	26.9
women	22.0	23.9	24.5

Source: Department of Commerce, Bureau of the Census and the Department of Health and Human Services, National Center for Health Statistics.

EXAMPLE:
The number of marriages has decreased since 1980.
In 1980 a total of 2,406,708 people got married.
In 1995 2,336,000 got married.

8 A COUNTRY YOU KNOW WELL

Work in small groups. Tell your classmates about some changes in a country you know well.

EXAMPLE:
In 1999, a new president took office. Since then, the economy has improved.

❾ LOOKING BACK

Work in pairs. Look at Maria's records from last year and this year. It's now the beginning of August. Compare what Maria did last year with what she's done this year.

LAST YEAR					
January	**February**	**March**	**April**	**May**	**June**
• business trip to N.Y. • L.A.—2X	• L.A.—2X • 1 seminar	• business trip to N.Y. • L.A.—1X	• L.A.—3X • 1 lecture	• 10 vacation days • Jay's wedding	• 2 seminars • L.A.—2X
July	**August**	**September**	**October**	**November**	**December**
• L.A.—1X • Sue's wedding	• L.A.—1X	• L.A.—2X • 1 lecture	• business trip to Little Rock	• 1 seminar	• 10 vacation days
THIS YEAR					
January	**February**	**March**	**April**	**May**	**June**
• L.A.—1X	• business trip to N.Y • 1 lecture	• L.A.—1X • Nan's wedding	• L.A.—1X	• business trip to Miami • L.A.—1X	• 5 vacation days • 1 seminar
July	**August**	**September**	**October**	**November**	**December**
• Barry's wedding	• L.A.—1X • 1 lecture				

EXAMPLE:

A: Last year she went on three business trips.

B: So far this year she's only gone on two.

❿ WRITING

How has your family changed in the last five years? Write a paragraph about some of the changes. Use the present perfect and the simple past tense.

EXAMPLE:

Five years ago, all my brothers and sisters lived at home. Since then, we have all moved away . . .

PRESENT PERFECT PROGRESSIVE

GRAMMAR **IN CONTEXT**

BEFORE YOU READ   Look at the photo. What can you guess about the man? Where is he? Look at the statistics at the end of the article. In which categories do you think the man belongs?

A journalist has been writing a series of articles about the problem of homelessness in the United States. Read this second in a series of five articles.

LIVING ON THE STREETS

Part two in a five-part series

BY ENRICO SANCHEZ

It **has been raining.** The ground is still wet. John Tarver **has been sitting** on the same park bench for hours. His clothes are soaked and he **has been coughing** all morning. A while ago someone gave him a bowl of hot soup. It's no longer warm, but John **has been eating** it anyway.

How did he end up like this? John, a former building superintendent, lost his job and his apartment when he hurt his back. He **has been living** on the street since then. And he is not alone. John is just one of a possible seven million Americans who **have been making** their homes in the streets, parks, and subway stations of our cities. The number of homeless men, women, and children **has been climbing** steadily since 1980 and will continue to rise until the government takes action.

Who's Homeless in the United States?

Age	Percentages
children under the age of 18	27%
adults between 31 and 50	50%
adults between 55 and 60	2.5%–19.4%
Gender and Marital Status	
single men	45%
single women	14%
families with children	40%

Source: The National Coalition for the Homeless

GRAMMAR **PRESENTATION**
PRESENT PERFECT PROGRESSIVE

STATEMENTS

SUBJECT	HAVE / HAS (NOT)	BEEN	BASE FORM OF VERB + -ING		(SINCE / FOR)
I You* We They	have (not)	been	sitting	here	(since 12:00). (for hours).
He She It	has (not)				

YES / NO QUESTIONS

HAVE / HAS	SUBJECT	BEEN	BASE FORM OF VERB + -ING		(SINCE / FOR)
Have	I you* we they	been	sitting	here	(since 12:00)? (for an hour)?
Has	he she it				

SHORT ANSWERS
AFFIRMATIVE

Yes,	you I / we you they	have.
	he she it	has.

SHORT ANSWERS
NEGATIVE

No,	you I / we you they	haven't.
	he she it	hasn't.

WH- QUESTIONS

WH- WORD	HAVE / HAS	SUBJECT	BEEN	BASE FORM OF VERB + -ING	
How long	have	I you* we they	been	sitting	here?
	has	he she it			

SHORT ANSWERS

Since 9:00.
For a few hours.

*You is both singular and plural.

NOTES	EXAMPLES

1. Use the **present perfect progressive** (also called the present perfect continuous) to talk about an action or situation that <u>began in the past and continues to the present</u>. The action or situation is usually not finished. It is continuing, and it will probably continue into the future.

REMEMBER: <u>Non-action (stative) verbs</u> are not usually used with the progressive. (*See page 5 and Appendix 2, page A-2.*)

- It**'s been raining** all day. When is it going to stop?
- They**'ve been looking** for work, but they haven't found anything yet.
- I**'ve been reading** an interesting book. I'll give it to you when I'm finished.

- He's known a lot of homeless people.
  NOT ~~He's been knowing a lot of homeless people.~~

2. Also use the **present perfect progressive** for <u>repeated actions</u> that <u>started in the past and continue up to the present</u>. Verbs that are frequently used in this way are: *hit, punch, knock, cough, jump, nod,* and *kick.*

- John **has been coughing** all morning.
- The interviewer **has been nodding** his head sympathetically.
- I**'ve been knocking** on the door for two minutes. I don't think anyone is home.

3. Use the **present perfect progressive** to describe actions that have <u>stopped in the recent past</u>. The action is not happening right now, but there are <u>results</u> of the action that you <u>can still see</u>.

- It**'s been raining**. The streets are still wet.
- John **has been fighting**. He has a black eye.

FOCUSED PRACTICE

① DISCOVER THE GRAMMAR

*Read the information about John and Enrico. Then circle the letter of the sentence (**a** or **b**) that best describes the situation.*

1. John has been sitting on that park bench for hours.
　a. He is still sitting on the park bench.
　b. He is no longer sitting on the park bench.

2. John's been coughing.
　a. He coughed several times.
　b. He coughed only once.

3. John's been living on the streets for two years.
　a. He used to live on the streets.
　b. He still lives on the streets.

4. Enrico has been writing an article.
　a. The article is finished.
　b. The article isn't finished yet.

5. Enrico looks out the window and says, "It's been snowing."
　a. It is definitely still snowing.
　b. It is possible that it stopped snowing a little while ago.

6. It's been snowing since 8:00.
　a. It's still snowing.
　b. It stopped snowing a little while ago.

② AN INTERVIEW　　　　　　　　　　　　　Grammar Notes 1–3

The newspaper interviewed John Tarver. Complete the interview. Use the present perfect progressive form of the verbs in the box.

ask	do	eat	~~live~~	look	read	sleep	spend	think	worry

INTERVIEWER: How long _____have_____ you ___been living___ on the streets, Mr. Tarver?
　　　　　　　　　　　　　　　　　　　　　　1.

MR. TARVER: For almost two years now.

INTERVIEWER: Where do you sleep?

MR. TARVER: It's been pretty warm, so I _____ in the park. But winter will be
　　　　　　　　　　　　　　　　　　2.
　　　　　　　　here soon, and it'll be too cold to sleep outside. I _____ about that.
　　　　　　　　　　　　　　　　　　　　　　　　　　　　3.

INTERVIEWER: What _____ you _____ about food?
　　　　　　　　　　　　　　　　4.

MR. TARVER: I _____ much lately. Sometimes someone gives me money, and
　　　　　　　5. (negative)
　　　　　　　I buy a sandwich and something to drink.

INTERVIEWER: How _____ you _____ your time?
6.

MR. TARVER: I do a lot of thinking. Recently, I _____ a lot about my past and
7.

how I ended up without a home.

INTERVIEWER: Do you see any way out of your present situation?

MR. TARVER: I want to work, so I _____ for a job. I _____ the want
8.   9.

ads every day in the paper, and I _____ everyone I know for a job.
10.

INTERVIEWER: Any luck?

MR. TARVER: So far, no.

---

3 **WHAT'S BEEN HAPPENING?** **Grammar Notes 1–3**

*Look at the two pictures of journalist Enrico Sanchez. Write sentences describing
what is going on in these two pictures. Use the present perfect progressive form of
the verbs in parentheses. Choose between affirmative and negative forms.*

1. He has been writing an article about the homeless.
   (write an article about the homeless)

2. _____
   (read the newspaper)

3. _____
   (drink coffee)

4. _____
   (drink tea)

5. _____
   (eat)

6. _____
   (watch TV)

7. _____
   (rain)

COMMUNICATION PRACTICE

4 LISTENING

Listen to Dave, a counselor at a job training program, talk to Martha, a homeless woman. Listen again and check the things Dave is still doing. Listen a third time and check the things Martha is still doing.

Dave

☑ **1.** Reviewing Martha's test results

☐ **2.** Teaching Martha to use the fax

☐ **3.** Setting up a day care program

Martha

☐ **1.** Working with computers

☐ **2.** Writing a resume

☐ **3.** Making a list of places to send her resume

☐ **4.** Walking to her job training program

☐ **5.** Looking for business clothes

☐ **6.** Taking care of her children all day

5 JOBLESSNESS AROUND THE WORLD

Work in pairs. Look at these government statistics. Discuss them with your partner. Make sentences using the present perfect progressive. Use the words in the box below.

joblessness	the unemployment rate	unemployment	
improve / get worse	go up and down	decrease / increase	fall / rise

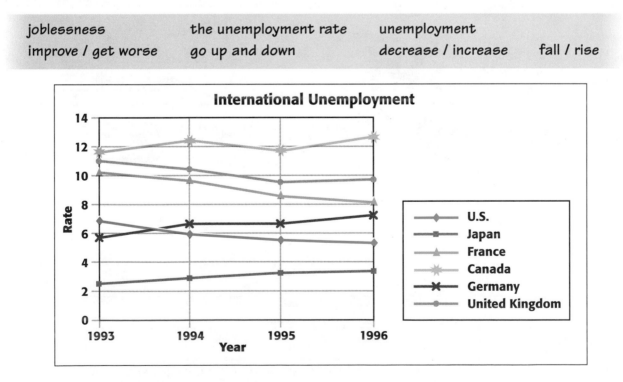

International Unemployment

Legend: U.S. · Japan · France · Canada · Germany · United Kingdom

EXAMPLE:

A: What's been happening in the United States?

B: The unemployment rate has been falling.

6 EXPLANATIONS

Work in pairs. Think of as many explanations as possible for the following situations.

1. John looks exhausted.

2. Martha is wearing a new suit.

3. Alexis and Tom look angry.

4. The streets are all wet.

5. Gina's wallet is stuffed with $100 bills.

6. Jason lost five pounds.

> **EXAMPLE:**
> Janet's eyes are red.
> **A:** Maybe she's been crying.
> **B:** Or maybe she's been suffering from allergies.
> **A:** She's probably been rubbing them.

7 WHAT ABOUT YOU?

Complete this form with information about your present life.

address:	_____
job:	_____
hobbies / interests:	_____
favorite school subjects:	_____
plans:	_____
concerns:	_____

Work in pairs. Look at each other's forms. Ask and answer questions with
How long + *the present perfect progressive. The verbs in the box can help you.*

> **EXAMPLE:**
> **A:** How long have you been
>   working as a cook?
> **B:** For two years.
>   OR
>   Since I moved here.

live at	study
work at / as	plan to
play / collect / do	worry about

8 WRITING

Write a paragraph about your present life. Use the present perfect progressive. You can use the form you filled out in Exercise 7 for ideas.

> **EXAMPLE:**
> I've been working at McDonald's for about a year. . . .

21 PRESENT PERFECT AND PRESENT PERFECT PROGRESSIVE

GRAMMAR **IN CONTEXT**

BEFORE YOU READ Look at the key facts about African elephants. Why do you think the elephant population has changed so much? Look at the map of Africa. What parts of Africa have elephants?

Professor Jane Owen has been studying elephants for several decades. Read this excerpt from her latest article in Science Today.

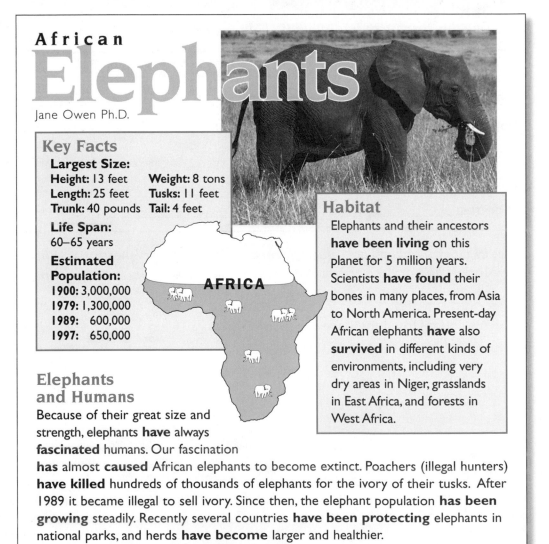

African Elephants
Jane Owen Ph.D.

Key Facts

Largest Size:
Height: 13 feet **Weight:** 8 tons
Length: 25 feet **Tusks:** 11 feet
Trunk: 40 pounds **Tail:** 4 feet

Life Span:
60–65 years

Estimated Population:
1900: 3,000,000
1979: 1,300,000
1989: 600,000
1997: 650,000

AFRICA

Habitat

Elephants and their ancestors **have been living** on this planet for 5 million years. Scientists **have found** their bones in many places, from Asia to North America. Present-day African elephants **have** also **survived** in different kinds of environments, including very dry areas in Niger, grasslands in East Africa, and forests in West Africa.

Elephants and Humans

Because of their great size and strength, elephants **have** always **fascinated** humans. Our fascination **has** almost **caused** African elephants to become extinct. Poachers (illegal hunters) **have killed** hundreds of thousands of elephants for the ivory of their tusks. After 1989 it became illegal to sell ivory. Since then, the elephant population **has been growing** steadily. Recently several countries **have been protecting** elephants in national parks, and herds **have become** larger and healthier.

GRAMMAR **PRESENTATION**
PRESENT PERFECT AND PRESENT PERFECT PROGRESSIVE

PRESENT PERFECT
Elephants **have roamed** the earth for thousands of years.
I**'ve read** two books about elephants.
Dr. Owen **has written** many articles.
She**'s lived** in many countries.

PRESENT PERFECT PROGRESSIVE
Elephants **have been roaming** the earth for thousands of years.
I**'ve been reading** this book since Monday.
She**'s been writing** articles since 1990.
She**'s been living** in France for a year.

NOTES

EXAMPLES

1. The **present perfect** often shows that an activity or state is <u>finished</u>. The emphasis is on the result of the action.

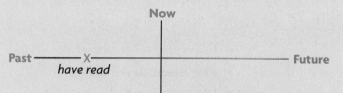

The **present perfect progressive** often shows that an activity or state is <u>unfinished</u>. It started in the past and is still continuing.

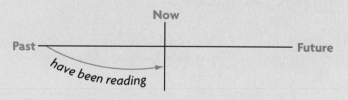

- I**'ve read** a book about elephants.
  (I finished the book.)
- She**'s written** an article.
  (She finished the article.)

- I**'ve been reading** a book about elephants.
  (I'm still reading it.)
- She**'s been writing** an article.
  (She's still writing it.)

(continued on next page)

2. Sometimes you can use either the **present perfect** OR the **present perfect progressive**. The meaning is basically the same. This is especially true when you use verbs such as *live, work, study,* and *teach* with *for* or *since*.

- She**'s studied** African elephants for three years.

  OR

- She**'s been studying** African elephants for three years.

  (In both cases, she started studying elephants three years ago, and she is still studying them.)

---

3. The **present perfect** places more emphasis on the permanence of an action or state.

The **present perfect progressive** emphasizes the temporary nature of the action.

- They**'ve** always **lived** in Africa.

- They**'ve been living** in Africa for three years, but they are returning to France next month.

---

4. We often use the **present perfect** to talk about:
  –how much someone has done
  –how many times someone has done something
  –how many things someone has done

- I**'ve read** a lot about it.
- I**'ve been** to Africa twice.
- She**'s written** three articles.

We often use the **present perfect progressive** to talk about how long something has been happening.

- I**'ve been reading** books on elephants for two months.

▶ **BE CAREFUL!** We usually do not use the present perfect progressive when we describe a number of completed events.

- I**'ve read** that book twice.
  NOT ~~I've been reading that book twice.~~

FOCUSED PRACTICE

1 DISCOVER THE GRAMMAR

Read the first sentence. Then decide if the second sentence is **True (T)** *or* **False (F)**.

1. Professor Owen has been reading a book about African wildlife.
_F_   She finished the book.

2. She's read a book about African wildlife.
_____   She finished the book.

3. She's written a magazine article about the rain forest.
_____   She finished the article.

4. She's been waiting for some supplies.
_____   She received the supplies.

5. They've lived in Uganda since 1992.
_____   They are still in Uganda.

6. They've been living in Uganda since 1992.
_____   They are still in Uganda.

7. We've been discussing environmental problems with the leaders of many countries.
_____   The discussions are probably over.

8. We've discussed these problems with many leaders.
_____   The discussions arc probably over.

2 PROFESSOR OWEN'S WORK   Grammar Notes 1–4

Complete these statements. Circle the correct form of the verbs. In some cases, both forms are correct.

1. Professor Owen is working on two articles for *National Wildlife Magazine.* She

has written / (has been writing) these articles since Monday.

2. *National Wildlife Magazine* has published / has been publishing its annual report on

the environment. It is an excellent report.

3. Hundreds of African elephants have already died / have been dying this year.

4. Professor Owen has given / has been giving many talks about wildlife preservation in

past lecture series.

5. She has spoken / has been speaking at our school many times.

(continued on next page)

6. Congress <u>has created / has been creating</u> a new study group to discuss the problem of endangered animals. The group has already met twice.

7. The new group has a lot of work to do. Lately, the members <u>have studied / have been studying</u> the problem of the spotted owl.

8. Professor Owen was late for a meeting with the members of Congress. When she arrived the chairperson said, "At last, you're here. We <u>have waited / have been waiting</u> for you."

9. Professor Owen <u>has lived / has been living</u> in England for the last two years, but she will return to the United States in January.

10. She <u>has worked / has been working</u> with environmentalists in England and France.

3 **GRANDAD**   Grammar Notes 1–4

Complete this entry from Dr. Owen's field journal. Use the present perfect or the present perfect progressive form of the verb in parentheses.

We ___'ve been hearing___ about Grandad since we arrived here in
　　　　1. (hear)

Amboseli Park. He is one of the last "tuskers." Two days ago, we finally saw

him. His tusks are more than seven feet long. I'_____ never

_____ anything like them.
　　2. (see)

Grandad _____ here for more than sixty years. He
　　　　　　3. (live)

_____ everything, and he _____
　　4. (experience)　　　　　　　　　　　　　　　　　5. (survive)

countless threats from human beings. Young men _____
　　　　　　　　　　　　　　　　　　　　　　　　　　6. (test)

their courage against him, and poachers _____ him for
　　　　　　　　　　　　　　　　　　　7. (hunt)

his ivory. His experience and courage _____ him so far.
　　　　　　　　　　　　　　　　　8. (save)

For the last two days, he _____ slowly through the
　　　　　　　　　　　　9. (move)

tall grass. He _____ and _____.
　　　　　　10. (eat)　　　　　　　　　　11. (rest)

Luckily, it _____ a lot this year, and the biggest
　　　　　12. (rain)

elephants _____ enough food and water.
　　　　　　13. (find)

4 HOW LONG AND HOW MUCH?

Professor Owen is doing fieldwork in Africa. Imagine you are about to interview her. Use the words below to ask her questions. Use her notes to complete her answers. Choose between the present perfect and present perfect progressive.

FIELD NOTES
3/23/00

GRANDAD
    Order: *Proboscidea*
    Family: *Elephantidae*
    Genus and Species: *Loxodonta africana*

—eats about 500 pounds of vegetation/day
—drinks about 40 gallons of water at a time
—walks 5 miles/hour (50 miles/day)

1. How long / you / observe / Grandad?

    You: How long have you been observing Grandad? _____

    Owen: I've been observing him for _____ two days.

2. How much vegetation / he / eat?

    You: _____

    Owen: _____

3. How often / he / stop for water?

    You: _____

    Owen: _____ four times.

4. How much water / he / drink?

    You: _____

    Owen: _____

5. How long / he / walk today?

    You: _____

    Owen: _____ nine hours.

6. How far / he / travel so far today?

    You: _____

    Owen: _____

COMMUNICATION PRACTICE

5 LISTENING

Listen to the conversations. Then listen again and circle the letter of the pictures that illustrate the situations.

1.

a.

(b.)

2.

a.

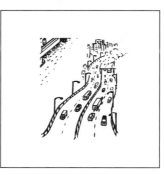

b.

3.

a.

b.

4.

a.

b.

5.

a.

b.

6 GIVING ADVICE

Sometimes we are asked to give advice, but we don't have enough information. Read the following situations and list the questions you might ask to get the information you need. Work with a partner. Take turns asking and answering questions and giving advice. Try to use the present perfect or the present perfect progressive. Then role-play these situations.

1. Your friend calls you. He says that he is tired of waiting for his girlfriend. She is always late. This time he wants to leave to teach her a lesson.

   Questions:
   a. How long have you been waiting?
   b. How often . . .
   c. How many times . . .
   d. Have you ever . . .

   Advice: _____

2. Your father is trying to quit smoking. He's having a hard time and tells you that he needs to have just one more cigarette.

   Questions:
   a. How long . . .
   b. How many times . . .
   c. Have you ever . . .

   Advice: _____

3. Your friend is an author. She has published several books and is working on a new one. She is getting very frustrated and thinks she will never finish.

   Questions:
   a. How many pages . . .
   b. How long . . .
   c. Have you ever . . .

   Advice: _____

7 FIND OUT MORE

These two creatures have been on the World Wildlife Fund's list of the ten most endangered species. Do research about one of the animals.

Find out about its . . .

- size

- geographic location (habitat)

- habits

Learn . . .

- why it has become endangered

- what governments or other groups have been doing to save it

Arabian Oryx

Monarch Butterfly

Now get together in small groups and discuss your findings.

8 WRITING

Write a paragraph about one of the animals discussed in this unit. Use the topics from Exercise 7 to guide your writing.

EXAMPLE:
The Arabian oryx is about three feet tall. Its horns are . . .

REVIEW OR SELFTEST

I. *Complete the following conversations. Use the present perfect form of the verbs in parentheses.*

1. A: I've just rented a truck to move our things.

    B: _____Have_____ you ever _____driven_____ a truck before?
                                  (drive)

    A: Sure, I have. It's not that hard.

2. A: How long _____ you _____ a comedian?
                                       (be)

    B: Since I was born. I made people laugh even when I was a baby.

3. A: Shh. The baby _____ just _____ asleep.
                                        (fall)

    B: Sorry. We'll be more quiet.

4. A: It's time to pay the bills.

    B: They're not as bad as they look. I _____ already

    _____ the phone bill.
     (pay)

5. A: _____ you ever _____ a letter of complaint?
                                      (write)

    B: Yes, I have. I got great results.

6. A: Can I throw this magazine out yet?

    B: Not yet. Jennifer _____ it yet.
                       (not read)

7. A: I win!

    B: I quit! You _____ every card game so far this evening.
                       (win)

8. A: What have you told the kids about our holiday plans?

    B: I _____ them anything yet. Let's wait until our
          (not tell)

    plans are definite.

9. A: _____ the letter carrier _____ yet?
                                   (come)

    B: Yes, he has. About an hour ago. You got two letters.

10. A: Would you like some coffee?

    B: No, thanks. I _____ three cups already.
                   (have)

II. *Complete the conversations with* **since** *or* **for.**

1. A: What happened? I've been waiting for you _____since_____ 7:00.

    B: My train broke down. I sat in the tunnel for an hour.

2. A: How long have you lived in San Francisco?

    B: _____ I was born. How about you?

    A: I've only been here _____ a few months.

3. A: When did you and Alan meet?

    B: I've known Alan _____ ages. We went to elementary school together.

4. A: Has Greg worked at Cafe Fidelio for a long time?

    B: Not too long. He's only been there _____ 1998.

5. A: Why didn't you answer the door? I've been standing here ringing the doorbell

    _____ five minutes.

    B: I didn't hear you. I was taking a shower.

6. A: How long have you had trouble sleeping, Mr. Yang?

    B: _____ March. It started when I moved.

7. A: Celia has been studying English _____ she was ten.

    B: That's why she speaks so well.

8. A: Did you know that Gary plans to change jobs?

    B: He's been saying that _____ the past two years. He never does anything

    about it.

III. *Each sentence has four underlined words or phrases. The four underlined parts of the sentences are marked A, B, C, or D. Circle the letter of the one underlined word or phrase that is NOT CORRECT.*

1. I've wanted to visit Hawaii since years, but I haven't been there yet.   A (B) C A
     A   B   C   D

2. We went there last year after we have visited Japan.   A B C D
         A   B   C   D

3. Have you been living in California since a long time?   A B C D
     A   B   C   D

4. I lived here since I got married in 1998.   A B C D
     A   B   C   D

5. We've been wait for Ju-yen for an hour, but she hasn't arrived yet.   A B C D
      A   B   C   D

6. Todd <u>is</u> excited right now <u>because</u> he's <u>lately</u> <u>won</u> an Emmy.　　　　　A　B　**C** D
   　　A　　　　　　　　　　B　　　　C　　D

7. <u>It's</u> only 9:00, and <u>she already</u> <u>had</u> four cups of tea <u>this</u> morning.　　A　B　**C** D
   　A　　　　　　　B　　　C　　　　　　　　D

8. I<u>'m watching</u> television <u>for</u> the last three <u>hours</u> and now I <u>feel</u> worried　　A　B　**C** D
   　　A　　　　　　　B　　　　　　　C　　　　　　D
   about that test tomorrow.

9. Paz <u>been working</u> <u>for</u> Intellect <u>since</u> he <u>moved</u> to Silicon Valley.　　　A　B　**C** D
   　　　A　　　　B　　　　　　C　　　D

10. <u>Has he moved</u> here a long time <u>ago</u>, or <u>has</u> he just <u>arrived</u>?　　　　A　B　**C** D
    　A　　　　　　　　　　　　B　　C　　　　D

IV. *Circle the letter of the correct answer to complete each sentence.*

1. _____ you ever appeared on a game show, Mr. Smith?　　A　B　Ⓒ　D
   (A) Did　　　　　　　　　　(C) Have
   (B) Has　　　　　　　　　　(D) Was

2. No, but I've _____ wanted to.　　　　　　　　　　　　A　B　C　D
   (A) ever　　　　　　　　　　(C) don't
   (B) yet　　　　　　　　　　 (D) always

3. Why _____ you decide to try out for Risk?　　　　　　A　B　C　D
   (A) did　　　　　　　　　　 (C) have
   (B) were　　　　　　　　　　(D) are

4. My wife _____ your show for years now.　　　　　　　A　B　C　D
   (A) watches　　　　　　　　(C) was watching
   (B) is watching　　　　　　 (D) has been watching

5. She has always _____ I should apply as a contestant.　　A　B　C　D
   (A) saying　　　　　　　　　(C) said
   (B) says　　　　　　　　　　(D) say

6. You're a librarian. How long _____ that kind of work?　A　B　C　D
   (A) did you do　　　　　　　(C) do you do
   (B) have you done　　　　　 (D) were you doing

7. I've been a reference librarian since _____.　　　　　A　B　C　D
   (A) a long time　　　　　　　(C) 1990
   (B) three years　　　　　　　(D) I've graduated from
   　　　　　　　　　　　　　　　　　library school

8. Have you been interested in game shows since you _____　A　B　C　D
   a librarian?
   (A) became　　　　　　　　　(C) become
   (B) have become　　　　　　 (D) have been becoming

(continued on next page)

9. I've only _____ them for about a year.   **A B C D**
    (A) watching   (C) been watching
    (B) watch   (D) watches

10. Have you been studying the rules for the show _____
    we called?   **A B C D**
    (A) for   (C) since
    (B) when   (D) as soon as

11. I _____ them for weeks, but I still don't understand them.   **A B C D**
    (A) read   (C) was reading
    (B) reading   (D) 've been reading

V. *Complete each conversation with the correct form of the verb in parentheses. Choose between affirmative and negative forms.*

  1. (see)

    A: _____Have_____ you _____seen_____ *Triassic Park* yet?
                              a.

    B: Yes, I have. I _____ it last night. Why?
                      b.

    A: I'm seeing it on Friday. Is it good?

  2. (drink)

    A: Who _____ all the soda?
              a.

    B: Not me. I _____ any soda at all since last week. I _____ water
                  b.   c.

    all week. It's much healthier.

  3. (write)

    A: Susan Jackson _____ a lot of books lately.
                        a.

    B: _____ she _____ *Wildest Dreams*?
                           b.

    A: Yes, she did. She _____ that one about five years ago.
                         c.

  4. (cook)

    A: You _____ for hours. When are we eating dinner?
              a.

    B: I just finished. I _____ something special for you. It's called "ants on a tree."
                      b.

    A: Gross!

    B: Actually, I _____ it for you many times before. It's just meatballs with rice.
                  c.

5. (have)

A: I _____ a lot of trouble with my new car lately.
a.

B: Really? You _____ it very long!
b.

A: I know. I _____ it for only a year. I _____ my old car for ten
c. d.

years before I sold it. I _____ any trouble with it at all!
e.

6. (look)

A: Linda _____ really discouraged yesterday afternoon.
a.

B: I know. She _____ for a new apartment and hasn't found anything yet.
b.

A: There's an apartment available on the fourth floor in our building. _____

she _____ at it?
c.

B: She _____ at it last week, but she didn't rent it because it's too small.
d.

VI. *Find and correct the mistake in each sentence.*

       have
1. I ~~am~~ applied for the position of junior accountant in my department.

2. I have been working as a bookkeeper in this company since four years.

3. I have did a good job.

4. I have already been getting a promotion.

5. I has gained a lot of experience in retail sales.

6. In addition, I have took several accounting courses.

7. Since February my boss liked my work a lot.

8. She has gave me more and more responsibility.

9. I have already show my accounting skills.

10. This has been being a very good experience for me.

▶ *To check your answers, go to the Answer Key on page 224.*

FROM GRAMMAR TO WRITING THE TOPIC SENTENCE AND PARAGRAPH UNITY

A paragraph is a group of sentences about one main idea. Writers often state the main idea in one sentence, called the topic sentence. For beginning writers, it is a good practice to put the topic sentence near the beginning of the paragraph.

 Read this personal statement for a job application. Cross out any sentences that do not belong in the paragraph.

While I was in high school, I worked as a server at Darby's during the summer and on weekends. ~~Summers here are very hot and humid.~~ I worked with many different kinds of customers, and I learned to be polite even with difficult people. They serve excellent food at Darby's. I received a promotion after one year. Since high school, I have been working for Steak Hut as the night manager. I have developed management skills because I supervise six employees. One of them is a good friend of mine. I have also learned to order supplies and to plan menus. Sometimes I am very tired after a night's work.

Now choose one of the sentences below as the topic sentence, and write it on the rules above the text.

- I feel that a high school education is necessary for anyone looking for a job.
- My restaurant experience has prepared me for a position with your company.
- Eating at both Darby's and Steak Hut in Greenville is very enjoyable.
- I prefer planning menus to any other task in the restaurant business.

You can use a tree diagram to develop and organize your ideas.
Complete the tree diagram for the paragraph in Exercise 1.

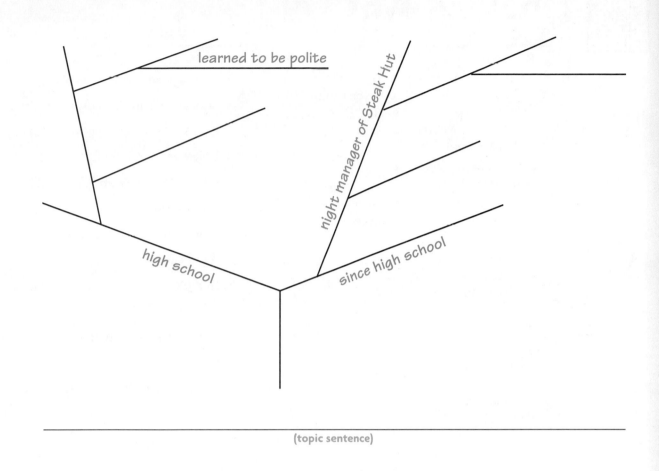

(topic sentence)

 Before you write . . .

- On a separate piece of paper, make a tree diagram for your accomplishments. Do not include a topic sentence.

- Work with a small group. Look at each other's diagrams and develop a topic sentence for each one.

- Ask and answer questions to develop more information about your accomplishments.

4 *On a separate piece of paper, write a personal statement about your accomplishments. Use your tree diagram as an outline.*

PART IV

REVIEW OR SELFTEST
ANSWER KEY

I. (Unit 16)

2. have . . . been
3. has . . . fallen
4. 've* . . . paid
5. Have . . . written
6. hasn't read
7. 've won
8. haven't told
9. Has . . . come
10. 've had

II. (Unit 16)

2. Since, for
3. for
4. since
5. for
6. Since
7. since
8. for

III. (Units 17 and 18)

2. C
3. D
4. A
5. B
6. C
7. B
8. A
9. A
10. A

IV. (Unit 21)

2. D
3. A
4. D
5. C
6. B
7. C
8. A
9. C
10. C
11. D

V. (Units 16–21)

1. **b.** saw
2. **a.** drank OR drunk
   b. haven't drunk
   c. 've been drinking
3. **a.** has written
   b. Did . . . write
   c. wrote
4. **a.** 've been cooking
   b. cooked
   c. 've cooked
5. **a.** 've had OR 've been having
   b. haven't had
   c. 've had
   d. had
   e. didn't have
6. **a.** looked
   b. 's been looking
   c. Has . . . looked OR Did . . . look
   d. looked

VI. (Units 16–21)

2. I have been working as a
   bookkeeper in this company ~~since~~ *for*
   four years. OR since four years ago.

3. I have ~~did~~ *done* a good job.

4. I have already ~~been getting~~ *gotten* a
   promotion.

5. I ~~has~~ *have* gained a lot of experience in
   retail sales.

6. In addition, I have ~~took~~ *taken* several
   accounting courses.

7. Since February my boss ~~like~~ *has liked* my
   work a lot.

8. She has ~~gave~~ *given* me more and more
   responsibility.

9. I have already ~~show~~ *shown* my
   accounting skills.

10. This has been ~~being~~ a very good
    experience for me.

*Where a contracted form is given, the long
form is also correct.

224

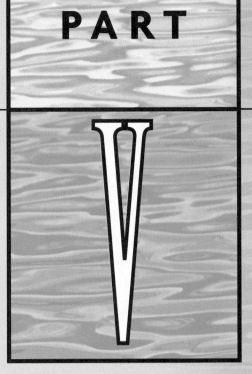

PART V

ADJECTIVES AND ADVERBS:
REVIEW AND EXPANSION

ADJECTIVES AND ADVERBS

GRAMMAR **IN CONTEXT**

BEFORE YOU READ What do you think this conversation is about? Look at the circled ad. What information does it give? What information is missing?

A young couple is looking at an apartment for rent. Read this transcript of their conversation with the apartment owner.

OWNER: As you can see, this is a **nice, quiet** building. We've never had any trouble with **noisy** neighbors. You're both **serious** students, aren't you?

MAGGIE: Oh, yes. **Very serious.**

LUIS: Uhm, isn't this apartment a **little small** for two people? I mean, there's **hardly enough** room for the three of us to stand here.

OWNER: **Small?** It's not **small**! It's **warm** and **cozy**, just as the ad says.

LUIS: Now that you mention it—it *is* **warm**. Is there something **wrong** with the heater?

OWNER: Not at all. The heater works **perfectly well**. But if it's **too warm** for you, just open the windows.

MAGGIE: Luis, don't be **silly**. This is a **lovely** apartment. It looks **great**. It's **perfect** for us.

OWNER: Yes. It's **absolutely perfect**. I know I'll rent this apartment **very quickly**. Take it before it's **too late**. You won't be **disappointed**.

LUIS: Not **so fast**. How much is the rent? The ad doesn't say.

OWNER: Oh. Well, that's a **very interesting** question. Please sit down.

EAST SIDE 2 BR w/priv grdn, $578/mo. Ideal for shares, immediate occupancy 555-8453

EAST SIDE Studio w/separate kitchen in excellent building. $250 per month 555-2335

SUNNYSIDE Cozy 1BR on quiet street. Perfect for students. Reasonable rent. Call owner 555-3428

EAST SIDE Attractive elevator building, laundry rooms, 1 BR $454, Studios $265, utilities included 555-5436

SUNNYSIDE Beautiful, bright 1 BR + study, near trains, shopping, $362/mo + utilities 555-5460

SUNNYSIDE 3 BR, very modern, near transp/shopping $775/mo + util/heat. NO PETS. Call owner 555-7769

WEST SIDE Large 1 BR + den, in owner occupied house. $432/mo. Utilities included. No pets. 555-3209

GRAMMAR **PRESENTATION**
ADJECTIVES AND ADVERBS

ADJECTIVES	ADVERBS
They are **quiet** students.	They work **quietly**.
It's a **fast** elevator.	It moves **very fast**.
The building looks **nice**.	She described it **nicely**.
It's absolutely **perfect**.	It's **absolutely** perfect.

PARTICIPIAL ADJECTIVES	
-ING ADJECTIVE	*-ED* ADJECTIVE
The apartment in Sunnyside is **interesting**. It's an **interesting** one-bedroom apartment.	One couple is **interested** in the apartment. The **interested** couple hasn't called back.

NOTES

1. Use **adjectives** when you are describing or giving more information about nouns (people, places, or things).

Adjectives usually come immediately before the noun they describe.

Adjectives can also come after the verb when it is a non-action (stative) verb such as *be, look, seem, appear, smell,* or *taste.*

(See Appendix 2, page A-2, for a list of non-action verbs.)

2. Use **adverbs** when you are giving more information about verbs, adjectives, or other adverbs.

EXAMPLES

• It's a *quiet* **building**.
  (Quiet *tells you more about the building.*)
  <small>adjective   noun</small>

• This is a *small* **house**.
  <small>adjective   noun</small>

• This apartment **is** *small*.
  <small>verb adjective</small>

• This house **looks** *small*.
  <small>verb   adjective</small>

• They **furnished** it *nicely*.
  <small>verb   adverb</small>

• It's an *extremely* nice house.
  <small>adverb   adjective</small>

• They got it *very* **quickly**.
  <small>adverb   adverb</small>

(continued on next page)

3. Use **adverbs of manner** when you are <u>describing</u> or giving more information about <u>action verbs</u>. These adverbs often answer *"How?"* questions.

▶ **BE CAREFUL!** Do not put an adverb of manner between the verb and the direct object.

(See Grammar Notes 6 and 7 for more information on adverbs of manner.)

- She **described** the apartment *perfectly*.
  (Perfectly *tells you how she* described *the apartment.*)

- He**'ll rent** this apartment *quickly*.
  NOT ~~He'll rent quickly this apartment.~~

---

4. Also use **adverbs** when <u>describing</u> or giving more information about <u>adjectives</u> or other <u>adverbs</u>.

These adverbs usually come immediately <u>before the adjective or adverb</u> they describe.

-      adverb   adjective
  It's ***absolutely* perfect**.
  (Absolutely *tells you just how* perfect *the apartment really is.*)

-      adverb   adverb
  It will rent ***very* quickly**.
  (Very *tells you how* quickly *the apartment will rent.*)

---

5. Use **adverbs of frequency** to express <u>how often</u> something happens.

(See Unit 1, page 4, for a discussion of adverbs of frequency.)

- She ***usually* rents** to students.

---

6. Adverbs of manner are often formed by <u>adding **-ly** to adjectives</u>.

(See Appendix 19 on page A-7 for spelling rules for forming -ly adverbs.)

▶ **BE CAREFUL!** <u>Some adjectives also end in *-ly*</u>—for example, *silly, friendly, lovely,* and *lonely.*

-               adjective
  We need a **quick** decision.
-               adverb
  You should decide ***quickly***.
  (*quickly = quick + ly*)

-        adjective
  It's a **lovely** apartment.

7. Some **adverbs of manner** have <u>two forms</u>: one with -*ly* and one without -*ly*.

> **slowly** OR **slow**
> **quickly** OR **quick**
> **loudly** OR **loud**
> **clearly** OR **clear**

- Don't speak so **loudly**; the neighbors will hear.

  OR

- Don't speak so **loud**, the neighbors will hear.

USAGE NOTE: The form without -*ly* is often used in informal speech.

---

8. Some **common adverbs** <u>do not end in -*ly*</u>—for example, the adverb form of *good* is *well*.

- She's a **good** manager. She manages the building **well**.

A few **adjectives** and **adverbs** have the <u>same form</u>—for example, *early, fast, wrong, late,* and *hard*.

ADJECTIVE
- The visitor was **late**.
- She is a **hard** worker.

ADVERB
- He woke up ***late***.
- She works ***hard***.

▶ **BE CAREFUL!** Adding -*ly* to the adjectives *late* and *hard* <u>changes the meaning</u> of these words.

Lately is not the adverb form of *late*. *Lately* means "recently."

Hardly is not the adverb form of *hard*. *Hardly* means "almost not."

- We haven't seen any nice apartments ***lately***. We are getting discouraged.
- There's ***hardly*** enough room for a bed. The bed takes up most of the room.

---

9. Participial adjectives are adjectives that end with ***-ing*** and ***-ed***. The two forms have different meanings.

- This fly is **disgusting**. (*Causes feelings of disgust.*)
- The woman looks **disgusted**. (*Feels disgust.*)

- Your story is **amazing**. (*Causes amazement.*)
- I'm **amazed** at your story. (*Feel amazement.*)

(See Appendix 6, page A-4, for a list of participial adjectives.)

FOCUSED PRACTICE

1 DISCOVER THE GRAMMAR

Read this notice which the owner of an apartment for rent put on a bulletin board at the local university. Underline the adjectives and circle the adverbs. Then draw an arrow from the adjective or adverb to the word it is describing.

APT. FOR RENT

Students! Are you looking for a special place to live? Come to 140 Grant Street, Apt. 4B. This apartment is absolutely perfect for two serious students who are looking for a quiet neighborhood, just 15 minutes from campus. This lovely apartment is in a new building. It is a short walk to the bus stop. The express bus goes directly into town. At night the bus hardly makes any stops at all. You can walk peacefully through the wonderful parks on your way home. The rent is very affordable. Call for an appointment: 555-5050. Don't wait! This apartment will rent fast.

2 DID YOU LIKE IT?   Grammar Notes 1–4, 6–9

Many different people went to see the apartment described in Exercise 1. Complete their comments about the apartment. Use the correct form of the words in parentheses.

1. I am very interested. I think the apartment is _____extremely nice_____.
                                                        (extreme / nice)

2. I was expecting much bigger rooms. I was _____.
                                              (terrible / disappointed)

3. I thought it would be hard to find the apartment, but it wasn't. It was

_____.
   (surprising / easy)

4. I think it's a great place—and the price is very reasonable. I am sure it will rent

_____.
   (incredible / fast)

5. I thought the notice said it was a quiet place. I heard the neighbors

_____.
   (very / clear)

6. I heard them, too. I thought their voices were _____.
                                                     (unusual / loud)

3 WRITING HOME   Grammar Notes 1–4, 6 and 8

Complete Maggie's letter. Choose the correct word in parentheses.

Dear Mom and Dad,

    Life in New York is very _____exciting_____. Luis and
               1. (exciting / excitingly)

I weren't sure we'd like living in a _____ city, but
                             2. (large / largely)

we do. In fact, we love it! You'd be surprised to see us. We walk

_____ down the busy streets, and the noise doesn't
   3. (happy / happily)

bother us at all.

    There's always something to do. Yesterday, when we left class, we

saw a street musician. He played the violin so _____
                          4. (beautiful / beautifully)

we couldn't believe he was on the street and not in a big concert hall.

    We like our new apartment. The enclosed photograph shows the

outside of the building. It looks very _____, doesn't it?
                 5. (nice / nicely)

It's so _____ we can _____ believe we're
    6. (quiet / quietly)   7. (hard / hardly)

in New York. Our next door neighbor is very _____.
                         8. (nice / nicely)

She seemed _____ at first, but now we're
     9. (shy / shyly)

_____ friends.
  10. (good / well)

    We hope you're both well. Please give our love to everyone and

write back soon!

    Love,

    Maggie

④ STUDENT EVALUATION

Read this evaluation Luis wrote about his teacher. Fill in the blanks. Use either the adjective or adverb form of the word in parentheses.

English 206   **EVALUATION**

Instructions: Please write your _____*general*_____ impression of your teacher this
                 1. (general)
year. All information will be _____ _____.
             2. (strict)   3. (confidential)

This English teacher was _____. He was always ready with an
                 4. (exceptional)

_____ lesson. Obviously, he prepared _____ for each class. His
   5. (interesting)   6. (careful)

class was not _____, but the time always passed _____ because
         7. (easy)   8. (quick)

it was so _____. In conclusion, I recommend this teacher _____.
     9. (interesting)   10. (high)

I did very _____ in his class, and I'm sure other students will, too.
       11. (good)

---

⑤ IT'S HARD TO TELL WITH ALICE

Maggie and Luis are talking about Maggie's sister. Read their conversation. Circle the correct adjectives to complete the sentences.

MAGGIE: What's the matter with Alice?

LUIS: Who knows? She's always (annoyed) / annoying about something.
                              1.

MAGGIE: I know, but this time I'm really puzzled / puzzling.
                                2.

LUIS: Really? Why is this time so puzzled / puzzling?
                            3.

MAGGIE: Oh, I thought she was happy. She met an interested / interesting man last week.
                                                4.

LUIS: That's nice. Was she interested / interesting in him?
                            5.

MAGGIE: I thought she was. She said they saw a fascinated / fascinating movie together.
                                               6.

                So I thought . . .

LUIS: Maybe she was fascinated / fascinating by the movie, but it sounds to me like she
                                7.

                might be disappointed / disappointing with the guy.
                           8.

MAGGIE: Maybe you're right. It's hard to tell with Alice. Her moods are always very

                surprised / surprising.
                9.

COMMUNICATION PRACTICE

6 LISTENING

A couple is discussing newspaper apartment ads. Read the ads. Then, listen to the conversation. Listen again, and number the ads from 1 to 4 to match the order in which the couple discusses them.

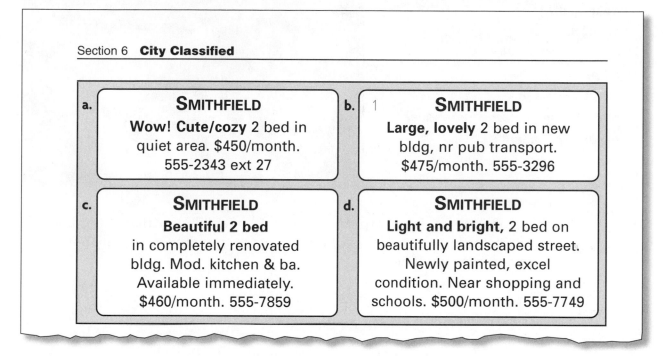

Section 6 **City Classified**

a.
SMITHFIELD
Wow! Cute/cozy 2 bed in quiet area. $450/month. 555-2343 ext 27

b. 1
SMITHFIELD
Large, lovely 2 bed in new bldg, nr pub transport. $475/month. 555-3296

c.
SMITHFIELD
Beautiful 2 bed in completely renovated bldg. Mod. kitchen & ba. Available immediately. $460/month. 555-7859

d.
SMITHFIELD
Light and bright, 2 bed on beautifully landscaped street. Newly painted, excel condition. Near shopping and schools. $500/month. 555-7749

7 APARTMENT ADS

Bring in four apartment ads from a newspaper, or choose four from page 226. Work with a partner. Talk about the ads.

EXAMPLE:

A: Here's an ad for a cozy one-bedroom apartment on a quiet street.

B: Cozy? That probably means small.

8 WHERE DO YOU LIVE?

Work in small groups. Describe where you live. Tell each other how you found the place. Explain how you first felt about it (pleased, disappointed, etc.). Describe what it looks like. Tell how you decorated it. What is special about your place?

EXAMPLE:

I found my apartment last summer when I was walking down the street. I saw an "Apartment for Rent" sign. I knocked on the door.

At first, I was disappointed. It's a small apartment . . .

9 HOME SWEET HOME

Work with a partner. There are many different types of housing. Describe the different types listed below. How are they similar? How are they different? Use your dictionaries to help you. Do these types of housing exist in other places you have lived?

> apartment
> boarding house
> dorm (dormitory)
> mansion
> private home
> rented room in someone's house
> studio apartment
> trailer

EXAMPLE:

A mansion is a very large, expensive house. It's much bigger than an ordinary private home. There are a lot of old mansions in my country. Usually only very wealthy people own them.

10 YOUR IDEAL ROOMMATE

Work in small groups. Take turns describing your ideal roommate. Describe the person and his or her activities. Here are some words you might want to use:

Adjectives			Adverbs		
cheerful	helpful	neat	early	late	politely
considerate	loud	reliable	easily	loudly	quietly
gloomy	messy	serious	happily	noisily	seriously

EXAMPLE:

My ideal roommate is not **messy** and doesn't get up too **early**.

11 WRITING

Read the student's evaluation of his teacher in Exercise 4 again. Now write your own evaluation of your teacher, your class, or this grammar book. Use as many adjectives and adverbs as you can. Share your evaluation with a classmate. Do you agree or disagree with your classmate's evaluation?

EXAMPLE:

My terrific teacher explains new grammar very clearly.
She tries extremely hard and seems quite happy with her work.

ADJECTIVES:
COMPARATIVES AND EQUATIVES

GRAMMAR IN CONTEXT

BEFORE YOU READ What information does the box at the end of the restaurant review give you? Talk about the dessert in the photograph.

Read this restaurant review from a neighborhood newspaper.

DINING OUT

Bigger and (Often) Better

By Dana Lee

Almond cake à la mode

The COUNTRY INN has just reopened under new management. The new owners have done a wonderful job redecorating the inn. The dining room looks **bigger, brighter,** and **prettier than** the old one. The food is just **as good as** before, but, unfortunately,

The Country Inn
★★★
(very good)
27 Waterside Place
555-3465
Open 11:00 A.M.–11:00 P.M.
Tuesday–Sunday
Reservations not accepted
Average cost of dinner:
$12–$23

the menu is **less varied** and **more expensive.** Good choices are the roast chicken with mashed potatoes, the lobster, and the homemade spaghetti with fresh tomatoes and olives. Be sure to leave room for the desserts. The selection keeps getting **better and better.** The homemade almond cake is **as good as**

you can get, and the chocolate soufflé is **as light as** air.

The staff is friendly but not able to handle large numbers of people—**the more crowded** the restaurant, **the slower** the service. At dinner time the lines outside this popular restaurant are getting **longer and longer.** Try lunchtime for a **quieter, more relaxed** meal.

GRAMMAR **PRESENTATION**
ADJECTIVES: COMPARATIVES AND EQUATIVES

COMPARATIVES

	COMPARATIVE ADJECTIVE FORM		*THAN*	
The new restaurant is	brighter friendlier better		than	the old one.
	more less	comfortable beautiful		

COMPARATIVES

	COMPARATIVE ADJECTIVE FORM	*AND*	COMPARATIVE ADJECTIVE FORM	
The food is getting	better	and	better.	
	worse		worse.	
	more		more	delicious.*
	less		less	interesting.*

* Note that the adjective is used only with the second *more/less*.

COMPARATIVES

THE	COMPARATIVE ADJECTIVE FORM		*THE*	COMPARATIVE ADJECTIVE FORM	
The	more crowded	the restaurant,	the	slower	the service.

EQUATIVES

	(NOT) AS	ADJECTIVE	AS	
The new restaurant is	(not) as	bright friendly good comfortable beautiful	as	the old one.

NOTES	EXAMPLES
1. Use the **comparative** form of adjectives to focus on a <u>difference</u> between people, places, and things.	• The new room is **bigger than** the old room. • The new waiters are **more experienced than** the old waiters.

2. There is more than one way to **form the comparative of adjectives**.

a. For one-syllable adjectives and two-syllable adjectives ending in *-y*, use **adjective + -er**.

▶ **BE CAREFUL!** There are often <u>spelling changes</u> when you add *-er*.
(See Appendix 18, page A-7, for spelling rules for the comparative form of adjectives.)

▶ **BE CAREFUL!** Some adjectives have <u>irregular comparative</u> forms.
(See Appendix 7, page A-4, for a list of irregular adjectives.)

b. For most other adjectives of two or more syllables, use:

more + **adjective**

AND

less + **adjective**

c. For some adjectives, use either *-er* or *more / less*.
(See Appendix 8, page A-4, for a list of adjectives that use both forms of the comparative.)

ADJECTIVE	COMPARATIVE
bright	**brighter**
friendly	**friendlier**
nice	**nicer**
big	**bigger**
pretty	**prettier**
good	**better**
bad	**worse**
comfortable	**more comfortable** **less comfortable**
expensive	**more expensive** **less expensive**

• The Inn is **pleasanter** than Joe's.
• The Inn is **more pleasant** than Joe's.
• Joe's is **less pleasant** than the Inn.

| **3.** Use the comparative **with *than*** when you mention the things you are comparing.

Use the comparative **without *than*** when it is clear from the context which things you are comparing. | • The apple pie is **better *than*** the cake.

• The new desserts are **better**.
(The new desserts are better than the old desserts.) |

(continued on next page)

4. To talk about change—<u>an increase or a decrease</u>—use:

comparative adjective	+ *and* +	comparative adjective
	OR	
more *less*	+ *and* +	comparative adjective

- It's getting **harder and harder** to find an inexpensive restaurant.

- It's becoming **more and more difficult**.
  (Both sentences mean the difficulty is increasing.)
- I'm **less and less interested** in cooking.

---

5. To show <u>cause-and-effect</u>, use:

the + comparative adjective + *the* + comparative adjective

- **The more crowded** the restaurant, **the slower** the service.
  (When the restaurant gets more crowded, the service gets slower.)

---

6. You can also use the **equative** (***as* + adjective + *as***) to compare people, places, and things. Use the equative to express both <u>similarities and differences</u>.

Use ***as* + adjective + *as*** to compare people, places, or things that are <u>equal</u> in some way. Use ***just*** to emphasize the equality.

Use ***not as* + adjective + *as*** to compare people, places, and things that are <u>different</u> in some way.

REMEMBER: It is not always necessary to mention both parts of the comparison. Sometimes the meaning is clear from the context.

- The waiter is **as polite as** the waitress, but he's **not as fast as** she is.
  (The waiter and waitress are equally polite, but they are not equally fast.)

- The new menu is ***just* as good as** the old menu.
  (The new menu and the old menu are equally good.)

- The new menu is**n't as expensive as** the old menu.
  (The new and old menus have different prices. The items on the new menu cost less.)

- I liked the old menu. The new one is**n't as varied**.
  (The new menu isn't as varied as the old menu.)

---

7. Comparatives and **equatives** often <u>express the same meaning</u> in different ways.

USAGE NOTE: With <u>one-syllable adjectives</u>, we usually use ***not as . . . as***. We do not use *less . . . than*.

- The Inn is **more expensive than** Joe's.
- Joe's is**n't as expensive as** the Inn.
- Joe's is **less expensive than** the Inn.

- Our table is**n't as big as** theirs.
  NOT ~~Our table is less big than theirs.~~

FOCUSED PRACTICE

1 DISCOVER THE GRAMMAR

Consumers are testing two brands of rice pudding. Look at the information about each brand. Then decide if each statement is **True (T)** *or* **False (F).**

PER SERVING	CLASSIC	LITE
Weight	45 grams	30 grams
Calories	220	150
Cost	$0.79	$1.25
Cooking time*	4 minutes	12 minutes

*Pudding becomes thicker with longer cooking time.

TASTE AND TEXTURE 1 = less 5 = more	CLASSIC	LITE
Sweet	3	5
Creamy	4	2
Sticky	1	3
Thick	4	1
Chewy	2	2

___T___ **1.** A serving of Classic is heavier than a serving of Lite.

_____ **2.** Lite is more fattening than Classic.

_____ **3.** Classic is less expensive.

_____ **4.** The cooking time for Lite is shorter.

_____ **5.** The longer the cooking time, the thicker the pudding.

_____ **6.** Classic is sweeter than Lite.

_____ **7.** Lite is creamier.

_____ **8.** Classic is not as sticky as Lite.

_____ **9.** Lite is thicker.

_____ **10.** Classic is as chewy as Lite.

2 NOT ALL RICE IS EQUAL   Grammar Note 6

Look at this consumer magazine chart comparing three brands of rice. Complete the sentences. Use **as . . . as** *or* **not as . . . as** *and the correct form of the words in parentheses.*

RICE		Better ● ◒ ○ Worse	
Brand	**Price** (per serving)	*Taste*	*Smell*
X	7¢	◒	●
Y	3¢	◒	◒
Z	3¢	○	◒

1. Brand Z ___is as expensive as___ Brand Y.
  (be / expensive)

2. Brand Y _____ Brand X.
  (be / expensive)

3. Brand X _____ Brand Y.
  (taste / good)

4. Brand Z _____ Brand Y.
  (taste / good)

5. Brand Y _____ Brand X.
  (smell / nice)

6. Brand Y _____ Brand Z.
  (smell / good)

③ MENU

Look at the menu. Then complete the comparisons. Use **-er, more, less** *and* **than** *in your comparisons.*

The Golden Palace
Take Out Menu

Open 7 days a week
Mon–Thurs: 11:00 A.M.–10:00 P.M.
Fri–Sat: 11:00 A.M.–11:00 P.M.
Sunday: 12:00 noon–10:00 P.M.

2465 Mineral Springs Rd.
Tel.: (401) 555-4923

Place your order by phone and it will be ready when you arrive.

*Broccoli with Garlic Sauce	$6.25
Beef with Broccoli	$7.75
*Beef with Dried Red Pepper	$7.75
Chicken with Broccoli	$7.25
*Chicken with Orange Sauce	$7.25
Sweet and Sour Shrimp	$8.25
Pork with Scallions	$6.25
♥Steamed Mixed Vegetables	$5.50
♥Steamed Scallops with Broccoli	$7.75

*Hot and Spicy   ♥No sugar, salt, or oil

---

1. The sweet and sour shrimp is __more expensive than__ the steamed scallops with broccoli.
   (expensive)

2. The beef with dried red pepper is _____ the beef with broccoli.
   (hot)

3. The sweet and sour shrimp is _____ the pork with scallions.
   (expensive)

4. The chicken with orange sauce is _____ the steamed scallops with broccoli.
   (spicy)

5. The steamed mixed vegetables are _____ the pork with scallions.
   (salty)

6. The chicken with broccoli is _____ the chicken with orange sauce.
   (mild)

7. The steamed mixed vegetables are _____ the beef with dried red pepper.
   (healthy)

8. The broccoli with garlic sauce is _____ chicken with broccoli.
   (cheap)

9. The pork with scallions is _____ the steamed mixed vegetables.
   (oily)

10. The scallop dish is _____ the shrimp dish.
    (sweet)

11. The restaurant's business hours on Sunday are _____ they are on Saturday.
    (short)

④ EDITING

Read this student's essay. Find and correct nine mistakes in the use of comparisons. The first mistake is already corrected.

When I was a teenager in the Philippines, I was an expert on snacks and fast foods. I was growing fast, so the more I ate, the ~~hungry~~ *hungrier* I felt. The street vendors in our town had the better snacks than anyone else. In the morning, I used to buy rice muffins on the way to school. They are much sweeter that American muffins. After school, I ate fish balls on a stick or *adidas* (chicken feet). Snacks on a stick are small than American hot dogs and burgers, but they are much varied. My friend thought *banana-cue* (banana on a stick) was really great. However, they weren't as sweet from *kamote-cue* (fried sweet potatoes and brown sugar), my favorite snack.

When I came to the United States, I didn't like American fast food at first. To me, it was interesting than my native food and less tastier too. Now I'm getting used to it, and it seems deliciouser and deliciouser. Does anyone want to go out for a pizza?

⑤ THE MORE THE MERRIER   Grammar Note 5

Complete these comments about a restaurant. Use the comparative forms of the words in parentheses to show cause and effect.

1. A: I can't believe the size of this menu. It's going to take me forever to make up my mind.

    B: I know what you mean. ___The longer___ the menu,
                   (long)
    ___the more difficult___ the choice.
         (difficult)

2. A: People say the food here is getting better and better.

    B: And _____ the food, _____ the prices.
               (good)   (high)

3. A: The cigarette smoke in here is really bothering me.

    B: Me, too. And I have a cold. Our table is too close to the smoking section.
    _____ the room, _____ my cough gets.
        (smoky)   (bad)

4. A: It's pretty loud in here. I can hardly hear myself think.

    B: That can happen when a restaurant becomes popular. _____
                                     (crowded)
    the restaurant, _____ the room.
                (noisy)

(continued on next page)

5. **A:** Why do they have to put so much salt in the soup?

   B: Well, _____ the food, _____ it tastes.
   (salty)   (good)

   A: Oh, I don't agree. Besides, you can always add your own salt.

6. **A:** They certainly give you a lot of food. I can't eat another bite.

   B: _____ the portions, _____ it is to finish.
   (big)   (hard)

6 MORE AND MORE   Grammar Note 4

Look at these statistics for food in the United States. Read the statements. Write
That's right *or* **That's wrong.** *Then write a true statement. Use* **get,** *plus the words in parentheses and the comparative form, to talk about change.*

FOOD IN THE UNITED STATES	1992	1993	1994	1995
1. Cost of food per year (family of three)	$4,273	$4,399	$4,411	$4,691
2. Cost of a slice of pizza	$1.50	$1.55	$1.60	$1.65
3. Sales (in millions of $) of frozen pizza	$1,289	$1,360	$1,529	$1,547
4. Consumption* of cheese	26.0 lbs.	26.3 lbs.	26.8 lbs.	27.3 lbs.
5. Consumption of ice cream	16.3 lbs.	16.1 lbs.	16.1 lbs.	15.7 lbs.
6. Consumption of candy	21.5 lbs.	21.9 lbs.	22.5 lbs.	23.4 lbs.

*Consumption numbers = average number of pounds that a person eats (consumes) each year

1. The cost of food is rising.

   That's right. It's getting higher and higher.
   (high)

2. The cost of a slice of pizza is decreasing.

   _____
   (expensive)

3. The frozen pizza industry is growing.

   _____
   (big)

4. The consumption of cheese is increasing.

   _____
   (high)

5. The consumption of ice cream is rising.

   _____
   (low)

6. Candy is increasing in popularity.

   _____
   (popular)

COMMUNICATION PRACTICE

7 LISTENING

A couple is trying to choose between two brands of frozen pizza in the supermarket. Listen to their conversation. Then listen again and check the pizza that is better in each category.

	Di Roma's	Angela's
1. cheap	☑	☐
2. big	☐	☐
3. healthy	☐	☐
4. tasty	☐	☐
5. fresh	☐	☐

8 INFORMATION GAP: THICK AND CHUNKY

Work in pairs (A and B). Student B, look at the Information Gap on p. 246 and follow the instructions there. Student A, look at the chart below comparing two brands of spaghetti sauce. Ask your partner questions to complete the chart. Fill in a circle completely (●) for the brand that has more of a certain quality. Draw a line through the circle (⊖) if the brands are equal. Fill in a circle half-way (◒) for the brand that has less of a certain quality. Answer your partner's questions.

Spaghetti Sauce:

● more   ⊖ equal   ◒ less

Quality	Frank's	Classic's
smooth	●	◒
thick	⊖	⊖
chunky	○	○
flavorful	◒	●
sweet	○	○
salty	●	◒

Quality	Frank's	Classic's
spicy	○	○
garlicky	●	◒
fresh-tasting	○	○
fattening	◒	●
nutritious	○	○
expensive	●	◒

EXAMPLE:

A: Which brand is smoother?

B: Frank's is smoother than Classic's.
Which brand is thicker?

A: Frank's is as thick as Classic's.

When you are finished, compare your charts. Are they the same? Choose a spaghetti sauce to buy. Explain your choice.

9 PIZZA AROUND THE WORLD

Look at some of these favorite international pizza toppings. Discuss them with a partner. Make comparisons using some of the adjectives in the box.

interesting   healthy   filling   spicy   unusual   traditional   delicious   tasty

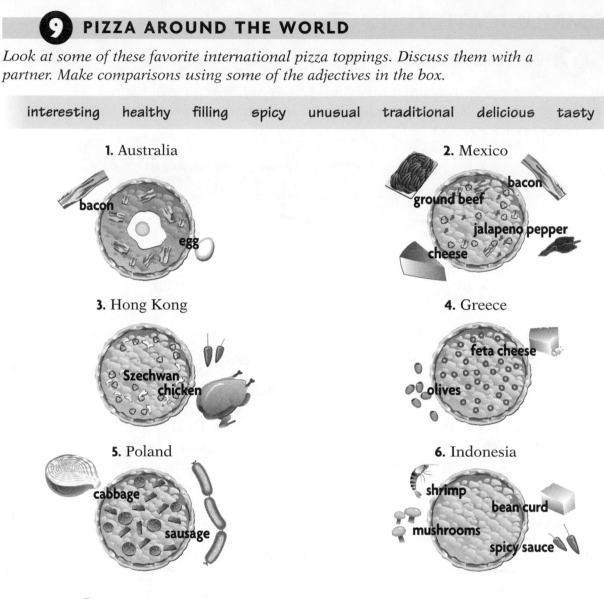

1. Australia — bacon, egg

2. Mexico — ground beef, bacon, jalapeno pepper, cheese

3. Hong Kong — Szechwan chicken

4. Greece — feta cheese, olives

5. Poland — cabbage, sausage

6. Indonesia — shrimp, bean curd, mushrooms, spicy sauce

EXAMPLE:

A: The pizza from Poland seems more filling than the one from Greece.

B: Yes, and it's not as spicy.

10 THINGS CHANGE

Think of how something in your life is changing. Tell a partner. Use the comparative form and **get, become,** *or* **grow**. *Here are some ideas you can talk about. Your:*

English   city or town   job   apartment

EXAMPLE:

I'm getting more and more fluent in English.

11 THE ESL DINER

Work in groups. Design a menu for a restaurant. Use a separate piece of paper.
Decide on dishes for each category and include prices. Give your restaurant a name.

EXAMPLE:

A: We need one more soup. How about chicken noodle?

B: Too boring! Gazpacho is more interesting.

Soups and Starters

_____ . . . . $ _____
_____ . . . . $ _____
_____ . . . . $ _____
_____ . . . . $ _____

Entrees

_____ . . . . $ _____
_____ . . . . $ _____
_____ . . . . $ _____
_____ . . . . $ _____

Salads and Side Dishes

_____ . . . . $ _____
_____ . . . . $ _____
_____ . . . . $ _____
_____ . . . . $ _____

Desserts

_____ . . . . $ _____
_____ . . . . $ _____
_____ . . . . $ _____

Beverages

_____ . . . . . $ _____   _____ . . . . . $ _____
_____ . . . . . $ _____   _____ . . . . . $ _____

With your group, roleplay ordering from your menu.

EXAMPLE:

CUSTOMER: Is the gazpacho as spicy as the hot and sour soup?

SERVER: No, the hot and sour soup is much spicier.

12 WRITING

Write a paragraph comparing your country's food with the food of
another country.

EXAMPLE:

Food in Taiwan is fresher than food in the United States.
Taiwan is a small island and there are a lot of farms. . . .

INFORMATION GAP FOR STUDENT B

Student B, look at the chart below comparing two brands of spaghetti sauce.
Answer your partner's questions. Ask your partner questions to complete the
chart. Fill in a circle completely (●) for the brand that has more of a certain
quality. Draw a line through the circle (⊖) if the brands are equal. Fill in a circle
half-way (◐) for the brand that has less of a certain quality.

Spaghetti Sauce:

● more   ⊖ equal   ◐ less

Quality	Frank's	Classic's
smooth	●	◐
thick	⊖	⊖
chunky	◐	●
flavorful	○	○
sweet	●	◐
salty	○	○

Quality	Frank's	Classic's
spicy	◐	●
garlicky	○	○
fresh-tasting	⊖	⊖
fattening	○	○
nutritious	◐	●
expensive	○	○

EXAMPLE:

A: Which brand is smoother?

B: Frank's is smoother than Classic's.
   Which brand is thicker?

A: Frank's is as thick as Classic's.

When you are finished, compare your charts. Are they the same? Choose a
spaghetti sauce to buy. Explain your choice.

ADJECTIVES: SUPERLATIVES

GRAMMAR **IN CONTEXT**

BEFORE YOU READ   Look at the cards. Which card looks the most romantic? Which one looks the cutest?

Read the following greeting cards.

I think that you're
the best,
And **the nicest**
Grandpa too,
So here's **the biggest**
hug and kiss
Especially for you!

HAPPY BIRTHDAY!

. . . AND SAY,

"THINGS
ARE REALLY
LOOKING
UP!"

FEEL BLUE?
DO WHAT I DO!
CLIMB
THE HIGHEST
MOUNTAIN
FIND **THE**
BRIGHTEST STAR
TAKE **THE DEEPEST**
BREATH

Grandpa,
You're
the Best!

TO DO LIST
Buy card for my
☑ **Best** friend
☑ **Coolest** friend
☑ **Oldest** friend
☑ **Nicest** friend

*So expect a lot of
cards this year!*
Happy Holidays

To the **loveliest**
Most original
Most vibrant
Most exciting
Woman I know...

Who just
happens to be
my wife!

HAPPY
VALENTINE'S
DAY!

GRAMMAR **PRESENTATION**
ADJECTIVES: SUPERLATIVES

	SUPERLATIVES	
	SUPERLATIVE ADJECTIVE FORM	
You are	**the sweetest the funniest the best the most wonderful the least selfish**	person in the world.
That's	**the nicest the loveliest the worst the most amusing the least original**	card I've ever received.

NOTES

EXAMPLES

1. Use the **superlative** form of adjectives to <u>single out one thing</u> from two or more things.

- You are **the nicest** person in the world.
- You are **the most wonderful** friend I've ever had.

2. There is more than one way to **form the superlative of adjectives**.

a. For one-syllable adjectives or two-syllable adjectives ending in -*y*, use: *the* **+ adjective +** *-est*.

ADJECTIVE	SUPERLATIVE
bright	**the brightest**
friendly	**the friendliest**

▶ **BE CAREFUL!** There are often <u>spelling changes</u> when you add *-est*.
(*See Appendix 18, page A-7, for spelling rules for the superlative form of adjectives.*)

nice	**the nicest**
big	**the biggest**
pretty	**the prettiest**

▶ **BE CAREFUL!** Some adjectives have <u>irregular superlative</u> forms.
(*See Appendix 7, page A-4, for a list of irregular adjectives.*)

good	**the best**
bad	**the worst**

ADJECTIVE	SUPERLATIVE
comfortable	**the most comfortable**
	the least comfortable
expensive	**the most expensive**
	the least expensive

b. For most other adjectives of two or more syllables, use:
the most **+ adjective**
OR
the least **+ adjective**

c. For some adjectives, use either *the . . . -est* or *the most / the least*. *(See Appendix 8, page A-4, for a list of more of these adjectives.)*

- My third trip was **the pleasantest**.
- My third trip was **the most pleasant**.
- My first trip was **the least pleasant**.

3. The superlative is often **used with expressions beginning with** *in* **and** *of*, such as *in the world* and *of all*.

- You're **the best** mother *in the world*.
- You're **the most wonderful** brother *in the universe*.
- He is **the smartest** one *of us all*.
- This is **the most practical** gift *of all the gifts* I've received.

4. The superlative is sometimes **followed by a clause**. Often the clause uses the present perfect with *ever*. *(See p. 186 for the present perfect with* ever.*)*

- That's **the nicest** card *I've ever received*.
- You have **the loveliest** smile *I've ever seen*.

FOCUSED PRACTICE

1 DISCOVER THE GRAMMAR

Read this Mother's Day card written by a young child. Underline all the superlative adjectives.

You are <u>the best</u> mother
in the whole wide world.
You are the smartest, the brightest, and
the funniest of all moms I've ever known.
You are the nicest mom I've ever had.
You are the most wonderful and definitely
the least mean.
No mom in the whole wide world is
better than you.
You are the greatest mother of all.
I love you very, very much!
Happy Mother's Day!

Love,
Erin

2 VALENTINE'S DAY   Grammar Notes 1–3

In Canada and the United States, Valentine's Day (February 14) is a time when many people think about the special friends and relatives in their lives. They send cards and letters and tell these people their feelings. Complete the sentences from Valentine's Day cards. Use the superlative form of the adjectives in parentheses and the expressions in the box.

in the world	of my life	in the school
of the year	of all	in our family

1. You are so good to me. I am _____the luckiest_____ person _____in the world_____.
(lucky)

2. The day we were married was _____ day _____.
(happy)

3. You are a terrific teacher. You are _____ teacher _____.
(good)

4. You make me feel warm, even in _____ months _____.
(cold)

5. You are _____ cousin _____.
(nice)

6. Grandma, you are _____ person _____. Maybe that's
(wise)

why I love you the most.

3 A SPECIAL GIFT   Grammar Notes 1–2

Look at the pictures. Write sentences about the gift items. Use the words in parentheses and **the most**, **the least**, *or* **-est**.

1. The painting ___is the most unusual gift._____
(unusual)

2. The scarf _____
(practical)

3. The book _____
(expensive)

4. The scarf _____
(expensive)

5. The book _____
(small)

6. The painting _____
(big)

7. The toy _____
(funny)

4 **WHAT ABOUT YOU?**

*Write questions. Use the words in parentheses with the superlative and the present perfect with **ever**.*

1. ___What's the strangest gift you've ever received?_____
   (What / strange / gift / you / receive?)

2. _____
   (What / funny / thing / you / do?)

3. _____
   (Who / smart / person / you / know?)

4. _____
   (What / nice / place / you / see?)

5. _____
   (Where / hot / place / you / be?)

6. _____
   (What / bad / experience / you / have?)

7. _____
   (What / silly thing / you / say?)

8. _____
   (What / long / book / you / read?)

9. _____
   (What / valuable / lesson / you / learn?)

10. _____
   (What / difficult / thing / you / do?)

11. _____
   (What / enjoyable / thing / you / do?)

5 **EDITING**

Read this paragraph from a student's essay. Find and correct five mistakes in the use of superlative adjectives. The first mistake is already corrected.

Ramadan is the ~~seriousest~~ *most serious* time in Muslim culture. During Ramadan, we do not eat from sunup to sunset. This is difficult for everyone, but teenagers have the hardest time. Right after Ramadan is the Eid al-Fitr. This holiday lasts three days, and it's the most happiest time of the year. The morning of Eid, my family gets up early and goes to the mosque. After we greet our neighbors by saying "Eid Mubarek" (Happy Eid), we go home. We eat the big breakfast you have ever seen. Our parents give us gifts, usually new clothes and money. One year, Eid came around the time I graduated from high school. That year, I got the most beautiful clothes and the fatter envelope of money of all the children in my family. Eid Mela is part of Eid al-Fitr. On that day, we all go to a big park. Last year at Eid Mela, I had the better time of my life. I met my old high school friends, and we all ate junk food and showed off our new clothes.

COMMUNICATION PRACTICE

6 LISTENING

 Timothy is trying to pick a gift for his wife. Listen to the conversation. Then listen again and check the appropriate column.

	Bracelet	Winter Coat	Picture Frame	Soap and Bubble Bath	Star
1. most practical	☐	☐	☐	☐	☐
2. sweetest	☐	☐	☐	☐	☐
3. least expensive	☑	☐	☐	☐	☐
4. most romantic	☐	☐	☐	☐	☐
5. silliest	☐	☐	☐	☐	☐

7 THE MOST . . .

Work in small groups. Answer the questions in Exercise 4.

EXAMPLE:

The strangest gift I've ever received is a singing birthday card.

8 WHAT ABOUT YOUR HOLIDAYS?

Work in small groups. Discuss the chart. When do people in the U.S. send cards? What are some important holidays in other cultures? Do people send cards? How else do they celebrate?

NUMBER OF CARDS SOLD IN THE U.S. EACH YEAR	
Halloween	28 million
Thanksgiving	40 million
Father's Day	101 million
Mother's Day	150 million
Valentine's Day	1 billion
Christmas	2.3 billion

Source: Droste K., and J. Dye. *Gale Book of Averages.*
Michigan: © Gale Research, Inc., 1994.

9 WRITING

Write your own card for a special day. Use superlatives. Then work in groups. Decide which card is the:

funniest	most original	most artistic	most serious	most sentimental

EXAMPLE:

Sam's card is the funniest, but Juan's card is definitely the most sentimental.

25 ADVERBS: EQUATIVES, COMPARATIVES, SUPERLATIVES

GRAMMAR **IN CONTEXT**

BEFORE YOU READ   Look at the photograph. What game are the people playing? What do you think the two players are trying to do?

▷ *Two TV sportscasters are talking about a game in their program, "The Halftime Report." Read this transcript of "The Halftime Report."*

RON: Hi, this is Ron Martin . . .

WILL: . . . and I'm Willie Roth. We're your hosts for "The Halftime Report."

RON: Have you ever seen these teams play **more aggressively**?

WILL: No, Ron, I haven't. Folks, we're watching the Bulls battle the Lakers, and both teams are playing **as well as** they've played all year. At the end of the first half, the Bulls are leading 47 to 44.

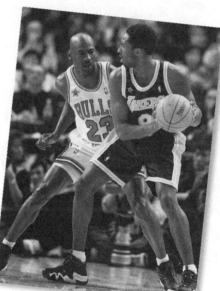

RON: Each team has lost its top player. Michael Jordan sprained his left ankle, and Shaquille O'Neal is out of the game because of his fouls.

WILL: But with Jordan out, that's going to hurt the Bulls **worse than** the Lakers.

RON: They still have Toni Kukoc. Have you been watching him lately? He's been playing **more and more aggressively** as the season goes on.

WILL: Kukoc is good, all right. In recent games, he's been scoring **more frequently than** any player except Jordan, and he's been playing **the most consistently** of the Bulls.

RON: **The more** he plays, **the better** he looks.

WILL: The second half is ready to begin! See you again after the game.

GRAMMAR **PRESENTATION**
ADVERBS: EQUATIVES, COMPARATIVES, SUPERLATIVES

EQUATIVES

		As	ADVERB	*As*	
The Bulls	played didn't play	**as**	**hard well aggressively consistently**	**as**	the Lakers.

COMPARATIVES

	COMPARATIVE ADVERB FORM		*THAN*	
The Bulls played	**harder better**		**than**	the Lakers.
	more less	**aggressively consistently**		

COMPARATIVES

	COMPARATIVE ADVERB FORM	*AND*	COMPARATIVE ADVERB FORM	
The Bulls are playing	**harder**	**and**	**harder.**	
	better		**better.**	
	more		**more**	**aggressively.***
	less		**less**	**consistently.***

* Note that the adverb is used only with the second *more/less*.

COMPARATIVES

THE	COMPARATIVE ADVERB FORM		*THE*	COMPARATIVE ADVERB FORM	
The	**harder**	he played,	**the**	**better**	he performed.

SUPERLATIVES

	SUPERLATIVE ADVERB FORM	
He threw	**the fastest the best the most accurately the least accurately**	of anyone in the game.

NOTES	**EXAMPLES**
1. Use the **equative**, (*as* + **adverb** + *as*) to talk about actions that are <u>the same or equal</u>. Use *just* to emphasize the equality. Use *not as* + **adverb** + *as* to talk about actions that are <u>not the same or equal</u>.	• Kerr played *just* **as well as** most players. *(He and the other players played equally well.)* • Jordan did**n't** play **as aggressively as** O'Neal. *(Jordan and O'Neal played differently. Jordan played aggressively, but he played less aggressively than O'Neal.)*
2. Use the **comparative form of adverbs** to focus on the <u>differences</u> between actions.	• The Bulls played **better than** the Lakers. • Jordan ran **faster than** O'Neal. • He played **more skillfully than** O'Neal. • He played **less aggressively than** O'Neal.
3. It is not always necessary to name the second person or thing. Sometimes it is clear from the context who or what that is.	• Jordan played hard. O'Neal played *just* **as hard** (as Jordan). • Jordan shot **more consistently** (than O'Neal).
4. Use the **superlative form of adverbs** to <u>single out something about an action</u>. We often use the superlative with expressions beginning with *of*, such as *of any player*.	• Kukoc worked **the hardest**. • He scored **the most frequently** *of any player* on the team.

5. There is more than one way to **form the comparative and superlative of adverbs**.

a. For one-syllable adverbs or for adverbs whose forms are the same as adjectives, use **-er** or **-est**.

▶ **BE CAREFUL!** Some adverbs have <u>irregular</u> <u>comparative and superlative</u> forms. *(See Appendix 7, page A-4, for a list of irregular adverbs.)*

ADVERB	COMPARATIVE	SUPERLATIVE
fast	**faster**	*the fastest*
hard	**harder**	*the hardest*
well	**better**	*the best*
badly	**worse**	*the worst*

b. For other adverbs of two or more syllables, use **more / less** or **the most / the least**. Most of these adverbs end in *-ly*.

skillfully	**more / less skillfully**	*the most / the least skillfully*

c. Note that some adverbs of manner have <u>two comparative</u> and <u>two superlative</u> forms.

USAGE NOTE: Although *more quickly, more slowly,* and *the most quickly* and *the most slowly* are the traditional comparative and superlative forms of these adverbs, *quicker, slower,* and *the quickest,* and *the slowest* are often heard in informal speech.

ADVERB	COMPARATIVE	SUPERLATIVE
quickly	**more quickly** **quicker**	*the most quickly* *the quickest*
slowly	**more slowly** **slower**	*the most slowly* *the slowest*

---

6. To talk about change—<u>an increase or a decrease</u>—use:

comparative adverb + *and* + **comparative adverb**

OR

more / *less* + *and* + **comparative adverb**

- Kukoc is playing **better and better** as the season continues.
- He is playing **more and more aggressively**.

---

7. To show a <u>cause-and-effect</u> relationship, use:

the + **comparative adverb** + *the* + **comparative adverb**

- **The harder** he played, **the better** he performed.

FOCUSED PRACTICE

1 DISCOVER THE GRAMMAR

Read this feature story from the sports section of the newspaper. Underline all the equative, comparative, and superlative adverb forms.

Section 3 **Sports**

Golds Beat Silvers!

In the first soccer game of the season, the Golds beat the Silvers, 6 to 3. The Silver team played a truly fantastic game, but its defense is still weak. The Golds defended the ball much <u>more aggressively than</u> the Silver team did. Of course, Ace Jackson certainly helped win the game for the Golds. The Golds' star player was back on the field today to the delight of his many fans. He was hurt badly at the end of last season, but he has recovered quickly. Although he didn't play as well as people expected, he still handled the ball like the old Ace. He certainly handled it the most skillfully of anyone on the team. He controlled the ball the best, kicked the ball the farthest, and ran the fastest of any of the players on either team. He played hard and helped the Golds look good. In fact, the harder he played, the better the Golds performed. Watch Ace this season.

And watch the Silvers. They have a new coach, and they're training more seriously this year. I think we'll see them play better and better as the season progresses.

---

2 NOT ALL BIKES ARE EQUAL Grammar Notes 1 and 5

*Read this chart comparing several models of bicycles. Complete the sentences. Use **(not) as** + adverb + **as** and the words in parentheses. Change the adjectives to adverbs.*

BICYCLES Better ← → Worse

Model	Braking Speed (Dry Ground)	Braking Speed (Wet Ground)	Shifting Ease	On-Road Handling
A	●	◒	●	◒
B	●	○	●	○
C	○	○	◒	◒

1. Model C __doesn't stop as quickly as__ Model A.
   (stop / quick)

2. On wet ground, Model B

   _____ Model C.
   (stop / slow)

3. On dry ground, Model C

   _____ Model B.
   (stop / quick)

4. Model A _____ Model B.
   (shift / easy)

5. Model C _____ Model B.
   (shift / easy)

6. On the road, Model B

   _____ Models A and C.
   (handle / good)

7. Model A _____ Model C.
   (handle / good)

3 SPEED READING   Grammar Notes 1, 5, and 7

*Complete the conversation with the equative or comparative form of the words in parentheses. Add **as** or **than** where necessary.*

BILLY: Did you hear about the new speed-reading course? It helps you read

_____ faster _____ and _____.
      1. (fast)   2. (well)

MIGUEL: No! The _____ you read, the _____ you understand.
         3. (fast)   4. (little)

BILLY: But the ad says after the course you'll read ten times _____,
                                5. (rapidly)

understand five times more, and you won't work any _____.
                                    6. (hard)

MIGUEL: I'd like to see that. I read _____ most people, but I remember details
                      7. (slowly)

_____ and _____ most people do.
  8. (clearly)   9. (long)

BILLY: Maybe you could read _____ and still remember details.
                   10. (quickly)

MIGUEL: Did you read the course description completely?

BILLY: I read it _____ I always read things.
          11. (completely)

4 THE ALL-AROUND ATHLETE   Grammar Notes 2, 4, and 5

Look at the chart. Then complete the sentences. Use the comparative or superlative form of the words in the box.

| far | good | fast | bad | slow | high |

	BROAD JUMP	**POLE VAULTING**	**5-MILE RUN**
Athlete 1	14.3 feet	7 feet 3 inches	24 minutes
Athlete 2	14.1 feet	7 feet 2 inches	28 minutes
Athlete 3	15.2 feet	7 feet 8 inches	30 minutes
Athlete 4	15.4 feet	8 feet 2 inches	22 minutes

1. Athlete 1 jumped ___ farther than ___ Athlete 2.

2. Athlete 4 vaulted ___ the highest ___ of all.

3. Athlete 3 ran _____.

4. Athlete 2 ran _____ Athlete 4.

5. Athlete 4 jumped _____.

6. Athlete 1 ran _____ Athlete 2.

7. Athlete 4 vaulted _____ Athlete 2.

8. All in all, Athlete 4 did _____.

9. All in all, Athlete 2 did _____.

COMMUNICATION PRACTICE

5 LISTENING

Listen to the radio announcer. He is describing a horse race. Then listen again and rank the horses from first place (1) to last place (5).

_____ Exuberant King

_1_ Get Packin'

_____ Inspired Winner

_____ Señor Speedy

_____ Wild Whirl

6 SPORTS AROUND THE WORLD

Work as a class. Name several famous athletes for one sport. Compare their abilities. Use the comparative and superlative forms of adverbs. Use your own ideas or the ideas in the box to help you.

Activities	Adverbs
catch	carefully
hit	defensively
kick	easily
play	powerfully
race	regularly
run	seriously
throw	straight
train	successfully

EXAMPLE:

Fatuma Roba is a runner from Ethiopia. She runs faster and more gracefully than most other runners.

7 A QUESTIONNAIRE

Answer the questionnaire.

1. How many hours do you work every week? _____

2. How many books have you read this month? _____

3. When did you last watch a sports event? _____

4. How many hours a week do you participate in sports? _____

5. How many trips have you taken in the last year? _____

6. How many countries have you visited? _____

Now add your own questions.

7. _____

8. _____

9. _____

10. _____

Work in groups. Compare your answers to questions 1–6 with those of your classmates. Ask the group your own questions (7–10) and compare the answers.

Find out:

1. Who works the hardest?

2. Who reads the most?

3. Who has watched a sports event the most recently?

4. Who participates in sports the most regularly?

5. Who has traveled the most frequently?

6. Who has traveled the most extensively?

> EXAMPLE:
> Sharif works the hardest. He works 45 hours every week.

8 WRITING

Write a paragraph comparing two sports figures. Choose either two people that you know or two famous athletes. You can use the ideas from the box in Exercise 6.

> EXAMPLE:
> My friends Paul and Nick are both good soccer players, but they have different styles. Nick plays more aggressively than Paul, but Paul runs faster and passes more frequently. Nick scores more often, but Paul plays more cooperatively. . . .

REVIEW OR SELFTEST

PART
V

I. *Complete the advertisements by choosing the correct words in parentheses.*

1. FOR RENT. Live ___comfortably___ in this
a. (comfortable / comfortably)

_____ studio apartment.
b. (cozy / cozily)

_____ rent makes it a _____
c. (Cheap / Cheaply)   d. (perfect / perfectly)
home for one student.

2. FOR SALE. Woman's bicycle. I'm asking the _____
a. (incredible / incredibly)

low price of $65 for this _____ five-speed bike. I've
b. (new / newly)

_____ used it at all. Don't miss this
c. (hard / hardly)

_____ bargain.
d. (terrific / terrifically)

3. FREE to a _____ family. Skipper is a
a. (good / well)

_____ and friendly puppy. He behaves
b. (beautiful / beautifully)

_____ with children, and he is very
c. (good / well)

_____. We are moving very soon, so if you want
d. (obedient / obediently)

Skipper, please act _____.
e. (quick / quickly)

II. *Circle the letter of the correct answer to complete each sentence.*

1. I passed my driver's test. It seemed much _____   A ⓑ C D
this time.
(A) easy   (C) easiest
(B) easier   (D) easily

2. Our team didn't play _____ I expected. I was   A B C D
disappointed.
(A) as well as   (C) as badly as
(B) well   (D) better

3. The faster Tranh walks, _____.   A B C D
(A) more tired   (C) the more tired he gets
(B) he gets tired   (D) he gets more tired

262

4. Could you talk _____ ? I'm trying to work.   **A B C D**
(A) more quietly   (C) more quiet
(B) quieter   (D) quiet

5. Lisa is staying home. Her cold is a lot _____ today.   **A B C D**
(A) bad   (C) worst
(B) worse   (D) the worst

6. Sorry we're late. Your house is much _____ than we thought.   **A B C D**
(A) far   (C) farther
(B) the farthest   (D) the farther

7. The movie was so _____ that we couldn't sleep last night.   **A B C D**
(A) excitingly   (C) excite
(B) excited   (D) exciting

8. Chris is working very _____ these days.   **A B C D**
(A) hardly   (C) harder
(B) hard   (D) hardest

9. Write the report first. It's more important _____ your other work.   **A B C D**
(A) than   (C) from
(B) as   (D) then

10. The lunch menu is very short. It's _____ than the dinner menu.   **A B C D**
(A) varied   (C) less varied
(B) more varied   (D) the least varied

11. Thank you! That's _____ I've ever received.   **A B C D**
(A) the nicer gift   (C) nicest gift
(B) a nice gift   (D) the nicest gift

12. It's getting more _____ to find a cheap apartment.   **A B C D**
(A) hardly   (C) the most difficult
(B) and more difficult   (D) and very difficult

III. *Each sentence has four underlined words or phrases. The four underlined parts of the sentences are marked A, B, C, or D. Circle the letter of the <u>one</u> underlined word or phrase that is NOT CORRECT.*

1. My Spanish isn't <u>very good</u>, so I make <u>some</u> <u>embarrassed</u> mistakes.   **A B C (D)**
                A   B   C   D

2. <u>The harder</u> Sylvia <u>tries</u>, <u>less</u> she <u>succeeds</u>.   **A B C D**
     A   B   C   D

3. This <u>has</u> been <u>the</u> <u>best</u> day <u>than</u> my whole life!   **A B C D**
        A   B   C   D

4. We're <u>always</u> <u>amazing</u> <u>by</u> John's <u>incredible</u> travel stories.   **A B C D**
         A   B   C   D

5. We took <u>a lot of</u> photos because she was <u>such</u> a <u>cutely</u> <u>little</u> baby.   **A B C D**
           A   B   C   D

6. Our <u>new</u> car is <u>hard</u> to drive <u>than</u> our <u>old</u> one.   **A B C D**
     A   B   C   D

(continued on next page)

7. Patrick doesn't <u>run quickly</u> as Lee, <u>but</u> he can run <u>farther</u>.   **A B C D**
               A   B   C   D

8. You did <u>much</u> <u>more</u> <u>better</u> in the last test <u>than</u> in this one.   **A B C D**
            A   B   C   D

9. What's <u>the</u> <u>more</u> <u>popular</u> of all the <u>new</u> TV shows?   **A B C D**
            A   B   C   D

10. <u>The</u> <u>more</u> I practice my English, the <u>most</u> <u>fluent</u> I get.   **A B C D**
      A   B   C   D

11. The garbage in the street <u>is</u> <u>more</u> <u>disgusted</u> <u>than</u> the potholes.   **A B C D**
                      A   B   C   D

12. Today seems <u>as</u> <u>hotter</u> <u>as</u> yesterday, but the humidity is <u>lower</u>.   **A B C D**
                A   B   C   D

IV. *Complete the sentences with the comparative form of the adjectives and adverbs.*
Use the information in parentheses to help you.

1. Ann's criticism was very unfair.
(I thought about it thoroughly. I became angry.)

The ___*more thoroughly*___ I thought about it, the ___*angrier*___ I became.

2. My teacher tried to explain the lesson, but she talked very fast.
(She talked fast. I felt confused.)

The _____ she talked, the _____ I felt.

3. Bruce gets really silly when he's tired. Last night he studied until midnight.
(It got late. He became silly.)

The _____ it got, the _____ he became.

4. Sylvia studied hard for her French course last semester.
(She studied hard. She spoke fluently.)

The _____ she studied, the _____ she spoke.

5. Greg takes good care of his garden.
(He often waters his tomatoes. They get big.)

The _____ he waters his tomatoes, the _____ they get.

6. My neighbors' dog always barks at me when I run near their house.
(He barks loud. I run fast.)

The _____ he barks, the _____ I run.

7. Sal felt guilty when his girlfriend apologized for their argument.
(She apologized profusely. Sal felt bad.)

The _____ she apologized, the _____ he felt.

V. *Read the sentences. Complete the summary sentence with the word in parentheses and* **as . . . as** *or* **not as . . . as**. *Use an appropriate verb.*

1. The rent for Apartment 5-G is $550.

The rent for Apartment 22-G is $720.

(expensive) Apartment 5-G __isn't as expensive as Apartment 22-G.__

2. Apartment 5-G has five rooms.

Apartment 22-G has five rooms.

(large) Apartment 5-G _____

3. Tony's pizzeria is two blocks away.

Sal's pizzeria is around the corner.

(far) Sal's pizzeria _____

4. A slice of Tony's pizza costs $2.15.

A slice of Sal's pizza also costs $2.15.

(expensive) Sal's pizza _____

5. The Mets have won six games. They've played very well.

The Pirates have won six games, too. They've played very well also.

(well) The Mets _____

6. Player number 12 runs a six-minute mile.

Player number 20 runs a five-and-a-half-minute mile.

(fast) Player number 12 _____

VI. *Complete each paragraph with the words from the box. Use each word once.*

> the   best   of   ~~successful~~   hardest

1. Pat's the most ____successful____ salesperson in her office, and she deserves to be. She
                              a.

works the longest hours. Sometimes she works until 10:00 at night. She also works the

_____. When she works with a client, she talks _____ most
        b.   c.

persuasively _____ all our salespeople. She's really the _____.
                    d.   e.

(continued on next page)

big sooner than many much exciting

2. Communications equipment used to be only for _____ companies, but
a.

recently more and more small offices are buying it. Fax machines are cheaper

_____ they used to be, and _____ home offices have them
b.   c.

now. Car telephones are also becoming _____ more common. The most
d.

_____ new development is the videophone. An inexpensive model will be
e.

available for home offices _____ than you think—probably by next year.
f.

VII. *Read this diary entry. Find and correct ten mistakes in the use of comparisons.*
The first mistake is already corrected.

> $\overset{worst}{}$
> I think today has been the ~~bad~~ day of my life. My car broke down on the
>
> expressway during rush hour this morning—a busiest time of day. I sat there
>
> for an hour waiting for a tow truck. The longer I sat, the nervous I got. I was a
>
> wreck when I got to work. Of course, this was the day we were closing biggest
>
> deal of the year. My boss called me five times about one letter. And more
>
> frequently he called, the worse I typed. My next worry is the repair bill for the
>
> car. I hope it isn't as high the last time.
>
> I'm going to try to relax now. There's an interested movie on cable TV
>
> tonight. Jan saw it last week and says it's the better film she's seen in a long
>
> time. After the movie, I'll take a hotter bath and go to bed. I'm looking forward
>
> to tomorrow. It can't be as badly as today!

▶ *To check your answers, go to the Answer Key on page 269.*

FROM GRAMMAR TO WRITING USING DESCRIPTIVE ADJECTIVES

Descriptive adjectives can help your reader better understand or picture what you are writing about.

> **EXAMPLE:**
> I live in an apartment. ⟶
> I live in a **small, comfortable, one-bedroom** apartment.

1 *Read this paragraph. Circle all the adjectives that describe the writer's apartment.*

I live in a (small,) comfortable, one-bedroom apartment that is close to school. The living room is my favorite room. It's sunny, warm, and cheerful. There's an old brick fireplace, which I use on cold winter nights. In the corner there's a large, soft, green couch. I like to sit there and read. Next to it is a small, wood table with a beautiful antique lamp from my grandmother. It's a cozy living room, and I enjoy spending time there.

2 *Complete this word map with the circled words from Exercise 1.*

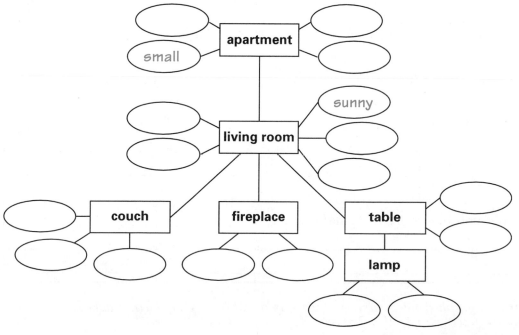

3 *Before you write . . .*

- Work in small groups. Put the adjectives from the box into the correct categories. Brainstorm other adjectives for each category. You can use a dictionary for help.

attractive	~~beautiful~~	coarse	comfortable	cozy
cute	enormous	gorgeous	~~hard~~	hideous
huge	~~large~~	~~little~~	lovely	rough
~~run-down~~	smooth	~~soft~~	tiny	ugly

things that are big: __large,_____

things that are small: __little,_____

things that look good: __beautiful,_____

things that look bad: __run-down,_____

things that feel good: __soft,_____

things that feel bad: __hard,_____

- Think about a room you know. On a separate piece of paper, construct a word map like the one in Exercise 2. Use some of the adjectives in the box above.

- Discuss your map with a partner. Do you want to add or change any adjectives?

> **EXAMPLE:**
> **A:** How small is the kitchen?
> **B:** Oh, it's tiny.

4 *Write a paragraph about the room from Exercise 3. Use your word map.*

5 *Exchange paragraphs with a new partner. Complete the chart.*

Did the writer use adjectives that describe how things _____?			
	Yes	**No**	**Example(s)**
look	☐	☐	_____
feel	☐	☐	_____
smell	☐	☐	_____
sound	☐	☐	_____
What would you like more information about? _____
_____
_____

Revise your paragraph if necessary. Answer any questions your partner asked.

REVIEW OR SELFTEST
ANSWER KEY

I. (Unit 22)

1. **b.** cozy
   c. Cheap
   d. perfect
2. **a.** incredibly
   b. new
   c. hardly
   d. terrific
3. **a.** good
   b. beautiful
   c. well
   d. obedient
   e. quickly

II. (Units 23 and 25)

2. A
3. C
4. A
5. B
6. C
7. D
8. B
9. A
10. C
11. D
12. B

III. (Unit 22)

2. C
3. D
4. B
5. C
6. B
7. A
8. B
9. B
10. C
11. C
12. B

IV. (Units 23 and 25)

2. faster, more confused
3. later, sillier
4. harder, more fluently
5. more often, bigger
6. louder, faster
7. more profusely, worse

V. (Units 23 and 25)

2. Apartment 5-G is as large as Apartment 22-G.
3. Sal's pizzeria isn't as far (away) as Tony's pizzeria.
4. Sal's pizza is as expensive as Tony's pizza.
5. The Mets play OR are playing OR have played as well as the Pirates.
6. Player number 12 doesn't run as fast as OR isn't as fast as player number 20.

VI. (Units 24 and 25)

1. **b.** hardest
   c. the
   d. of
   e. best
2. **a.** big
   b. than
   c. many
   d. much
   e. exciting
   f. sooner

VII. (Units 22–25)

I think today has been the ~~bad~~ *worst* day of my life. My car broke down on the expressway during rush hour this morning—~~a~~ *the* busiest time of day. I sat there for an hour waiting for a tow truck. The longer I sat, the *more* nervous I got. I was a wreck when I got to work. Of course, this was the day we were closing *the* biggest deal of the year. My boss called me five times about one letter. And *the* more frequently he called, the worse I typed. My next worry is the repair bill for the car. I hope it isn't as high *as* the last time.

I'm going to try to relax now. There's an ~~interested~~ *interesting* movie on cable TV tonight. Jan saw it last week and says it's the ~~better~~ *best* film she's seen in a long time. After the movie, I'll take a ~~hotter~~ *hot* bath and go to bed. I'm looking forward to tomorrow. It can't be as ~~badly~~ *bad* as today!

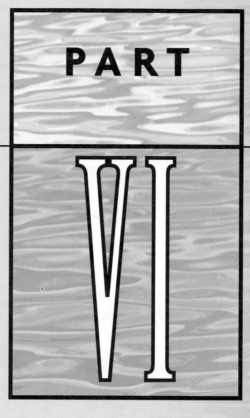

PART

VI

GERUNDS AND INFINITIVES

26

GERUNDS: SUBJECT AND OBJECT

GRAMMAR **IN CONTEXT**

BEFORE YOU READ Where can you find signs like these? How do you feel about them?

NO SMOKING   PROHIBIDO FUMAR   SİGARA İÇİLMEZ   禁煙

Read these messages from an online bulletin board about smoking.

Re: Can't Stand Seeing Those Signs!

[**Follow Ups**] [**Post a Reply**] [**Message Board Index**]

Posted by Cigarman on February 16, 2000, at 15:30:03
I **can't stand seeing** all the new No Smoking signs. **Eating** in a restaurant and **traveling** by plane are no fun anymore! Junk food is worse than **smoking**. But I bet the government won't **prohibit ordering** burgers and fries for lunch!

Reply posted by Nuffsed on February 17, 12:15:22
Hey, Cigarman—I don't get sick when my boyfriend goes to McDonald's, but **sitting** in a room full of his cigarette smoke makes my hair and clothing stink.

Reply posted by Swissfriend on February 17, 20:53:11
Hello, U.S. Smokers! I am a member of Freunde der Tabak, a Swiss group of smokers and nonsmokers. We **suggest practicing** courtesy to nonsmokers and tolerance of smokers. I **enjoy smoking**, but I **understand not wanting** to inhale second-hand smoke.

Reply posted by Cleanaire on February 18, 9:53:11
Friend—Have you ever tried to **stop smoking**? If so, then you know you are addicted to nicotine. The younger you **start smoking**, the harder it is to quit.

GRAMMAR **PRESENTATION**
GERUNDS AS SUBJECTS AND OBJECTS

GERUND AS SUBJECT		
GERUND (SUBJECT)	**VERB**	
Smoking	harms	your health.
Not smoking	is	healthier.

GERUND AS OBJECT		
SUBJECT	**VERB**	**GERUND (OBJECT)**
You	should quit	**smoking**.
I	suggest	**not smoking**.

NOTES

1. Gerunds (base form of verb + **-ing**) are <u>verbs that function like nouns</u>. The gerund can be the **subject** of a sentence.

Notice that the gerund is always singular and is followed by the third-person-singular form of the verb.

▶ **BE CAREFUL!** Don't confuse the gerund with the progressive form of the verb.

EXAMPLES

- *Smoking* is bad for your health.
- *Traveling* by plane was fun.

- *Eating* junk food **makes** me sick.
- *Inhaling* smoke **gives** me bronchitis.

    gerund
- *Drinking* coffee isn't healthy.

   progressive form
- He **is drinking** coffee right now.

---

2. Gerunds are also used as the **object** of certain verbs.

To the right is a short list of <u>verbs that can be followed by gerunds</u>.

(See Appendices 9 and 11, page A-5, for more complete lists.)

- I **enjoy** *exercising*.
- I've **considered** *joining* a gym.

admit	deny	miss	resent
avoid	enjoy	practice	suggest
consider	finish	quit	understand

---

3. There are many common expressions with **go + gerund**. These expressions usually describe <u>activities</u>, such as shopping, fishing, skiing, swimming, and camping.

- We often **go** *swimming* in the lake.
- Yesterday I **went** *shopping* for a new pair of running shoes.

FOCUSED PRACTICE

1 DISCOVER THE GRAMMAR

Read part of an article from a health newsletter. Underline the words ending in **-ing** *that are gerunds.*

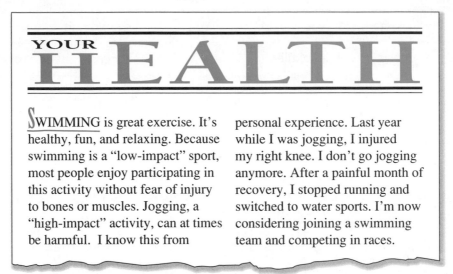

SWIMMING is great exercise. It's healthy, fun, and relaxing. Because swimming is a "low-impact" sport, most people enjoy participating in this activity without fear of injury to bones or muscles. Jogging, a "high-impact" activity, can at times be harmful. I know this from personal experience. Last year while I was jogging, I injured my right knee. I don't go jogging anymore. After a painful month of recovery, I stopped running and switched to water sports. I'm now considering joining a swimming team and competing in races.

2 HEALTH ISSUES

Grammar Notes 1–2

Complete these statements with gerunds. Use the verbs in the box.

increase	eat	do	walk
~~smoke~~	swim	run	go

1. _____Smoking_____ is bad for your heart and lungs.

2. _____ too much fat and sugar is also unhealthy.

3. Doctors suggest _____ the number of fruits and vegetables in your diet.

4. Avoid _____ too many high-impact sports such as jogging and jumping

   rope. Instead, consider _____ in a pool every day. It's an excellent

   low-impact sport.

5. Many health experts think that _____ is better than _____

   because there is less stress on your body when your feet come into contact with

   the ground.

6. Many people postpone _____ to the doctor or dentist, but regular

   checkups are important.

3 **A QUESTION OF HEALTH**

Read these conversations. Write a summary sentence for each conversation.
Choose the appropriate verb from the box, and use the gerund form of the verb
in parentheses.

admit	avoid	consider	deny	~~enjoy~~	go	mind	quit

1.   **ANN:** Do you want to go jogging with me before work?

   TOM: No, thanks. I really don't like that kind of exercise.

   SUMMARY: Tom doesn't ___enjoy jogging._____
                                    (jog)

2.   **RALPH:** Would you like a cigarette?

   MARTA: Oh, no, thanks. I don't smoke anymore.

   SUMMARY: Marta _____.
                              (smoke)

3.   **CHEN:** What are you doing after work?

   AN-LING: I'm going to that new swimming pool. Would you like to go with me?

   SUMMARY: An-ling is going to _____.
                                             (swim)

4.   **JIM:** I smell smoke in here. You had a cigarette, didn't you?

   ELLEN: No, I didn't.

   SUMMARY: Ellen _____.
                             (smoke)

5.   **IRENE:** You're lazy. You really need to exercise more.

   MIKE: You're right. I *am* lazy.

   SUMMARY: Mike _____ lazy.
                            (be)

6. MONICA: Would you like a piece of chocolate cake?

   PHIL: No, thanks. I try to stay away from sweets.

   SUMMARY: Phil _____ sweets.
                            (eat)

7.   **CRAIG:** I know exercise is important, but I hate it. What about you?

   VILMA: Well, I don't *love* it, but it's OK.

   SUMMARY: Vilma doesn't _____.
                                    (exercise)

8.   **ALICE:** We've been working too hard. Maybe we need a vacation.

   ERIK: A vacation? Hmm. That's an interesting idea. Do you think we can afford it?

   SUMMARY: Erik and Alice _____ a vacation.
                                        (take)

COMMUNICATION PRACTICE

4 LISTENING

A doctor is giving advice to a patient. Some things are OK for this patient to do, but other things are not. Listen to the conversation. Listen again and check the correct column.

	OK to do	Not OK to do
1. smoking	☐	☑
2. drinking coffee	☐	☐
3. losing more weight	☐	☐
4. eating more complex carbohydrates	☐	☐
5. running every day	☐	☐
6. riding a bike every day	☐	☐
7. working eight hours a day	☐	☐

5 AN OPINION SURVEY

Take a class survey. How many students agree with the statements below? Write the numbers in the appropriate column.

	AGREE	DISAGREE	NO OPINION OR DON'T KNOW
Seeing someone with a cigarette turns me off.*			
I'd rather date** people who don't smoke.			
It's safe to smoke for only a year or two.			
Smoking can help you when you're bored.			
Smoking helps reduce stress.			
Smoking helps keep your weight down.			
I strongly dislike being around smokers.			

Source: Based on a survey by Centers for Disease Control

 * *turns me off* = disgusts me
** If your classmate doesn't date, change the statement to "I'd rather be married to someone who doesn't smoke."

Discuss your survey results.

> **EXAMPLE:**
> Ten people say that seeing someone smoke turns them off.

6 POSTER TALK

Work in small groups. Discuss this poster. Complete some of the sentences below to help you in the discussion.

The message of this poster is . . .

The man wants / doesn't want to quit . . .

The camel enjoys . . .

The camel keeps . . .

Lighting up a cigarette . . .

After six years, most people can't resist . . .

I can't imagine . . .

I can't stand . . .

This poster makes me feel like . . .

Smoking is . . .

7 NO SMOKING?

Many people agree with laws that prohibit smoking in all public places. What is your opinion? Work in small groups. Think of arguments for and against allowing smoking in public places. Take notes.

EXAMPLE:
Going outside to smoke wastes a lot of time at work.

8 WRITING

Write a letter to a friend who wants to stop smoking. Give your friend tips on how to quit. Use gerunds.

EXAMPLE:
Avoid being around people who smoke.

GERUNDS AFTER PREPOSITIONS

GRAMMAR **IN CONTEXT**

BEFORE YOU READ   Look at the notice board. When can students attend a Student Council meeting? Where can students go if they want to meet some international students?

Many schools have boards with information for students. Read these notices on a school bulletin board.

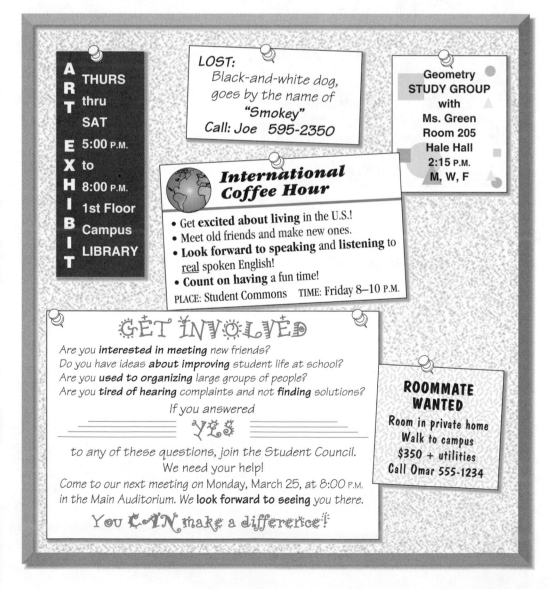

A
R
T

E
X
H
I
B
I
T

THURS
thru
SAT
5:00 P.M.
to
8:00 P.M.
1st Floor
Campus
LIBRARY

LOST:
Black-and-white dog,
goes by the name of
"Smokey"
Call: Joe 595-2350

Geometry
STUDY GROUP
with
Ms. Green
Room 205
Hale Hall
2:15 P.M.
M, W, F

International Coffee Hour

• Get **excited about living** in the U.S.!
• Meet old friends and make new ones.
• **Look forward to speaking** and **listening** to real spoken English!
• **Count on having** a fun time!

PLACE: Student Commons   TIME: Friday 8–10 P.M.

GET INVOLVED

Are you **interested in meeting** new friends?
Do you have ideas **about improving** student life at school?
Are you **used to organizing** large groups of people?
Are you **tired of hearing** complaints and not **finding** solutions?

If you answered

YES

to any of these questions, join the Student Council.
We need your help!
Come to our next meeting on Monday, March 25, at 8:00 P.M.
in the Main Auditorium. We **look forward to seeing** you there.

You **CAN** make a difference!

ROOMMATE
WANTED
Room in private home
Walk to campus
$350 + utilities
Call Omar 555-1234

GRAMMAR **PRESENTATION**
GERUNDS AFTER PREPOSITIONS

PREPOSITION + GERUND			
Do you have ideas	**about**	**improving**	life at school?
Are you tired	**of**	**hearing**	complaints?
They insist	**on**	**coming**	to the meeting.
She is used	**to**	**organizing**	large groups.

NOTES

EXAMPLES

1. Prepositions are words such as *about, against, at, by, for, in, instead of, of, on, to, with,* and *without.* Prepositions can be followed by nouns or pronouns.

Since **gerunds** (base form of the verb + *-ing*) act as nouns, they <u>can follow prepositions</u> too.

- The council is **against** *tuition increases*.
- The council is **against** *them*.

- The council is **against** *raising* tuition.

2. Many common **expressions** are made up of a verb or an adjective followed by a preposition. These expressions can be <u>followed by a gerund</u>.

(See Appendices 13 and 14, pages A-5, A-6, for more expressions followed by prepositions.)

advise **against**	be afraid **of**
believe **in**	be bored **with**
count **on**	be excited **about**

- She **dreams of** *going* to college.
- He **is bored with** *working* in a shop.

3. In the expressions to the right, *to* is a <u>preposition</u>, not part of an infinitive form. For this reason it can be <u>followed by the gerund</u>.

look forward **to**	be accustomed **to**
object **to**	be opposed **to**
resort **to**	be used **to**

- I'm looking forward **to** *seeing* you.
  NOT I'm looking forward to see you.

▶ **BE CAREFUL!** *Be used to* + gerund means "be accustomed to." *Get used to* + gerund means "get accustomed to."

- I **am used to** *driving* to work.
- I have to **get used to** *taking* the train.

FOCUSED PRACTICE

1 DISCOVER THE GRAMMAR

The Student Council wrote a letter to Ana Rivera, the president of the college.
Read the letter and underline all the preposition + gerund combinations.

October 4, 1999

Dear President Rivera:

We, the members of the Student Council, would like to share with you the thoughts and concerns of the general student body. As you probably know, many students are complaining about life on campus. We are interested in meeting with you to discuss our ideas for dealing with these complaints.

We know that you are tired of hearing students complain, and that you are not used to working with the Student Council. However, if you really believe in giving new ideas a try, we hope you will think about speaking with our representatives soon.

We look forward to hearing from you soon.

Respectfully submitted,

The Student Council

2 **SPRING BREAK**   **Grammar Notes 2 and 3**

Read the school newspaper. Complete the students' statements. Choose the appropriate preposition from the box. (You will use one of the prepositions several times.) Add the gerund form of the verb in parentheses.

at	on	in	to	about	for

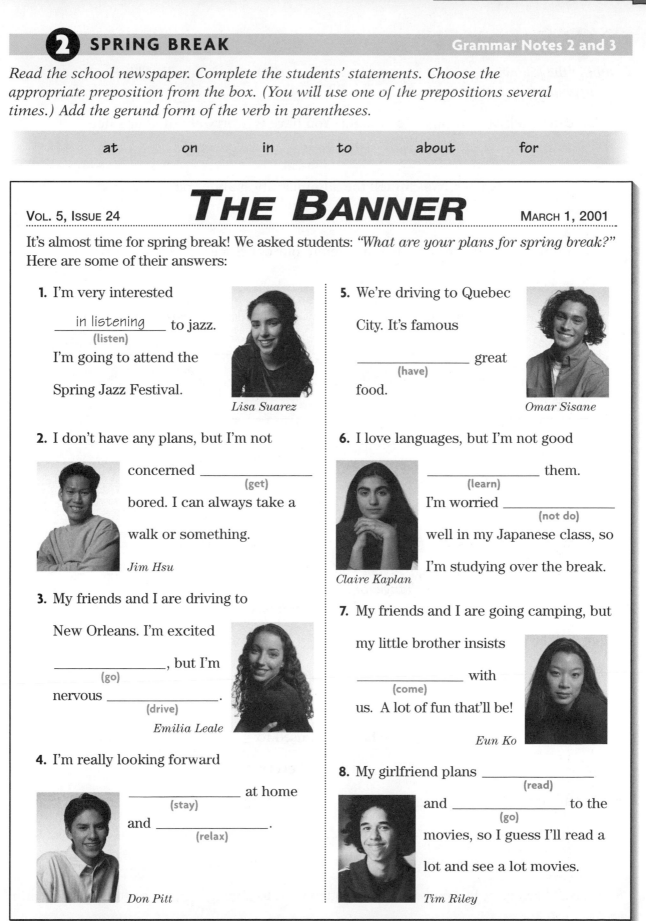

THE BANNER

VOL. 5, ISSUE 24   MARCH 1, 2001

It's almost time for spring break! We asked students: *"What are your plans for spring break?"* Here are some of their answers:

1. I'm very interested <u> in listening </u> to jazz.
(listen)
I'm going to attend the Spring Jazz Festival.

Lisa Suarez

2. I don't have any plans, but I'm not concerned _____
(get)
bored. I can always take a walk or something.

Jim Hsu

3. My friends and I are driving to New Orleans. I'm excited _____, but I'm
(go)
nervous _____.
(drive)

Emilia Leale

4. I'm really looking forward _____ at home
(stay)
and _____.
(relax)

Don Pitt

5. We're driving to Quebec City. It's famous _____ great
(have)
food.

Omar Sisane

6. I love languages, but I'm not good _____ them.
(learn)
I'm worried _____
(not do)
well in my Japanese class, so I'm studying over the break.

Claire Kaplan

7. My friends and I are going camping, but my little brother insists _____ with
(come)
us. A lot of fun that'll be!

Eun Ko

8. My girlfriend plans _____
(read)
and _____ to the
(go)
movies, so I guess I'll read a lot and see a lot movies.

Tim Riley

③ SCHOOL ISSUES

Combine the following pairs of sentences to make statements about school life.
Use the prepositions in parentheses.

1. You can't walk on campus late at night. You have to worry about your safety.

<u>You can't walk on campus late at night without worrying about your safety.</u>
(without)

2. We can make changes. We can tell the administration about our concerns.

_____
(by)

3. The administration can help. It can listen to our concerns.

_____
(by)

4. In some cases, students just complain. They don't make suggestions for improvements.

_____
(instead of)

5. Students get annoyed with some teachers. Some teachers come late to class.

_____
(for)

6. You can improve your grades. Study regularly.

_____
(by)

④ MAKING CHANGES

Larry Jones quit school after high school and had various jobs. Then he decided
to go to college. That was a big change for him. Complete the sentences about
Larry. Use the appropriate form of the verb in parentheses.

1. Larry used to _____ *be* _____ a student, but he quit after high school.
(be)

2. He used to _____ a job.
(have)

3. In fact, he used to _____ a lot of different jobs.
(have)

4. When he went back to college, he had to get used to _____ a student again.
(be)

5. He wasn't used to _____ to school every day.
(go)

6. He had to get used to _____ homework again and _____ for tests.
(do) (study)

7. When Larry was working, he used to _____ quite a bit of money. He used to
(earn)

_____ everything, too. Now he has to get used to _____ less.
(spend) (spend)

8. It hasn't been easy, but now Larry has gotten used to _____ a student's life again.
(live)

COMMUNICATION PRACTICE

5 LISTENING

 *Listen to this speech by a candidate for the office of Student Council president. Listen again and mark the following statements* **True (T)** *or* **False (F)**.

___T__ **1.** Latoya has experience in working for student government.

_____ **2.** She believes in raising student activity fees.

_____ **3.** There are only two kinds of food on campus.

_____ **4.** The computer labs and libraries close early.

_____ **5.** Students feel safe on the campus at night.

_____ **6.** Latoya is most interested in improving campus safety.

6 VOTE FOR ME

Pretend you are running for president of the Student Council. Prepare your campaign speech and read it to the class. Answer some of these questions.

What are you most interested in?   What are you opposed to?

What do you believe in?   What are you excited about?

What will you insist on?   What are you good at?

> **EXAMPLE:**
> Vote for me. I'm interested in making our lives better by improving . . .

Then have an election.

7 STRESS

Below are some life events, both positive and negative, that can lead to stress. Work by yourself and rank them from most stressful (1) to least stressful (8). Then in small groups compare and discuss your lists. Use **be used to** *and* **get used to** *to explain your choices.*

_____ starting college   _____ getting divorced

_____ moving to a new city   _____ having or adopting a baby

_____ changing jobs or schools   _____ death of a close family member

_____ getting married   _____ getting fired at work

> **EXAMPLE:**
> I think getting married is the third most stressful life event. You have to get used to living with another person.

8 WRITING

Read this letter to the editor of a school newspaper. Then complete the exercise below.

TO THE EDITOR . . .

I have been attending Longtree College for a year. I am an international student in the Chemistry Department. I am very happy about studying here. However, I have had some problems with academic advisors. The academic advisors are not used to talking to international students, so they get nervous about understanding us.

In addition, the school delays looking at the records of transfer students. I attended a university in Ukraine for two years, and I took several chemistry courses. The Chemistry Department has not yet looked at my records. My advisor recommends taking basic courses, but I am afraid of repeating courses and wasting my time.

I suggest giving a workshop for advisors. In the workshop they can practice talking clearly and organizing their information for international students. I also recommend looking at student records as soon as possible.

Respectfully,
Galina Terela

Mark the following statements **True (T)** *or* **False (F)**.

___F___ **1.** Galina is complaining about being a chemistry student.

_____ **2.** The advisors have a lot of experience in talking to international students.

_____ **3.** They feel confident about communicating with international students.

_____ **4.** Galina is a freshman.

_____ **5.** The Chemistry Department has been slow in reviewing Galina's records.

_____ **6.** Galina objects to taking basic chemistry courses.

_____ **7.** Galina thinks that advisors should learn about dealing with international students.

Write a letter to the editor of your school newspaper. Write about the things you like and dislike about your school. Use Galina's letter as a model.

INFINITIVES AFTER CERTAIN VERBS

GRAMMAR **IN CONTEXT**

BEFORE YOU READ   What kind of questions do you think Annie answers?
Do you think this is a good place to get advice?

Read this letter to the newspaper advice column, "Ask Annie."

Lifestyles Section 4

ASK ANNIE

Dear Annie,

I've just moved to Seattle and started going to a new school. I **try hard to meet** people but nothing **seems to work**. The last guy I went out with **asked to borrow** money from me on our first date. He also **wanted to correct** my pronunciation (I'm from Louisiana). Obviously, I **decided not to see** him again. My problem is that I'**d** really **like to find** someone special to date. My roommate **advised** me **to put** an ad in the newspaper, but I really **don't want to do** that. Do you have any suggestions?

Lonely in Seattle

Dear Lonely,

You **seem to be** very focused on meeting someone right away. Perhaps you **need to relax** a bit. Tell friends and acquaintances that you **want to meet** someone, but **don't expect to fall** in love with the first person you meet. Do things that you'**d like to do** anyway. Join a sports club. **Learn to dance. Try not to focus** on meeting the man of your dreams, and just have fun. You'll come into contact with people who have similar interests. Even if you **fail to meet** Mr. Right immediately, you will at least have a good time! Don't give up!

Annie

GRAMMAR **PRESENTATION**
INFINITIVES AFTER CERTAIN VERBS

STATEMENTS				
SUBJECT	**VERB**	**(OBJECT)**	**INFINITIVE**	
I You He	**decided**		**(not) to write**	to Annie.
	urged	John	**(not) to take**	her advice.
	wanted	(her)	**to advise**	John.

NOTES

EXAMPLES

1. Certain **verbs** can be **followed by an infinitive** (*to* + base form of the verb).

- I **want** *to make* some new friends.
- I **asked** Annie *to help* me.
- She **advised** me *to relax*.
- She **told** me *not to worry*.

2. Some of these verbs are followed **directly by an infinitive**.

The verbs to the right can be followed directly by an infinitive.

(See Appendix 10, page A-5, for a more complete list of verbs that are followed directly by the infinitive.)

- He **decided** *to join* a health club.
- He **hoped** *to meet* new people.
- She **promised** *to go* with him.
- She **tried** *not to be* late.

begin	plan
decide	promise
fail	refuse
hope	seem
learn	try

3. Some verbs require an **object** (noun or pronoun) **before the infinitive**.

object
- I **invited Mary** *to celebrate* with us.

object
- I **reminded her** *to come*.

The verbs to the right require an object before the infinitive.

advise	order
allow	remind
encourage	tell
force	urge
invite	warn

(See Appendix 12, page A-5, for a more complete list of verbs that require an object before the infinitive.)

---

4. Some verbs can be followed by either:

    an infinitive
      OR
    an object + infinitive

infinitive
- He **wants** *to leave*.

object + infinitive
- He **wants** *you to leave*.

The verbs to the right can be followed either directly by an infinitive or by an object + infinitive.

ask	need
expect	want
help	would like

(See Appendix 12, page A-5, for a more complete list of these verbs.)

---

5. Form the **negative infinitive** by placing *not* before the infinitive.

- Lee remembered **not** *to call* after 5:00. (*Lee didn't call after 5:00.*)

- Ana told me **not** *to go* to class. (*Ana: "Don't go. The teacher is sick."*)

▶ **BE CAREFUL!** A sentence with a negative infinitive can have a very different meaning from a sentence with a negative main verb.

- Van told me **not** *to give up*. (*Van: "Don't give up. You'll meet someone soon."*)

- Van **didn't tell** me to give up. (*Van didn't say anything.*)

FOCUSED PRACTICE

1 DISCOVER THE GRAMMAR

Read this entry in a personal diary. Underline all the verbs + infinitive and the verbs + object + infinitive.

> Annie <u>advised me to join</u> a club or take a class, and I finally did it! I decided to join the school's Outdoor Adventure Club, and I went to my first meeting last night. I'm really excited about this. The club is planning a hiking trip next weekend. I definitely want to go. I hope it won't be too hard for my first adventure. Last night they also decided to go rafting in the spring. At first I didn't want to sign up, but the leader was so nice. He urged me not to miss this trip, so I put my name on the list. After the meeting, a group of people asked me to go out with them. We went to a coffee shop and talked for hours. Well, I hoped to make some new friends when I joined this club, but I didn't expect everyone to be so friendly. I'm glad Annie persuaded me not to give up.

2 PLAN TO SUCCEED   Grammar Notes 1–5

Complete the article with the correct form of the verbs in parentheses. Use the simple present or the imperative form for the first verb.

Most people make careful plans when they ___decide to take___ a vacation.
                                             1. (decide / take)

Yet when they _____ a mate, they depend on luck.
                2. (attempt / find)

Edward A. Dreyfus, PhD, _____ love to chance. He
                          3. (warn / single people / not / leave)

_____ his Master Relationship Plan when they search
4. (urge / them / use)

for a life partner. Remember: when you _____, you
                                          5. (fail / plan)

_____.
6. (plan / fail)

STEP ONE: Make a list. What kind of person do you _____?
                                                        7. (wish / meet)

Someone intelligent? Someone who loves sports? List everything.

STEP TWO: Make another list. What kind of person are you? List all your

characteristics. _____ this list and comment on it.
                  8. (Ask / two friends / read)

_____ about hurting your feelings. The two lists should match.
9. (Tell / them / not / worry)

STEP THREE: Increase your chances. _____ in activities you like.
                                        10. (Choose / participate)

STEP FOUR: Ask for introductions. Dr. Dreyfus _____
                                              11. (advise / people / not / feel)
embarrassed to ask. Everyone _____ a matchmaker!
                                  12. (want / be)

3 IN OTHER WORDS   Grammar Notes 2–4

*For each short conversation, use a verb from the box, followed by an infinitive or
an object + infinitive.*

| agree | remind | ~~would like~~ | invite | need | forget | encourage |

1. **KAREN:** *(Yawn)* Don't you have a meeting tomorrow? Maybe you should go home
   and get some sleep.

   TOM: It's only eleven. And *Star Wars* is on in five minutes!

   SUMMARY: Karen _would like Tom to go home._

2. **KURT:** Hey, honey, are you planning to buy gas soon?

   LILY: I was just leaving.

   SUMMARY: Kurt _____

3. **JOHN:** We're going out for coffee. Would you like to join us?

   MARY: I'd love to.

   SUMMARY: John _____

4. **DAD:** I expect you to come home by 10:30. Do you understand? If you don't, I'm
   grounding you for two weeks.

   JASON: OK, OK. Take it easy, Dad.

   SUMMARY: Jason _____

5. **DON:** You didn't go to the staff meeting. We missed you.

   JEFF: Oh, no! The staff meeting!

   SUMMARY: Jeff _____

6. **MOM:** Don't be scared, sweetie. Just try once more. You'll love it.

   LISA: I hate to ice skate. I always fall down.

   SUMMARY: Lisa's Mom _____

7. **BRAD:** Are you using the car tonight?

   TERRY: Well . . . I have a lot of shopping to do. And I promised Susan I'd give her
   a ride.

   SUMMARY: Terry _____

COMMUNICATION PRACTICE

4 LISTENING

Listen to a couple talk about their family. Listen again and circle the letter of the sentences that you hear.

1. **a.** I really wanted to discuss their problems.
   b. I really wanted them to discuss their problems.

2. **a.** I finally learned to argue with my stepdaughter.
   b. I finally learned not to argue with my stepdaughter.

3. **a.** I expected to have problems with my daughter.
   b. I expected you to have problems with my daughter.

4. **a.** Sometimes I just wanted to leave the house for a few hours.
   b. Sometimes I just wanted her to leave the house for a few hours.

5. **a.** After all, she didn't choose to live with us.
   b. After all, she chose not to live with us.

6. **a.** Then, one day, she asked to go on a family vacation.
   b. Then, one day, she asked me to go on a family vacation.

7. **a.** I didn't expect to have a good time.
   b. I didn't expect her to have a good time.

8. **a.** In fact, sometimes I'd like to stop talking for a few minutes.
   b. In fact, sometimes I'd like her to stop talking for a few minutes.

5 DESCRIBE YOUR PARENTS

Work in pairs. Tell each other about your parents.

What did they encourage you to do?   Why did they advise you to do that?

How did they encourage you to do that?   What would they like you to do?

What didn't they allow you to do?   What do they expect you to do?

What did they force you to do?   What would *you* prefer to do?

What did they advise you to do?   Why would you prefer to do that?

EXAMPLE:
   My parents encouraged me to learn other languages.

Add your own questions.

_____

_____

_____

6 SOCIALIZING AROUND THE WORLD

Discuss how people in your culture socialize. Do young men and women go out together? If so, do they go out in couples or in groups? What are some ways people meet their future husbands or wives?

7 WRITING

Imagine you would like to meet one of the people in these personal ads. Write a letter to that person and introduce yourself. Use verbs followed by infinitives.

EXAMPLE:

Dear Nice Guy,

I'm a friendly female student. I like to take walks in the country . . .

City Classified Section 6

3 Meeting Place

300 Women Seeking Men

Can't wait to meet you!—friendly, but lonely, foreign student would like to meet a nice, thoughtful guy who enjoys good conversation, books, music, and the outdoors. Please send note. 3512

We deserve to be together—I love to travel, but I also like to stay home with friends and family. My hobbies include tennis, dancing, and gardening. You are a nice guy with many interests. Please write me about them. 6534

310 Men Seeking Women

Nice Guy—would like to meet warm, friendly female who enjoys the city, country, reading, movies and traveling. You don't need to send a photo, but please write. 3543

Attractive single male—refuses to believe that the woman of his dreams does not exist! She is smart, funny, and has a warm heart. Send note with photo, please. 2073

Want to dance?—athletic man wants to meet partner for dancing,

GRAMMAR **IN CONTEXT**

BEFORE YOU READ   In your opinion, are electronic organizers useful? Does this electronic organizer look easy to use?

Read this ad for an electronic pocket organizer.

DATALATOR 534 F

Electronic
Talking Dictionary / Organizer
$89.95

Are you still using

- pencil and paper **to make** notes?
- reference books **to find** basic information?

If so, you need to start using the DATALATOR **to organize** your studies and **save** precious time. Use it

✔ **to make** study notes

✔ **to listen** to pronunciation of basic conversational English, Chinese, Japanese, French, and German

✔ **to take** practice tests for the TOEFL while you wait for the bus

✔ **to look up** words in the built-in dictionary
(*and* **listen** to the correct pronunciation)

✔ **to check** your class schedule

✔ **to download** information from the Datalator to your computer

Of course, you can also use it **to store** names and phone numbers, and **to add** and **subtract**.

Available at all Lacy's Department Stores.
To locate the one nearest you,
call 1 800 555-LACY or visit our website at www.lacy.com.

GRAMMAR **PRESENTATION**
INFINITIVES OF PURPOSE

AFFIRMATIVE	**NEGATIVE**
I borrowed her car **to go** to Lacy's. I left at 9:00 **(in order) to arrive** early.	I left at 9:00 **in order not to arrive** late.

NOTES

EXAMPLES

1. Use an **infinitive** (*to* + **base form** of the verb) to explain the <u>purpose of an action</u>. It often answers the question *Why?*

USAGE NOTE: In spoken English, you can answer the question *Why?* with an <u>incomplete sentence</u> beginning with *To*.

A: *Why* did you go to Lacy's?

B: I went there **to buy** one of those Datalators I saw in an ad.

OR

To buy an electronic organizer.

2. You can also use the longer form, *in order to* + **base form** of the verb to explain a purpose.

USAGE NOTE: *To* + **base form** of the verb is more common in <u>informal</u> speech and writing.

- I bought an organizer **in order to store** names and phone numbers.

- I bought an organizer **to store** names and phone numbers.

3. Use *in order not to* + **base form** of the verb to express a <u>negative purpose</u>.

- I use my Datalator **in order not to make** mistakes in pronunciation. *(I don't want to make mistakes.)*

4. You can also use:

   noun / pronoun + infinitive

to express the <u>purpose of an object</u>.

- I need an **organizer to help** me remember my schedule.
- I need **it to help** me remember my schedule.

FOCUSED PRACTICE

1 DISCOVER THE GRAMMAR

 Read the conversation. Underline all the infinitives that express a purpose.

YOKO: It's 5:00. Aren't you going home?

LEE: No. I'm staying late <u>to finish</u> this report. What about you? Are you going straight home?

YOKO: No. I'm going to stop at the bank to get some cash. Then I'm going to Lacy's Department Store to take advantage of the sale they're having.

LEE: Oh, what are you going to get?

YOKO: One of those new electronic organizers they're advertising. I've been looking for something to help me with my work.

LEE: What's wrong with just a regular calculator?

YOKO: Nothing. But sometimes I have to convert other currencies to dollars.

LEE: What else are you going to use it for?

YOKO: Oh, to store important names and phone numbers and to balance my checkbook.

LEE: What did we do before they invented all these electronic gadgets?

YOKO: We made a lot of mistakes!

2 TELL ME WHY   Grammar Note 2

Look at Yoko's list of things to do. Then write a phrase to answer each question.

To Do
—Get gas
—Make dental appointment
—Buy batteries
—Withdraw $100
—Invite Rika and Taro to dinner
—Buy milk and eggs

1. Why did she call Dr. Towbin's office? __To make a dental appointment.__

2. Why did she go to the bank? _____

3. Why did she call Mrs. Watanabe? _____

4. Why did she go to the supermarket? _____

5. Why did she go to the electronics store? _____

6. Why did she go to the service station? _____

3 **THE REASON IS . . .**

Match each action with its purpose.

Action		Purpose
_g_	**1.** He enrolled in Chinese 101 because he	**a.** didn't want to get any phone calls.
_b_	**2.** She took a bus because she	**b.** didn't want to be late.
_____	**3.** She went to the store because she	**c.** wanted to store information.
_____	**4.** We disconnected our phone because we	**d.** wanted to listen to the news.
_____	**5.** He turned on the radio because he	**e.** didn't want to worry me.
_____	**6.** He didn't tell me he was sick because he	**f.** needed to buy some dishes.
_____	**7.** She bought a Datalator because she	**g.** wanted to learn the language.

Now combine the sentences. Use the infinitive of purpose.

1.   He enrolled in Chinese 101 to learn the language.
   _____

2.   She took a bus in order not to be late.
   _____

3.   _____

4.   _____

5.   _____

6.   _____

7.   _____

4 **EDITING**

Read Yoko's journal entry. Find and correct six mistakes in the use of the
infinitive of purpose. The first mistake is already corrected.

>   to get
> I went to Dr. Towbin ~~for getting~~ my teeth cleaned today. While I was waiting, I used my
> Datalator to study for the TOEFL. Then I used it to helps me pronounce "novocaine" and
> "dental floss" for my appointment. After the dentist, I checked my schedule and saw
> "Rika and Taro, dinner, 7:30." I should use it in order to not forget appointments! Luckily,
> my recipes are already on the Datalator, so I used them for making a quick shopping
> list. When I got home, there was a note on my door—"Call bldg. super." I checked the
> Datalator dictionary to find "bldg. super." The "building superintendent" wanted to come
> up in order fix the doorbell! Rika and Taro and I played with the Datalator all evening.
> You can program it for to play computer games, too. I don't know how I lived without it!

COMMUNICATION PRACTICE

5 LISTENING

You are calling Lacy's Department Store to get information. Read the list below. Listen to Lacy's automatic telephone message. Then listen again and write the number of the telephone key that you should press for each of the following purposes.

1. place an order ☐

2. find out when the store opens ☐

3. report a lost or stolen credit card ☐

4. ask about a bill ☐

5. ask about a delivery ☐

6. speak to a customer service representative ☐ 1

7. listen to the message again ☐

6 WHAT'S IT FOR?

Work in groups. Think of uses for the following objects. Use the infinitive of purpose and your imagination!

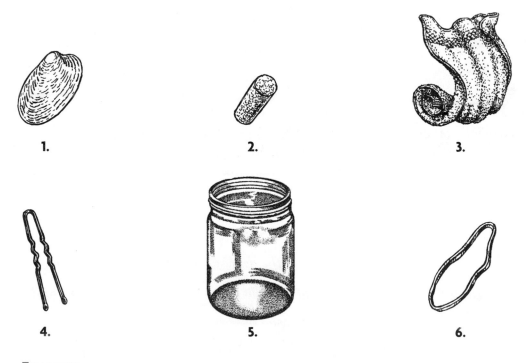

1.

2.

3.

4.

5.

6.

EXAMPLE:
You can use a shell to hold coins, to keep soap in, or to eat from.

 THE DATALATOR

Reread the ad on p. 292. Would you like to have an electronic organizer? What would you use it to do? What wouldn't you use it to do? Discuss your answers with a partner.

> **EXAMPLE:**
> **A:** I'd use it to keep a record of my appointments.
> **B:** I wouldn't use it to add two plus two!

8 REMOTE CONTROL

Read this ad for a remote control.

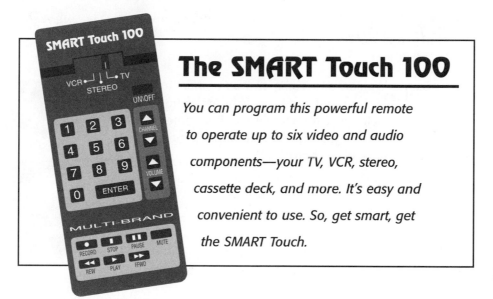

Work in small groups. Discuss the Smart Touch 100. Would you like to have one? Imagine that it could control everything in your house—not only electronic equipment. What would you use it to do?

> **EXAMPLE:**
> **A:** I'd use it to turn on the shower.
> **B:** I'd use it to open and close the windows.

9 WRITING

Write an ad for a new electronic gadget. Describe a real item, or invent one. Use the infinitive of purpose.

30 INFINITIVES WITH *TOO* AND *ENOUGH*

GRAMMAR **IN CONTEXT**

BEFORE YOU READ Look at the photographs. How old do you think each person is? In your opinion, are they old enough to vote?

Read this transcript of a radio talk show about voting rights for people under age eighteen.

SMITH: Welcome to *Voice of the People.* I'm Ed Smith, and tonight our topic is youth voting rights. Kyle, you're only sixteen. For someone your age, is getting the vote really **important enough to fight** for?

KYLE: Sure. Without it, teenagers are **too powerless** for politicians **to listen to**.

SMITH: I don't get it. In the 1960s when military service was required, eighteen-year-olds had an argument—"if we're **old enough to fight** for our country, we're **old enough to vote**." What's *your* argument?

Kyle

Tina

TINA: Well, there are a lot of laws that discriminate against us.

MICAH: For example, my parents are divorced. I see my father every week. I don't want to, but the law says I'm **too young to decide**.

KYLE: My city has curfew laws. I'm **responsible enough to work** and **pay** taxes, but **too immature to stay** out until 10:00. That's fair?

TINA: Women, racial minorities, and people with disabilities have already won their civil rights. Now it's our turn.

MICAH: That's right. Things are changing, but not **quickly enough** for us **to get** anything out of it.

Micah

GRAMMAR **PRESENTATION**
INFINITIVES WITH *TOO* AND *ENOUGH*

INFINITIVES WITH *TOO*

	TOO	ADJECTIVE / ADVERB	(FOR + NOUN / OBJECT PRONOUN)	INFINITIVE	
We're (not)		**young**	(for people)	**to trust**.	
People answered	**too**	**quickly**	(for me)	**to consider**	all the issues.
It's		**hard**	(for us)	**to decide**.	

INFINITIVES WITH *ENOUGH*

	ADJECTIVE / ADVERB	ENOUGH	(FOR + NOUN / OBJECT PRONOUN)	INFINITIVE	
They're (not)	**old**		(for people)	**to trust**.	
We have(n't) voted	**often**	**enough**	(for them)	**to understand**	our role.
It's	**easy**		(for us)	**to decide**.	

NOTES

1. Use *too* + adjective / adverb + infinitive to give a <u>reason</u>.

EXAMPLES

- I'm **too young** *to vote*.
  (*I'm too young, so I can't vote.*)

- She isn't **too young** *to vote*.
  (*She isn't too young, so she can vote.*)

- I arrived **too late** *to vote*.
  (*I arrived too late, so I couldn't vote.*)

- She didn't arrive **too late** *to vote*.
  (*She didn't arrive too late, so she could vote.*)

(continued on next page)

2. You can also use **adjective / adverb + enough + infinitive** to give a <u>reason</u>.

- I'm **old enough** *to go* into the army.
  (I'm old enough, so I can go into the army.)
- He isn't **old enough** *to go* into the army.
  (He isn't old enough, so he can't go into the army.)
- I ran **fast enough** *to pass* the physical.
  (I ran fast enough, so I passed the physical.)
- She didn't run **fast enough** *to pass* the physical.
  (She didn't run fast enough, so she didn't pass the physical.)

---

3. Notice that you <u>don't need</u> to use the <u>infinitive</u> when the meaning is clear from the context.

▶ **BE CAREFUL!** Note the placement of *too* and *enough*.

Too comes before the adjective or adverb.

Enough comes after the adjective or adverb.

- I'm seventeen years old, and I can't vote yet. I'm **too young**. I'm not **old enough**.

- She's *too* old.
- I'm not **old** *enough*.
  NOT I'm not enough old.

---

4. Sometimes we use *for* + **noun or pronoun** before the infinitive.

- We are too young **for people** *to trust* us.
  (People don't trust us.)
- We are too young **for them** *to trust* us.
  (They don't trust us.)

FOCUSED PRACTICE

1 DISCOVER THE GRAMMAR

*People have different opinions about public issues. Read each statement of opinion. Then choose the sentence (**a** or **b**) that summarizes that opinion.*

1. Teenagers are responsible enough to stay out past 10:00 P.M.

   a. Teenagers should have permission to stay out past 10:00 P.M.

   b. Teenagers shouldn't have permission to stay out past 10:00 P.M.

2. Teenagers are too immature to vote.

   a. Teenagers should be able to vote.

   b. Teenagers shouldn't be able to vote.

3. Women are strong enough to be good soldiers.

   a. Women can be good soldiers.

   b. Women can't be good soldiers.

4. Children are mature enough to choose which parent to live with.

   a. Children can choose which parent to live with.

   b. Children can't choose which parent to live with.

5. Teenagers are responsible enough to use the Internet without censorship.

   a. Teenagers can use the Internet without censorship.

   b. Teenagers can't use the Internet without censorship.

6. Adults are too afraid of change to listen to children's ideas.

   a. Adults can listen to children's ideas.

   b. Adults can't listen to children's ideas.

7. People with disabilities have worked too hard to give up the fight for equal rights.

   a. People with disabilities can give up the fight for equal rights.

   b. People with disabilities can't give up the fight for equal rights.

8. At age seventy, people are not too old to work.

   a. At age seventy, people can work.

   b. At age seventy, people can't work.

2 CAN YOU GET BY?

Match the pictures with the sentences below.

1. ___e___

2. _____

3. _____

4. _____

5. _____

6. _____

7. _____

8. _____

9. _____

a. The buttons are too high for him to reach.

b. The buttons are low enough.

c. The steps are too steep for him to get up.

d. The box is too heavy.

e. The street is too busy for them to cross.

f. The traffic is slow enough for them to cross.

g. She's too old to join the army.

h. She is too young to vote.

i. She is old enough to vote.

3 **CURFEW!**

Some teenagers are leaving a concert. Complete their conversations. Use the words in parentheses with the infinitive and **too** *or* **enough**.

1. A: Phish is so cool! Did you catch what Mike Gordon said in that last song?

   B: No. The guitar was _____too loud for me to hear_____ the words.
   (loud / me / hear)

2. A: They're playing in Hampton Stadium next month.

   B: Let's go. The tickets are _____.
   (cheap / us / afford)

3. A: I don't think the Stadium has wheelchair access yet.

   B: We'll sit on the grass. This concert is going to be _____.
   (good / you / miss)

4. A: It's 9:30. Do we have time to get a slice of pizza?

   B: No. It's _____.
   (late / stop)

5. A: I hate this curfew!

   B: Me too! I think we're _____ out past 10:00!
   (old / stay)

6. A: Where's Kyle tonight?

   B: Working. He didn't get out _____.
   (early / come)

7. A: The new recreation center just opened. Do you want to play basketball tomorrow?

   B: Sure. But I'm still _____ you!
   (slow / beat)

8. A: We can take my car. My brother repaired it today.

   B: Ummm. Is that thing really _____?
   (safe / drive)

4 **EDITING**

Read this student's journal entry. Find and correct six mistakes in the use of infinitives with **too** *or* **enough**. *The first mistake is already corrected.*

> The Phish concert was awesome! Now I'm too excited ~~for sleeping~~ to sleep. That Mike Gordon can
> really sing. My voice isn't enough good to sing in the shower! After the concert we were
> really hungry, but it was to late to go for pizza. I HATE this stupid curfew! It's too weird
> understand. My friend Todd works and has to pay taxes, but the law says he's too
> young for staying out past 10:00! That's crazy enough to make me want to scream.
> Well, I'd better try to get some sleep or I'll be too tired too get up in the morning.

COMMUNICATION PRACTICE

5 LISTENING

Listen to the description of a new youth recreation center. It has been built so that people in wheelchairs can get around easily. Then listen again and circle the number of the picture that best fits the description.

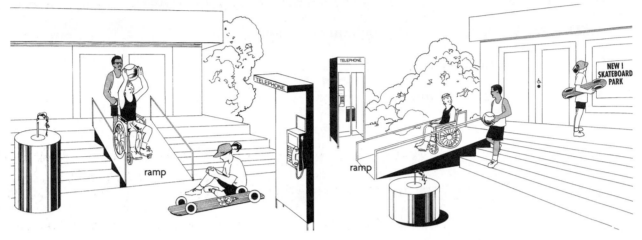

1.   **2.**

3.   **4.**

6 YOUTH RIGHTS

Discuss one of these questions as a class. Then vote on your opinions.

• At what age should people start to vote?

• Should towns have curfews for people younger than age eighteen?

> **EXAMPLE:**
> **A:** I think fifteen-year-olds are mature enough to vote. They can read newspapers and understand issues.
> **B:** I disagree. I don't think fifteen-year-olds are concerned enough about politics to vote.

7 COMMON EXPRESSIONS

What do you think these expressions mean? When would you use them?
Discuss your ideas in small groups.

1. She's old enough to know better.

2. Life is too short to worry about every little thing.

3. You're never too old to try.

4. It looks good enough to eat.

5. It's too hot to handle.

8 WHAT'S YOUR OPINION?

Complete the following sentences. In small groups, compare your opinions.

1. Elderly people are too . . .

   EXAMPLE:
   A: People over age seventy are too old to drive.
   B: Oh, I don't agree. Some elderly people drive better than young people.

2. The leaders of this country are powerful enough . . .

3. Teenagers are too crazy . . .

4. Guns are too dangerous . . .

5. Taxes aren't high enough . . .

6. Women are strong enough . . .

7. Radio and TV broadcasters speak (or don't speak) clearly enough . . .

8. Time goes by too quickly . . .

9 WRITING

Write a letter to the editor of a newspaper. Choose a topic from Exercise 8.

   EXAMPLE:
   To the Editor:

   I'm in favor of gun control. I believe that guns are too dangerous for ordinary
   people to own and use. . . .

GERUNDS AND INFINITIVES

GRAMMAR **IN CONTEXT**

BEFORE YOU READ   Look at the cartoon. What is the man trying to do?
What are your strategies for remembering names?

Read this excerpt from a magazine article.

STOP *FORGETTING* ☞

Marta **wanted to go** to the party. She's friendly and **enjoys meeting** people. But as Marta looked at the invitation, part of her **kept saying**, "I won't know anyone there! How will I remember all those new names?" Marta's problem is not unusual. **Remembering** names is a problem for many people. For international travelers like Marta (she's a Mexican student studying in the United States), **it** is even harder **to recall** unfamiliar foreign names. What can Marta and others like her do? Here are some tips from memory experts:

☞ **Decide to remember. Making** an effort can really help.

☞ Listen carefully when you hear someone's name for the first time. **It**'s important **to pay** attention.

☞ **Keep repeating** the name. **Calling** the person by name more than once will help fix the name in your mind.

☞ Write the name down. **Putting** things in writing is the most common memory aid.

☞ **Don't hesitate to ask** the person **to repeat** the name. Most people **don't mind doing** this.

And last, but not least,

☞ **Stop worrying.** Anxiety only makes the problem worse.

*"Hi. I'm, I'm, I'm . . . You'll have to forgive me,
I'm terrible with names."*

GRAMMAR **PRESENTATION**
GERUNDS AND INFINITIVES

GERUNDS
Marta **enjoys going** to parties.
She **loves meeting** new people.
She **stopped buying** ice cream.
She's worried **about forgetting** people's names.
Meeting new people is fun.

INFINITIVES
Marta **wants to go** to parties.
She **loves to meet** new people.
She **stopped to buy** ice cream
It's fun **to meet** new people.

NOTES

EXAMPLES

1. Some **verbs** are **followed by the gerund**.

To the right is a list of verbs that can be followed by the gerund.

(See Appendix 9, page A-5, for a more complete list of these verbs.)

- Marta **enjoys** *meeting* people.
- She **misses** *going* to parties.

appreciate	prohibit
can't stand	recall
mind	resist

2. Some **verbs** are **followed by the infinitive**.

To the right is a list of verbs that can be followed by the infinitive.

(See Appendix 10, page A-5, for a more complete list of these verbs.)

- Marta **wants** *to meet* people.
- She**'d like** *to go* to parties.

afford	need
agree	offer
expect	want

3. Some verbs can be followed by either **the gerund or the infinitive**.

To the right is a list of verbs that can be followed by the gerund or the infinitive.

(See Appendix 11, page A-5, for a more complete list of these verbs.)

- Marta **loves** *meeting* new people.
  OR
- Marta **loves** *to meet* new people.

begin	like
continue	love
hate	prefer

(continued on next page)

4. BE CAREFUL! A few verbs (for example, *stop, remember,* and *forget*) can be followed by either the gerund or the infinitive, but the **meanings are very different**.

- Marta **stopped eating** ice cream.
  (She doesn't eat ice cream anymore.)
- Marta **stopped to eat** ice cream.
  (She stopped another activity in order to eat some ice cream.)

- Richard **remembered mailing** the invitation.
  (First he mailed the invitation. Then he remembered that he did it.)
- Richard **remembered to mail** the invitation.
  (First he remembered. Then he mailed the invitation. He didn't forget.)

- Marta **forgot meeting** Richard.
  (Marta met Richard, but afterwards she didn't remember the event.)
- Marta **forgot to meet** Richard.
  (Marta had plans to meet Richard, but she didn't meet him because she forgot about the plans.)

5. The **gerund** is the only verb form that **can follow a preposition**.

(See page 279 in Unit 27.)

- Marta's worried **about** *forgetting* people's names.
  preposition
- She apologized **for** *not remembering* his name.
  preposition

6. To make **general statements**, you can use:

    gerund as subject

        OR

    it **+ infinitive**

- **Meeting** new people is fun.

        OR

- **It**'s fun **to meet** new people.

FOCUSED PRACTICE

1 DISCOVER THE GRAMMAR

*Read the first sentence. Then decide if the second sentence is **True (T)** or **False (F)**.*

1. Marta remembered meeting Mr. Jackson.

___T___ Marta has already met Mr. Jackson.

2. Richard stopped smoking.

_____ Richard doesn't smoke anymore.

3. She didn't remember to buy a cake for the party.

_____ She bought a cake.

4. She stopped eating desserts.

_____ She used to eat desserts.

5. Richard forgot to invite his boss to the party.

_____ Richard invited his boss.

6. Richard forgot inviting his neighbor to the party.

_____ Richard invited his neighbor.

7. Richard thinks giving a party is fun.

_____ Richard thinks it's fun to give a party.

8. Marta likes going to parties.

_____ Marta likes to go to parties.

2 SUPER MEMORY   Grammar Notes 1–2, 4–6

Circle the correct words to complete these ideas from a book called
Super Memory.*

1. Get in the habit of (repeating) / to repeat things aloud.

2. Never rely on someone else's memory. Learn trusting / to trust your own.

3. It's easy forgetting / to forget what you don't want remembering / to remember.

4. Study immediately before going / to go to sleep. You'll remember a lot more the next day.

5. Our memories are filled with things we never even meant remembering / to remember.

6. Make it a habit to pass in front of your car every time you get out, and you'll never forget turning off / to turn off your headlights.

7. Playing / To play games is a fun way of improving / to improve your memory skills.

*Douglas J. Hermann, *Super Memory: A Quick Action Program for Memory Improvement*
  (Avenel, NJ: Wings Books, 1991).

3 **PARTY TALK**

Read these conversations that took place at Richard's party. Complete the summary statements. Use the gerund or the infinitive.

1. **RICHARD:** Hi, Roger. Did you bring the soda?

   ROGER: Yes. Here it is.

   SUMMARY: Roger remembered _to bring the soda._____

2. **FRANK:** Marta, do you remember Natalya and Viktor?

   MARTA: Oh, yes. We met last year.

   SUMMARY: Marta remembers _____

3. **NATALYA:** Oh, no. Someone spilled grape juice all over the couch.

   ROGER: Don't look at me! I didn't do it!

   SUMMARY: Roger denied _____

4. **MARTA:** What do you do in your free time, Natalya?

   NATALYA: I listen to music a lot.

   SUMMARY: Natalya enjoys _____

5. **LEV:** Would you like to go dancing some time?

   MARTA: Sure. I'd like that very much.

   SUMMARY: Lev suggested _____

   Marta agreed _____ with Lev.

6. **VIKTOR:** I'm tired. Let's go home.

   NATALYA: OK. Just five minutes more.

   SUMMARY: Viktor wants _____

7. **NATALYA:** Marta, can we give you a ride home?

   MARTA: Thanks, but I think I'll stay a little longer.

   SUMMARY: Natalya offered _____

   Marta decided _____

8. **RICHARD:** Good night. Please drive carefully.

   VIKTOR: Don't worry. I will.

   SUMMARY: Viktor promised _____

4 REMEMBER TO STUDY

Complete this advice. Use the gerund or infinitive form of the verb in parentheses.

_____Studying_____ for an exam is different from _____ _____
        1. (Study)   **2. (try)**   **3. (remember)**

someone's name. Here are some tips:

* Group information by dates, people, or places. It may help _____ a chart.
                                                                                 4. (make)

* Color code. _____ colored pens helps many people retain new information.
                    5. (Use)

* Use different senses. Try _____ new information by _____,
                                     6. (learn)   **7. (read)**

_____, _____, and _____. Some people need
      8. (write)   **9. (speak)**   **10. (listen)**

_____ two or more senses.
     11. (use)

* Remember _____ frequently. It's important _____
                      12. (review)   **13. (go over)**

information again and again.

5 IN OTHER WORDS

Marta and Lev are on their first date. They agree on everything. Read one person's opinion and write the other's. If the first person used the gerund, use the infinitive. If the first person used the infinitive, use the gerund.

1. MARTA: It's fun to meet new people

    LEV: I agree. __Meeting new people is fun._____

2. MARTA: Remembering names is hard, though.

    LEV: I know. __It's hard to remember names._____

3. MARTA: It's difficult to make new friends.

    LEV: That's true. _____

4. MARTA: It's important to relax.

    LEV: You're right. _____

5. MARTA: Dancing is fun.

    LEV: I agree. _____

6. MARTA: It's nice to get to know someone like you.

    LEV: I feel the same way. _____

7.   LEV: Being with you is wonderful.

    MARTA: Thanks. _____, too.

6 EDITING

Read Marta's letter about Richard's party. Find and correct six mistakes in the use of the gerund and infinitive. The first mistake is already corrected.

Dear Lisa,

    I expected ~~hearing~~ *to hear* from you by now. I hope you're OK. I'm busy but happy. Last night I went to a party at one of my classmate's homes. I was really nervous. You know how I usually avoid to go to parties because I have trouble remembering people's names. Well, last night things were different. Before the party I read a book about improving your memory, and I practiced doing some of the memory exercises. They really helped. As a result, I stopped to worry about what people would think of me, and I tried to pay attention to what people were saying. And guess what? I had a good time! I'm even planning going dancing with this guy from my class.

    I have an English test tomorrow, so I should stop writing now and start studying! That book I told you about had some pretty good tips, too.

    Why don't you consider to visit me? I really miss seeing you.

    Please write. I always enjoy to hear from you.

                   Marta

P.S. I'm sending a photo of
    two classmates and me.

COMMUNICATION PRACTICE

7 **LISTENING**

 The school newspaper is interviewing Marta about her opinions on dating.
Read the list of activities. Listen to the interview. Then listen again and check the
things Marta does and doesn't do when she is first getting to know someone.

	Things Marta does	**Things Marta doesn't do**
1. go for walks	☑	☐
2. go dancing	☐	☐
3. go bowling	☐	☐
4. go to the movies	☐	☐
5. have pizza out	☐	☐
6. make dinner at home	☐	☐
7. have a picnic	☐	☐

8 **SOCIAL SITUATION SURVEY**

How do you feel and act in new social situations? Complete these sentences.
Use the gerund or the infinitive. Then discuss your answers with a partner.

When I'm in a new social situation, I . . .

1. enjoy _____

2. always expect _____

3. never hesitate _____

4. dislike _____

5. don't mind _____

6. am afraid of _____

7. avoid _____

8. often regret _____

9. keep _____

10. always try _____

11. believe it's important _____

12. feel nervous about _____

❾ INFORMATION GAP: REMEMBER THE PARTY?

Work in pairs (A and B). Student B, look at the Information Gap on page 316 and follow the instructions there. Student A, look at the picture below. Ask your partner questions to complete what people said at the party. Answer your partner's questions.

EXAMPLE:

A: What does Sue remember doing?

B: She remembers meeting Lev.
What does Lev hope to do?

A: He hopes to see Sue again.

When you are done, compare your pictures. Are they the same?

Close your books. Try to remember each person's name and what each person said. Write down the information and then check your answers with your book.

EXAMPLE:

A: Uta enjoys dancing.

B: I don't think that's right. Uta enjoys jogging.

 STOP FORGETTING

Work in small groups. Reread the article on page 306. Discuss these questions:

1. Do you have trouble remembering people's names?

2. Do you follow any of the experts' memory tips?

3. What other things do you have trouble remembering?

4. What tricks do you use to remember things?

> **EXAMPLE:**
>
> **A:** I sometimes forget to pay my rent.
>
> **B:** Oh, I always make a note on my calendar when the rent is due.

11 WRITING

Write a short letter to someone you know. Describe your recent social activities.
Try to use some of the verbs from Exercise 8.

> **EXAMPLE:**
>
> Last week I went to a party. I felt nervous about speaking English, but
> I enjoyed dancing . . .

INFORMATION GAP FOR STUDENT B

Student B, look at the picture below. Answer your partner's questions. Ask your partner questions to complete what people said at the party.

EXAMPLE:

A: What does Sue remember doing?

B: She remembers meeting Lev.
What does Lev hope to do?

A: He hopes to see Sue again.

When you are done, compare your pictures. Are they the same?

Close your books. Try to remember each person's name and what each person said. Write down the information and then check your answers with your book.

EXAMPLE:

A: Uta enjoys dancing.

B: I don't think that's right. Uta enjoys jogging.

REVIEW OR SELFTEST

I. *Complete the conversation. Use the prepositions in the box and the gerund form of the verbs in parentheses.*

for   to   in   without   ~~by~~   about

A: Carla, your English is just great. How did you learn so quickly?

B: _____By using_____ some special strategies.
    1. (use)

A: Like what?

B: Well, first I got used _____ my time. I scheduled time
                              2. (plan)

_____ television and writing letters in English to my pen pal.
3. (watch)

A: How did you practice speaking?

B: At first I was very nervous _____ English. I had to learn to talk
                                    4. (speak)

_____ about mistakes. I used deep breathing exercises and
5. (worry)

music to calm myself down.

A: What else helped you relax?

B: Jokes. I got interested _____ jokes in English. That way I always
                                6. (learn)

had something to say, and I also learned a lot about Amcrican culture.

II. *Complete each conversation with the correct phrase in parentheses.*

1. A: Let's go jogging.

B: I don't know. You always run _____too fast_____ for me to
                              (too fast / fast enough)

keep up with you.

A: OK. Let's go swimming, then.

2. A: Why did I get an F on this paper?

B: Your handwriting was _____ for me to read.
                            (messy enough / too messy)

A: Then how did you know the answers were wrong?

(continued on next page)

3. A: Have you tried the coffee?

   B: I will in a minute. It's _____ to drink yet.
                                    (too cool / not cool enough)

4. A: This steak is _____ to eat.
                         (too tough / tough enough)

   B: Send it back and ask for something else.

5. A: John didn't make the soccer team.

   B: Why not? He's a good player.

   A: But he doesn't play _____ to win.
                        (too aggressively / aggressively enough)

6. A: What did the forecaster say about thunderstorms?

   B: I'm not sure. The radio wasn't _____ for me to hear.
                             (loud enough / too loud)

III. *Complete the paragraph with the correct form of the verbs in the box. Choose between the gerund or the infinitive of purpose.*

drink	eat	feel	follow	give up	~~quit~~	read
reward	save	shop	smoke	take	tell	

Cigarettes. They're bad for your health. Your doctor recommends _____quitting_____. Your
                                                      1.

friends keep _____ you to stop. Even your dry cleaner suggests that you stop
                  2.

_____. (He says you burned holes in your suit jacket.) You want to stop, but
   3.

_____ an old habit is difficult. _____ these suggestions can help.
   4.   5.

- List your reasons for quitting. Are you quitting _____ better?
                                          6.

  _____ money? Keep your list nearby _____ when you want
  7.   8.

  a cigarette.

- Stop _____ coffee and tea. Caffeine causes people to want a cigarette.
        9.

- When you feel the desire to light up, put it off for five minutes. Use the time

  _____ some deep breaths. The urge will pass quickly.
  10.

- Avoid _____ big meals for a few weeks.
  11.

- Save the money that you aren't spending on cigarettes. Go _____ for
                                                                          12.

  something special _____ yourself for your success.
                              13.

If you follow these suggestions, it shouldn't be too hard to give up this unhealthy habit.

IV. *Complete the conversation by writing the words and phrases in parentheses in the correct order.*

A: Why are so many people starting home-based businesses?

B: In offices, work hours are often ___too long for people to spend___ time with their
                                   1. (people / to spend / too long / for)
 families.

A: What are some keys to home business success?

B: Networking is one. _____ organizations. After you join,
                          2. (necessary / to / It's / join)
 you must _____ a lot of people. But don't get
              3. (enough / get to know / participate / to)
 _____ people who sound interested in your product.
         4. (too / to / busy / call)

A: Do business owners really work fewer hours?

B: No, they work more. But they can arrange their time. Their hours

 _____ family time, too.
     5. (to have / enough / for them / are flexible)

A: What do you warn new business owners about?

B: I _____ their privacy. Remember, the business
       6. (them / to think about / advise)
 phone is always going to ring in the middle of the family dinner. Also,

 _____ the loneliness of working alone, especially
     7. (important / It's / to know about)
 when you're used to a big office.

A: Anything else?

B: Home business owners often find that they don't get paid

 _____ their own bills. In my seminars,
     8. (for /enough / to pay / soon / them)
 I teach strategies for getting paid on time.

A: What kind of home businesses are people starting?

B: Well, as I said, a lot of working people are _____ care of
                9. (take / to / too / busy)
 certain family responsibilities anymore. Many home-based businesses supply services

 like shopping and planning parties.

A: You mean, someone will pay me for shopping?

B: Sure. In fact, I _____ planning your own shopping
       10. (you / to start / encourage)
 business. My class for new business owners starts next week.

V. *Circle the letter of the correct answer to complete each sentence.*   A   B   C   (D)

1. Tom is late because he stopped _____ dinner.
   (A) buying   (C) and buy
   (B) buy   (D) to buy
   A   B   C   D

2. My keys were in my pocket, but I don't remember _____ them there.   A   B   C   D
   (A) to put   (C) I put
   (B) putting   (D) to put

3. Bob's seventeen years old, so he's still _____ vote.   A   B   C   D
   (A) too young to   (C) too old to
   (B) young enough to   (D) too young for

4. I bought a Datalator _____ my appointments.   A   B   C   D
   (A) by organizing   (C) to organize
   (B) I organized   (D) organize

5. _____ everything in advance, Sandra finished the project quickly.   A   B   C   D
   (A) To plan   (C) She plans
   (B) By planning   (D) Planned

6. Chris _____, so her grades are low this semester.   A   B   C   D
   (A) stopped studying   (C) stopped to study
   (B) stopping to study   (D) was stopping to study

7. As military officers, women work _____ the job done.   A   B   C   D
   (A) hardly get   (C) not enough to get
   (B) too hard to get   (D) hard enough to get

8. He's used _____ a big breakfast.   A   B   C   D
   (A) ate   (C) to eating
   (B) to eat   (D) eats

9. I used to be very nervous _____, but I'm not anymore.   A   B   C   D
   (A) to drive   (C) to driving
   (B) for driving   (D) about driving

10. I forgot _____ my check, so I paid the rent twice this month.   A   B   C   D
    (A) mailed   (C) mailing
    (B) to mail   (D) I mail

11. Sal enjoyed _____ in Texas.   A   B   C   D
    (A) live   (C) living
    (B) to live   (D) lived

VI. *Complete the interview with the gerund or infinitive forms of the verbs in parentheses.*

INTERVIEWER: You're one of the best baseball players today, Cliff. Who taught you
_____*to play*_____?
1. (play)

CLIFF: I learned _____ a ball with my dad. We used to play together for
2. (hit)
hours on weekends.

INTERVIEWER: What was the most important thing he taught you?

CLIFF: Dad believed in _____ fun. He always forgot about
3. (have)
_____ when he played. By _____ with him,
4. (win)   5. (play)
I developed the same attitude.

INTERVIEWER: When did you decide _____ a professional?
6. (become)

CLIFF: Too early—in elementary school. That was a mistake. I was too young
_____ that decision.
7. (make)

INTERVIEWER: Why?

CLIFF: My schoolwork suffered. I thought a lot about _____ a pro ball
8. (become)
player, and I didn't think much about _____ homework.
9. (do)

INTERVIEWER: Did anything happen to change your mind about school?

CLIFF: Yes, I planned _____ to City High School, which had a great
10. (go)
team. Then I found out that my grades were probably too low for the school
_____ me.
11. (accept)

INTERVIEWER: But you did graduate from City High School.

CLIFF: Yes, I did. My parents urged me _____ harder. I followed their
12. (study)
advice and I've never stopped _____.
13. (study)

INTERVIEWER: Well, thank you for _____ to this interview.
14. (agree)

CLIFF: You're welcome. I enjoyed _____ your questions. I hope my
15. (answer)
experience encourages other young athletes _____ their education.
16. (continue)

VII. *Each sentence has four underlined words or phrases. The four underlined parts of the sentence are marked A, B, C, or D. Circle the letter of the one underlined word or phrase that is NOT CORRECT.*

1. It's <u>difficult</u> <u>study</u> in a foreign country, so students <u>need</u> <u>to prepare</u>   A Ⓑ C D
        A   B   C   D
for the experience.

2. Students <u>look forward</u> <u>to traveling</u>, but they <u>worry about</u> <u>don't make</u>   A B C D
            A   B   C   D
a good impression.

3. They're afraid <u>of</u> <u>not understanding</u> the culture, and they <u>don't want</u>   A B C D
               A   B   C
<u>making</u> mistakes.
   D

4. Advisors can <u>advise</u> them <u>against wear</u> the wrong <u>clothing</u> and   A B C D
            A   B   C
<u>making</u> the wrong gestures.
   D

5. It's <u>natural</u> <u>to have</u> some problems because no one can <u>get used to</u>   A B C D
      A   B   C
<u>live</u> in a new culture immediately.
   D

6. No one escapes <u>from</u> <u>feeling</u> some culture shock, and <u>it's important</u>   A B C D
               A   B   C
<u>realizing</u> this fact.
   D

7. Jan <u>stopped</u> <u>to feel</u> uncomfortable after she <u>started</u> <u>to make</u>   A B C D
      A   B   C   D
new friends.

8. Now she is <u>looking</u> <u>forward to</u> <u>stay</u> here and <u>getting</u> a job.   A B C D
        A   B   C   D

▶ *To check your answers, go to the Answer Key on page 325.*

FROM GRAMMAR TO WRITING
COMBINING SENTENCES with *and, but, so, or*

PART VI

You can combine two sentences with a coordinating conjunction such as *and, but, so,* and *or*. The new sentence has two main clauses.

EXAMPLE:

Commuting to school is hard. I prefer to live in the dorm. ———▶
main clause   main clause
Commuting to school is hard, **so** I prefer to live in the dorm.

Note that a comma comes after the first clause and before the conjunction.

---

1 *Circle the correct conjunctions to complete this letter.*

Dear Dania,

   I have just a little time before my next class, (so)/ but I'm trying to catch up
a.
with my letter writing. This semester has been difficult, but / or I'm enjoying it.
b.
I'm taking two English classes, and / so I'm also on the student council. Being on
c.
the council has taught me a lot, but / so it takes up a lot of time.
d.

   Studying takes up most of my time, and / but I try to find time for sports too.
e.
I've got to keep in shape! This weekend I'm going hiking with some classmates. Do

you remember the time we went hiking, and / so we couldn't find our way back?
f.

   Your visit is in just two weeks! I'm really looking forward to seeing you,

and / but I'm sure we'll have a great time. You can stay in my dorm, and / or
g.   h.
I can arrange for us both to stay with my parents. Which would you prefer to do?

My parents don't live far away, and / but I know they will want to see you.
i.

   Let me know which train you're taking, so / and I can meet you at the station.
j.
                                                            Love,

                                                            Monica

---

Note these different ways to close a personal letter: *Love,* for family and close
friends; *Warmly,* for friends; *Best wishes,* for colleagues and acquaintances.

2 Look at the letter in Exercise 1, and complete these rules about coordinating conjunctions.

a. Use _____*and*_____ when the second sentence adds information.

b. Use _____ when the second sentence gives a contrasting idea.

c. Use _____ when the information in the second sentence is a result of

the information in the first sentence.

d. Use _____ when the second sentence gives a choice.

3 Complete these sentences with your own ideas.

a. It has started to rain, but _____

b. I don't really want to study tonight, so _____

c. This weekend my friends and I will go to a movie, or _____

d. I'm reading a lot of books in English, and _____

e. After class I'm going shopping, so _____

f. I used to go dancing a lot, but _____

g. I'm looking forward to graduating, and _____

h. Ed is too young to vote, but _____

i. We can take a train, or _____

j. Dan is tired of staying home evenings, so _____

4 Before you write . . .

Talk to a partner about your life these days. Answer some of these questions.

What are you doing these days?

What do you enjoy doing?

What can't you stand?

What do you plan to do next semester?

What are you looking forward to?

5 Write a letter to a friend. Use the letter in Exercise 1 as a model. Describe your present life. Include some of the ideas you spoke about in Exercise 4. Use coordinating conjunctions.

6 Exchange letters with a new partner. Answer your partner's letter.

REVIEW OR SELFTEST
ANSWER KEY

I. (Unit 27)

2. to planning
3. for watching
4. about speaking
5. without worrying
6. in learning

II. (Unit 30)

2. too messy
3. not cool enough
4. too tough
5. aggressively enough
6. loud enough

III. (Units 26 and 29)

2. telling
3. smoking
4. giving up
5. Following
6. to feel
7. To save
8. to read
9. drinking
10. to take
11. eating
12. shopping
13. to reward

IV. (Unit 28)

2. It's necessary to join
3. participate enough to get to know
4. too busy to call
5. are flexible enough for them to have
6. advise them to think about
7. It's important to know about
8. soon enough for thcm to pay
9. too busy to take
10. encourage you to start

V. (Units 26–31)

2. B
3. A
4. C
5. B
6. A
7. D
8. C
9. D
10. C
11. C

VI. (Units 26–31)

2. to hit
3. having
4. winning
5. playing
6. to become
7. to make
8. becoming
9. doing
10. to go
11. to accept
12. to study
13. studying
14. agreeing
15. answering
16. to continue

VII. (Units 26–31)

2. D
3. D
4. B
5. D
6. D
7. B
8. C

325

PART

VII

MORE **MODALS**
AND
RELATED VERBS
AND **EXPRESSIONS**

32 PREFERENCES: PREFER, WOULD PREFER, WOULD RATHER

GRAMMAR **IN CONTEXT**

BEFORE YOU READ Look at the chart below. What is *leisure time*? Which leisure time activity is most popular?

Read this questionnaire about leisure time preferences.

Market Survey, Inc.

Leisure Time Activities

Check the answer closest to your preference.

1 When you go to the movies, **would** you **rather see** an action adventure or a romantic comedy?

☐ I **prefer seeing** an action-adventure film. ☐ I**'d rather watch** a romantic comedy.

2 When you choose a restaurant, do you look for interesting new foods or big portions and fast service?

☐ I **prefer** big portions. ☐ I**'d rather try** interesting foods.

3 Which **would** you **prefer**: tickets to a rock concert, or tickets to a football game?

☐ I**'d rather go** to the rock concert. ☐ I**'d prefer** the football game.

4 Which **do** you **prefer**—eating out or cooking at home?

☐ I almost always **prefer eating out**. ☐ I**'d rather cook** at home.

5 What is your favorite way to use the computer in your free time?

☐ I **prefer using** it to play games. ☐ I**'d rather use** it to surf the Internet.

Preferred Pastimes Around the World

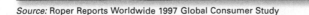

Source: Roper Reports Worldwide 1997 Global Consumer Study

GRAMMAR **PRESENTATION**
PREFERENCES: *PREFER, WOULD PREFER*

STATEMENTS		
SUBJECT	**PREFER / WOULD PREFER***	**NOUN / GERUND / INFINITIVE**
I You We They	**prefer** **would prefer**	**newspapers** (to magazines). **reading** newspapers (to reading magazines). **(not) to read** newspapers.
He She	**prefers** **would prefer**	

*Like modals, *would prefer* does not have *-s* in the third-person singular.

CONTRACTIONS
would prefer = **'d prefer**

YES / NO QUESTIONS			
DO / WOULD	**SUBJECT**	**PREFER**	**NOUN / GERUND / INFINITIVE**
Do **Would**	I you we they	**prefer**	**newspapers**? **reading** newspapers? **to read** newspapers?
Does **Would**	he she		

SHORT ANSWERS		
AFFIRMATIVE		
Yes,	you I you they	**do.** **would.**
	he she	**does.** **would.**

SHORT ANSWERS		
NEGATIVE		
No,	you I you they	**don't.** **wouldn't.**
	he she	**doesn't.** **wouldn't.**

(continued on next page)

PREFERENCES: *WOULD RATHER*

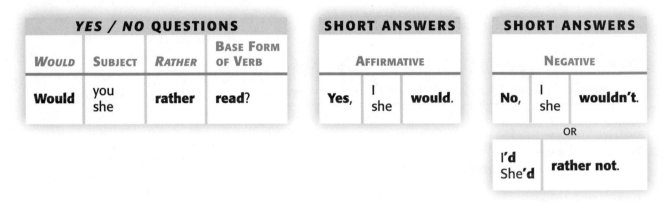

	STATEMENTS		
SUBJECT	WOULD RATHER*	BASE FORM OF VERB	
I You He She We They	would rather	read / (not) read	newspapers (than read magazines). newspapers.

CONTRACTIONS

would rather = **'d rather**

*Like modals, *would rather* does not have -s in the third-person singular.

YES / NO QUESTIONS			
WOULD	SUBJECT	RATHER	BASE FORM OF VERB
Would	you she	**rather**	**read?**

SHORT ANSWERS		
AFFIRMATIVE		
Yes,	I she	**would.**

SHORT ANSWERS		
NEGATIVE		
No,	I she	**wouldn't.**

OR

| I'd She'd | **rather not.** |

NOTES

1. Use *prefer, would prefer,* and *would rather* to talk about <u>things or activities that you like better</u> than other things or activities.

USAGE NOTE: We usually use the contraction for *would* in speech and in informal writing.

We often use *prefer* to express a <u>general</u> preference.

We use *would prefer* or *would rather* to talk about a preference in a <u>particular</u> situation.

▶ **BE CAREFUL!** Do not use *will* to talk about preferences.

EXAMPLES

- We usually **prefer *Italian food***.
- **I'd prefer *to have*** Chinese food tonight.
- **I'd rather *cook*** at home.

- I**'d rather** go.
  NOT <s>I would rather go.</s>

A: Which **do** you **prefer**—action movies or romantic comedies?

B: I usually **prefer** action movies, but tonight I**'d rather see** a romantic comedy.

- I**'d rather go** to the rock concert next weekend.
  NOT <s>I will rather go to the rock concert next weekend.</s>

2. *Prefer* and *would prefer* may be followed by a <u>noun</u>, a <u>gerund</u>, or an <u>infinitive</u>.

- I usually **prefer** the *newspaper*. *(noun)*
- **I'd prefer** a *newspaper*.
- Does Bill **prefer** *reading* magazines? *(gerund)*
- **Would** Bill **prefer** *reading* a magazine?
- He **prefers** *to watch* TV. *(infinitive)*
- He **would prefer** *to watch* soccer.

3. *Would rather* can only be followed by the <u>base form of the verb</u>.

We often use **I'd rather not**, by itself, <u>to refuse</u> an offer, suggestion, or invitation.

▶ **BE CAREFUL!** The negative of *I'd rather* is *I'd rather not*.

- **A:** Would you like to eat out tonight?
- **B:** **I'd rather** *cook* dinner at home. *(base form)*

- **A:** Would you like some dessert?
- **B:** **I'd rather not**. I've had enough to eat.

- **I'd rather not** have dessert.
  NOT ~~I wouldn't rather have dessert.~~

4. A **comparison with** *to* may follow *prefer / would prefer* + <u>noun</u>.

A **comparison with** *to* may also follow *prefer / would prefer* + <u>gerund</u>.

- Lani **prefers** comedies **to** action movies. *(noun ... noun)*
- She**'d prefer** *Dave* **to** *Speed*. *(noun ... noun)*

- I **prefer** visiting friends **to** attending big parties. *(gerund ... gerund)*
- Tonight **I'd prefer** visiting Lani **to** going to the office party. *(gerund ... gerund)*

5. A **comparison with** *than* may follow *would rather* + <u>base form of the verb</u>.

- They**'d rather** eat out **than** cook. *(base form ... base form)*
  (They like eating out better than cooking.)
- **I'd rather** watch football **than** play it. *(base form ... base form)*
  (I like watching football better than playing it.)

FOCUSED PRACTICE

1 DISCOVER THE GRAMMAR

Terry and Grace are spending the afternoon at the mall. Underline the sentences that talk about preferences.

TERRY: <u>Which would you rather do first, get stuff for your project or shop?</u>

GRACE: I think I'd rather get the things for my project first. There's ABC Crafts.

TERRY: Have you tried Franklin's? I really prefer them for science projects.

GRACE: So let's go there.

* * * *

GRACE: Do you want to look at computer games at Nerdly's?

TERRY: I'd prefer shopping for CDs. What about you?

GRACE: I'd rather do that, too. Let's check out the new Dylan CD.

* * * *

TERRY: There's Stella Blue. Do you want to exchange the earrings you got for your birthday?

GRACE: I've been thinking about it, and I'd rather not.

* * * *

TERRY: Have you seen *Total Power* yet?

GRACE: No, but you know me. I always prefer romantic comedies to action movies.

TERRY: We can see *New York Stories* at 5:00. That's romantic.

GRACE: Sounds good. Are you hungry? Let's get a pizza.

TERRY: The line's awfully long. I'd rather just have a taco.

GRACE: You're right. The movie starts in about ten minutes.

Look at the Mall Directory. Check the places that Grace and Terry decide to go to.

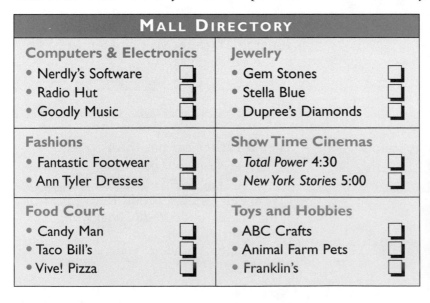

MALL DIRECTORY			
Computers & Electronics		**Jewelry**	
• Nerdly's Software	☐	• Gem Stones	☐
• Radio Hut	☐	• Stella Blue	☐
• Goodly Music	☐	• Dupree's Diamonds	☐
Fashions		**Show Time Cinemas**	
• Fantastic Footwear	☐	• *Total Power* 4:30	☐
• Ann Tyler Dresses	☐	• *New York Stories* 5:00	☐
Food Court		**Toys and Hobbies**	
• Candy Man	☐	• ABC Crafts	☐
• Taco Bill's	☐	• Animal Farm Pets	☐
• Vive! Pizza	☐	• Franklin's	☐

2 MUSHROOMS OR PEPPERONI? Grammar Notes 1 and 3

Arlene and Jim are discussing their evening plans. Complete their conversation.
Use **would rather (not)** *in a short answer or with one of the verbs in the box.*

have	cook	see	~~stay~~

ARLENE: Would you like to go to a movie tonight?

JIM: _____I'd rather stay_____ home and watch TV.
1.

ARLENE: Sounds good. Maybe we could make dinner later.

JIM: _____ tonight. Let's order out for some pizza.
2.

ARLENE: OK. Mushrooms or anchovies?

JIM: I'm in the mood for pepperoni. Let's get a pepperoni pizza.

ARLENE: _____. Pepperoni gives me heartburn.
3.

_____ mushrooms than pepperoni, if that's OK.
4.

JIM: Mushrooms it is! Now, what should we watch on TV? How about the new

Stephen King thriller?

ARLENE: _____. His movies give me the creeps.
5.

JIM: Well . . . there's a comedy on at 8:00 and a documentary at 8:30.

ARLENE: _____ the comedy. I need a laugh.
6.

3 DECISIONS Grammar Notes 1–3

Complete the questions with **prefer**, **would prefer**, *or* **would rather**. *Use* **prefer**
to state general preferences.

1. A: When we go to St. Louis next week, _____would_____ you _____rather_____

travel by train or by plane?

B: Let's take the train. It's cheaper.

2. A: _____ Jim usually _____ an aisle or a window seat?

B: He always asks for an aisle seat. He says there's more room.

(continued on next page)

3. A: Look—our ticket won the prize. We have two choices. _____ you

_____ going to a World Series game or getting a new television set?

B: Let's go to the baseball game. I've always wanted to watch the World Series.

4. A: I'm looking for a movie.

B: What do you like? _____ you _____ to watch comedies

or thrillers?

5. A: Listen up, everyone! We're going on a field trip next week. You have a choice.

_____ you _____ go to the Science Museum or to

the Capitol?

B: Science Museum!

6. A: Waiter, this cigarette smoke is really bothering us.

B: _____ you _____ a table in the nonsmoking section?

4 EDITING

Read Jim's report. Find and correct six mistakes in the use of **prefer** *and*
would rather. *The first mistake is already corrected.*

> For my study, I interviewed fifty men and women. There was
> no difference in men's and women's preferences for television.
> I found that everyone prefers watching television t͟h͟a͟n͟ going
> to the movies. Men and women both enjoy news programs and
> entertainment specials. However, men would rather watching
> adventure programs and science fiction, while women prefer soap
> operas. Men also like to watch all kinds of sports, but women
> would rather see game shows to sports events.
>
> I found a big difference in reading preferences. Men prefer
> to reading newspapers, while women would much rather read
> magazines and books. When men read books, they prefer read
> nonfiction and adventure stories. Women will prefer novels.

5 **SPORTS PREFERENCES** Grammar Notes 4–5

*Complete this report about sports preferences around the world. Use the words in parentheses plus **to** or **than** to make a comparison. If there is a verb, choose the correct form.*

The Wide World of Sports

Soccer or Basketball?

You're going to play ball today. Would you prefer

_____playing soccer to playing basketball_____? Your answer depends a lot

1. (play soccer / basketball)

on your age, your gender, and your nationality. Boys age thirteen and

older prefer _____, but girls prefer

2. (soccer / basketball)

_____. Because of girls' preferences,

3. (shoot hoops / make goals)

teens as a group would rather _____.

4. (play basketball / soccer)

In this age group, basketball is as popular in Colombia and Thailand as it is

in the United States.

Play or Watch?

People of all ages prefer _____.

5. (watch / play)

Seventy percent of Latin Americans prefer

_____, but Filipinos would rather

6. (soccer / other TV sports)

see a basketball game (85 percent watch regularly). Worldwide, cricket is not

a popular sport on TV, but in India, a whopping 80 percent prefer

_____. In general, people watch

7. (it / basketball or soccer)

the sports they love to play.

No, Thanks.

This is not true of car racing, figure skating, and wrestling. For these sports,

almost everyone would rather _____.

8. (watch a pro / participate)

Source of statistics: Roper Reports Worldwide, 1997 Global Consumer Study.

COMMUNICATION PRACTICE

6 LISTENING

Arlene is ordering in a restaurant. Listen to her conversation with the waiter. Then listen again and circle the items on the menu that Arlene wants.

FISH DINNER
Comes with your choice of
Soup (tomato or onion)
or salad
rice or potato
coffee, tea, soda (diet or regular)
apple pie or ice cream

STEAK DINNER
Comes with
salad and baked potato
coffee, tea, or
soda (diet or regular)
apple pie

7 WHAT'S ON TV?

Work in small groups. Look at the TV schedule and try to agree on something to watch at 8:00 P.M. Use **would rather** *or* **would prefer** *to talk about your preferences.*

	8:00
2	**Baseball** The Mets vs. the Dodgers. Third game in a five-game series.
4	**Science Watch** Are we alone in the universe?
8	**My Life with Henry** Henry meets an old girlfriend.
12	**World News**
CNN	**Washington Report**
35	**Movie★** (1987) *The Monster of Monroe Street* Man turns into a monster and terrorizes neighborhood. Frightening.
42	**Movie★★★★** (1988) *Who's There?* Comedy about computer programmer. Light and entertaining.
50	**Movie★★★** (1955) *It's My Life* Black-and-white drama about the lives and relationships of four friends. Serious and moving.

EXAMPLE:

A: Let's watch the ball game at 8:00.

B: I don't really like baseball. I'd prefer to watch "My Life with Henry."

8 IF I HAD MY WAY

Read the choices below. In pairs, discuss your preferences. Give reasons for your choices.

1. live in the city / live in the country
2. work in an office / work at home
3. be married / be single
4. be a man / be a woman

EXAMPLE:

A: I'd rather live in the city than in the country. There's a lot more to do.

B: Really? I'd prefer the country. It's quieter.

Now ask your partner about some other choices.

Would you rather . . . ?

9 INFORMATION GAP: PREFERRED SNACKS

Work in pairs (A and B). Student B, look at the Information Gap on p. 339 and follow the instructions there. Student A, look at the bar graphs below. Ask your partner for the information you need to complete each graph. Draw the missing bar(s) on each graph. Answer your partner's questions.

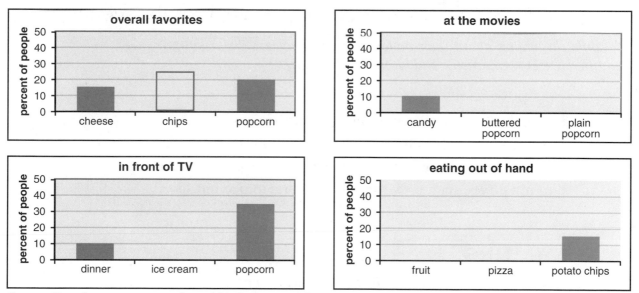

Source: Based on a survey conducted by *Bon Appétit* (January 1998, p. 64)

EXAMPLE:

A: In the overall favorites: What percentage of people would rather eat chips than any other snack?

B: About 25 percent. What percentage prefer eating cheese?

A: 15 percent prefer cheese to chips or popcorn.

B: What percentage of people . . . ?

When you are finished, compare graphs. Are they the same?

 **CHOICES**

*Complete the leisure time activities questionnaire on p. 328. Discuss your
answers with a partner. Give reasons for your choices.*

> **EXAMPLE:**
>
> **A:** I prefer seeing action-adventure films. They're more exciting.
>
> **B:** Not me. I prefer romantic comedies. I'd rather laugh than be frightened.

11 RANK ORDER

*Look at the list of some favorite leisure time activities. Rank them in the order of
your own preferences. (1 = most favorite, 12 = least favorite)*

Favorite Leisure Time Activities

_____	Watch television	_____	Watch sports
_____	Go to the movies	_____	Play sports
_____	Listen to popular music	_____	Read books
_____	Travel	_____	Read newspapers or magazines
_____	Cook	_____	Play cards
_____	Eat in restaurants	_____	Do crafts (woodworking, sewing, etc.)

*Ask some classmates about their preferences. Have a class discussion. Is there
any difference between men's and women's preferences?*

> **EXAMPLES:**
>
> Would you rather listen to music than cook?
>
> Would you prefer playing sports to watching sports?
>
> Do you prefer books or magazines?
>
> In my survey, men prefer watching sports to playing sports.

 **WRITING**

*Compare your top five activities from Exercise 11 with another person's favorites.
Write a paragraph comparing your preferences.*

> **EXAMPLE:**
>
> After school, I like to play sports, but Marissa prefers listening to music . . .

INFORMATION GAP FOR STUDENT B

Student B, look at the bar graphs below. Answer your partner's questions. Ask your partner for the information you need to complete each bar graph. Draw the missing bar(s) on each graph.

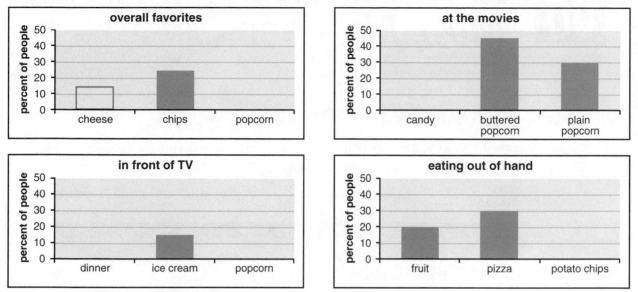

Source: Based on a survey conducted by *Bon Appétit* (January 1998, p. 64)

EXAMPLE:

A: In the overall favorites: What percentage of people would rather eat chips than any other snack?

B: About 25 percent. What percentage prefer eating cheese?

A: 15 percent prefer cheese to chips or popcorn.

B: What percentage of people . . . ?

When you are finished, compare graphs. Are they the same?

33 NECESSITY: HAVE (GOT) TO, DON'T HAVE TO, MUST, MUST NOT, CAN'T

GRAMMAR **IN CONTEXT**

BEFORE YOU READ What kind of information can you find in a driver's manual? What does the Buckle Up sign mean?

Read this excerpt from the introduction to a driver's manual.

⚠ Becoming a Safe Driver

In our society, people are always on the move, and most people **have to drive** to get from one place to another. With so many people on the roads, it is necessary for everyone to know how to drive safely. That's why you—and all other drivers—**must pass** a test to get a driver's license before you drive.

It takes time and practice to become a safe driver. You **will have to learn** how to drive safely in fog, snow, and other dangerous weather conditions. You **will** also **have to learn** how to drive in different traffic situations. In the city, for example, you **have to be** careful about traffic at cross-streets. On expressways you **don't have to deal** with cross-traffic, but you **must know** how to change lanes and pass other cars.

Finally, you **have to learn** the driving laws. Many of these are common sense. For example, according to the law you **must wear** your seat belt when you drive. And, of course, you **must not drive** under the influence of alcohol.

BUCKLE UP EVERYBODY

WE CARE ABOUT YOU!

GRAMMAR **PRESENTATION**
NECESSITY: *HAVE (GOT) TO, DON'T HAVE TO*

AFFIRMATIVE STATEMENTS

SUBJECT	HAVE TO / HAVE GOT TO	BASE FORM OF VERB
I You We They	**have to** **have got to**	**stop**.
He She It	**has to** **has got to**	

NEGATIVE STATEMENTS

SUBJECT	DO NOT	HAVE TO	BASE FORM OF VERB
I You We They	**don't**	**have to**	**stop**.
He She It	**doesn't**		

CONTRACTIONS

have got to = **'ve got to**
has got to = **'s got to**

Note: There are no contractions for *have to* and *has to*.

YES / NO QUESTIONS

DO	SUBJECT	HAVE TO	BASE FORM OF VERB
Do	I you we they	**have to**	**stop**?
Does	he she it		

SHORT ANSWERS

	AFFIRMATIVE	
Yes,	you I / we you they	**do**.
	he she it	**does**.

SHORT ANSWERS

	NEGATIVE	
No,	you I / we you they	**don't**.
	he she it	**doesn't**.

WH- QUESTIONS

WH- WORD	DO	SUBJECT	HAVE TO	BASE FORM OF VERB
Why	**do**	I you we they	**have to**	**stop**?
	does	he she it		

(continued on next page)

NECESSITY: *MUST, MUST NOT, CAN'T*

MUST			
SUBJECT	**MUST* (NOT)**	**BASE FORM OF VERB**	
I You He She It We They	**must**	**stop**	at the stop sign.
	must not	**go**	above the speed limit.

CONTRACTION

must not = **mustn't**

*Must is a modal. Modals have only one form. They do not have *-s* in the third-person singular.

CAN'T			
SUBJECT	**CAN'T**	**BASE FORM OF VERB**	
You They	**can't**	**park**	here.

NOTES

1. Use *have to, have got to*, and *must* to express **necessity**. Note these differences among the three expressions:

a. *Have to* is the <u>most common</u> expression in everyday use.

b. *Have got to* is usually only used in <u>spoken English</u> and <u>informal writing</u>. When it is used orally, it often expresses strong feelings on the part of the speaker.

c. *Must* is used to express <u>obligation in writing</u>, including official forms, signs, and notices.

USAGE NOTE: Americans do not usually use *must* when speaking to or about another adult. Sometimes people use *must* to tell a child there is no choice in a situation.

EXAMPLES

- Everyone **has to pass** a road test before getting a driver's license.

- We**'ve got to stop** for lunch soon. I'm starving.

- You **must stop** completely at a stop sign.

- Jess, you **must clean** your room before Grandma gets here.

PRONUNCIATION NOTE
In informal speech, *have to* is usually pronounced /hæftə/, and *got to* is usually pronounced /gɑt̬ə/.

2. You can use *have to* for **all tenses**.

- Everyone **has to pass** a road test.
- She**'ll have to renew** her license next year.

Have got to and *must* refer only to the <u>present</u> or the <u>future</u>.

- I**'ve got to get** glasses soon because I didn't pass the eye test.
- Everyone **must take** an eye test in order to get a driver's license.

Use the correct form of *have to* for <u>all other tenses</u>.

- Sheila **has had to drive** to work for two years. *(present perfect)*
- After his traffic accident, Sal **had to take** a driver-improvement class. *(past tense)*

---

3. Use *have to* for most **questions**.

USAGE NOTE: We almost never use *must* or *have got to* in questions.

- **Does** Paul **have to drive**? He always goes too fast.
- **Did** he **have to drive** all night?
- When **will** he **have to leave**?

---

4. BE CAREFUL! *Have (got) to* and *must* have similar meanings. However, *must not* and *don't / doesn't have to* have very <u>different meanings</u>.

a. *Must not* expresses **prohibition**.

USAGE NOTE: We often use *can't* instead of *must not* to express prohibition in spoken English

- You **must not drive** without a license. It's against the law.
- You **can't drive** without a license. It's against the law.

b. *Don't / doesn't have to* expresses that something is **not necessary**. It means that there is a choice.

- You **don't have to drive** tomorrow. I can do it.

REFERENCE NOTE
Have (got) to and *must* are also used to make assumptions *(see Unit 36).*
Can't is also used to express ability *(see Unit 11),* refuse requests *(see Unit 13),* and make assumptions *(see Unit 36).*

FOCUSED PRACTICE

1 DISCOVER THE GRAMMAR

Read Ben Leonard's telephone conversation with a clerk from the California Department of Motor Vehicles. Underline the words in the conversation that express necessity, lack of necessity, or prohibition.

CLERK: Department of Motor Vehicles. May I help you?

BEN: I'm moving to California soon, and I have some questions. My Illinois license is good for five years. <u>Will I have to get</u> a California driver's license when I move?

CLERK: Yes, <u>you will</u>. It's the law—California residents must have a California driver's license.

BEN: When will I have to get my California license?

CLERK: You can't use your old license longer than ten days after you become a resident. So, come in and apply for your California license right after you get here.

BEN: Do I have to take any tests?

CLERK: Since you already have an Illinois license, you probably won't have to take the road test here in California. But you will have to take the written test.

BEN: How about the eye test?

CLERK: Oh, everyone has got to take the eye test.

BEN: OK. Thanks a lot. You've been very helpful.

Now check the appropriate box for each instruction.

	Necessary	Not Necessary	Prohibited
1. get a California driver's license	☑	☐	☐
2. use the Illinois license for longer than ten days	☐	☐	☐
3. take the written test	☐	☐	☐
4. take the road test	☐	☐	☐
5. take the eye test	☐	☐	☐

② GETTING READY

The Leonards have checked off the things they've already done to get ready to move to California. Read the lists and write sentences about what the Leonards **have to do** *and* **don't have to do**.

Ben
✓ Clean car
buy gas
check the oil

Ann
buy a road map
✓ call the moving company again
get the kids' school records
✓ buy film

Jim and Sue
✓ pack clothes and toys for the trip
say goodbye to friends
buy gifts for teachers

Ben doesn't have to clean the car.

He has to buy gas, and he has to check the oil.

_____

_____

_____

_____

_____

_____

_____

_____

3 **CAR GAMES**

Ben's family is driving to their new home in California. Complete the conversations with short answers or the correct form of **have to**, **have got to**, *or* **can't** *and the verb in parentheses.*

1. Use *have to* or *can't*.

   BEN: What time _____*do*_____ we ____*have to leave*____?
   a. (leave)

   ANN: We _____ later than 9:00. We _____ at the Holiday
   b. (start)   c. (check in)
   Motel in Centerville by 5:00.

2. Use *have to*.

   BEN: _____ we _____ for lunch? We're running late already.
   a. (stop)

   ANN: Yes, _____. The kids are starving, and so am I.
   b.

3. Use *have to*.

   BEN: We _____ never _____ for a table at Ardy's before.
   a. (wait)

   ANN: I know. There are a lot of people on the road today.

4. Use *have to*.

   SUE: Mom, _____ you _____? I want you to sit back here.
   a. (drive)

   ANN: Yes, _____. It's a long trip, and your father drove all morning.
   b.

5. Use *have got to* or *can't*.

   ANN: Hey kids, here's a good car game. Each player chooses a kind of car. You get a

   point for every one you see.

   JIM: Toyota! There's one! And there's another!

   SUE: Hey! That's not fair! He _____ me a turn, too.
   a. (give)

   ANN: You _____, kids. I _____ attention to the road.
   b. (shout)   c. (pay)

6. Use *have got to*.

   ANN: We _____ gas soon. There's only a quarter tank left.
   a. (buy)

   BEN: There'll be a rest stop in about ten miles.

7. Use *have to*.

   JIM: Where did you go, Dad?

   BEN: To call the motel. I _____ them we'll be late.
   a. (tell)

4 **FOLLOWING THE RULES**

Complete these rules from a driver's handbook. Use **must** *or* **must not**.

1. You _____must not_____ drive on a public road without a license or permit.

2. Bicycle riders _____ ride on freeways. Cars drive fast on freeways, and bicycles can cause accidents.

3. A parent or guardian _____ sign the driver's license application of anyone under eighteen years of age.

4. You _____ speed up when another driver is trying to pass you.

5. You _____ pay a fee when you apply for a license.

6. You _____ take an eye test.

7. All drivers _____ be able to read and understand the simple English in highway traffic and direction signs.

8. You _____ park within fifteen feet of a fire hydrant. Fire trucks must be able to reach the fire hydrant in case of a fire.

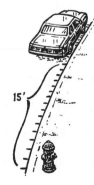

9. The driver and front-seat passenger _____ wear seat belts. Seat belts save lives.

10. You _____ signal before you turn.

5 **AT THE POOL**

*Read the sign at the Holiday Motel swimming pool and complete each statement,
using* **must not** *or* **don't have to**.

Holiday Motel
Swimming Pool Rules and Regulations

Pool Hours 10 A.M.–10:00 P.M.

Children under 12 years NOT ALLOWED in pool
without an adult.   **NO**

Towels available at front desk.

- ball playing
- radios
- diving
- glass bottles
- alcoholic beverages

---

1. Children under age 12 _____ must not swim _____ without an adult.
   (swim)

2. You _____ your own towel.
   (bring)

3. You _____ ball in or around the pool.
   (play)

4. You _____ into the pool.
   (dive)

5. Teenagers _____ with an adult.
   (be)

6. You _____ the pool at 8:00 P.M.
   (leave)

6 **EDITING**

*Read Jim's postcard home. Find and correct five mistakes in expressing necessity.
The first mistake is already corrected.*

Holiday Motel, Rte. 55

Hi Jason!

We're almost halfway to California! Dad drove all day
                  had to
yesterday, but we ~~must~~ stop at 4:00 when he got tired. We're

staying at this really cool motel. The only problem is, you have

to be twelve years old in order to go swimming alone. It's

almost 9:00 P.M. now, and we gotta get up early tomorrow.

Even though we must not leave until 10:00 (checkout time), Mom

and Dad want to get an early start. We <u>must</u> get to California

by Thursday. That's when Mom and Dad have to signing the

papers for the new house. You'll really hafta come visit us

next summer!

                              Jim

USA 22

To:

Jason Harter
433 Red Oak Lane
Galena, IL 60173

COMMUNICATION PRACTICE

7 LISTENING

Listen to the conversations. Then listen again and write the number of each conversation next to the appropriate sign.

a. _____

b. _____

c. _____

d. __1__

e. _____

f. _____

8 **READING THE SIGNS**

Work in pairs. Where can you find these signs? Discuss what they mean. What do you have to do when you see each one? What are you not allowed to do? What do you think of these rules?

9 INVENT A SIGN

Draw your own sign to illustrate something people **have to do** *or* **must not do**.
*Show it to a classmate. See if he or she can guess the meaning. Decide where
the sign belongs.*

10 DRIVING AROUND THE WORLD

Discuss different driving rules around the world. Consider some of the ideas below.

seatbelts	car insurance
airbags	side of the road
driver's license	yellow lights
learner's permit	minimum and maximum age
speed limits	license plates

EXAMPLE:

A: In England, you have to drive on the left side of the road.

B: Do you have to drive on the left in any other countries?

11 TAKING CARE OF BUSINESS

*Make a list of your most important tasks for this week. Check off the things
you've already done. Tell a partner what you* **have to do** *and what you* **don't
have to do**. *Report to a group.*

EXAMPLES:

I don't have to do English homework. I've already done it.

Hamed has to wash the car. He doesn't have to go shopping because he went
on Monday.

12 WRITING

*Write about the application procedure for getting a driver's license, a passport, a
work permit, citizenship, school admission, or a new job. What do you have to
do? What don't you have to do? Use* **have to**, **don't have to**, **must**, *and* **must not**.

34 EXPECTATIONS:
BE SUPPOSED TO

GRAMMAR **IN CONTEXT**

BEFORE YOU READ   What do you think the letter to Ms. Etiquette is about? What does *etiquette* mean?

Read this page from Ms. Etiquette's book, Wedding Wisdom.

Dear Ms. Etiquette:

What **is** the maid of honor **supposed to do** in a wedding ceremony? My best friend is getting married soon. She has invited me to be her maid of honor. I am new in this country, and I'm not sure what my friend expects of me.

Dear Reader:

You should be very proud. In the past, the bride's sister **was supposed to serve** as her maid of honor, and the groom's brother **was supposed to be** his best man. Today, however, the bride and groom can ask anyone they want. Your friend's invitation means that she values your friendship very highly.

The maid of honor is the bride's assistant, and the best man is the groom's. Before the wedding, these two **are supposed to help** the couple prepare for the ceremony. You might help the bride send the wedding invitations, for example. The day of the wedding, the best man **is supposed to drive** the groom to the ceremony. During the ceremony, the maid of honor holds the bride's flowers. After the wedding, the maid of honor and the best man **are** both **supposed to sign** the marriage certificate as witnesses.

GRAMMAR **PRESENTATION**
EXPECTATIONS: *BE SUPPOSED TO*

SUBJECT	BE	(NOT) SUPPOSED TO	BASE FORM OF VERB	
I	am was			
You We They	are were	(not) supposed to	sign	the marriage certificate.
He She	is was			
It			be	a small wedding.

(Table heading: STATEMENTS)

YES / NO QUESTIONS

BE	SUBJECT	SUPPOSED TO	BASE FORM OF VERB
Am Was	I		
Are Were	you	supposed to	stand?
Is Was	she		

SHORT ANSWERS

AFFIRMATIVE		
	you	are. were.
Yes,	I	am. was.
	she	is. was.

SHORT ANSWERS

NEGATIVE		
	you	aren't. weren't.
No,	I	'm not. wasn't.
	she	isn't. wasn't.

WH- QUESTIONS

WH- WORD	BE	SUBJECT	SUPPOSED TO	BASE FORM OF VERB
Where	am was	I		
	are were	you	supposed to	stand?
	is was	she		

NOTES	**EXAMPLES**

1. Use *be supposed* **to** to talk about different kinds of <u>expectations</u>:

a. rules and **usual ways** of doing things

- You**'re not supposed to run** near the swimming pool. It's a safety rule.
- The groom **is supposed to arrive** at the ceremony early. It's a custom.

b. predictions

- It**'s not supposed to rain** tomorrow. I heard it on the radio.
- It**'s supposed to be** a lovely day.

c. hearsay (what everyone says)

- The beach **is supposed to be** beautiful in August. Everyone says so.
- I've never met them, but the groom's family **is supposed to be** very nice. People are always saying good things about them.

d. plans or **arrangements**

- Let's hurry. We**'re supposed to meet** the Smiths in front of the movie theater at 8:00.
- **Am** I **supposed to send** these invitations today?
- Bob's plane **is supposed to arrive** at noon.
- The ceremony **isn't supposed to begin** yet.

---

2. Use *be supposed to* only in the **simple present** tense or in the **simple past** tense.

- The bride **is supposed to wear** white.
- The ceremony **was supposed to begin** at 7:00.

Use the simple present tense to refer to both the <u>present</u> and the <u>future</u>.

- I**'m supposed to be** at the wedding rehearsal *tomorrow*.
  NOT ~~I will be supposed to be there tomorrow.~~

▶ **BE CAREFUL!** *Was / were supposed to* often suggests that <u>something did not happen</u>.

- Carl **was supposed to bring** flowers, *but* he forgot.
- The Hamptons **were supposed to come** to the wedding, *but* they had to leave town.

FOCUSED PRACTICE

1 DISCOVER THE GRAMMAR

Read the article and underline the phrases that express expectations.

It wasn't supposed to be a big wedding.

BY MATT PEDDLER

PROVIDENCE, JULY 19—The Stricklands wanted a small, quiet wedding—that's why they eloped to Block Island, off the Atlantic Coast of the United States.

The ferry they took to their wedding site doesn't carry cars, so the Stricklands packed their bikes for the trip.

The couple found a lonely hill overlooking the ocean. The weather was supposed to be beautiful, so they asked the mayor to marry them there the next afternoon. They planned to have a private ceremony in this romantic setting.

"When we got there, we found a crowd of bikers admiring the view," laughed Beth Strickland.

When Bill kissed his bride, the audience burst into loud applause and rang their bicycle bells. "We weren't supposed to have fifty wedding guests, but we love biking, and we're not sorry," Bill said.

When they packed to leave the island the next day, Beth left her wedding bouquet at the hotel. She remembered it minutes before the ferry was supposed to leave. Bill jumped on his bike, recovered the flowers, and made it back to the ferry before it departed.

"Bikers are supposed to stay fast and fit," he said. "Now I know why."

Read the article again. Circle **True (T)** *or* **False (F)** *for each statement.*

1. The Stricklands planned a big wedding.   T   (F)
2. The weather forecaster predicted rain.   T   F
3. The Stricklands invited fifty wedding guests.   T   F
4. The ferry followed a schedule.   T   F
5. People believe that bikers are in good shape.   T   F

2 **GETTING READY**

Complete the conversations with the verb in parentheses and a form of
be supposed to.

1. **A:** Netta, Gary called while you were out.

   B: _____Am_____ I __supposed to call__ him back?

a. (call)

   A: No, he'll call you later in the afternoon.

2. **A:** The dress store called, too. They delivered your wedding dress to your office.

   _____ they _____ that?

a. (do)

   B: No, they weren't! They _____ it here. That's why I stayed home today.

b. (deliver)

3. **A:** Let's get in line. The rehearsal _____ in a few minutes.

a. (start)

   B: We're bridesmaids. Where _____ we _____?

b. (stand)

   A: Right here, behind Netta.

4. **A:** Hi. Where's Netta?

   B: Gary! You _____ here!

a. (be)

   A: Why not?

   B: The groom _____ the bride on the day of the wedding until the

b. (see)

   ceremony. It's bad luck.

5. **A:** Sophie, could I borrow your handkerchief, please?

   B: Sure, but why?

   A: I _____ something old, something new, something borrowed, and

a. (wear)

   something blue. I don't have anything borrowed.

   B: It _____ this afternoon. Maybe I should lend you my umbrella instead.

b. (rain)

6. **A:** Where are Gary and Netta going on their honeymoon?

   B: Aruba.

   A: Oh, that _____ a really nice island.

a. (be)

3 EDITING

Read Sophie's letter to a friend. Find and correct five mistakes in the use of **be supposed to**. *The first mistake is already corrected.*

May 6, 1999

Dear Kasha,

I have some wonderful news. My friend Netta is getting married soon, and she's asked me to be her maid of honor. She and Gary want a big wedding—they ^are^ supposed to have about two hundred guests. I have a lot of responsibilities. I will be supposed to give Netta a shower before the wedding. (That's a party where everyone brings presents for the bride.) I am also suppose to help her choose the bridesmaids' dresses. The best man's name is Jim. He'll help Gary get ready. I haven't met him yet, but he's supposed to be very nice.

I'd better say goodbye now, or I'll be late for the rehearsal. I supposed to leave five minutes ago.

Love,

Sophie

P.S. Aren't you supposing to get time off soon? How about a visit? I miss you!

COMMUNICATION PRACTICE

4 LISTENING

It's the day of the wedding. Listen to the conversations. Then listen again and circle the correct words.

1. Netta is / **isn't** supposed to be at the church by 2:00.

2. The photographer <u>is</u> / <u>isn't</u> supposed to take pictures during the ceremony.

3. Members of the bride's family <u>are</u> / <u>aren't</u> supposed to sit on the right.

4. The maid of honor <u>is</u> / <u>isn't</u> supposed to walk behind the bride.

5. Guests <u>are</u> / <u>aren't</u> supposed to say "congratulations" to the groom.

6. Guests <u>are</u> / <u>aren't</u> supposed to throw rice at the bride and groom.

5 INTERNATIONAL CUSTOMS

Work in small groups. Discuss these important events. What are people in your culture supposed to do and say at these times? Are people expected to give certain gifts? Report to the class.

• a wedding

• an important birthday

• a graduation ceremony

• an engagement to be married

• an anniversary

• a birth

• a funeral

EXAMPLE:
In traditional Japanese weddings, the bride and groom are supposed to wear kimonos.

6 WRITING

Write a short essay about one of the events listed in Exercise 5. Use **be supposed to** *to describe customs.*

FUTURE POSSIBILITY: MAY, MIGHT, COULD

GRAMMAR **IN CONTEXT**

BEFORE YOU READ Look at the weather map. Are temperatures in Celsius or Fahrenheit? How warm might it get in Ankara? How cool? What's the weather prediction for Madrid?

Read this transcript of a weather report on British TV.

CAROL: Good morning. I'm Carol Johnson, and here's the local forecast. The cold front that has been affecting much of northern Europe is moving toward Great Britain. Temperatures **may drop** as much as eleven degrees by tomorrow morning. In London, expect a high of only two and a low of minus four degrees. We **might** even **see** some snow flurries later on in the day. By evening, winds **could reach** 40 mph. So, bundle up, it's going to be a cold one! And now it's time for our traveler's forecast with Jim Harvey. Jim?

JIM: Thanks, Carol. Take your umbrella if you're traveling to Paris. Stormy conditions **may move** into France by tomorrow morning. Rain **could turn into** snow by evening when temperatures fall to near or below freezing. On a warmer note—you **may not need** your coat at all if you plan to be in Rome. Expect to see partly cloudy skies with early morning highs around ten. Temperatures **could climb** to above twenty as skies clear up in the afternoon. It looks like it will turn out to be a beautiful, sunny day in central Italy.

CAROL: Italy sounds great! Will you join me on a Roman holiday?

JIM: I might!

GRAMMAR **PRESENTATION**
FUTURE POSSIBILITY: *MAY, MIGHT, COULD*

STATEMENTS			
SUBJECT	*MAY / MIGHT / COULD**	**BASE FORM OF VERB**	
I You He She It We You They	**may (not)** **might (not)** **could**	**get**	cold.

*May, might, and *could* are modals. Modals have only one form.
They do not have *-s* in the third-person singular.

YES / NO **QUESTIONS**
Are you going to fly to Paris? Are you taking the Concorde?

Are you going to Will you Is it possible you'll	**be**	there long?

SHORT ANSWERS			
I	**may (not)**. **might (not)**. **could**.		
We	**may** **might** **could**	**be**.	

Note: *May not* and *might not* are
not contracted.

WH- **QUESTIONS**
When are you **going** to Paris?
How long are you going to **be** there?

ANSWERS			
I	**may** **might**	**go**	next week.
We	**could**	**be**	there a week.

NOTES	EXAMPLES
1. Use *may*, *might*, and *could* to talk about **future possibility**.	• It **may be** windy later. • It **might get** cold. • It **could rain** tomorrow.
▶ **BE CAREFUL!** Notice the difference between *may be* and *maybe*. Both express possibility. *May be* is a <u>modal + verb</u>. It is always two words. *Maybe* is not a modal. It is an <u>adverb</u>. It is always one word, and it comes at the beginning of the sentence.	 • He **may be** late today. • **Maybe** he'll take the train. NOT ~~He'll maybe take the train.~~

2. Use *may not* and *might not* to express the possibility that something <u>will not happen</u>.	• There are a lot of clouds, but it **might not rain**.
Use *couldn't* to express the idea that something is <u>impossible</u>.	A: Why don't you ask John for a ride? B: I **couldn't do** that. He's too busy.
▶ **BE CAREFUL!** We usually do not contract *might not*, and we never contract *may not*.	• You **may not** need a coat. NOT ~~You mayn't need a coat.~~

3. **Questions about possibility** usually are not formed with *may*, *might*, or *could*. Instead, they are formed with the future (*will, be going to*, the present progressive) or phrases such as *Do you think . . . ?* or *Is it possible that . . . ?*	A: When *will* it *start* snowing? B: It **might start** around lunch time. A: *Are* you *going to drive* to work? B: I **might take** the bus instead.
The **answers** to these questions often contain *may*, *might*, or *could*.	A: When *are* you *leaving*? B: I **may leave** now. A: *Do you think it'll snow* tomorrow? B: It **could stop** tonight.
In <u>short answers to *yes / no* questions</u>, use *may*, *might*, or *could* alone.	A: Will your office close early? B: It **might**.
If *be* is the main verb, it is common to include *be* in the short answer.	A: Will our flight *be* on time? B: It **might be**.

FOCUSED PRACTICE

1 DISCOVER THE GRAMMAR

Alice is a college student who works part time; Bill is her boyfriend. Read their conversation. Underline the words that express future possibility.

ALICE: Are you going to drive to work tomorrow?

BILL: I <u>might</u>. Why?

ALICE: I just heard the weather report. It may snow tonight.

BILL: Then I might take the 7:30 train instead. I have a 9:00 meeting, and I don't want to miss it. Do you have a class tomorrow morning?

ALICE: No, but I'm going to go to the library to work on my paper. Maybe I'll take the train with you.

BILL: We could have lunch together after you go to the library.

ALICE: Oh, I'm sorry. I have a class at noon every day this week.

BILL: Cut class tomorrow. One day won't make any difference.

ALICE: I couldn't do that. I'll meet you at six at the train station, OK? I'm going to take the 6:30 train home.

BILL: I might not catch the 6:30 train. My boss said something about working late tomorrow. I'll call you and let you know what I'm doing.

Read the conversation again. Check the appropriate box for each activity.

BILL'S SCHEDULE	certain	possible	impossible
shovel snow from front steps	☐	✔	☐
take 7:30 A.M. train	☐	☐	☐
9:00 A.M. meeting	☐	☐	☐
meet Alice for lunch	☐	☐	☐
call Alice	☐	☐	☐
work until 8:00 P.M.	☐	☐	☐

ALICE'S SCHEDULE	certain	possible	impossible
ride train with Bill	☐	☐	☐
go to library—work on paper	☐	☐	☐
go to class	☐	☐	☐
lunch with Bill	☐	☐	☐
6:00 P.M.—meet Bill at station	☐	☐	☐
take 6:30 train home	☐	☐	☐

2 MAKING PLANS

*Alice is graduating from college with a degree in Early Childhood Education.
Complete this paragraph from her diary. Choose the appropriate words in
parentheses.*

I just got the notice from my school. I _____'m going to_____ graduate in June, but
1. (might not / 'm going to)

I still don't have plans. Some day-care centers hire students before they graduate, so I

_____ apply for a job now. On the other hand, I _____
2. (could / couldn't) 3. (might / might not)

apply to a graduate school and get my master's degree.

I'm just not sure, though—these past two years have been hard, and I

_____ be ready to study for two more years. At least I *am* sure about my
4. (may / may not)

career. I _____ work with children—that's certain. I made an
5. ('m going to / might)

appointment to discuss my plans with my teacher, Mrs. Humphrey, tomorrow. I

_____ talk this over with her. She _____ have an idea
6. (maybe / may) 7. (won't / might)

about what I should do.

3 I MIGHT

Look at Alice's schedule for Monday. She put a question mark **(?)** *next to each item
she wasn't sure about. Write sentences about Alice's plans for Monday. Use* **may** *or*
might *(for things that are possible) and* **be going to** *(for things that are certain).*

MONDAY

call Bill at 9:00   go to work at 1:00

buy some notebooks before class **?**   go shopping after work **?**

go to meeting with Mrs. Humphrey at 11:00   take 7:00 train **?**

have coffee with Sue after class **?**

 Alice is going to call Bill at 9:00.

_____

_____

_____

_____

_____

_____

4 STORM WARNING

Write short answers with **could** *or* **couldn't**. *Use* **be** *when necessary.*

1. Do you think the roads will be dangerous? It's snowing really hard.

_____ They could be _____. It's a big storm.

2. Will the schools stay open?

Oh, no. _____. It's too dangerous for school buses in a storm like this.

3. Will it be very windy?

_____. The winds are very strong already.

4. Will it get very cold?

_____. The temperature in Centerville is below zero.

5. Is it possible that the storm will be over by Monday?

_____. It's moving pretty quickly now.

6. Do you think it will be warmer on Tuesday?

_____. It has stopped snowing in Centerville already.

5 EDITING

Read this student's report about El Niño. Find and correct seven mistakes in the use of modals. The first mistake is already corrected.

Every few years, the ocean near Peru becomes warmer. This change
is called El Niño. Meteorologists predict this year we will
experience the effects of El Niño. An El Niño ~~maybe~~ ^{may} cause big
weather changes all over the world. The west coasts of North and
South America might have very heavy rains. On the other side of
the Pacific, New Guinea might becomes very dry. Northern areas
could have warmer, wetter winters, and southern areas maybe
become much colder. These weather changes affect plants and
animals. Some fish mayn't survive in warmer waters. They die or
swim to colder places. In addition, dry conditions could causing
crops to die. When that happens, food may get very expensive. El
Niño does not happen regularly. It may happen every two years,
or it could not come for seven years. Will El Niños get worse in
the future? They could be. Pollution that holds heat in the air
might increase the effects of El Niño, but no one is sure yet.

COMMUNICATION PRACTICE

6 LISTENING

Listen to the weather forecast. Then listen again and check **Certain** *or* **Possible** *for each forecast.*

	Certain	Possible		Certain	Possible		Certain	Possible
Friday			**Saturday**			**Sunday**		
Dry	☑	☐	Sunny	☐	☐	Cold	☐	☐
Sunny	☐	☐	60°	☐	☐	Windy	☐	☐
Low fifties	☐	☐	Windy	☐	☐	Snow	☐	☐

7 POSSIBILITIES

Look at these student profiles from a school newspaper. Work in a group. Talk about what these students might do in the future. Use the information in the box or your own ideas.

Name: Alice Lane

Major: Early Childhood Education

Activities: Caribbean Students' Association, school newspaper

Likes: adventure, new people

Dislikes: snow, boring routines

Plans and Dreams: "I plan to teach in a preschool. I dream about traveling around the world."

Name: Nick Vanek

Major: Information Systems

Activities: Computer Club, Runners' Club

Likes: learning something new

Dislikes: crowded places

Plans and Dreams: "I plan to go to a four-year college. I dream about becoming an inventor."

FUTURE POSSIBILITIES		
Occupations	**Hobbies**	**Achievements**
• computer programmer	• dancing	• fly on space shuttle
• teacher	• skiing	• teach in Alaska
• manager, day-care center	• creative writing	• develop a computer program for making word puzzles

EXAMPLE:

A: Alice is on the school newspaper. She might do creative writing as a hobby.

B: Nick hates crowded places. He couldn't work on the space shuttle.

Now write your own profile. Discuss your future possibilities with your group.

8 WRITING

Write a paragraph about your future plans. Use **will** *and* **be going to** *for the things you are certain about. Use* **may, might,** *and* **could** *for the things you think are possible.*

36 ASSUMPTIONS: MUST, HAVE (GOT) TO, MAY, MIGHT, COULD, CAN'T

GRAMMAR **IN CONTEXT**

Who is Sherlock Holmes? What kind of a story is this?

Read an excerpt from "The Red-Headed League," a Sherlock Holmes story.

*W*hen Dr. Watson arrived, Sherlock Holmes was with a visitor.

"Dr. Watson, this is Mr. Jabez Wilson," said Holmes. Watson shook hands with a fat, red-haired man.

"Mr. Wilson **must write** a lot," Dr. Watson said.

Holmes smiled. "You **could be** right. But why do you think so?"

"His right shirt cuff looks very old and worn. And he has a small hole in the left elbow of his jacket. He probably rests his left elbow on the desk when he writes."

Wilson looked amazed. "Dr. Watson is correct," he told Holmes. "Your methods **may be** useful after all."

"Please tell Dr. Watson your story," said Holmes.

"I have a small shop," began the red-haired man. "I don't have many customers, so I was very interested in this advertisement. My clerk, Vincent, showed it to me." He handed Watson a piece of newspaper.

An American millionaire started the Red-Headed League to help red-headed men.

The League now has one position open. The salary is £4 per week for four hours of work every day.

The job is to copy the encyclopedia in our offices.

"They **couldn't pay** someone just for having red hair and copying the encyclopedia," Watson laughed. "This **has to be** a joke."

"It **might not be**," said Holmes. "Listen to Wilson tell the rest of his story."

"I got the job, and I worked at the League for two months. Then this morning I found a note on the door." Wilson gave Holmes the note. . . .

38

GRAMMAR **PRESENTATION**
ASSUMPTIONS: *MUST, HAVE (GOT TO), MAY, MIGHT, COULD, CAN'T*

AFFIRMATIVE STATEMENTS

SUBJECT	*MUST / MAY / MIGHT / COULD**	BASE FORM OF VERB	
I You He She We You They	**must may might could**	**write work**	a lot. at a desk.
It		**be**	a joke.

*Must, may, might, and *could* are modals. Modals have only one form. They do not have *-s* in the third-person singular.

NEGATIVE STATEMENTS

SUBJECT	*MUST / MAY / MIGHT / COULD / CAN*	NOT	BASE FORM OF VERB	
I You He She We They	**must may might could can**	**not**	**write work**	a lot. at a desk.
It			**be**	a joke.

CONTRACTIONS

could not = **couldn't**	
cannot OR can not	= **can't**

Note: We usually do not contract *must not, may not,* and *might not* when we make assumptions.

AFFIRMATIVE STATEMENTS WITH *HAVE (GOT) TO*

SUBJECT	HAVE (GOT) TO	BASE FORM OF VERB	
I You We They	**have (got) to**	**write work**	a lot. at a desk.
He She	**has (got) to**		
It		**be**	a joke.

(continued on next page)

YES / NO QUESTIONS

CAN / COULD	SUBJECT	BASE FORM OF VERB	
Could **Can**	he	**work**	there?

DO	SUBJECT	BASE FORM OF VERB	
Does	he	**work**	there?

SHORT ANSWERS

SUBJECT	MODAL
He	must (not). may (not). might (not). could (n't). has (got) to. can't.

YES / NO QUESTIONS WITH BE

CAN / COULD	SUBJECT	BE	
Could **Can**	he	**be**	a detective?

BE	SUBJECT	
Is	he	a detective?

SHORT ANSWERS

SUBJECT	MODAL	BE
He	must (not) may (not) might (not) could (n't) has (got) to can't	be.

WH- QUESTIONS WITH CAN AND COULD

WH- WORD	CAN / COULD	SUBJECT	BASE FORM OF VERB
Who What	**can** **could**	it they	**be?** **want?**

NOTES	EXAMPLES

1. We often make **assumptions**, or "best guesses," based on information we have. <u>The modal</u> that we choose depends on <u>how certain</u> we are about our assumption.

	100 % certain	
POSITIVE	↑	NEGATIVE
must		**can't, couldn't**
have (got) to		**must not**
may		**may not**
might, could		**might not**
	0% certain	

2. When the facts make us <u>almost 100 percent certain</u>, we state a **conclusion**.

Use **must**, **have to**, or **have got to** to state affirmative conclusions.

USAGE NOTE: We use **have got to** in informal speech and writing. We usually contract *have* or *has*.

FACT	CONCLUSION
Wilson has only one clerk.	• His shop **must be** quite small.
Wilson applied for a job.	• He **has to need** money.
The League pays men for having red hair.	• It**'s got to be** a joke.

PRONUNCIATION NOTE

In informal speech, **have to** is usually pronounced /hæftə/, and **got to** is usually pronounced /gɑṭə/.

---

3. When we are <u>less certain</u>, we express **possibilities**.

Use **may**, **might**, or **could** to express affirmative possibilities.

FACT	POSSIBILITY
Wilson has a hole in his sleeve.	• He **may write** a lot.
Watson knows a lot about medicine.	• He **might be** a doctor.
Vincent knows a lot about cameras.	• He **could be** a photographer.

(continued on next page)

4. To express **negative assumptions**, use the following modals:

Use *can't* and *couldn't* when you are almost 100 percent certain that something is **impossible**.

Use *must not* when you are slightly less certain.

Use *may not* and *might not* when you are less certain.

▶ **BE CAREFUL!** *Have to* and *have got to* are not used to make negative assumptions.

- He **can't be** dead! I think he's still breathing!

- Vincent **couldn't be** dishonest! I trust him completely!

- He **must not have** enough money. He never buys new clothes.

- He **may not know** about the plan. His boss doesn't tell him everything.

- It **can't be** true!
  NOT ~~It doesn't have to be true!~~

---

5. Use *can* and *could* in **questions about possibility**.

USAGE NOTE: We rarely use *might* in questions about possibility, and we never use *may* in this type of question.

- Someone's coming. Who **can** it **be**?
- **Could** Vincent **be** in the shop?

- RARE **Might** he **be** in the shop?
  NOT ~~May he be in the shop?~~

---

6. In **short answers**, use *have (got) to* or a modal alone.

▶ **BE CAREFUL!** Use *be* in short answers to questions that include *be*.

A: Could Ann know Marie?
B: She **has to**. They're neighbors.

A: Does she still work at Wilson's?
B: She **may not**. I saw a new clerk there.

A: *Is* Ron still with City Bank?
B: I'm not sure. He **might not** *be*.

A: *Are* his parents still alive?
B: They**'ve got to** *be*. He still talks about them.

REFERENCE NOTE
May, can, and *could* are also used to express permission *(see Unit 12).*
Must, have to, and *have got to* are also used to express necessity *(see Unit 33).*
May, might, and *could* are also used to express future possibilities *(see Unit 35).*

FOCUSED PRACTICE

1 DISCOVER THE GRAMMAR

Read the next part of "The Red-Headed League." Underline the phrases that express possibilities or state conclusions.

Sherlock Holmes studied the note:

The Red-Headed League does not exist anymore.

"This <u>could be serious</u>," Holmes told Wilson. "What can you tell us about your clerk Vincent?"

"Vincent couldn't be dishonest," replied Wilson. "In fact, he took this job for half-pay because he wanted to learn the business. His only fault is photography."

"Photography?" Holmes and Watson asked together.

"Yes," replied Wilson. "He's always running down to the basement to work with his cameras."

Wilson left soon after that.

"Wilson's clerk might be the key to this mystery," Holmes told Watson. "Let's go see him." An hour later, Holmes and Watson walked into Wilson's shop. The clerk was a man of about thirty, with a scar on his forehead. Holmes asked him for directions. Then he and Watson left the shop.

"My dear Watson," Holmes began. "It's very unusual for a thirty-year-old man to work for half-pay. This clerk has to have a very special reason for working here."

"Something to do with the Red-Headed League?" Watson asked.

"Yes. Perhaps the clerk placed that ad in the newspaper. He may want to be alone in the shop. Did you look at his legs?"

"No, I didn't."

"He has holes in his trouser knees. He must spend his time digging a tunnel from Wilson's basement. But where is it?"

Holmes hit the ground sharply with his walking stick. "The ground isn't hollow, so the tunnel must not be here in front of the shop. Let's walk to the street in back of Wilson's shop."

39

Read the second part of the story again. What does Holmes believe about each of the statements that follow? Check **Possibility** *or* **Conclusion** *for each statement.*

	Possibility	Conclusion
1. Something serious is happening.	☑	☐
2. The clerk is the key to the mystery.	☐	☐
3. The clerk has a special reason for working in Wilson's shop.	☐	☐
4. He put the ad in the newspaper because he wants to be alone in the shop.	☐	☐
5. He's digging a tunnel from Wilson's basement.	☐	☐
6. The tunnel isn't in front of the shop.	☐	☐

2 **PICTURE THIS**

Look at the picture. Think about it in connection to the story, "The Red-Headed League." Make assumptions and circle the appropriate words.

1. It (must) / could be nighttime.

2. Number 27 <u>might / can't</u> be a bank.

3. The delivery <u>couldn't / might</u> be for the bank.

4. The box <u>could / must not</u> contain gold.

5. The two men on the sidewalk <u>must not / could</u> notice the delivery.

6. The manager <u>might not / must</u> want people to know about this delivery.

7. He <u>couldn't / may</u> worry about robbers.

3 **EDITING**

Read this student's reading journal for a mystery novel. Find and correct six mistakes in the use of modals. The first mistake is already corrected.

> The main character, Molly Smith, is a college ESL teacher. She is trying to find her
>   be
> dead grandparents' first home in the United States. It may ~~being~~ in a nearby town.
> The townspeople there seem scared. They could be have a secret, or they must just
> hate strangers. Molly has some old letters that might lead her to the place. They are
> in Armenian, but one of her students mights translate them for her. They hafta be
> important, because the author mentions them right away. The letters must contain
> family secrets. Who is the bad guy? It couldn't be the student because he wants to
> help. It might to be the newspaper editor in the town.

4 **DRAWING CONCLUSIONS** Grammar Notes 1, 2, and 4

*Look at the poster and the map of Wilson's neighborhood. Use the evidence and the words in parentheses to write sentences with **must** and **must not**.*

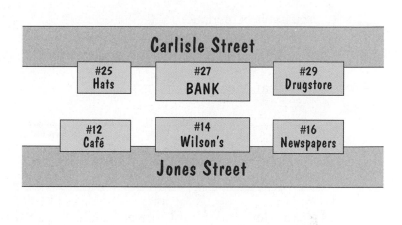

1. Wilson's clerk is the man on the poster.

   He must be a criminal.
   _____
   (He / be a criminal)

2. The man on the poster is named John Clay.

   _____
   (Vincent / be the clerk's real name)

3. He's committed a lot of crimes, but the police haven't caught him.

   _____
   (He / be very careful)

4. The address of the bank on the map above and the address in the picture for Exercise 2 are the same.

   _____
   (Number 27 Carlisle Street / be City Bank)

5. The hat shop and the drugstore don't make much money.

   _____
   (Vincent's tunnel / lead to those shops)

6. There's a lot of money in the bank, and it's very close to Wilson's shop.

   _____
   (Vincent's tunnel / lead to the bank)

5 **IT'S GOT TO BE**

Ann and Marie are buying hats. Read the dialogue and rewrite the underlined sentences another way. Use **have got to** *or* **can't** *and the word in parentheses.*

ANN: Look at this hat, Marie. What do you think?

MARIE: Oh, come on. <u>That's got to be a joke.</u>

You can't be serious.
                                              1. (serious)

Anyway, it's much too expensive. Look at the price tag.

ANN: $100! <u>That can't be right.</u>

_____
                                              2. (wrong)

MARIE: I know. <u>It can't cost more than $50.</u>

_____
                                              3. (less)

Anyway, let's talk about it over lunch. I'm getting hungry.

ANN: It's too early for lunch. <u>It has to be before 11:00.</u>

_____
                                              4. (after)

MARIE: Look at my watch. It's already 12:30.

ANN: Then let's go to Café Au Lait. It's on Jones Street. <u>It can't be far.</u>

_____
                                              5. (nearby)

MARIE: Let's go home after lunch. I don't feel well.

ANN: Oh come on. <u>You're fine.</u> You must be hungry.

_____
                                              6. (sick)

6 **SPECULATIONS**

Write a short answer to each question. Use **might** *or* **must** *and include* **be** *where necessary.*

A: You sound terrible. Are you sick?

B: I _____<u>must be</u>_____. I have a headache and my throat is starting to hurt.
        1.

A: This bottle of cough medicine is empty. Do we need some more?

B: We _____. I'm not sure. Check the shelf in the bathroom.
        2.

A: There isn't any cough medicine here. Are we all out of it?

B: We _____. That was the last bottle. Never mind. I can drink tea with honey.
           3.

A: I'll go get you some cough medicine. Does that nighttime cough medicine work?

B: It _____. It's worth a try.
         4.

A: I forgot to cash a check today. Do you have any money?

B: I _____. Look in my wallet. It's on the table downstairs.
      5.

A: I found it. Does Drake's Drugstore stay open after nine?

B: It _____. Their advertisement says "Open 'til eleven."
      6.

---

7 MAYBE IT'S THE CAT   **Grammar Notes 3–6**

Mr. and Mrs. Wilson are trying to get to sleep. Write questions and answers with
could / couldn't be *and* **can / can't be**.

1. (could be)

    MRS. WILSON: Shh! I hear someone at the door. It's 9:30. Who _____could_____

                    it _____be_____?
                               a.

    MR. WILSON: It _____could be_____ a late customer.
                           b.

    MRS. WILSON: No, it _____. The shop has been closed for hours. Maybe
                             c.

          it's the cat.

2. (can be)

    MR. WILSON: It _____. I put the cat out before we went to bed.
                   a.

    MRS. WILSON: _____ it _____ Vincent? He's always down
                                 b.

         in the basement with his cameras.

    MR. WILSON: No, Vincent went out an hour ago. He _____ back this early.
                                          c.

3. (could be)

    MRS. WILSON: What _____ it _____ then?
                             a.

    MR. WILSON: That door rattles whenever the wind blows. It _____
                                                   b.

         the wind.

    MRS. WILSON: That must be it. Let's go to sleep.

COMMUNICATION PRACTICE

8 LISTENING

*Holmes, Dr. Watson, and a police captain meet in front of City Bank. Listen to their conversation. Then listen again and check **Possibility** or **Conclusion** for each statement below.*

	Possibility	Conclusion
1. It's 10:00.	☐	☑
2. They have a long wait.	☐	☐
3. There are 2,000 gold coins in one box.	☐	☐
4. John Clay knows about the gold.	☐	☐
5. Clay's tunnel is finished.	☐	☐
6. The tunnel is under the bank floor.	☐	☐
7. John Clay is dangerous.	☐	☐
8. Clay is waiting for Wilson to go to sleep.	☐	☐
9. There's someone in the tunnel.	☐	☐
10. The man is John Clay.	☐	☐

9 TELL-TALE SIGNS

Look at the pictures. Make guesses about the owner of each item. Compare your ideas with your classmates'.

1.

2.

EXAMPLE:
Bob must be a very good student.
He could be the best in the class.
He may study hard.

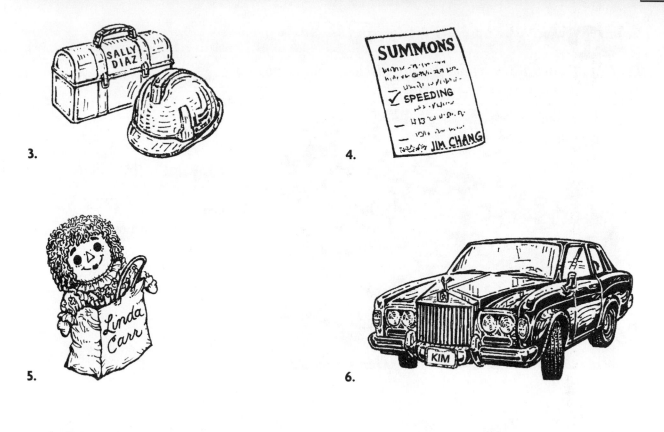

3.

4.

5.

6.

---

⑩ POSSIBLE EXPLANATIONS

Read the following situations. In pairs, discuss possible explanations for each situation. Then come to a conclusion. Discuss your explanations with the rest of the class. Use your imagination!

1. You've been calling your sister on the phone for three days. No one has answered.

> **EXAMPLE:**
> **A:** She might be at the library. She always studies hard for her exams.
> **B:** I don't think so. She's already finished her exams.
> **A:** You could have the wrong number.
> **B:** This is the number I always call. I think she's been on vacation this week.
> **A:** Then she must be away.

2. You are on the street. You have asked a woman three times for the time. She hasn't answered you.

3. You go to dinner with a good friend. Your friend hardly says a word all evening.

4. You went on a picnic in the park. You ate strawberries and cheese. Now you are sneezing and your eyes are watering.

5. You're at a party, and no one is talking to you.

11 WHAT COULD IT BE?

Look at this picture. In small groups, discuss what it might be.
Then check the Answer Key on page 385.

EXAMPLE:

A: It could be a picture of a Martian.

B: You must be kidding! Martians don't exist!

12 WRITING

Agatha James, the mystery writer, starts a new novel by writing story outlines about each one of her characters. Read about the murder suspect's activities on the day of the crime.

```
MARCH 1
7:00-8:00      gym—aerobics class—Talks to exercise instructor!
9:30           calls Dr. Lorenzo
11:00-1:00     hairdresser—changes hair color
1:30           pharmacy—picks up prescription
2:00           bank—withdraws $10,000
3:00           Mr. Jordan
4:30           calls travel agency—vegetarian meal?
```

Work in small groups to speculate about the story and the characters. Consider questions like these:

• Is the murder suspect a man or a woman?

• Who is Dr. Lorenzo?

• Who is Mr. Jordan? What is his relationship with the suspect?

• Why does the suspect need $10,000?

EXAMPLE:

A: The suspect must be a woman. She's going to the hairdresser.

B: It could be a man. Men go to hairdressers too.

Now write possibilities and conclusions about the story and the characters.

REVIEW OR SELFTEST

I. *Circle the letter of the appropriate response to each question.*

1. Are we supposed to bring a gift?
   a. Yes, we are.
   b. Yes, we were.

2. Do you think Fred has the report?
   a. Yes, he may. It's OK with me.
   b. He might. Let's ask him.

3. Will the weather improve tomorrow?
   a. It might.
   b. It might be.

4. Do you have to practice every day?
   a. Yes, I have.
   b. Yes, I do.

5. Do we have any more orange juice?
   a. We might.
   b. We might have.

6. Would you prefer to go out or stay home?
   a. Yes, I would.
   b. Let's stay home.

7. Should I turn left at the corner?
   a. You can't turn left. It says, Do Not Enter.
   b. You don't have to turn left. It says, Do Not Enter.

8. Is it going to rain?
   a. It might.
   b. It can.

9. Was I supposed to call you?
   a. No, you weren't.
   b. Yes, I was.

10. There's someone at the door. Who can it be?
   a. It can be Melissa.
   b. It could be Melissa.

11. I'd rather stay home. What about you?
   a. So had I.
   b. So would I.

II. *Read each sentence. Write its function. Use the words in the box. You will use some words more than once.*

assumption	expectation	future possibility
necessity	preference	prohibition

1. She might arrive around noon. _____future possibility_____

2. You must fill out the entire form. _____

3. I'd rather not see that movie. _____

4. He might be sick. _____

5. We're supposed to take the test on Friday. _____

6. You can't drive without a license. _____

7. Because of the cold front, the temperature could fall below freezing.

   _____

8. There is only one Maple Street, so this has got to be the correct street.

   _____

9. That new restaurant is supposed to be very good. _____

10. She must be very happy about her promotion. _____

III. *Circle the letter of the correct answer to complete each sentence.*

1. I'd rather _____ the movie. It's supposed to be good.　　Ⓐ B C D
   (A) watch 　　　　　　 (C) watching
   (B) to watch 　　　　　(D) not watch

2. Take your umbrella. It _____ rain.　　　　　　　　　A B C D
   (A) might not 　　　　 (C) 's supposed to
   (B) must 　　　　　　　(D) going to

3. There are two umbrellas. This one is definitely mine, so the other　A B C D
   _____ be yours.
   (A) must not 　　　　　(C) might
   (B) might not 　　　　 (D) must

4. Don't forget your sweater. I'm afraid the movie theater _____ be cold.　A B C D
   (A) might 　　　　　　 (C) couldn't
   (B) has to 　　　　　　(D) must

5. We _____ bring a gift, but we can if we want to.　　　　A B C D
   (A) have to 　　　　　 (C) must
   (B) don't have to 　　　(D) must not

6. I _____ have dessert. I'm trying to lose some weight.　　　　**A　B　C　D**
    (A) 'd rather   (C) 'd prefer
    (B) 'd rather not   (D) 'd prefer not

7. That's a beautiful gold watch. It _____ be expensive.　　　**A　B　C　D**
    (A) couldn't   (C) must
    (B) doesn't have to   (D) maybe

8. Hurry up. We _____ be home by 11:00.　　　　　　　　　**A　B　C　D**
    (A) have to   (C) must not
    (B) might   (D) prefer

9. We _____ be late, or we'll get into trouble.　　　　　　　**A　B　C　D**
    (A) don't have to   (C) couldn't
    (B) can't   (D) might

IV. *Write a sentence about each situation. Use the negative or affirmative form of the modal and the words in parentheses.*

1. John has a lot of headaches. At school, he can't see the board unless he sits in the front row.

    He might need glasses.
    ————————————————————————————————
                      (might / need glasses)

2. Your sister won't go see *Visitor from Another Planet* with you, and she turns off the TV when *Star Ship* starts.

    ————————————————————————————————
                (prefer / watch science fiction)

3. Carmen is looking at some jewelry. It's beautiful and it's made of gold.

    ————————————————————————————————
                  (must / be expensive)

4. In Thai culture it's impolite to open a gift in front of the giver. Somchai felt embarrassed when Linda opened his birthday gift.

    ————————————————————————————————
          (be supposed to / open it in front of him)

5. You've called your friend at work several times today. He doesn't answer, and he hasn't returned your messages.

    ————————————————————————————————
                (must / be at work today)

6. You've invited some friends to dinner, and you've served curry. Everyone except Sue has had two servings. Sue hasn't even finished the first one.

    ————————————————————————————————
                  (might / like curry)

(continued on next page)

7. In the United States, international travelers must arrive at the airport three hours before their flight. Your flight from New York to Los Angeles leaves at 3:00 P.M.

_____
(have to / arrive at the airport by noon)

8. Your sister often forgets important appointments. You want her to come to your graduation. You're worried. She has an invitation, but you haven't called to remind her.

_____
(might / remember to come)

9. Carl has just left for a trip to Hong Kong. You've seen him off at the airport. A few minutes after you get home, the doorbell rings.

_____
(could / be Carl)

10. You just bought a painting for ten dollars at a garage sale. Your friend Tim thinks it looks a lot like a Whistler. First you laughed, but then you looked at some art books.

_____
(could / be very valuable)

V. *Read this journal entry. Find and correct eight mistakes in the use of modals and related verbs and expressions. The first mistake is already corrected.*

>   am
> I supposed to take my road test tomorrow. I'm a little nervous because
> I heard that there might be a storm. I'd not rather drive in the rain! My
> instructor, John, is supposed to pick me up at 8:00 and drive me to the test
> area. Then he have to wait for me while I take the test. He doesn't have to be in
> the car with me during the test—it's not allowed. I like John. I don't know much
> about him. He says he's been driving for more than forty years, so I guess he
> got to be at least sixty. He maybe even older than that.
>   Well, it's getting late, and I should go to bed. I'd rather watching some TV,
> but I hafta get up early tomorrow.

▶ *To check your answers, go to the Answer Key on page 385.*

FROM GRAMMAR TO WRITING
COMBINING SENTENCES with
because, although, even though

You can combine two sentences with a subordinating conjunction such as *because*, *although*, and *even though*.

> **EXAMPLE:**
> It was my mistake. I think the cashier was rude. ⟶
> <u>subordinate clause</u>   <u>main clause</u>
> **Even though** it was my mistake, I think the cashier was rude.

The subordinate clause can come first or second. When it comes first, a comma separates the two clauses.

1 *Circle the correct conjunctions to complete this business letter. Underline the main clauses once and the subordinate clauses twice.*

---

                                               23 Creek Road
                                               Provo, UT 84001
                                               September 10, 2001

Customer Service Representative
Hardly's Restaurant
12345 Beafy Court
Provo, UT 84004

Dear Customer Service Representative:

    I am writing this letter of complaint although / (**because**) one of your cashiers treated me rudely. Because / Even though I was sure I paid her with a $20 bill, I only received change for $10. I told her that there was a mistake. She said, "You're wrong." Later the manager called. He said the cashier was right although / because the money in the cash drawer was correct.

    Because / Even though the mistake was mine, I believe the cashier behaved rudely. Although / Because I like Hardly's, I also value polite service. I hope I won't have to change restaurants although / because I can't get it there.

Sincerely,
Ken Nelson
Ken Nelson

---

2 *Look at the letter in Exercise 1. Circle the correct words in the sentences below to complete these rules about subordinating clauses and business letters.*

a. Use *because* to give a (reason)/ contrasting idea.

b. Use *although* or *even though* to give a reason / contrasting idea.

c. When you begin a sentence with a subordinate clause, use a colon / comma after the clause.

d. When a sentence has a subordinate / main clause, it must also have a subordinate / main clause.

e. When a sentence has a subordinate / main clause, it doesn't have to have a subordinate / main clause.

f. In a business letter, the sender's / receiver's address comes first.

g. The date comes before / after the receiver's address.

h. Use a colon / comma after the receiver's name.

3 *Before you write . . .*

• Work with a partner. Complete these complaints with subordinate clauses and correct punctuation. Use your own ideas.

a. _____ I will not bring my car to your mechanic again.

b. The server brought me a hamburger _____.

c. _____ I missed my plane.

d. _____ Ms. Vo in Apartment B still won't turn down the TV.

• Choose one of the above situations. Plan a role play about the conflict. Act out your role play for another pair of students.

• Discuss what to write in a letter of complaint.

4 *Write a letter of complaint. Use information from your role play in Exercise 3.*

5 *Exchange letters with another student. Complete the chart. Discuss any problems with the writer. Revise your letter if necessary.*

Did the writer . . .		
a. use subordinate clauses correctly?	**Yes** _____	**No** _____
b. use modals correctly?	**Yes** _____	**No** _____
c. give enough information about the complaint?	**Yes** _____	**No** _____
d. use correct business letter form?	**Yes** _____	**No** _____

REVIEW OR SELFTEST
ANSWER KEY

I. (Units 32–36)

2. b
3. a
4. b
5. a
6. b

7. a
8. a
9. a
10. b
11. b

II. (Units 32–36)

2. necessity
3. preference
4. assumption
5. expectation
6. prohibition

7. future possibility
8. assumption
9. expectation
10. assumption

III. (Units 32–36)

2. C
3. D
4. A
5. B

6. B
7. C
8. A
9. B

IV. (Units 32–36)

2. She prefers not to watch science fiction.
3. It must be expensive.
4. She *or* Linda wasn't supposed to open it in front of him.
5. He must not be at work today.
6. She *or* Sue might not like curry.
7. You *or* I don't have to arrive at the airport by noon.
8. She might not remember to come.
9. It couldn't be Carl.
10. It could be very valuable.

V. (Units 32–36)

   I ~~^~~ supposed to take my road test *[am]* tomorrow. I'm a little nervous because I heard that there might be a storm. I'd ~~not rather~~ drive in the rain! My instructor, *[rather not]* John, is supposed to pick me up at 8:00 and drive me to the test area. Then he ~~have~~ *[has]* to wait for me while I take the test. He ~~doesn't have to~~ be in the car with me during *[must not OR can't]* the test —it's not allowed. I like John. I don't know much about him. He says he's been driving for more than forty years, so I guess he ~~^~~ got to be at least sixty. He *['s]* ~~maybe~~ even older than that. *[may be]*

   Well, it's getting late, and I should go to bed. I'd rather ~~watching~~ some TV, but I ~~hafta~~ *[watch]* *[have to]* get up early tomorrow.

Answer to Exercise 11 on page 378
This is a photo of the eye of a fly.

PART

VIII

NOUNS AND ARTICLES

37

NOUNS AND QUANTIFIERS

GRAMMAR **IN CONTEXT**

BEFORE YOU READ Look at the map. Where did each journey start and end? Look at the photo of the boat. When do you think these journeys took place?

Read this history text about a modern explorer.

WHO REALLY DISCOVERED AMERICA?

Was **Columbus** really the first **explorer** to discover the **Americas**? The great Norwegian **explorer Thor Heyerdahl** didn't think so. He believed that ancient **people** were able to build **boats** that could cross **oceans**.

To test his **ideas**, **Heyerdahl** decided to build a **copy** of the reed **boats** pictured in ancient Egyptian **paintings** and sail across the **Atlantic** from **North Africa** to **Barbados**. **Heyerdahl's team** also copied ancient Middle Eastern **pots** and filled them with *enough* **food** for their **journey**—dried **fish, honey, oil,** *some* **eggs** and **nuts,** and *a little* fresh **fruit**. **Ra**, the **expedition's boat**, carried an international

group including a **Norwegian**, an **Egyptian**, an **Italian**, a **Mexican**, and a **Chadian**.

On **May** 25, 1969, **Ra** left **Safi** in **Morocco** and headed across the widest **part** of the **Atlantic**. **Ra** fell apart just before it reached **Barbados**, but everyone survived and wanted to try again.

On **May** 17, 1970, **Ra II**, sailing under the **flag** of the **United Nations**, successfully crossed the **Atlantic** in 57 **days**. The **expedition** proved that ancient **civilizations** had *enough* **skill** to reach the **Americas** long before **Columbus** did.

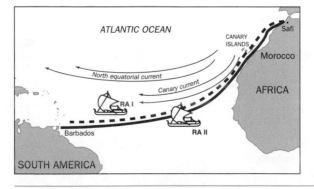

GRAMMAR **PRESENTATION**
NOUNS AND QUANTIFIERS

COUNT NOUNS			
ARTICLE / NUMBER	**NOUN**	**VERB**	
A One	**sailor**	is	brave.
(The) Two	**sailors**	are	

NON-COUNT NOUNS		
NOUN	**VERB**	
Oil	is	necessary.
Sailing		dangerous.

QUANTIFIERS AND COUNT NOUNS		
	QUANTIFIER	**NOUN**
I saw	*some* *enough* *a lot of*	**sailors**. **islands**. **ships**.
	a few *several* *many*	
I didn't see	*any* *enough* *a lot of* *many*	

QUANTIFIERS AND NON-COUNT NOUNS		
	QUANTIFIER	**NOUN**
I used	*some* *enough* *a lot of*	**oil**. **salt**. **honey**.
	a little *a great deal of* *much*	
I didn't use	*any* *enough* *a lot of* *much*	

NOTES	EXAMPLES

1. Proper nouns are the names of <u>particular people, places, or things</u>. They are usually unique (there is only one). To the right are some categories and examples of proper nouns.

People	Heyerdahl, Chadians
Places	Bolivia, Egypt, the Atlantic
Months	September, October
Days	Monday, Tuesday
Holidays	Easter, Passover, Ramadan
Languages / Nationalities	Arabic, Italian, Norwegian
Seasons	spring, summer, fall, winter

Capitalize the first letter of most proper nouns. We do not usually use an article (*a / an* or *the*) with a proper noun.

- The ancient **Egyptians** called their sun god **Ra**.
- The ship sailed in **May**.
- We spent **Passover** at sea.

Seasons are usually not spelled with a capital letter, and they are often preceded by *the*.

- We arrived in **the spring**.

2. Common nouns refer to people, places, and things, but <u>not by their individual names</u>. For example, *explorer* is a common noun, but *Heyerdahl* is a proper noun. To the right are some categories and examples of common nouns.

People	explorer, sailor, builder
Places	continent, country, city
Things	pots, eggs, fish, honey

3. Common nouns can be either count or non-count. **Count nouns** (also called countable nouns) are things that you can <u>count separately</u>. They can be singular or plural. For example, you can say *a ship* or *three ships*. You can use *a / an* or *the* before count nouns.

(See Unit 38, page 398, for more information about articles.)

- **a** sailor, **the** sailor, **two** sailors
- **an** island, **the** island, **three** islands
- **a** ship, **the** ship, **four** ships

4. Non-count nouns (also called uncountable or mass nouns) are things that you <u>cannot count separately</u>. For example, in English you can say *gold,* but you cannot say *a gold* or *two golds.* Non-count nouns usually have no plural forms. We usually <u>do not use *a / an* with non-count nouns</u>. To the right are some categories and examples of non-count nouns.

Abstract words	courage, education, time
Activities	exploring, sailing, farming
Fields of study	geography, history
Foods	corn, chocolate, fish
Gases	air, oxygen, steam
Liquids	water, milk, gasoline
Materials	cotton, plastic, silk
Natural forces	cold, electricity, weather
Particles	dust, sand, sugar, salt

Some common non-count nouns do not fit into the above categories. You must memorize nouns such as the ones to the right.

advice	homework	mail
equipment	information	money
furniture	jewelry	news
garbage	luggage	work

▶ **BE CAREFUL!** When a non-count noun is the subject of a sentence, its verb must be <u>singular</u>. Pronouns that refer to non-count nouns must also be singular.

- ***Reed* is** a good material for boats. ***It* floats** in the heaviest storm.

5. You can use the **quantifiers *some,* *enough,* *a lot of,* and *any*** with both <u>count and non-count nouns.</u>

- We have *some* eggs and *some* honey.
  (count) (non-count)
- Are there *enough* pots and *enough* oil?
  (count) (non-count)
- There were *a lot of* good times.
  (count)
- There was *a lot of* danger too.
  (non-count)

Use *any* in negative sentences and in questions.

- We didn't see *any* sharks.
  (count)
- Is there *any* tea left?
  (non-count)

(continued on next page)

6. You can use *a few, several*, and *many* with <u>plural count nouns</u> in <u>affirmative</u> sentences.

- *A few* team **members** got sick.
- They experienced *several* large **storms**.
- *Many* **people** worried about them.

You can use *a little, a great deal of*, and *much* with <u>non-count nouns</u> in <u>affirmative</u> sentences

- They had *a little* **trouble** with the sail.
- They threw away *a great deal of* **food**.
- *Much* **planning** went into this.

USAGE NOTE: In <u>affirmative sentences</u>, *many* is more formal than *a lot of*; *much* is very formal.

count
MORE FORMAL: *Many* **people** agreed.
LESS FORMAL: *A lot of* **people** agreed.

non-count
VERY FORMAL: We saw *much* **pollution**.
LESS FORMAL: We saw *a lot of* **pollution**.

▶ **BE CAREFUL!** Don't confuse *a few* and *a little* with *few* and *little*. *Few* and *little* usually mean "not enough."

- They received *a little* **news** during their voyage.
  (not a lot, but enough)
- They received *little* **news** during their voyage.
  (probably not enough news)

7. Use *many* with count nouns and *much* with non-count nouns in <u>questions</u> and <u>negative sentences</u>.

A: **How** *many* **ships** did they see?
B: They **didn't** see *many*.

A: **How** *much* **water** did they carry?
B: They **didn't** carry *much*.

USAGE NOTE: In questions and negative sentences *many* and *much* are appropriate for both formal and informal English.

FOCUSED PRACTICE

1 DISCOVER THE GRAMMAR

Tina Arbeit sailed around the world alone on a small boat. Read her interview with Adventure Travel (AT) *magazine. Underline the nouns.*

ADVENTURE TRAVEL

AT: It took a lot of <u>courage</u> to make this journey. Why did you decide to sail around the world alone?

TINA: I needed a goal. I didn't want any more formal education, but I didn't know what else to do. I got my boat, *Katya*, for my nineteenth birthday, and I knew right away that I wanted to do this.

AT: When did you start?

TINA: I left New York on May 15, two and a half years ago, and I headed for Panama.

AT: How far did you travel?

TINA: 30,000 miles.

AT: How much were you able to take with you?

TINA: I didn't have much money, so I didn't bring many things. I used the stars to navigate by, not electronic equipment.

AT: What did you eat?

TINA: I bought food in different ports. I loved going to markets and learning about local cooking. And I collected water when it rained.

AT: How did you spend your time when you were sailing?

TINA: At first I listened to the news a lot, but after a while I preferred music. And I did a lot of reading.

AT: What was difficult for you?

TINA: The loneliness. I had my cat, Typhoon, but I missed my family.

AT: What did you like best about the trip?

TINA: The sight of this harbor. I'm so glad to be back for Thanksgiving.

Write each noun in the correct column.

PROPER NOUNS

Katya		

COMMON NOUNS

Count Nouns	**Non-count Nouns**
journey	courage

2 MAKING PLANS

Megan and Jason are planning a hiking trip. Complete their conversation with the correct form of the words in parentheses.

JASON: There ___'s___ still a lot of ___work___ to do this evening. We
           1. (be)   2. (work)

    have to plan the food for the trip.

MEGAN: I've been reading this book about camping. There _____ some good
          3. (be)

    _____ about food in it.
    4. (advice)

JASON: What does it say?

MEGAN: We should bring a lot of _____ and _____.
          5. (bean)   6. (rice)

JASON: _____ _____ good on camping trips, too.
    7. (Potato)   8. (be)

MEGAN: Fresh _____ _____ too heavy to carry. Maybe we can
          9. (vegetable)   10. (be)

    get some when we pass through a town.

JASON: _____ the _____ ready? We should go over the checklist.
    11. (be)   12. (equipment)

MEGAN: I did that. We need some _____ for the radio.
          13. (battery)

JASON: Why do we need a radio? I thought we were running away from civilization.

MEGAN: But the _____ never _____. I still want to know
          14. (news)   15. (stop)

    what's happening.

JASON: That's OK with me. By the way, do we have enough warm _____?
          16. (clothing)

    It gets chilly in the mountains.

MEGAN: That's true. And the

    _____ really
    17. (cold)

    _____ me
    18. (bother)

    at night.

JASON: But we have warm

    sleeping _____.
    19. (bag)

MEGAN: And I have you!

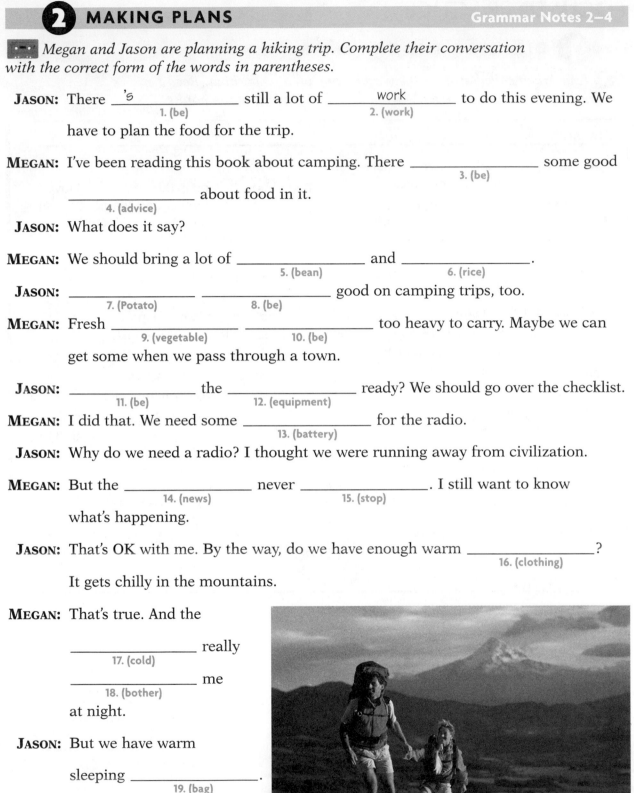

3 **HAPPY CAMPERS**

Complete these excerpts from a book about family camping. For each paragraph, use the quantifiers in parentheses.

1. (a little / a few)

Try to get _____a little_____ exercise before a long camping trip. It will help you feel
a.

better on the trip. _____ good stretching exercises every day will help.
b.

_____ walking or swimming is also useful.
c.

2. (many / a great deal of)

You will need _____ information for a long trip. Your public library has
a.

_____ books about family camping. The National Park Service can also
b.

provide _____ advice.
c.

3. (a / some) (much / many)

Making a fire is _____ skill, but it's easy to learn. You won't need
a.

_____ practice before you can build a roaring campfire. Start with
b.

_____ paper and leaves. Place the wood on top of these, and leave
c.

spaces for air. Don't use _____ big pieces of wood.
d.

4. (any / enough) (How much / How many)

"There isn't _____ milk left! Who used it all?" _____
a.   b.

times have you heard this cry? To avoid this problem, plan your food in advance.

_____ sandwiches are you going to make? _____ bread
c.   d.

will you need? Are you planning to have popcorn and pancakes? Do you have

_____ butter for these treats **and** your morning toast?
e.

_____ eggs will you need? Make sure you have _____ food
f.   g.

and beverages before you leave.

(continued on next page)

5. (few / a few) (little / a little)

On our family's first camping trip, we had _____ equipment and almost
a.

no experience, but we still had a lot of fun. It was a blast. We swam, we hiked, and we

made new friends. Of course, we had _____ problems, but not many.
b.

Anyway, _____ inconvenience didn't interfere with our fun.
c.

Today millions of people enjoy camping. In fact, _____ campsites are
d.

available in the summer without a reservation.

4 EDITING

*Read Tina's diary entries. There are fourteen mistakes in the use of nouns and
verb and pronoun agreement. Find and correct them. The first two mistakes are
already corrected.*

> October 27. I've been on the ~~canary~~ ^{Canary} Islands for three days now. I'll start
> home when the ~~weathers are~~ ^{weather is} better. I was so surprised when I picked
> up my mails today. My family sent some birthday presents to me.
> My Birthday is the 31st. I won't open any gifts until then.
>
> october 29. I think the weather is getting worse. I heard thunders
> today, but there wasn't many rain. Typhoon and I stayed in bed.
> I started reading a novel, brave New World.
>
> October 30. I left the Canary Islands today—just like columbus. There's
> a strong wind and plenty of sunshine now. I went 250 miles.
>
> October 31. I'm 21 today. To celebrate, I drank little coffee for breakfast
> and I opened my presents. I got some perfume and some pretty
> silver jewelries.
>
> November 1. The electricities are very low. I'd better save them until
> I get near New York. I'll need the radio then. It rained today,
> so I collected a few waters for cooking.

COMMUNICATION PRACTICE

5 LISTENING

 *Megan and Jason are planning to make cookies for their trip. Listen to them talk about the recipe. Then listen again and check the ingredients that they have enough of. Listen a third time and make a shopping list of ingredients that they need to buy.*

Ingredients		Shopping List	
2 cups of butter	1 cup of cornflakes	butter	_____
✔ 3 cups of brown sugar	8 eggs	_____	_____
2 cups of oatmeal (uncooked)	1 cup of raisins	_____	
4 cups of flour	2 cups of chocolate chips	_____	

6 DESERT ISLAND

Work with a group. Imagine that you are about to be shipwrecked near a deserted tropical island. You have room in your lifeboat for all the members of your group plus five of the things on the list that follows. Decide what to take, and give your reasons. Compare your choices with other groups' choices.

sugar	fishing equipment	telescope
flour	portable TV set	compass
pasta	radio	maps of the area
beans	batteries	a book, *Navigating by the Stars*
chocolate	ax	a book, *Tropical Plants You Can Eat*
fresh water	cooking pot	fireworks

EXAMPLE:

I think we should take a lot of beans. We might not find any food on the island.

7 WRITING

Describe a trip that you have taken. Where did you go, and when? How long did you stay? Who went with you? What did you take along? What did you do there?

EXAMPLE:

Three years ago, I went to Amsterdam with my family. My father was on a short vacation, so we couldn't spend much time there . . .

38 ARTICLES: INDEFINITE AND DEFINITE

GRAMMAR **IN CONTEXT**

BEFORE YOU READ Look at the picture. Try to identify the people and the objects. What kind of games do *you* enjoy playing?

Read this advertisement for a new video game.

An evil **magician** from **a universe** beyond ours is trying to conquer **the Earth.**
The magician is Zado, and he has four helpers—they are all monsters, and they all
have magic powers like Zado's. Fortunately, you are also **a magician** and can destroy
Zado and his team. Here's how **the game** works.

You are **a Space Defender**, and it is your job to save **the Earth** from Zado. At
the start, you have **some gold** and **some weapons**, but you are alone. You must train
fighters to defeat **the magician**. When **the fighters** win **a battle**, you can use **the gold**
to buy magic tools and medicine. Your team becomes stronger each time it wins.

Music is **a powerful force** in Space Defender—it tells you when Zado is near,
and it signals your new magic power. Hurry and defend your planet. Save **the world**
before it's too late!

GRAMMAR **PRESENTATION**
ARTICLES: INDEFINITE AND DEFINITE

INDEFINITE
A / AN + SINGULAR COUNT NOUN
Let's play **a video game**. *Super Mario Brothers* is **a good game**. It's **an adventure**.
Ø* + NON-COUNT NOUN Ø + PLURAL COUNT NOUN
This game has great **music**. **Graphics** are very important.

DEFINITE
THE + SINGULAR COUNT NOUN
The game we rented is *Space Defender*. It's **the best game** of all. **The adventure** takes place on Mars.
THE + NON-COUNT NOUN *THE* + PLURAL COUNT NOUN
The music in this game is weird. **The graphics** are fantastic.

*Ø = no article

NOTES

1. A noun is **indefinite** (not specific) when either you or your listener do not have a particular person, place, or thing in mind. Use the indefinite article *a / an* with <u>singular count nouns</u> that are **not specific**.

Use *a* before <u>consonant sounds</u>.

Use *an* before <u>vowel sounds</u>.

▶ **BE CAREFUL!** It is the <u>sound</u>, not the letter, that determines if you use *a* or *an*.

2. Use *some* or **no article** with <u>plural count nouns</u> and with <u>non-count nouns</u> that are **not specific**. In thcsc types of statements, *some* means an unspecified number.

PRONUNCIATION NOTE: Do not stress *some* in these sentences.

EXAMPLES

A: Let's buy *a video game*.
B: Good idea.
(A and B are not talking about a specific game.)

- *a* **m**agician, *a* **g**reat adventure

- *an* **e**vil magician, *an* **a**dventure

- *a* **u**niverse (universe = /ˈyunəˌvɚs/)

- *an* **ho**nest warrior (honest = /ˈɑnɪst/)

count, plural
- There are *(some)* **games** on the shelf.
(The speaker doesn't mention which games or the number of games.)

non-count
A: I had to buy *(some)* **medicine**.

B: Oh. Are you sick?
(B doesn't know what kind of medicine A bought.)

(continued on next page)

3. A noun is **definite** when you and your listener both know which person, place, or thing you mean. Use the definite article, **the**, with <u>nouns</u> that are **specific** for you and your listener. You can use *the* with most nouns, <u>count and non-count, singular and plural</u>.

count, singular

A: I bought *the* **video game** yesterday.

B: Great! We've been talking about it for a long time. Is it fun?
(B knows which game A means. They've spoken about it before.)

count, plural

A: *The* **new video games** are great.

B: I know. I'm glad we bought them.
(B knows which games A means. They have talked about them before.)

non-count

A: I bought *the* **medicine**.

B: Good. Why don't you take some now?
(B knows which medicine A means. They have already spoken about it.)

---

4. Use *the* when a person, place, or thing is <u>unique</u>—there's only one.

- There's a hole in *the* **ozone layer**.
- *The* **moon** is 250,000 miles away.

---

5. Use *the* when the <u>context makes it clear</u> which person, place, or thing you mean.

A: What do you do?

B: I'm *the* **pilot**.
(A and B work on a plane with only one pilot. A is a new crew member.)

A: *The* **music** was great.

B: I enjoyed it, too.
(A and B are coming out of a concert.)

Often, <u>a phrase or an adjective</u> such as *right*, *wrong*, *first*, *best*, or *only* <u>identifies which one</u>.

- *Donkey Kong* was *the first* **video game** with a story.
- Ben pushed *the wrong* **button**.

6. A noun is often **indefinite** <u>the first time</u> a speaker mentions it. It is usually **definite** <u>after</u> the first mention.

- ***An* evil magician** is trying to conquer the Earth. ***The* magician** is very powerful.

- You have ***some* gold**. Use ***the* gold** to buy magic tools.

- Buy **medicine** too. ***The* medicine** makes you stronger.

---

7. Use ***a / an*** for <u>singular count nouns</u> when you **classify** (say what something or someone is).

A: What do you do for a living?

B: I'm ***a* pilot**. And you?

A: I'm ***a* doctor**.

---

8. Use **no article** for <u>plural count nouns</u> and for <u>non-count nouns</u> when you **classify**.

▶ **BE CAREFUL!** Do not use *some* when you classify.

A: What are those?

B: They're **magic tools**.

A: And what's that?

B: It's **gold**. I just won it.

A: Look at those sharks!

B: Those aren't **sharks**. They're **dolphins**. NOT ~~They're some dolphins.~~

---

9. Use **no article** with <u>plural count nouns</u> and <u>non-count nouns</u> to make **general statements**.

Some in general statements means *some, but not all*.

PRONUNCIATION NOTE: Stress *some* in these sentences.

- Sue loves **video games**.
  (video games in general)

- **Music** is relaxing.
  (music in general)

- I like ***some* video games**, but a lot of them are boring.

FOCUSED PRACTICE

1 DISCOVER THE GRAMMAR

Read the conversations. Circle the letter of the statement that best describes each conversation.

1. **CORA:** I'm bored. Let's rent a video game.
   FRED: OK.
       a. Fred knows which game Cora is going to rent.
       (b.) Fred and Cora aren't talking about a particular game.

2. **CORA:** Mom, where's the new video game?
   MOM: Sorry, I haven't seen it.
       a. Mom knows that Cora rented a new game.
       b. Mom doesn't know that Cora rented a new game.

3. **FRED:** I'll bet it's in the hall. You always drop your things there.
   CORA: I'll go look.
       a. There are several halls in Fred and Cora's house.
       b. There is only one hall in Fred and Cora's house.

4. **FRED:** Was I right?
   CORA: You weren't even close. It was on a chair in the kitchen.
       a. There is only one chair in the kitchen.
       b. There are several chairs in the kitchen.

5. **FRED:** Wow! Look at that! The graphics are awesome.
   CORA: So is the music.
       a. All video games have good pictures and music.
       b. The game Cora rented has good pictures and music.

6. **CORA:** This was fun. But why don't we rent a sports game next time?
   FRED: Good idea. I love sports games.
       a. Fred is talking about sports games in general.
       b. Fred is talking about a particular sports game.

2 GAMES PEOPLE PLAY   Grammar Notes 1–9

Circle the correct article to complete this paragraph. Circle Ø if you don't need an article.

Board games are popular all over (the)/ Ø world. Mah Jong is an / the example of a / an
                                                     1.   2.   3.

very old one. I had an / a uncle who had an / the old set from the / Ø Singapore. He kept
                4.   5.   6.

a / the set in the / a beautiful box. He used to open the / a box and tell me about the / Ø
7.   8.   9.   10.

pieces. They were made of a / Ø bamboo, and each one had a / the Chinese character
                      11.   12.

on it. To me, they were the / some most fascinating things in a / the world.
                      13.   14.

3 FUN AND GAMES

Complete the conversations with **a**, **an**, *or* **the**.

1. A: _____A_____ car just pulled up. Are you expecting someone?

   B: No, I'm not. I wonder who it is.

2. A: Can we use _____ car?

   B: OK, but bring it back by 11:00 o'clock.

3. A: Let's turn off _____ game system before we leave.

   B: We don't have to. We can just leave it on *Pause*.

4. A: Do you have _____ game system?

   B: Yes, I do. I just bought a Mega Genesis.

5. A: Do you see the video store? I was sure it was on Main Street.

   B: I think it's on _____ side street, but I'm not sure which one.

   A: I'll try this one.

6. A: There it is.

   B: You can park right across _____ street.

7. A: Can I help you?

   B: Do you have any new games?

   A: _____ newest games are in the front of the store.

8. A: We'd better go. We've been here for _____ hour.

   B: That was _____ fastest hour I've ever spent.

   A: I know. Let's take the Marco Brothers game, OK?

9. A: Excuse me. I'd like to rent this game.

   B: Just bring it to _____ cashier. She's right over there.

10. A: My cousin just got _____ summer job.

   B: What does he do?

   A: He's a cashier at _____ amusement park.

   B: Really? Which one?

   A: Blare Gardens.

11. A: Whew! _____ sun got really hot. It must be almost noon.

   B: We were supposed to be home by 11:00. Let's hurry.

4 SCARY RIDES

Grammar Notes 2, 3, 5, 6, and 9

Complete the sentences with **the** *where necessary. Use* **the** *for specific statements.*
Use **Ø** *if you don't need an article.*

A: I'm going to Blare Gardens next weekend. You work there. What's it like?

B: That depends. Do you like ___Ø___ scary rides? If you do, then you're going to love
        1.

_____ rides at Blare Gardens.
   2.

A: What's _____ most exciting ride there?
                    3.

B: The Python. I've seen people actually shaking before they got on it.

A: Sounds like fun. By the way, how's _____ food? I hate _____ hot dogs.
                                          4.   5.

B: Then you might have a little problem. They sell _____ hot dogs and _____
                                                      6.   7.

pizza, and that's about it. But do you like _____ music?
                                            8.

A: I love it. I listen to _____ country music all the time. Why?
                              9.

B: _____ music at Blare Gardens is great. They have _____ best country music
       10.   11.

groups in the state.

A: What exactly do you do there? Maybe we'll see you.

B: I dress like a cartoon character and guide people around _____ park.
                                                                12.

5 PERSON, PLACE, OR THING?

Grammar Notes 1–9

This is a quiz game. For each item, complete the clues. Then, using the clues and
the pictures, write the answer. Use **a / an** *or* **the** *where necessary. Use* **Ø** *if you*
don't need an article.

1. He's ___*a*___ person in _____ story. In _____ story, he lives in _____ tree
  a.   b.   c.   d.
with his wife, Jane, and his son, Boy.

ANSWER: He's ___Tarzan._____

2. It's _____ longest structure in the world. _____ emperor built it. It's so big that
  a.   b.
_____ astronauts can see it from space.
  c.
ANSWER: It's _____

3. It's _____ smallest continent. There are _____ kangaroos and other interesting
  a.   b.
animals there. Europeans found _____ gold there in 1851.
  c.
ANSWER: It's _____

4. You can find one in _____ amusement park. It scares _____ people, but they
  a.   b.
still love it. _____ tallest one is in Japan.
  c.
ANSWER: It's _____

5. She was _____ intelligent and beautiful woman. She was _____ most famous
  a.   b.
queen of Egypt. She ruled _____ country with her brother.
  c.
ANSWER: She was _____

6. They are _____ biggest animals that have ever lived. They have _____ fins,
  a.   b.
but they aren't _____ fish.
  c.
ANSWER: They're _____

6 EDITING

Read the article about video games. Find and correct nine mistakes with **a**, **an**,
and **the**. *The first mistake is already corrected.*

                                      The plumber

Once there was a plumber named Mario. ~~Plumber~~ had beautiful girlfriend. One day, a ape fell in
love with the girlfriend and kidnapped her. The plumber chased ape to rescue his girlfriend.

    This simple tale became *Donkey Kong*, a first video game with a story. It was invented by
Sigeru Matsimoto, a artist with Nintendo, Inc. Matsimoto loved the video games, but he wanted to
make them more interesting. He liked fairy tales, so he invented story similar to a famous fairy
tale. Story was an immediate success, and Nintendo followed it with *The Mario Brothers*. The rest
is video history.

COMMUNICATION PRACTICE

7 LISTENING

Listen to the conversations. Then listen again and circle the correct article.

1. **A:** Let's go to an / the amusement park this weekend.
   B: That's a great idea. I haven't ridden a roller coaster in ages.

2. **A:** Is Mark a / the manager at Blare Gardens now?
   B: Yes, he is.

3. **A:** Have you played a / the video game yet?
   B: No, I haven't. I'm going to right now.

4. **A:** It's 6:00. Let's pick up a / the pizza.
   B: OK. Do you want me to go?

5. **A:** What's that?
   B: It's a / the new ride. Do you want to try it?

6. **A:** Look! A shark!
   B: That's not a shark, silly. It's a / the dolphin from the water show.

Read your completed conversations. Circle the letter of the statement that best describes each conversation.

1. **a.** A has a specific amusement park in mind.
   b. A isn't thinking of a particular amusement park.

2. **a.** There is only one manager at Blare Gardens.
   b. There are several managers at Blare Gardens.

3. **a.** A and B are in a video arcade. There are a lot of video games.
   b. A and B are at home. They have a new video game.

4. **a.** A and B have already ordered a pizza. Now it's time to pick it up.
   b. A and B haven't ordered a pizza. A is hungry and wants to order one.

5. **a.** There are several new rides. This is one of them.
   b. This is the only new ride. A and B have both heard about it.

6. **a.** There are several dolphins in the water show. This is one of them.
   b. There's only one dolphin in the show, and this is it.

8 QUIZ SHOW

Work with a group. Choose five interesting or famous things. Write three clues for each thing. Then join another group. Give your clues and ask the other group to guess what each thing is. Look at Exercise 5 for ideas.

EXAMPLE:
A: It protects you from the sun. It's getting thinner. There's a hole in it.
B: Is it the ozone layer?
A: Yes, it is.

9 INFORMATION GAP: STORY TIME

Work in Pairs (A and B). Student B, look at the Information Gap on p. 409 and follow the instructions there. Student A, look at the picture below. Ask your partner for the information you need to finish labeling the picture. Answer your partner's questions.

EXAMPLE:

A: Who's the man in the black cape?

B: It's the magician.
What's the magician holding?

A: A magic wand.

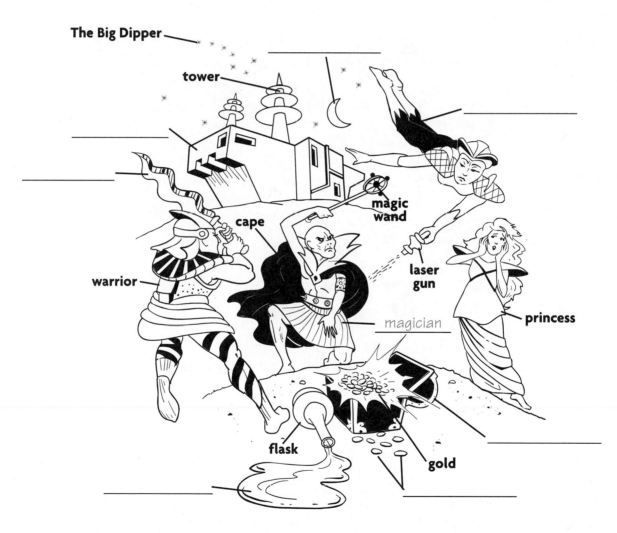

When you are finished, compare pictures. Are the labels the same?

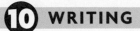

10 WRITING

This picture shows the end of the story in Exercise 9. Write a story based on the two pictures. Use your imagination!

INFORMATION GAP FOR STUDENT B

Student B, look at the picture below. Ask your partner for the information you need to finish labeling the picture. Answer your partner's questions.

EXAMPLE:

A: Who's the man in the black cape?

B: It's the magician.
What's the magician holding?

A: A magic wand.

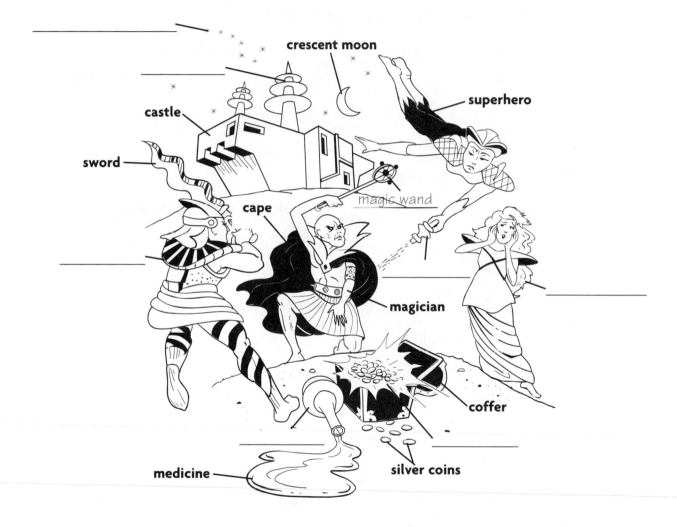

When you are finished, compare pictures. Are the labels the same?

REVIEW OR SELFTEST

I. *Complete each conversation with the correct form of the words in parentheses.*

1. A: We got _____ a lot of mail _____ today.
   <u>a. (many / a lot of) (mail / mails)</u>

   B: How _____ came?
   <u>b. (much / many) (letter / letters)</u>

2. A: Are you still majoring in mathematics?

   B: No, _____ interest me much anymore.
   <u>a. (it / they) (doesn't / don't)</u>

3. A: There _____ some new furniture in the office.
   <u>a. ('s / are)</u>

   B: I know. I saw _____ new
   <u>b. (several / a great deal of)</u>

   _____, too.
   <u>c. (computer / computers)</u>

4. A: Do you enjoy aerobics?

   B: _____ OK, but I prefer lifting weights.
   <u>a. (It's / They're)</u>

5. A: I put _____ in the tomato sauce.
   <u>a. (too much / too many) (salt / salts)</u>

   B: No, you didn't. _____ just fine to me.
   <u>b. (It / They) (tastes / taste)</u>

6. A: Did you watch the six o'clock news?

   B: No. I missed _____ today.
   <u>a. (it / them)</u>

7. A: I brought _____ luggage on this trip.
   <u>a. (a lot of / a)</u>

   B: How _____ do you have?
   <u>b. (much / many) (bag / bags)</u>

8. A: Jones is a very unpopular mayor. Many people are voting against him.

   He has _____ friends in politics.
   <u>a. (few / a few)</u>

   B: You're right. He won't get _____ support.
   <u>b. (much / many)</u>

9. A: I love Nancy Griffith's music.

   B: I like _____ too.
   <u>a. (it / them)</u>

II. *Complete the conversation with the correct words or phrases in parentheses.*

A: Joe's birthday is tomorrow. Let's surprise him and give a party.

B: That's not _____much_____ time.

        1. (much / many)

A: One day? That's _____. We still have candles and decorations left from

            2. (enough / too much)

the last party.

B: Let's just make _____ hamburgers and fries. And I'll bake a cake.

        3. (a lot of / a great deal of)

_____ chopped meat do we have?

4. (How much / How many)

A: Only _____. And we only have _____ rolls.

      5. (a few / a little)   **6. (a few / a little)**

B: Put them on the list. I'll also need _____ eggs for the cake.

            7. (some / any)

A: _____?

8. (How many / How much)

B: Two. Is there _____ flour and sugar?

       9. (any / many)

A: Not _____. I'll get more.

    10. (much / many)

B: I think that's it.

A: Not quite. Joe's got _____ friends. We'd better start calling them.

        11. (a lot of / much)

B: Why don't you go shopping? I'll call _____ people while you're gone.

           12. (few / a few)

III. *Complete the conversations with* **a, an** *or* **the**.

1. A: Did anyone feed ____*the*____ cat today?

   B: I did. Why?

   A: He's still hungry.

2. A: Look at my picture.

   B: It's lovely. What kind of cat is that?

   A: It's not _____ cat. It's _____

      dog.

   B: You're kidding! What _____

      unusual animal!

3. A: Shut _____ door. It just blew open.

   B: OK.

4. A: It was cold last night.

   B: I know. _____ ground is still

      frozen.

5. A: How's _____ weather in Phoenix?

   B: Sunny. How's New York?

   A: You can't even see _____ sun.

6. A: Who's that woman in the uniform?

   B: She must be _____ captain of this

      ship.

7. A: What does Martha do?

   B: She's _____ engineer. She works

      for World Cargo.

8. A: We need _____ new car.

   B: I know. But we'll have to wait.

9. A: I need _____ car today.

   B: OK. Can you drop me off at work?

   A: Sorry, I have _____ early

      appointment.

IV. *Complete the sentences with **the** where necessary. Use **Ø** and capitalize the first letter when you don't use **the**.*

1. ___Ø___ F̷riendship is very important to most people.

2. ___The___ friendship of my classmates is very important to me.

3. Sue used _____ money in her bank account to pay her tuition.

4. _____ money isn't everything.

5. _____ travel can be educational.

6. _____ staying at home can be educational too.

7. _____ vegetables in our garden aren't ripe yet.

8. _____ vegetables contain a lot of vitamins.

V. *Complete the paragraphs with **a**, **an**, **the**, or **some**.*

1. Yesterday, I went to ___the___ biggest video store downtown to rent _____
   a.   b.
   movies. I found _____ comedy and _____ adventure story. _____
                    c.   d.   e.
   comedy was very funny. I really enjoyed it. _____ adventure story wasn't that good.
                                               f.

2. We need to buy _____ office supplies fairly soon. We need _____ paper for
                   a.   b.
   _____ printer and _____ floppy disks. _____ paper is more
   c.   d.   e.
   important than _____ disks, though. We'd better buy it this week.
                  f.

VI. *Each sentence has four underlined words or phrases. The four underlined parts of the sentence are marked A, B, C, or D. Circle the letter of the <u>one</u> underlined word or phrase that is NOT CORRECT.*

1. <u>Many</u> popular <u>flavorings</u> <u>come</u> from <u>Native american</u> cultures. **A B C (D)**
     A   B   C   D

2. Chili <u>was</u> unknown in <u>an</u> <u>Asia or Europe</u> <u>a few</u> hundred years ago. **A B C D**
        A   B   C   D

3. Now <u>it's</u> <u>the</u> most popular spice in <u>a</u> <u>world</u>. **A B C D**
        A B   C D

4. It's hard to imagine <u>the</u> <u>Italian</u> or Szechuan <u>food</u> without <u>chili</u>. **A B C D**
                    A   B   C   D

5. <u>A</u> <u>chocolate</u> also <u>comes</u> from <u>America</u>. **A B C D**
    A   B   C   D

6. For <u>some</u> <u>American</u> cultures, it was <u>the</u> <u>medicine</u>. **A B C D**
       A   B   C   D

7. Now <u>People</u> all over <u>the world</u> <u>use</u> chocolate to flavor <u>food</u>. **A B C D**
        A   B   C   D

▶ *To check your answers, go to the Answer Key on page 415.*

From Grammar to Writing
The form of an Essay

 school essay is usually several paragraphs long and has a title. Capitalize the first letter of the first word in the title. Capitalize the first letter of the other words, except for articles and prepositions. Indent the first line of each paragraph.

1 *Read the following essay. Choose the best title and write it above the essay.*

A Mariachi Band	Mexican Halloween
An Altar in the Living Room	My Grandfather
Friendly Spirits	Gifts for Our Relatives

_____

    In my town in Mexico, we celebrate Los Días de los Muertos (The Days of the Dead) on November 1 and 2. It may sound like a sad occasion, but it is one of the best holidays of the year. We celebrate it with food, special gifts for the dead, and music.

    On The Days of the Dead, we remember our dead relatives. The first day is for children and babies who have died. The second day is for adult relatives. In my family, we set up an altar in the living room. We decorate it with yellow and red flowers, pictures of the people who have died, and foods. The foods for this altar are very special. We bake breads we call "souls." They are shaped like people. We also use candy skulls for decoration. We remember special things our relatives liked, and we buy them gifts. For my grandfather, we always put out some coffee, and for my sister, we offer toys. On the second day, all my family meets at the cemetery. This sounds sad, but it is really a big party. We bring picnics, and my family always hires a mariachi band. We all sing.

    Some people think that Los Días de los Muertos is like Halloween, but they are wrong. At Halloween, people pretend to be afraid of evil spirits, but during Los Días de los Muertos, we invite the friendly spirits of our family to visit us.

Complete this outline for the essay in Exercise 1.

Title: _____

I. First Paragraph (Introduction)

    A. Topic of the essay: _____

    B. Main idea: <u>It is one of the best holidays of the year.</u>

    C. Details to develop: food, _____ , and _____

II. Second Paragraph (Body of the Essay)

    A. Purpose of the holiday: _____

        1. Day 1: _____

        2. Day 2: _____

    B. Altar decorations: _____

        1. foods: _____

        2. gifts: _____

    C. A party at the cemetery

        1. _____

        2. _____

III. Last Paragraph (Conclusion)

    Why this holiday is special: _____

---

3 *Before you write . . .*

- Develop an outline like the one in Exercise 2 for an essay about a holiday that is special to you.

- Work with a partner. Exchange outlines. Ask questions about your partner's holidays. Answer your partner's questions.

---

4 *Write a three-paragraph essay about a special holiday. Include information your partner asked you about. Give your essay a title.*

---

5 *Exchange essays with a new partner. Complete the chart.*

a. Does the essay have three paragraphs?	Yes _____	No _____
b. Was the first line of each paragraph indented?	Yes _____	No _____
c. Does the title fit the essay?	Yes _____	No _____
d. Was it capitalized correctly?	Yes _____	No _____
e. What else would you like to know about this holiday? _____
_____		

Revise your essay if necessary.

REVIEW OR SELFTEST
ANSWER KEY

I. (Unit 37)

1. **b.** many letters
2. **a.** it doesn't*
3. **a.** 's
   b. several
   c. computers
4. **a.** It's
5. **a.** too much salt
   b. It tastes
6. **a.** it
7. **a.** a lot of
   b. many bags
8. **a.** few
   b. much
9. **a.** it

II. (Unit 37)

2. enough
3. a lot of
4. How much
5. a little
6. a few
7. some
8. How many
9. any
10. much
11. a lot of
12. a few

III. (Unit 38)

2. a, a, an
3. the
4. The
5. the, the
6. the
7. an
8. a
9. the, an

IV. (Unit 38)

3. the
4. Ø Money
5. Ø Travel
6. Ø Staying
7. The
8. Ø Vegetables

V. (Unit 38)

1. **b.** some
   c. a
   d. an
   e. The
   f. The
2. **a.** some
   b. some
   c. the
   d. some
   e. The
   f. the

VI. (Units 37 and 38)

2. B
3. C
4. A
5. A
6. C
7. A

*Where a contracted form is given, the long
form is also correct.

APPENDICES

1 Irregular Verbs

Base Form	Simple Past	Past Participle	Base Form	Simple Past	Past Participle
arise	arose	arisen	grind	ground	ground
awake	awoke	awoken	grow	grew	grown
be	was/were	been	hang	hung	hung
beat	beat	beaten	have	had	had
become	became	become	hear	heard	heard
begin	began	begun	hide	hid	hidden
bend	bent	bent	hit	hit	hit
bet	bet	bet	hold	held	held
bite	bit	bitten	hurt	hurt	hurt
bleed	bled	bled	keep	kept	kept
blow	blew	blown	kneel	knelt	knelt
break	broke	broken	knit	knit/knitted	knit/knitted
bring	brought	brought	know	knew	known
build	built	built	lay	laid	laid
burn	burned/burnt	burned/burnt	lead	led	led
burst	burst	burst	leap	leapt	leapt
buy	bought	bought	leave	left	left
catch	caught	caught	lend	lent	lent
choose	chose	chosen	let	let	let
cling	clung	clung	lie (lie down)	lay	lain
come	came	come	light	lit/lighted	lit/lighted
cost	cost	cost	lose	lost	lost
creep	crept	crept	make	made	made
cut	cut	cut	mean	meant	meant
deal	dealt	dealt	meet	met	met
dig	dug	dug	pay	paid	paid
dive	dived/dove	dived	prove	proved	proved/proven
do	did	done	put	put	put
draw	drew	drawn	quit	quit	quit
dream	dreamed/dreamt	dreamed/dreamt	read /rid/	read /rɛd/	read /rɛd/
drink	drank	drunk	ride	rode	ridden
drive	drove	driven	ring	rang	rung
eat	ate	eaten	rise	rose	risen
fall	fell	fallen	run	ran	run
feed	fed	fed	say	said	said
feel	felt	felt	see	saw	seen
fight	fought	fought	seek	sought	sought
find	found	found	sell	sold	sold
fit	fit	fit	send	sent	sent
flee	fled	fled	set	set	set
fling	flung	flung	sew	sewed	sewn/sewed
fly	flew	flown	shake	shook	shaken
forbid	forbade/forbad	forbidden	shave	shaved	shaved/shaven
forget	forgot	forgotten	shine	shone	shone
forgive	forgave	forgiven	shoot	shot	shot
freeze	froze	frozen	show	showed	shown
get	got	gotten/got	shrink	shrank/shrunk	shrunk/shrunken
give	gave	given	shut	shut	shut
go	went	gone	sing	sang	sung

(continued on next page)

Base Form	Simple Past	Past Participle	Base Form	Simple Past	Past Participle
sink	sank	sunk	sweep	swept	swept
sit	sat	sat	swim	swam	swum
sleep	slept	slept	swing	swung	swung
slide	slid	slid	take	took	taken
speak	spoke	spoken	teach	taught	taught
speed	sped	sped	tear	tore	torn
spend	spent	spent	tell	told	told
spill	spilled/spilt	spilled/spilt	think	thought	thought
spin	spun	spun	throw	threw	thrown
spit	spit/spat	spat	understand	understood	understood
split	split	split	upset	upset	upset
spread	spread	spread	wake	woke	woken
spring	sprang	sprung	wear	wore	worn
stand	stood	stood	weave	wove	woven
steal	stole	stolen	weep	wept	wept
stick	stuck	stuck	win	won	won
sting	stung	stung	wind	wound	wound
stink	stank/stunk	stunk	withdraw	withdrew	withdrawn
strike	struck	struck	wring	wrung	wrung
swear	swore	sworn	write	wrote	written

❷ Common Non-action (Stative) Verbs

EMOTIONS	MENTAL STATES		WANTS AND PREFERENCES	PERCEPTION AND THE SENSES	APPEARANCE	POSSESSION
admire	agree	imagine	desire	feel	appear	belong
adore	assume	know	need	hear	be	have
appreciate	believe	mean	prefer	notice	feel	own
care	consider	presume	want	observe	look	possess
detest	disagree	realize	wish	perceive	represent	
dislike	disbelieve	recognize		see	resemble	
doubt	estimate	remember		smell	seem	
envy	expect	see (*understand*)		taste	signify	
fear	feel (*believe*)	suppose			smell	
hate	find	suspect			sound	
hope	guess	think (*believe*)			taste	
like	hesitate	understand				
love	hope	wonder				
regret						
respect						
trust						

❸ Verbs and Expressions Commonly Used Reflexively

amuse oneself	cut oneself	look after oneself
ask oneself	deprive oneself of	look at oneself
avail oneself of	dry oneself	pride oneself on
be hard on oneself	enjoy oneself	push oneself
be oneself	feel sorry for oneself	remind oneself
be pleased with oneself	help oneself	see oneself
be proud of oneself	hurt oneself	take care of oneself
behave oneself	imagine oneself	talk to oneself
believe in oneself	introduce oneself	teach oneself
blame oneself	kill oneself	tell oneself

4 Some Common Transitive Separable Phrasal Verbs

(s.o. = someone   s.t. = something)

PHRASAL VERB	MEANING
ask s.o. **over**	invite to one's home
blow s.t. **out**	stop burning by blowing on it
blow s.t. **up**	make explode
bring s.o. or s.t. **back**	return
bring s.o. **up**	raise (children)
bring s.t. **up**	bring attention to
burn s.t. **down**	burn completely
call s.o. **back**	return a phone call
call s.t. **off**	cancel
call s.o. **up**	phone
clean s.o. or s.t. **up**	clean completely
clear s.t. **up**	clarify
close s.t. **down**	close by force
cover s.o. or s.t. **up**	cover completely
cross s.t. **out**	draw a line through
do s.t. **over**	do again
drink s.t. **up**	drink completely
drop s.o. or s.t. **off**	take someplace
empty s.t. **out**	empty completely
figure s.o. or s.t. **out**	understand (after thinking about)
fill s.t. **in**	complete with information
fill s.t. **out**	complete (a form)
find s.t. **out**	learn information
give s.t. **back**	return
give s.t. **up**	quit, abandon
hand s.t. **in**	submit work (to a boss/teacher)
hand s.t. **out**	distribute — give to somebody
help s.o. **out**	assist
keep s.o. or s.t. **away**	cause to stay at a distance
keep s.t. **on**	not remove (a piece of clothing/jewelry)
lay s.o. **off**	end employment
leave s.t. **on**	not remove (a piece of clothing/jewelry)
leave s.t. **out**	omit
let s.o. **down**	disappoint
let s.o. **in**	allow to enter
let s.o. **off**	allow to leave (a bus/car)
light s.t. **up**	illuminate
look s.o. or s.t. **over**	examine
look s.t. **up**	try to find (in a book/on the Internet)
make s.t. **up**	create
pass s.t. **on**	give to
pass s.t. **out**	distribute
pass s.o. or s.t. **over**	skip

PHRASAL VERB	MEANING
pass s.o. or s.t. **up**	decide not to use
pay s.o. or s.t. **back**	repay
pick s.o. or s.t. **out**	select
pick s.o. or s.t. **up**	lift
pick s.t. **up**	get (an idea, a new book, an interest)
point s.o. or s.t. **out**	indicate
put s.t. **away**	put in an appropriate place
put s.t. **back**	return to its original place
put s.o. or s.t. **down**	stop holding
put s.t. **off**	postpone
put s.t. **on**	cover the body
put s.t. **together**	assemble
put s.t. **up**	erect
set s.t. **up**	1. prepare for use 2. establish (a business/an organization)
shut s.t. **off**	stop (a machine/light)
start s.t. **over**	start again
straighten s.t. **up**	make neat
switch s.t. **on**	start (a machine/light)
take s.o. or s.t. **back**	return
take s.t. **off**	remove
talk s.o. **into**	persuade
talk s.t. **over**	discuss
tear s.t. **down**	destroy
tear s.t. **off**	remove by tearing
tear s.t. **up**	tear into small pieces
think s.t. **over**	consider
think s.t. **up**	invent
throw s.t. **away/out**	discard
try s.t. **on**	put clothing on to see if it fits
try s.t. **out**	use to see if it works
turn s.o. or s.t. **down**	reject
turn s.t. **down**	lower the volume (a TV/radio)
turn s.t. **in**	submit
turn s.o. or s.t. **into**	change from one form to another
turn s.o. **off**	(slang) destroy interest
turn s.t. **off**	stop (a machine/light)
turn s.t. **on**	start (a machine/light)
turn s.t. **up**	raise the volume (a TV/radio)
use s.t. **up**	use completely, consume
wake s.o. **up**	awaken
work s.t. **out**	solve
write s.t. **down**	write on a piece of paper
write s.t. **up**	write in a finished form

5 Some Common Intransitive Phrasal Verbs

PHRASAL VERB	MEANING
blow up	explode
break down	stop functioning
burn down	burn completely
call back	return a phone call

PHRASAL VERB	MEANING
clear up	become clear
close down	stop operating
come about	happen
come along	accompany

PHRASAL VERB	MEANING
come in	enter
come off	become unattached
come out	appear
come up	arise

(continued on next page)

Phrasal Verb	Meaning	Phrasal Verb	Meaning	Phrasal Verb	Meaning
dress up	wear special clothes	go on	continue	show up	appear
drop in	visit unexpectedly	grow up	become an adult	sign up	register
drop out	quit	hang up	end a phone call	sit down	take a seat
eat out	eat in a restaurant	keep away	stay at a distance	slip up	make a mistake
empty out	empty completely	keep on	continue	stand up	rise
find out	learn information	keep up	go as fast as	start over	start again
follow through	complete	lie down	recline	stay up	remain awake
fool around	be playful	light up	illuminate	straighten up	make neat
get along	relate well	look out	be careful	take off	depart (a plane)
get back	return	make up	reconcile	turn up	appear
get by	survive	play around	have fun	wake up	arise after sleeping
get together	meet	run out	not have enough of	watch out	be careful
get up	rise from bed	set out	begin a project	work out	1. be resolved
give up	quit				2. exercise

6 Common Participial Adjectives

-ed	-ing	-ed	-ing	-ed	-ing
alarmed	alarming	disturbed	disturbing	moved	moving
amazed	amazing	embarrassed	embarrassing	paralyzed	paralyzing
amused	amusing	entertained	entertaining	pleased	pleasing
annoyed	annoying	excited	exciting	relaxed	relaxing
astonished	astonishing	exhausted	exhausting	satisfied	satisfying
bored	boring	fascinated	fascinating	shocked	shocking
confused	confusing	frightened	frightening	surprised	surprising
depressed	depressing	horrified	horrifying	terrified	terrifying
disappointed	disappointing	inspired	inspiring	tired	tiring
disgusted	disgusting	interested	interesting	touched	touching
distressed	distressing	irritated	irritating	troubled	troubling

7 Irregular Comparisons of Adjectives, Adverbs, and Quantifiers

Adjective	Adverb	Comparative	Superlative
bad	badly	worse	worst
far	far	farther/further	farthest/furthest
good	well	better	best
little	little	less	least
many/a lot of	—	more	most
much*/a lot of	much*/a lot	more	most

*Much is usually only used in questions and negative statements.

8 Some Adjectives that Form the Comparative and Superlative in Two Ways

Adjective	Comparative	Superlative
common	commoner / more common	commonest / most common
cruel	crueler / more cruel	cruelest / most cruel
deadly	deadlier / more deadly	deadliest / most deadly
friendly	friendlier / more friendly	friendliest / most friendly
handsome	handsomer / more handsome	handsomest / most handsome
happy	happier / more happy	happiest / most happy
likely	likelier / more likely	likeliest / most likely
lively	livelier / more lively	liveliest / most lively
lonely	lonelier / more lonely	loneliest / most lonely
lovely	lovelier / more lovely	loveliest / most lovely
narrow	narrower / more narrow	narrowest / most narrow

ADJECTIVE	COMPARATIVE	SUPERLATIVE
pleasant	pleasanter / more pleasant	pleasantest / most pleasant
polite	politer / more polite	politest / most polite
quiet	quieter / more quiet	quietest / most quiet
shallow	shallower / more shallow	shallowest / most shallow
sincere	sincerer / more sincere	sincerest / most sincere
stupid	stupider / more stupid	stupidest / most stupid
true	truer / more true	truest / most true

9 Common Verbs Followed by the Gerund (Base Form of Verb + -ing)

acknowledge	delay	endure	give up (stop)	postpone	regret
admit	deny	enjoy	imagine	practice	report
appreciate	detest	escape	justify	prevent	resent
avoid	discontinue	explain	keep (continue)	prohibit	resist
can't help	discuss	feel like	mention	quit	risk
celebrate	dislike	finish	mind (object to)	recall	suggest
consider	dispute	forgive	miss	recommend	understand

10 Common Verbs Followed by the Infinitive (To + Base Form of Verb)

afford	can't afford	expect	learn	plan	request
agree	can't wait	fail	manage	prepare	seem
appear	choose	help	mean	pretend	want
ask	consent	hope	need	promise	wish
arrange	decide	hurry	offer	refuse	would like / 'd like
attempt	deserve	intend	pay		

11 Common Verbs Followed by the Gerund or the Infinitive

begin	forget*	love	start
can't stand	hate	prefer	stop*
continue	like	remember*	try

*These verbs can be followed by either the gerund or the infinitive, but there is a big difference in meaning *(see Unit 31)*.

12 Verbs Followed by Objects and the Infinitive

advise	convince	help*	pay*	remind	urge
allow	encourage	hire	permit	require	want*
ask*	expect*	invite	persuade	teach	warn
cause	forbid	need*	promise*	tell	would like*
choose*	force	order			

*These verbs can also be followed by the infinitive without an object (example: *ask to leave* or *ask someone to leave*).

13 Common Adjective + Preposition Expressions

be accustomed to	be bored with/by	be fond of	be pleased about	be slow at
be afraid of	be capable of	be glad about	be ready for	be sorry for/about
be amazed at/by	be careful of	be good at	be responsible for	be surprised at/about/by
be angry at	be concerned about	be happy about	be sad about	be terrible at
be ashamed of	be content with	be interested in	be safe from	be tired of
be aware of	be curious about	be nervous about	be satisfied with	be used to
be awful at	be excited about	be opposed to	be sick of	be worried about
be bad at	be famous for			

14 Common Verb + Preposition Combinations

admit to	believe in	deal with	look forward to	resort to
advise against	choose between	dream about/of	object to	succeed in
apologize for	complain about	feel like	plan on	talk about
approve of	count on	insist on	rely on	think about

15 Spelling Rules for the Present Progressive

1. Add -*ing* to the base form of the verb.

read	read*ing*
stand	stand*ing*

2. If a verb ends in a silent -*e*, drop the final -*e* and add -*ing*.

leave	leav*ing*
take	tak*ing*

3. In a one-syllable word, if the last three letters are a consonant-vowel-consonant combination (CVC), double the last consonant before adding -*ing*.

C V C
↓ ↓ ↓
s i t   sit*ting*

C V C
↓ ↓ ↓
r u n   run*ning*

However, do not double the last consonant in words that end in *w*, *x*, or *y*.

sew	sew*ing*
fix	fix*ing*
enjoy	enjoy*ing*

4. In words of two or more syllables that end in a consonant-vowel-consonant combination, double the last consonant only if the last syllable is stressed.

admít	admit*ting*	(The last syllable is stressed)
whísper	whisper*ing*	(The last syllable is not stressed, so you don't double the -*r*.)

5. If a verb ends in -*ie*, change the *ie* to *y* before adding -*ing*.

die	d*ying*

16 Spelling Rules for the Simple Present Tense: Third-Person Singular (*he, she, it*)

1. Add -*s* for most verbs.

work	work*s*
buy	buy*s*
ride	ride*s*
return	return*s*

2. Add -*es* for words that end in -*ch*, -*s*, -*sh*, -*x*, or -*z*.

watch	watch*es*
pass	pass*es*
rush	rush*es*
relax	relax*es*
buzz	buzz*es*

3. Change the *y* to *i* and add -*es* when the base form ends in a consonant + *y*.

study	stud*ies*
hurry	hurr*ies*
dry	dr*ies*

Do not change the *y* when the base form ends in a vowel + *y*. Add -*s*.

play	play*s*
enjoy	enjoy*s*

4. A few verbs have irregular forms.

be	is
do	does
go	goes
have	has

17 Spelling Rules for the Simple Past Tense of Regular Verbs

1. If the verb ends in a consonant, add -ed.

return	returned
help	helped

2. If the verb ends in -e, add -d.

live	lived
create	created
die	died

3. In one-syllable words, if the verb ends in a consonant-vowel-consonant combination (CVC), double the final consonant and add -ed.

```
C V C
↓↓↓
h o p        hopped
C V C
↓↓↓
r u b        rubbed
```

However, do not double one-syllable words ending in -w, -x, or -y.

bow	bowed
mix	mixed
play	played

4. In words of two or more syllables that end in a consonant-vowel-consonant combination, double the last consonant only if the last syllable is stressed.

preférr	preferred	(The last syllable is stressed.)
vísit	visited	(The last syllable is not stressed, so you don't double the t.)

5. If the verb ends in a consonant + y, change the y to i and add -ed.

worry	worried
carry	carried

6. If the verb ends in a vowel + y, add -ed. (Do not change the y to i.)

play	played
annoy	annoyed

Exceptions:

pay	paid
lay	laid
say	said

18 Spelling Rules for the Comparative (-er) and Superlative (-est) Forms of Adjectives

1. Add -er to one-syllable adjectives to form the comparative. Add -est to one-syllable adjectives to form the superlative.

cheap	cheaper	cheapest
bright	brighter	brightest

2. If the adjective ends in -e, add -r or -st.

nice	nicer	nicest

3. If the adjective ends in a consonant + y, change y to i before you add -er or -est.

pretty	prettier	prettiest

Exception:

shy	shyer	shyest

4. If the adjective ends in a consonant-vowel-consonant combination (CVC), double the final consonant before adding -er or -est.

```
C V C
↓↓↓
b i g        bigger       biggest
```

However, do not double the consonant in words ending in -w or -y.

slow	slower	slowest
coy	coyer	coyest

19 Spelling Rules for Adverbs Ending in -ly

1. Add -ly to the corresponding adjective.

nice	nicely
quiet	quietly
beautiful	beautifully

2. If the adjective ends in a consonant + y, change the y to i before adding -ly.

easy	easily

3. If the adjective ends in -le, drop the e and add -y.

possible	possibly

However, do not drop the e for other adjectives ending in -e.

extreme	extremely

Exception:

true	truly

4. If the adjective ends in -ic, add -ally.

basic	basically
fantastic	fantastically

1. SIMPLE PRESENT TENSE, PRESENT PROGRESSIVE, AND IMPERATIVE

Contractions with *Be*

I am	=	**I'm**
you are	=	**you're**
he is	=	**he's**
she is	=	**she's**
it is	=	**it's**
we are	=	**we're**
you are	=	**you're**
they are	=	**they're**

I am not	=	**I'm not**		
you are not	=	**you're not**	or	**you aren't**
he is not	=	**he's not**	or	**he isn't**
she is not	=	**she's not**	or	**she isn't**
it is not	=	**it's not**	or	**it isn't**
we are not	=	**we're not**	or	**we aren't**
you are not	=	**you're not**	or	**you aren't**
they are not	=	**they're not**	or	**they aren't**

SIMPLE PRESENT	**PRESENT PROGRESSIVE**
I**'m** a student.	I**'m studying** here.
He**'s** my teacher.	He**'s teaching** verbs.
We**'re** from Canada.	We**'re living** here.

SIMPLE PRESENT	**PRESENT PROGRESSIVE**
She**'s not** sick.	She**'s not reading**.
He **isn't** late.	He **isn't coming**.
We **aren't** twins.	We **aren't leaving**.
They**'re not** here.	They**'re not playing**.

Contractions with *Do*

do not	=	**don't**
does not	=	**doesn't**

SIMPLE PRESENT	**IMPERATIVE**
They **don't live** here.	**Don't run**!
It **doesn't snow** much.	

2. SIMPLE PAST TENSE AND PAST PROGRESSIVE

Contractions with *Be*

was not	=	**wasn't**
were not	=	**weren't**

SIMPLE PAST	**PAST PROGRESSIVE**
He **wasn't** a poet.	He **wasn't singing**.
They **weren't** twins.	They **weren't sleeping**.
We **didn't** see her.	

Contractions with *Do*

did not	=	**didn't**

3. FUTURE

Contractions with *Will*

I will	=	**I'll**
you will	=	**you'll**
he will	=	**he'll**
she will	=	**she'll**
it will	=	**it'll**
we will	=	**we'll**
you will	=	**you'll**
they will	=	**they'll**

will not	=	**won't**

FUTURE WITH *WILL*
I**'ll take** the train.
It**'ll be** faster that way.
We**'ll go** together.
He **won't come** with us.
They **won't miss** the train.

Contractions with *Be going to*

I am going to	=	**I'm going to**
you are going to	=	**you're going to**
he is going to	=	**he's going to**
she is going to	=	**she's going to**
it is going to	=	**it's going to**
we are going to	=	**we're going to**
you are going to	=	**you're going to**
they are going to	=	**they're going to**

FUTURE WITH *BE GOING TO*
I**'m going to buy** tickets tomorrow.
She**'s going to call** you.
It**'s going to rain** soon.
We**'re going to drive** to Boston.
They**'re going to crash**!

4. PRESENT PERFECT AND PRESENT PERFECT PROGRESSIVE

Contractions with *Have*

I have	=	**I've**
you have	=	**you've**
he has	=	**he's**
she has	=	**she's**
it has	=	**it's**
we have	=	**we've**
you have	=	**you've**
they have	=	**they've**
have not	=	**haven't**
has not	=	**hasn't**

You**'ve** already **read** that page.
We**'ve been writing** for an hour.
She**'s been** to Africa three times.
It**'s been raining** since yesterday.
We **haven't seen** any elephants yet.
They **haven't been living** here long.

5. MODALS AND MODAL-LIKE EXPRESSIONS

cannot or can not	=	**can't**
could not	=	**couldn't**
should not	=	**shouldn't**
had better	=	**'d better**
would prefer	=	**'d prefer**
would not	=	**wouldn't**
would rather	=	**'d rather**

She **can't dance.**
We **shouldn't go.**
They**'d better decide.**
I**'d prefer** coffee.
She **wouldn't.**
I**'d rather take** the bus.

(21) Pronunciation Table

These are the pronunciation symbols used in this text. Listen to the pronunciation of the key words.

VOWELS		CONSONANTS			
Symbol	**Key Word**	**Symbol**	**Key Word**	**Symbol**	**Key Word**
i	beat, feed	p	pack, happy	ʃ	ship, machine, station, special, discussion
ɪ	bit, did	b	back, rubber		
eɪ	date, paid	t	tie	ʒ	measure, vision
ɛ	bet, bed	d	die	h	hot, who
æ	bat, bad	k	came, key, quick	m	men
ɑ	box, odd, father	g	game, guest	n	sun, know, pneumonia
ɔ	bought, dog	tʃ	church, nature, watch	ŋ	sung, ringing
oʊ	boat, road	dʒ	judge, general, major	w	wet, white
ʊ	book, good	f	fan, photograph	l	light, long
u	boot, food, student	v	van	r	right, wrong
ʌ	but, mud, mother	θ	thing, breath	y	yes, use, music
ə	banana, among	ð	then, breathe	t̬	butter, bottle
ɚ	shirt, murder	s	sip, city, psychology		
aɪ	bite, cry, buy, eye	z	zip, please, goes		
aʊ	about, how				
ɔɪ	voice, boy				
ɪr	beer				
ɛr	bare				
ɑr	bar				
ɔr	door				
ʊr	tour				

> **STRESS**
> ' shows main stress.

22 Pronunciation Rules for the Simple Present Tense: Third-Person Singular *(he, she, it)*

1. The third-person singular in the simple present tense always ends in the letter *-s*. There are, however, three different pronunciations for the final sound of the third person singular.

/s/	/z/	/ɪz/
talks	loves	dances

2. The final sound is pronounced /s/ after the voiceless sounds /p/, /t/, /k/, and /f/.

top	tops
get	gets
take	takes
laugh	laughs

3. The final sound is pronounced /z/ after the voiced sounds /b/, /d/, /g/, /v/, /ð/, /m/, /n/, /ŋ/, /l/, and /r/.

describe	describes
spend	spends
hug	hugs
live	lives
bathe	bathes
seem	seems
remain	remains
sing	sings
tell	tells
lower	lowers

4. The final sound is pronounced /z/ after all vowel sounds.

agree	agrees
try	tries
stay	stays
know	knows

5. The final sound is pronounced /ɪz/ after the sounds /s/, /z/, /ʃ/, /ʒ/, /tʃ/, and /dʒ/. /ɪz/ adds a syllable to the verb.

relax	relaxes
freeze	freezes
rush	rushes
massage	massages
watch	watches
judge	judges

6. *Do* and *say* have a change in vowel sound.

say	/seɪ/	says	/sɛz/
do	/du/	does	/dʌz/

23 Pronunciation Rules for the Simple Past Tense of Regular Verbs

1. The regular simple past always ends in the letter *-d*. There are, however, three different pronunciations for the final sound of the regular simple past.

/t/	/d/	/ɪd/
raced	lived	attended

2. The final sound is pronounced /t/ after the voiceless sounds /p/, /k/, /f/, /s/, /ʃ/, and /tʃ/.

hop	hopped
work	worked
laugh	laughed
address	addressed
publish	published
watch	watched

3. The final sound is pronounced /d/ after the voiced sounds /b/, /g/, /v/, /z/, /ʒ/, /dʒ/, /m/, /n/, /ŋ/, /l/, /r/, and /ð/.

rub	rubbed	rhyme	rhymed
hug	hugged	return	returned
live	lived	bang	banged
surprise	surprised	enroll	enrolled
massage	massaged	appear	appeared
change	changed	bathe	bathed

4. The final sound is pronounced /d/ after all vowel sounds.

agree	agreed
play	played
die	died
enjoy	enjoyed

5. The final sound is pronounced /ɪd/ after /t/ and /d/. /ɪd/ adds a syllable to the verb.

start	started
decide	decided

INDEX

This Index is for the full and split editions. All entries are in the full book.
Entries for Volume A of the split edition are in black. Entries for Volume B are in color.